Black Canadians

Black Canadians

History, Experiences, Social Conditions

Joseph Mensah

Fernwood Publishing • Halifax

B·O·O·K·S
FOR EVERYBODY
The essential catalogue
of quality titles from
your independent bookseller

Editing: Donna Davis
Cover design: Larissa Holman and Beverley Rach
Design and production: Brenda Conroy
Printed and bound in Canada by: Hignell Printing Limited

A publication of:
Fernwood Publishing
Box 9409, Station A
Halifax, Nova Scotia
B3K 5S3

Fernwood Publishing Company Limited gratefully acknowledges the financial support of the Department of Canadian Heritage, the Nova Scotia Department of Tourism and Culture and the Canada Council for the Arts for our publishing program.

NOVASCOTIA
Tourism and Culture

Le Conseil des Arts | The Canada Council
du Canada | for the Arts

National Library of Canada Cataloguing in Publication

Mensah, Joseph, 1960–
    Black Canadians : history, experience, social conditions / Joseph Mensah.

Includes bibliographical references and index.
ISBN 1–55266–090–7

    1. Black Canadians. I. Title.

FC106.B6M45 2002   971'.00496   C2002-903647-X
F1035.N3M45 2002

This book is dedicated to my wife, Janet Mensah,
to our two children, Nicole and Cassandra,
and, with deep affection and a solemn sense of loss,
to the loving memories of
my aunt-in-law, Ms. Lurline Thomas of Kingston, Ontario,
and my two friends Mr. Alhassan Manu (Alass)
and Mr. Benjamin Effah-Kusi of Ghana.

Contents

Acknowledgements

It is both a duty and a pleasure to express my heartfelt thanks to many individuals who have made the writing of this book possible. In particular I wish to thank Dr. Augustine Akuoko-Asibey of Statistics Canada; Dr. Edward Osei Kwadwo Prempeh of Carleton University, Ottawa; Dr. Francis Adu Febiri of Camosun College, Victoria; and Dr. Senyo Adjibolosoo of Point Loma Nazarene University, San Diego, who have not only read and commented on the manuscript but who have been most forthright with their encouragement throughout the writing of this book. I am indebted to my students and colleagues at the Geography Department of Kwantlen University College in Surrey, British Columbia, who helped to lay some of the groundwork for this book during years of teaching and discussions. Fernwood Publishing has been all that one could hope for in a publisher. This book is a product of the labour of a number of people at Fernwood's production and design departments. My sincere thanks to Errol Sharpe, Donna Davis, Beverley Rach, Brenda Conroy, Tim Dunn, Debbie Mathers and Larissa Holman. Without their time and ingenuity the book could never have been produced to this high quality.

I wish to thank my wife, Janet Mensah, and my two daughters, Nicole and Cassandra, who, as always, have adjusted the rhythm of their lives to the demands of this project. Indeed, their patience has been tried by the weight of this book, and their understanding should not go unnoticed. I am also deeply indebted to my parents, Mr. and Mrs. M.Y. Mensah of Techiman, Ghana, and my brother Samuel Mensah and his family in Surrey, for their encouragement and support. I thank Mr. Lawrence Billey and his wife Susan Billey in Cloverdale, British Columbia; Mr. Kofi Owusu Addo and family in Surrey; Ms. Jacinta Kuma-Minta in Surrey; Dr. Stephen Ameyaw of Simon Fraser University; and Mr. Oti Bronya Moses of Techiman, Ghana, for their support and kindness.

Finally, with deep affection and a solemn sense of loss, I dedicate this book in loving memory of my aunt-in-law, Ms. Lurline Thomas of Kingston, Ontario, and my friends Mr. Alhassan Manu (Alass) and Mr. Benjamin Effah-Kusi of Ghana, all of whom passed away in the prime of their life.

Chapter One

The Black Presence in Canada

Toward an Integrated Study

Since the early 1960s when Canada officially took a non-racist stance with respect to immigration, the ethnic and racial composition of the country has become increasing heterogeneous. Studies show that the number of Asian, African, Caribbean and other non-European immigrants to Canada has increased substantially in recent years, while at the same time immigration from traditional sources such as the United Kingdom, Western Europe, and the United States has declined (Li 1999; Berry and Laponce 1994; Frideres 1992). The resulting increase in the proportion of visible minorities has made ethnicity and race such a battleground for clashing opinions and social tensions that even the most cursory observer can hardly ignore it. "Ethnicity," write Berry and Laponce (1994: 3), "is likely to be to the twenty-first century what class was to the twentieth—a major source of social and political conflict."

Prior to the 1960s, non-Whites, notably Chinese, East Indians, and Blacks, were brought to Canada mainly to perform the hard, dirty, hazardous, and low-paying jobs (e.g., coal mining, railroad construction, and farm clearing) that White Canadians generally did not want to perform. Most of these immigrants worked as indentured labourers, enduring race-related abuses and harassment at the hands of their White Canadian employers. Indeed, Blacks and Aboriginal people were subjected even to slavery. Indeed, Canada was built on the backs of ethnoracial minorities, most of whom "were welcomed when they came to perform hard and dirty work, [but] were often rejected when those duties were completed, or when economic recessions occurred and it appeared they were taking jobs away from White Canadians" (Head 1984: 8).

Many Canadians are reluctant to admit that racial oppression and inferiorization persist in this country. As Canadians, we have the tendency not only to ignore our racist past, but also to dismiss any contemporary racial incidence as nothing but aberration in an essentially peaceful, tolerant, charitable, and egalitarian nation. For the most part, we believe that we are superior to countries, such as the United States, that are struggling with racial problems (Boyko 1998: 16). Admittedly, some studies corroborate this perception. For instance, in *Continental Divide* (1989) Lipset finds that Canadians are generally more tolerant of ethnoracial minorities than Americans. And, more recently, Macionis and Gerber (1999: 327), deriving insights from Artibise (1988: 244), argued: "The fact that Toronto, in a short period of time, went from being a largely Anglo-Saxon Protestant city to one with a substantial immigrant and visible-minority component without major violence or disruptions suggests a fair degree of social tolerance."

But isn't the assertion that Toronto has not experienced any major race-based riots or disruptions in recent years problematic, considering the racial clashes that have erupted between Toronto's Black community and the police, culminating in the formation of the Stephen Lewis Commission of Inquiry?[1] Even that aside, isn't the argument that there have not been major racial disruptions in Toronto, therefore Canada (or Toronto) is a tolerant society logically specious? Can't one attribute the "absence" of major racial disruptions in Canada or Toronto to factors other than our presumed tolerance? The fact is, the "absence" of major racial distortions could be because ethnoracial minorities (e.g., Blacks) are not politically well-organized because minorities are afraid of the possible repercussions, in terms of public backlash, media lashing, and police brutality; because minorities have been oppressed to the extent that they cannot bear the financial burden of organizing a major resistance; or, worse still, because they are too oppressed to even fathom the thought of resisting.

Vic Satzewich (1998: 11) writes that "one of our most enduring Canadian national myths is that there is less racism here than in the United States." However, historical records and contemporary comparative studies suggest that, when it comes to the maltreatment of racial minorities, Canada has a disreputable past and present and, therefore, has little to be proud of (Reitz and Breton 1998; Boyko 1998; Bolaria and Li 1988; Head 1984). After a thorough empirical comparison of racial prejudice and discrimination in the United States and Canada—using variables such as overt racism and negative racial stereotypes, anti-Semitism, social distance, employment discrimination, and government action against discrimination—Reitz and Breton (1998: 65) conclude that "despite the historical differences between race relations in Canada and race relations in the United States, Canadians and Americans are roughly similar in their attitudes and behaviors toward racial minorities." Even Macionis and Gerber (1999: 330), citing the work of Mackie (1974), acknowledge that "When Canadians were asked to rank various racial and ethnic categories on the Bogardus-scale,[2] the ranking was very similar."

Non-Whites are commonly harassed and subjected to discriminatory practices in nearly all aspects of Canadian life. Perhaps nowhere do minorities face more discrimination than in the arena of employment. We thus find Bolaria and Li (1988: 22) asserting that racial problems basically are consequences of "racial encounter predicated by exploitation of labour and resources." Studies show that even when qualifications are equal, the incomes of visible minorities are generally lower than those of their White counterparts (Bolaria and Li 1988; Head 1984). In his recent thought-provoking paper "The Market Value and Social Value of Race," Peter Li (1998: 115) made a twofold observation in this regard: first, that there is a social hierarchy of races in Canada and that this is "manifested in Canadians' views of which groups are socially desirable or undesirable according to racial origin"; and second, that there is race-based disparity in earnings in the Canadian job market, "with those of European origin having higher earnings than non-White Canadians" who are equally qualified. Characteristically, Li (1998: 115) was able to support these hard-hitting claims with meticulous and persuasive empirical evidence.

Due to their high visibility and the legacy of slavery, Blacks in particular are stigmatized and discriminated against in a fashion that drastically undermines their social and economic status in Canada (Christensen and Weinfeld 1993). Undoubtedly, other visible minorities (e.g., East Indians and Chinese) continue to face racial denigration and discrimination; indeed, their much-touted socio-economic ascent in Canada has never been easy. But their racial problems, arguably,[3] pale in comparison to the wide-raging exploitation and dehumanization suffered by Blacks throughout the history of Canada. Not surprisingly, the available Canadian literature on social distance usually situates Blacks at the bottom of the hierarchy of acceptance (Moghaddam et al. 1994; Berry et al. 1977; Pineo 1977).

Even though the history of Black Canadians can be traced to the seventeenth century, it was only after the introduction of the point system in 1967 that Blacks began to arrive in Canada in significant numbers. The current Black population in Canada is highly heterogeneous. It includes the Canadian-born descendants of those who came through the slave trade; the descendants of those who migrated from the United States during and after the Civil War; and Blacks who have immigrated from Caribbean, African, and other countries in recent decades (Lampkin 1985). Needless to say, Canadian Blacks have a wide range of socio-economic and cultural backgrounds. Consequently, any analysis that treats them as a homogenous group is inherently flawed. The vast majority of Black Canadians lives in metropolitan centres such as Toronto, Montreal, Ottawa-Hull, Halifax, and Vancouver. And, contrary to popular belief, Black Canadians have higher levels of educational attainment than both the Canadian average (Christensen and Weinfeld 1993: 31) and people of

British and French ethnic origins in Canada (Macionis and Gerber 1999: 339). Notwithstanding the immense heterogeneity, Black Canadians invariably share one thing in common: the injuries and dehumanization of racism.

While there is a growing body of literature on the conditions of ethnoracial minorities, such as Chinese, East Indians, and Aboriginal people, very little research has been published on the Black presence in Canada, as determined through computer-assisted searches and consultation with numerous bibliographies and electronic abstract databases. Most of the available studies on the Canadian ethnic mosaic, including the pioneering work of John Porter (1965), either ignore the case of Blacks entirely or give it peripheral attention. Blacks are usually treated as a mere insightful accessory by lumping them into the ambiguous category of "others."[4] In fact, until the 1996 census, even the number of Black Canadians was always in doubt due to gaps and errors in official counts. Some observers (e.g., Christensen and Weinfeld 1993; Krauter and Davis 1978) attribute the ironic "obscurity" of the Black Canadians, despite their high visibility, to the lack of a charismatic Black leader (comparable to Martin Luther King or even Jesse Jackson) in Canada and the relative smallness of the Canadian Black population. Considering that any analysis of Blacks inevitably evokes the racist character of Canadian society, something many scholars are uncomfortable with, one can reasonably assert that the omission is strategic. Whatever the *raison d'être* may be, it is no insight to state that the dearth of research on Blacks is a serious lapse, since race continues to be a crucial factor in structuring inequality in Canada (Li 1998; Satzewich and Li 1987).

Although some noteworthy studies exist, the vast majority, including Calliste (1996), Henry (1994), Anderson (1993), Walker (1984), and Jean-Baptiste (1979), focuses exclusively on Caribbeans, relegating the experience of African-born and Canadian-born Blacks to the background. This academic regionalism has inhibited serious comparative analysis and sometimes has led to an explicit overgeneralization of the Black experience in Canada. The available studies are, undoubtedly, insightful, but the need for a comprehensive text on Black Canadians from a multidisciplinary perspective cannot be gainsaid. At present, there remain insufficient empirical and theoretical analyses from several social science disciplines— with the notable exception of sociology and, to some extent, history—to construct a comprehensive portrait of the Black presence in Canada.

Sociological and historical analyses have so successfully dominated the field that now the most notable works on Blacks (e.g., Boyko 1998; Alexander and Glaze 1996) project an image of the Black presence in Canada that seems to exist on "the head of a pin," with no spatial dimensions whatsoever. The relative lack of geographical analysis is particularly alarming in light of Michel Foucault's paradigmatic declaration that "the present epoch will perhaps be above all the epoch of space. We are in the epoch of simultaneity; we are in the epoch of juxtaposition, the epoch of near and far, of the side-by-side, of the disperse" (1986: 22). And who can forget John Berger's (1974: 40) astute observation that "prophesy now involves a geographical rather than historical projection: it is space not time that hides consequence from us"? Since the late 1990s, though, with the establishment of centres of excellence for research in immigration and integration at major universities across the country, more and more geographers are examining the spatial components of Canada's immigration and ethnoracial diversity. Notable examples of such geographic analyses include those of Hiebert (1999a 1999b), Owusu (1998), Teixeira and Murdie (1997), Ley and Smith (1997), and Lo and Wang (1997).

It is against this background that the present book examines the condition of Black Canadians from a multidisciplinary perspective. The main objective is to explore the incorporation of Blacks into Canadian society from the standpoint of their differential access to resources and rewards. The analysis pursued here cuts across a wide range of academic disciplines, notably history, sociology, geography, economics, psychology, political economy, and philosophy. And, as can be expected, a variety of theoretical paradigms, including postmodernism, structuralism, Marxism, and colonial/post-colonial discourse, inform the arguments presented in the book. Moreover, the book employs several descriptive, evaluative, comparative, and case study approaches to shore up the spatial and socio-economic variations within the Canadian Black population. The bulk of the empirical data is procured from the Canadian census; the *Historical Statistics of Canada,* published by Statistics Canada; and the *Immigration Statistics* compiled by Citizenship and Immigration Canada. A significant impetus for the book stems from the fact that a reasonable amount of reliable empirical data on Blacks now exists in Canada as a result of the 1996 census. Also, the size of the Black population in Canada now— estimated at 573,860[5]—is big enough to allow for meaningful statistical analyses and comparisons.

Even though Black Canadians are the main focus, there are several instances where the book carefully draws insights from the case of Blacks in the United States, where the literature is far more comprehensive. Also, while the spotlight remains on Blacks, some of the basic arguments are readily applicable to the circumstances of other ethnoracial minorities in Canada. The works of intersectional theorists, such as Daiva Stasiulis (1999) and Patricia Collins (1991), suggest that several significant axes of social organization, including race, gender, class, ethnicity, age, and sexual orientation, simultaneously and interactively intersect to determine the social reality of people, as well as the dynamics of their socio-economic and geopolitical contexts. Given the innumerable array of social divisions and their possible permutations and convoluted interrelationships, it is always difficult to determine the number of axes to include in a book like this and still preserve meaningful analytical focus. In this book the main point of entry is race. While the "iron triangle" (Stimpson 1993: 17) or the "three giants of modernist social critique" (Bordo 1990: 145), namely, gender, class, and race, are all featured in this book, the primacy belongs to the latter, given its enduring power and persistent salience in the life experiences of Black Canadians (Boyko 1998; Stasiulis 1999; Dei 1996). Implicit in this approach is the assumption that race is "a *central axis* of social relations which cannot be subsumed under or reduced to some broader category or conception" (Omi and Winant 1998: 16; emphasis in original).

Without question, the flow of power in a society such as ours is hardly unidirectional: "the oppressed can also be the oppressor, and the victim the victimizer, depending on the particular site of power one considers" (Stasiulus 1999: 381). Thus, not all Blacks are oppressed, just as not all Whites are the oppressors in all situations. Therefore, "White" is used in this book to imply only in broad theoretical terms the adversary or the antithesis of "Black." It is not meant to encompass all White people in Canada, many of whom have not only risen above the prevailing prejudice, but have undertaken invaluable positive steps to enhance the social and economic conditions of Black Canadians.

This book seeks to provide an authoritative reference for teachers, students, and other persons who need to know more about the Canadian component of the Black Diaspora in North America. But it bears stressing that some arguments made in the book may be uncongenial for those with little appetite for pointed, provocative analysis from the standpoint of Blacks. At the same time, those with genuine interest in venturing beyond established orthodoxies and simplistic solutions to the contentious ethnoracial problems of Canada will find the book to be insightful and worthy of close attention. To deny that, over the years, Canada has made remarkable progress towards multiculturalism, racial equality, and the settlement of refugees from around the world is to refute an evident truth.[6] But there remains work to be done, and only a candid acknowledgement of our racist past and present can help alleviate the racial tensions that continue to plague Canadian society.

Organization of the Book

Eight chapters follow. Chapter 2 deals with the conceptual framework of the book. "Race," "ethnicity," "Blacks," and kindred concepts are explored to provide some insights into how they are used in the context of this book. The controversial issues surrounding the origins of racial antagonism are also examined in this chapter. The chapter ends with an overview of Canada's relationships with the major Black societies of Africa and the Caribbean. Chapter 3 covers the history of Black Canadians, their experience with slavery in Canada and their settlement patterns during the pioneering years. The geography of Black Canadians is the focus of Chapter 4, where the immigration trends and spatial distribution of Blacks across Canada are examined.

Chapter 5 profiles the major Black groups in Canada, including "indigenous" Blacks in Nova Scotia; two Caribbean immigrant groups (Jamaicans and Haitians); and two African immigrant groups (Ghanaians and Somalis). The labour market characteristics and problems of Black Canadians are the focus of Chapter 6. Here, the racial and gender underpinnings of the employment problems faced by Blacks are unraveled. In Chapter 7 the focus shifts to the contribution of Blacks to Canadian sport; the controversial issues surrounding the "superiority" of Blacks in sport are explored as well. Chapters 8 and 9 concentrate on government initiatives on race-relations in Canada. More specifically, the policies of multiculturalism and employment equity are examined from the stand-point of Blacks. The book concludes with some general comments on the Black presence in Canada.

Many contemporary theoreticians rebuke the presumption of value neutrality, objectivity, or what some now call "the view from nowhere" or "God's eye view" in social discourse (Agnew 1996: 5). Critics such as Harding (1990) and Agnew (1996) argue, quite rightly, that all analyses stem from specific identities, backgrounds, and locations; consequently, they urge writers to identify their voices. Edward Carr (1961: 26) made a similar admonition decades ago in *What is History?* when he encouraged readers to study the historian before they study his or her history. To paraphrase Stephen Steinberg (1995): Who can candidly claim objectivity in the emotional issues surrounding race and ethnicity in Canada? Who can even pretend to see both sides of the issue when innocent Aboriginal people are allegedly[7] dragged into police cruisers and dropped off on the outskirts of town on chilly Prairie winter nights for no apparent reason other than the fact that they are Aboriginal people? Who can claim neutrality when Blacks are routinely harassed, arrested, and sometimes fatally shot in the streets of Toronto with little or no provocation?

Our presuppositions, which are almost always couched in our backgrounds and life experience, influence the way we approach issues. These presuppositions not only limit our selection of research data and information, but also dictate, sometimes unconsciously, how we interpret them. As Clyde Manschreck (1974: 3–4) shrewdly puts it: "No stance is without presuppositions, for to be without them is to be without a foundation. Presuppositions are our guidelines to truth; they undergird our values, standards, and ideals; they form the framework within which we move."

With this in mind, let me bring this introduction to a close by locating myself with brief biographical information that might help readers to engage in purposeful deconstruction of the discourse and counter-discourse presented in this book. I am a Black man who was born and raised in post-colonial Ghana, with a master's degree and a doctorate in human geography from the Wilfrid Laurier University in Waterloo, Ontario, and the University of Alberta in Edmonton, Alberta, respectively. For the past six years or so, I have taught various geography courses at the University of British Columbia in Vancouver, Simon Fraser University in Burnaby, Douglas College in New Westminster, Malaspina University College in Nanaimo, and the Kwantlen University College in Surrey, British Columbia; the latter is my current principal employer.[8] While my biographical information and presuppositions naturally have significant implications for the analysis pursued here, it bears stressing that good scholarship, in the form of reasonable substantiation of suppositions and sourcing of evidence, overrides sensationalism, propaganda, and egocentrism in this book.

Notes

1. Toronto has witnessed its share of major race riots. The Stephen Lewis Commission of Inquiry was set up in the early 1990s to help resolve the racism perpetrated against Blacks by the police and the criminal justice system in Toronto. Nelson and Fleras (1995: 253) estimate that between 1988 and 1993, the police in Metropolitan Toronto wounded or killed ten Black-Canadians. Most of these killings were followed by racial disruptions in the city. Similar killings and riots have occurred in Montreal. Nelson and Fleras (1995) observed that four (or 50 percent) of the last eight shootings in Montreal have involved Blacks, even though Blacks comprise less than 5 percent of the city's population. And who can forget the 1991 race riot in Montreal's east end, which started when a Black family moved into a neighbourhood and a group of young Whites planned an assault: It did not take long for the Black family to be beaten and chased out, their car set ablaze, and their apartment smashed to cries of "White Power!" Black youth got involved and the situation escalated into a race riot involving an estimated four hundred people and lasting for over five hours (See Boyko 1998).
2. Developed by Emory Bogardus in 1968, this scale is used to measure social distance or the extent to which people feel close to or distanced from mem-

bers of various ethnoracial groups.

3. The emphasis on "arguably" here is purposeful. At best, one can make only an academic comparison of the level of dehumanization suffered by different groups at the hands of others.

4. See, for instance, Rick Helmes-Hayes and James Curtis's edited monograph, *The Vertical Mosaic Revisited* (1998).

5. This figure is derived from the 1996 census, the *Nation Series*, based on 20 percent sample.

6. Note that in 1986 Canada was awarded the Nansen Medal by the United Nations for its role in international refugee work. The award is named after Fridtjof Nansen, the Norwegian explorer, oceanographer, statesman, humanitarian, and Nobel Peace Prize winner in 1922.

7. This incident allegedly occurred in Saskatoon in January 2000. The trial of the policemen involved had just started at the time of writing and so was then only an allegation, albeit a shocking one.

8. I have recently accepted a faculty position at the School of Social Sciences, Atkinson Faculty of Liberal and Professional Studies, York University, Toronto, Ontario.

Chapter Two

Conceptual Background

Race, of course, has no intrinsic significance, except to a racist.
(van den Berghe 1967: 21)

This chapter seeks to undo some of the obfuscating effects commonly produced by the use of such vague and polemical concepts as "race," "racism," "race relations," "ethnicity," "ethnocentrism," and "Blacks," and hence reach a clearer understanding of how they are used in the context of this book. Achieving such clarity from the outset is vital. Without a firm understanding of how these terms are used, one can neither appreciate the intricacies of the questions raised herein nor grasp what count as answers to them. As Tom Regan (1980: 11) aptly puts it: "Clarity by itself may not be enough, but thought cannot get far without it." In striving to understand these contentious concepts, we must guard against emotionalism; otherwise we run the risk of having our analysis clouded by prejudice.

Race and Related Concepts
It is believed that the term "race" entered the English language during the fifteenth century as a means of interpreting and classifying the variety of human life (Elliott and Fleras 1992). Despite this longevity, race is still hard to grasp in a scientifically manageable way. Indeed, few social science concepts are as contentious as that of race. Van den Berghe (1967: 9), a renowned chronicler of race and race relations, notes that the confusion stems from the fact that race has as many as four principal connotations:

a) As a sub-species of *homo sapiens* characterized by certain phenotypical and genotypic traits (e.g., the "Mongoloid race" or the "Negroid race").
b) As a human group that shares certain cultural characteristics such as language or religion (e.g., the "French race" or the "Jewish race").
c) As a synonym for species (e.g., the "human race").

11

d) As a human group that defines itself and/or is defined by other groups as different from other groups by virtue of innate and immutable physical characteristics. These physical characteristics are in turn believed to be intrinsically related to moral, intellectual, and other non-physical attributes or abilities.

This diverse usage of the term "race" has left analysts in a quandary over the frame of reference encompassed by the concept. Notwithstanding the confusion, many scholars (e.g., Omi and Winant 1998; Rex 1983; and Miles 1982) now reject the biological conception of race in favour of an approach that regards race as a social construct used to describe and explain certain physical and genetic differences among groups of people. The United Nations Educational, Scientific and Cultural Organization (UNESCO) played a pivotal role in casting doubt on the biological notion of race that was so prevalent in Anglo-European science prior to the 1950s. Through a number of scientific conferences (in 1950 1951, 1964, and 1967)[1] involving reputable scientists from a wide variety of social and physical sciences, including biology, genetics, physiology, anthropology, sociology, and population studies, UNESCO was able to come up with some definitive conclusions regarding the conception of race. Essentially, the UNESCO conferences noted that there is little or no correlation between the physical characteristics of groups of people and their social behaviour, and that "race" has a limited scientific value in classifying people into population groups. Many social analysts (e.g., Li 1999; Omi and Winant 1998; and Elliott and Fleras 1992) now acknowledge that physical and genetic attributes such as skin colour and the frequency distribution of blood type, commonly used for racial categorizations, are arbitrary and have no scientific basis. As Vic Satzewich (1999: 316) recently put it: "It is as irrational and senseless to use skin colour to define 'race' as it is to use the length of people's index fingers, or the number of moles that people have per square centimeter of skin." Indeed, there is a growing realization that biologically speaking, the differences *between* the "races" are far smaller than those *within* them. As Elliott and Fleras (1992: 29) point out, "discrete and distinct categories of racially pure people do not exist" due to the "intermingling effect of migration, social exchange, and intermarriages." In short, race is not a real phenotype.[2]

Not surprisingly, some scholars—notably Robert Miles (1989)—have called for an end to the use of the term "race" in social scientific discourse. In the blunt words of Miles (1989: 72), "'race' should be explicitly and consistently confined to the dustbin of analytically useless terms." In a recent critique of race-relations sociology, Vic Satzewich (1999) expresses a fairly similar sentiment from the standpoint of political economy. Among other things, Satzewich argues, with insights from Robert Miles (1982), Ashley Montagu (1964) and others, that the continued use of "race" contradicts the general recognition that no real race exists, helps reify the concept of race as though it were something concrete or real with ontological dimensions, and ultimately reproduces inaccurate and simplistic views about different groups of people. It is instructive to note that this line of reasoning goes back to the writings of Lloyd Warner (1941), who chose to avoid the term "race" altogether by describing race relations in caste terms.

Oliver C. Cox, in his *Caste, Class, and Race* (1959), criticizes Warner's approach, arguing that the Hindu caste system is based on consent, whereas race relations are usually characterized by conflict. In his contribution to the debate, van den Berghe (1967: 10) observed that, even in the United States, race relations have not always been conflictual, for "in the antebellum South slavery was accompanied by a considerable degree of accommodation of Negroes to their inferior status and by a lower degree of overt and violent conflict than in the post-bellum period." While it is not hard to subscribe to the view that the two concepts (caste and race) are different, at least theoretically, we must recall Frantz Fanon's (1967: 86) admonition: "It is utopian to try to ascertain in what ways one kind of inhuman behaviour differs from another kind of inhuman behaviour." Arguably, for the oppressed Black or the oppressed Hindu, the differences between the two systems are imperceptible. It is probably unnecessary to assert that no oppressed human group has ever given its consent to its own oppression unless consent is somehow defined as an agreement under duress. Because of the controversy surrounding "race," some sociologists, notably van den Berghe (1984: 216–18), advocate the use of "social race" to stress the fact that race is nothing but a social construct.

Given the varied and imprecise usage of "race," it is pertinent to specify the definition adopted here. After all, the way the concept is defined has a bearing on the sort of issues raised and the kind of explanations given. Drawing from the works of van den Berghe (1967, 1981), Rex (1983), Cashmore (1988), and Elliott and Fleras (1992), race is defined as a human population distinguished on the basis of socially perceived physical traits such as skin pigmentation, hair texture, facial features and the like. Thus one's racial group membership depends primarily on how society classifies him or her, regardless of the biological validity of the classification scheme utilized (Elliott and Fleras 1992). As already indicated, race is a social construct, a social myth; biologically speaking, there is only one race—the human race.

Given this basic fact, why do social scientists continue to use the concept? Why don't we just heed Robert Miles's call to discard the concept of race?[3] What justification do we have for the continued use of "man's [sic] most dangerous myth"?[4] There are no simple answers here, but one can argue plausibly that, since reality is usually socially constructed, it does not matter whether race is a sound biological concept or not. As long as race continues to have significant social connotations and consequences, it deserves our analytical attention as social scientists. As the now famous Thomas theorem in sociology posits: situations defined as real become real in their consequences (Thomas 1966: 301; orig. 1931).[5] The fact is, many people really believe in the reality of race and, indeed, act accordingly, regardless of what the physical science evidence suggests. One of the most powerful statements ever made in support of the continued use of race in social discourse can be found in the words of Daiva Stasiulis (1999: 365):

> Race endures because of the complexity and enduring power of racist discourses, the role of racial divisions in organizing relations of production and exploitation, the visceral, psychosexual responses evoked by racial differences, and psychically and politically affirming properties of racial existence. *These are all arguments for the fatality of colour blind political strategies that propose to do away with racism through its "unnaming."* (emphasis added)

The existence of racism in society is indisputable. But what really is racism? To what extent is it related to race? Does the presence of racism presuppose the existence of race as a concept? Can we analyze racism without any conception of race? Put differently, can we discursively deal with racism after discarding race into the dustbin of analytically useless terms (Miles 1989: 72)? Without question, race and racism are intricately interwoven. As van den Berghe (1967: 11) so brilliantly put it, "Without racism physical characteristics are devoid of social significance." Drawing upon the works of Macionis and Gerber (1999), Boyko (1998), Allahar (1993), and van den Berghe (1967), racism is defined in the context of this book as a philosophy of racial antipathy that asserts the superiority of one human group over another based on real or perceived genetically transmitted differences. Thus, racism occurs when the variation in skin colour, hair texture, eye colour, or any other biological attribute leads to a presumed superiority or inferiority of any classified group. For the most part, racism results in the exploitation of real or perceived physical differences to the advantage of the superior group and to the detriment of the "inferior" one.

Implicit in this account is the fact that the mere existence of physical differences among groups, regardless of how visible these differences may be, does not necessarily lead to racism. There will always be differences among human groups. It is only when such differences are considered a determinant of social behaviour and moral or intellectual qualities that we can properly speak of racism. Thus, only when real or perceived physical differences are seized upon as rationalization for prejudice and discrimination can we reasonably affirm racism.

Racism takes different forms. For instance, one can distinguish between individual racism and systemic racism. As the name suggests, individual racism is perpetrated by individuals; it may be overt or covert, but it is not imbedded in any institutional framework. Systemic racism, on the other hand, is inherent in societal institutions. It is normally covert, subtle, and sometimes unintentional, yet highly powerful in its consequences for ethnoracial minorities. A good example of systemic racism is the common practice, until quite recently, of requiring prospective transit drivers or police officers to be of a certain weight or height. On a *prima facie* basis, such a requirement seems non-racist but, as we now know, it invariably goes against some ethnoracial groups.

Two other forms of racism that are becoming increasingly popular in the Canadian literature are new racism and democratic racism. The term "new racism" is traced to the work of Martin Barker (1983) who describes it as a form of racism that is highly sophisticated and disguised through semantic manipulations. Unlike the old-fashioned racism, which relies on notions of innate biological superiority of Whites, new racism does not take such an extremist stance. It abandons such explicit racial language in favour of code words and race-neutral rhetoric. The works of Perera and Pugliese (1997) and Omi and Winant (1986) suggest that neoconservatives in the United States, Canada, Australia, and elsewhere in the West tend to *rearticulate* the meanings of concepts such as colour-blindness, racial equality, and race neutrality in ways that are disadvantageous to visible minorities. The new connotations accorded these concepts by the new right movement tend to disregard the historical and structural undertones of racial inequalities.

Through a skillful deconstruction, Della Kirkham (1998) has shown how the former Reform Party of Canada used the tactics of new racism to chastise federal policies such as employment equity, multiculturalism, and immigration. One of Kirkham's revelations will suffice here. The erstwhile Reform Party, Kirkham writes, called for an immigration policy that is "based on non-racial criteria—i.e., on Canada's economic needs and *adjustment potential* of the immigrant" (1998: 252; original emphasis). The party argued that immigrants "should possess the *human capital necessary to adjust quickly and independently* to the needs of Canadian society and the job market."[6] In a typical new-racist format, the "Reformers" began their argument with a non-racist rhetoric before resorting to code words to mask the basic thrust of their position on immigration. In this particular case, the semantic coding employed was not thick enough; we can all read through it.

Democratic racism, in the Canadian context, is normally traced to the works of Henry et al. (1995) and Li (1995, 1998), who use the term to describe the contradictory manner in which racist ideologies are simultaneously articulated with egalitarian and democratic principles in many Canadian social discourses. Thus, democratic racism occurs where racist ideologies and democratic principles coexist (Li 1998: 118). An example of the apparent contradiction involved in democratic racism is the ironic situation in Canada in which the *Charter of Rights and Freedoms*—which seeks to protect ethnoracial minorities—has ended up giving "legal ammunitions to extremists to advocate racial supremacism in the name of freedom of speech" (Li 1998: 118).

Given the intricate links between the concepts of race and racism, any attempt to discard race as a concept runs the risk of downplaying the realities of racism. Indeed, one wonders whether we can realistically address the problems of racism, either theoretically or practically, in the absence of "race." Analysts such as Satzewich (1999) and Appiah (1990) believe we can. As the former puts it, with insights from the latter:

> There is absolutely no connection between denying the analytical utility of the concept of "race" and whether one thinks that racism is a problem in our society. Racism is intellectually sustained by the belief in race; however, racism can be *studied and condemned* without believing in "race." (Satzewich 1999: 320; original emphasis)

Despite the tortuous arguments employed by Satzewich in support of this position, it is fairly similar to the claim: "Give me a place to stand and I will move the earth." It is impossible to find such a place, at least in this world, just as it would be to deal with racism in the absence of "race," given that racism is intellectually sustained by "race," as both Satzewich (1999) and Appiah (1990) acknowledge.

In fact, Vic Satzewich's position unintentionally plays into the hands of those who engage in the new racism. As Stasiulis (1999: 360) shrewdly points out, the fact that the tenets of the new racism are almost always articulated in code words "certainly supports argument for the continued need to provide manifest analytical attention to social divisions of race"; there is certainly no better code word than "unnaming." In practical terms, what can we possibly hope to gain by avoiding the use of "race" in our analysis of racism? At best, the impact of such a move in our attempts to alleviate the realities of racism would be minute, if existent at all. At worst, such a move may add more theoretical and semantic complications to the already-convoluted discourse on racism. Not surprisingly, some sociologists (e.g., Satzewich 1999; Bolaria and Li 1988; Miles 1982) have already started to use words such as "racialization" to connote the social process of grouping people—perhaps to undermine the concept of race in a way. In the context of this book, race remains a salient analytical concept. In fact, for the most part, it is not even put in quotation marks, except in specific instances where quotation marks are warranted for one reason or another.

"Race relation" is yet another term that requires elucidation. We can think of race relations as those patterns of human interaction that are based on a consciousness of racial differences. Not all social contacts among racial groups constitute race relations. Only those that are pursued with preoccupation with socially defined physical differences among people, or within the context of racial domination and exploitation, are considered race relations under the above conceptualization (Elliott and Fleras 1992; Cox 1959). As Cox (1959: 320) illustrates: if two people of different racial background deal with each other on their own merits, without any preoccupation with each other's race, then the pattern of interaction is not a race relation. However, if these people fashion their contacts on the basis of what they believe about the other person's race, then their interactions fall under race relations. The implication here is that race relation is ultimately a power relation couched in racial prejudice and stereotype.

Racial prejudice, as used here, connotes a set of negative or positive generalizations and beliefs about racial groups that are based primarily on faulty and unfounded presumptions. "Prejudiced beliefs," writes Boyko (1998: 11), "are betrayed by phrases such as 'They are all ...' 'Those people ...' and so on." Racial prejudices are based on stereotype. The latter derives from the Greek word *stereo,* which means "hard" or "solid" and connotes characteristics and behaviours attributed to a particular racial group and popularized through outlets such as newspapers, magazines, cartoons, movies, television, and racist jokes. Like prejudice, stereotypes are essentially fallacious in the sense that they leave no room for individuality.

Ethnicity and Related Concepts

The term "ethnic" originated from the Greek word *ethnos,* which means "heathen," "gentile," "non-Christian," "others." In contemporary usage, ethnicity shares several attributes with race as a means of human categorization and stratification. At times the distinction between these two concepts becomes so blurred that it raises the question of whether one is dealing with race or ethnicity, or both. In most cases, the mechanisms of social and psychological control used by the dominant group, the etiquette for inter-group behaviour, and the stereotypes, myths, and patterns of spatial segregation used against racial and ethnic minorities coincide directly (van den Berghe 1967).

Despite this overlap, ethnicity usually leads to a more flexible system of social stratification than race. Unlike racial groups, which are often distinguished by socially selected physical characteristics, ethnic groups are identified by socially selected cultural attributes. Simply put, "ethnicity is *a shared cultural heritage*" (Macionis and Gerber 1999: 324; original emphasis). As Jackson and Hudman (1990: 280) illustrate: "The combination of characteristics that make the Japanese distinct from the Koreans, or the Italians from Spaniards, is called ethnicity." For most practical purposes, one can move more easily across ethnic lines than across racial lines. Racial grouping invariably "results in a nearly impermeable caste system more easily than ethnic stratification" (van den Berghe 1967: 22). These distinctions notwithstanding, one really needs the context to be able to decipher whether a particular reference is to race or ethnicity, for, as Berry and Laponce (1994) indicate, "ethnic" sometimes means "race," and sometimes it does not.

Who really is ethnic? There are two conflicting views on this issue. Analysts such as Everett Hughes and Helen Hughes (1952: 7) insist, "We are all ethnic." Similarly, E.K. Francis wrote decades ago: "Not only the French Canadians or the Pennsylvanian Dutch would be ethnic but also the French in France and the Irish in Ireland (1947: 395). Other analysts disagree with this universalist connotation of ethnic, and rather use the term to cover only subordinate or minority groups—"others." This usage is what Werner Sollors (1999: 219) calls "ethnicity minus one"; the "one" being the dominant group—i.e., the White Anglo-Saxon Protestant (WASP) group in most Western industrialized nations. Obviously, in the Canadian context the "one" would refer to English and French Canadians as a group. This notion of ethnicity as otherness, non-standard, or in some sense not fully Canadian is far more prevalent in the Canadian social discourse than the former connotation of the concept. Thus we find people such as the former Quebec premier, Jacques Parizeau, blaming the "ethnic vote" for the loss of the *Yes* position in Quebec's sovereignty referendum in 1995. As Werner Sollors (1999) argues, members of the dominant group are generally hesitant to come under the ethnic umbrella; perhaps because of the nonreligious undertones of the concept.

It is instructive to note, however, that for the purpose of the Canadian census, Statistics Canada adopts the universalist definition in its "ethnic origins" count; it uses the term to cover both minority and majority groups. For this reason, one is somehow compelled to do likewise, as long as one relies on the census for empirical data. In this book, "ethnic" is used to imply otherness or ethnic minorities, in consonance with the most common deployment of the term in Canada, except in situations where the use of Statistics Canada data compels otherwise.

A term closely related to ethnicity is "ethnocentrism"—the belief that one's cultural practices or values are superior to those of other people. Ethnocentrism is not as overtly discriminatory or damaging as racism, yet it has the potential to breed intolerance, bigotry, and xenophobia toward ethnoracial minorities.

Writing in the Canadian context, Boyko (1998) has developed what he calls a "racist ladder" by arranging these race- and ethnic-related concepts in a hierarchical order based on their perceived impact on minorities. Situated at the bottom rung of Boyko's ladder is "stereotype," followed in ascending order by "prejudice," "discrimination," "attempts at racial purification" (which can take the form of ethnoracial segregation), and finally "genocide." As Boyko (1998: 13) skillfully demonstrates, Canada, as a nation, has occupied every rung of the racist ladder at one time or another. In his words: "[In Canada] the ladder is white… It is propped against a wall of suspicion, fear, pride and hatred. Without those emotions, and the ignorance from which they grow, the ladder would fall." Despite the obvious sensationalism, few can dispute Boyko's general argument that Canada is a racist country. Furthermore, as is shown by the simple

Figure 2.1 The Vicious Cycle of Racial Discrimination and Socio-economic Disadvantage

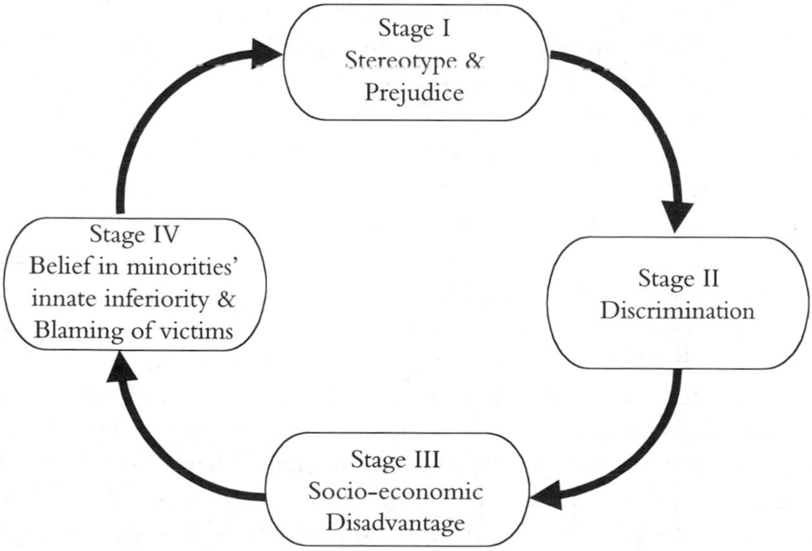

Source: Adapted from Macionis and Gerber, 1999, p. 331.

theoretical framework (Figure 2.1), adapted from Macionis and Gerber (1999: 331), the prejudice and discrimination, intrinsic in racism, work in a vicious cycle to perpetuate the socio-economic deprivations and subordination of minorities. Stereotypes and prejudices are usually at the root of racial discrimination; and the latter invariably lead to socio-economic disadvantages, such as poverty and unemployment. These disadvantages are then blamed on the victims' culture or attributed to their inherent inferiority, which, consequently, makes them unable to compete in a "tough" world. The framework (Figure 2.1) is broken down into stages for theoretical purposes only; one can conceivably enter the model from many different points or stages. In fact, it is usually difficult to locate the starting and end points of discrimination and its impacts, due to the intricacies, interrelationships, and overlaps inherent among the key components of racism.

The Concepts of Black and Visible Minority

We cannot take this theoretical discussion any further without offering some operational definition of the concept of "black," given its numerous connotations in social discourse. Colonial and post-colonial theoreticians contend that, time and again, Whites engage in a process of "othering" in which "White" becomes the yardstick against which all other communities of colour are judged (Weis and Fine 1996: 8). And as the works of Carl James (1998) and Allan James (1981) show, much of the othering, and its attendant marginalization of minorities, is accomplished through word usage. Not surprisingly, in the English language the word "black" or "blackness" is commonly associated with dirt, sin, evil, crime, anger, and dishonesty, as exemplified by phrases such "black lie," "black book," "black death," "black list," "black magic," "black sheep," "black market," "black-mail," etc. At the same time, "white," the antithesis of black, generally connotes honour, benevolence, righteousness, generosity, and grace. We even have "white lies," which we are told are neither significant nor harmful. The social construction of whiteness in these positive terms is somewhat problematic, given White culture's historical and contemporary ties to racial crimes and domination. We thus find some contemporary scholars calling for the reinterpretation of whiteness to imply the "space between guilt and denial" (Giroux 1997: 385; Frankenberg 1993: 232).

The most disturbing aspect of these semantic manipulations, as James (1981: 29) points out, is the tendency among many to regard these words as "natural" or a true reflection of humanity. For the purposes of this book, the term "Blacks" will be used to denote people of African descent in Canada. This category is made up of three sub-groups: Canadian-born descendants of Blacks who came from Africa during the slave trade; the descendants of Black Loyalists, refugees, fugitives, and settlers who immigrated during the American Civil War; and those who immigrated mostly from the Caribbeans and Africa after the Second World War in search of a better socio-economic and political environment. Until the 1996 census, Canadians, unlike Americans, were not officially disaggregated into races. Consequently, it was difficult to procure empirical data on Black Canadians from the censuses. The most commonly used surrogates for race in the available literature were "ethnicity," "country of birth," "mother tongue," and "country of last permanent residence." Needless to say, some of these proxies are very different from race. As a consequence, we need to note from the outset that some of the pre-1996 data on Blacks, used in this book, are problematic; they are mostly approximations derived from a variety of sources.

Because of these data difficulties, and the pejorative connotations of "Black," some Canadian researchers have chosen to use terms such as "Afro-Caribbeans" (Ray 1994), "West Indians" (Walker 1984), and "Caribbeans" (Henry 1994; Anderson 1993), instead of Blacks. Wolseley Anderson (1993), in particular, is highly critical of the use of the term "Blacks" with respect to Caribbean immigrants. He contends:

> "Black" refers to the biological correlates of race and colour; and not all West Indians possess the same biological properties. Second, race and colour may be important, but not sufficient, factors in determining the ethnicity of a people—how they think and behave; how they view the world; [and] how they esteem themselves. (Anderson 1993: 28)

Anderson raises other thought-provoking issues. For instance, he wonders whether the "readiness to denote all West Indians as Blacks makes it easier to apply [immigration] discrimination based on race?" "Does race transcend culture?" he also queries (Anderson 1993: 28–29). In fact, just as all West Indians are not Blacks, neither do all of them have the same ethnicity. Furthermore, while race may not transcend culture in some societies, one can argue that in Canada, for all practical purposes, race does transcend culture, at least from the standpoint of Blacks. And who can deny that skin colour overrides most attributes of Blacks' humanity and individuality in Canadian society?

Race is frequently taken as a decisive factor in several social and economic situations involving Black Canadians. There is, therefore, no need to shy away from the term "Blacks." The term is certainly distasteful, and even a misnomer, given that no human being is actually black in colour (or white, for that matter). Yet, for most Blacks, the term has a real meaning in their daily activities in Canadian society. Irrespective of their place of birth, Canadian Blacks share the common prejudicial experience that their presumed blackness engenders in their association with White Canada. While most White Canadians tolerate individual Blacks, there is no denying that some Whites look down upon Blacks, as a group, and treat Blacks with fear—and, sometimes, envy-coated condescension. "Race" and "Black" have such an overwhelming impact on people of African descent in Canada that we gain nothing at all by attempting to ignore these concepts in our analytical endeavours.

Also, it is worth noting that not all the connotations of "Black" are negative; in fact, the meaning of the concept varies considerably across space and time. The work of Sivanandan (1981) suggests that in contemporary Britain, for instance, the term Black is used to refer to all non-Whites. Sivanandan (1981) writes that this usage of "Black" did not emerge out of any racist discourse. Rather, Asian and Afro-Caribbean youth are increasingly adopting the term to assert their self-identity in their cultural and political movements. Renowned African-American feminist bell hooks makes a similar point in the context of the United States. She points out that African Americans often use "black" or "blackness" to signify and solidify their political resistance and self-affirmation (hooks 1992). Another significant impetus for the use of this term relates to data availability: Statistics Canada uses "Blacks" in its categorization of race in the Canadian census.

Another term that is increasingly gaining popularity as a substitute for "Blacks" and other non-White groups in Canada is "visible minorities." In the *Employment Equity Act* of 1986, visible minorities are officially defined as "persons, other than Aboriginal people, who are non-Caucasian in race or non-White in colour." The Act specifies the following groups as visible minorities in Canada: Chinese, South Asians, Blacks, Arabs and West Asians, Filipinos, Southeast Asians, Latin Americans, Japanese, Koreans, and Pacific Islanders. Clearly, of all the categories listed, "Blacks" is the only one that is based on skin colour and not on geographic location. This has inadvertently led to the distasteful and demeaning style in which some authors (e.g., Lampkin 1985: 651) list the visible-minority groups as: "blacks, Chinese, Japanese, South Asians, Southeast Asians, and Latin Americans." There is nothing inherently wrong with starting "black" with a lower case. Indeed, it is a common practice among many authors, but it is only fair in this instance to use an uppercase "B" for the sake of parity and also to avoid possible allegations of condescension. This is, perhaps, why Statistics Canada uses "Blacks" instead of "blacks" in its listings of visible minorities.

Like "Blacks," the term "visible minorities" (which is a Canadian original) has been variously criticized. Some denounce it as yet another nuance for "different" or "otherness." Critics, such as Bannerji (1986) and Carty and Brand (1989), argue that the term has a homogenizing effect, as it lumps diverse groups under one umbrella label. Bannerji claims that "visible minority" is derogatory, marking people as "not only different, but also inferior or inadequate" (1986: 27–29). Carty and Brand (1989: 39) argue that the term is both ahistorical and apolitical, in the sense that it is devoid of any appreciation of the class and racial struggles of the people it purports to capture. Some synonyms have been suggested as a substitute for "visible minorities." Notable among them are "Third World immigrants" and "non-White immigrants." Needless to say, these substitutes are equally, if not more, problematic (Agnew 1996).

Therefore, despite the problems associated with "visible minorities," it features prominently in this book, not only because there is no better substitute around, but also because, unlike the other terms, "visible minorities," like "Blacks," has a reliable database, as it is used by Statistics Canada in the Canadian census and also by many corporations for their employment equity data compilations. To appreciate the force with which race, ethnicity, and related concepts have been deployed in Canada to oppress Blacks and other minorities, it is necessary to explore, in some detail, the genesis of racial antagonism and its links with colonialism, capitalism, and slavery.

The Origins of Racial Antagonism

That differences exist among the human population is self-evident. Even a cursory observation of human groups will provide conclusive evidence of the variety of shades, sizes, and shapes of people living in different parts of the world. The implications of these differences, however, are not so obvious, and they have been characterized by centuries of debate and controversy (Head 1985a). Quite naturally, members of every society have a fairly good opinion of themselves compared with members of other societies. This is usually based on perceptions of cultural superiority or ethnocentrism. There is nothing intrinsically wrong with this allegiance or loyalty to one's own cultural values as long as these values are not projected as the standard for evaluating the behaviour of other groups; and, more importantly, as long as it does not lead to racial prejudice and oppression. A racist culture is automatically ethnocentric, but not vice versa. What we are concerned with here is not ethnocentrism but racial antagonism.

In his comprehensive exploration of the roots of racial antagonism, Cox (1959) notes that the Hellenistic empire (which extended into the territories of coloured people farther than any other European empire up to the end of the fifteenth century) did not exhibit racial antagonism. The basic mode of stratification in Hellenic Greece, according to Cox (1959), was cultural and not racial, as the main division of people was Greeks versus "barbarians." The term "barbarian" referred to people who did not possess Greek culture. It was especially used for someone who did not speak the Greek language. Undoubtedly, some Greek philosophers believed in the natural superiority and inferiority of people. For example, Aristotle in his *Politics* (Book I) espoused the view that for civilized people to be free, others must be exploited and denied human rights. He argued that social order should be based on slavery, which he believed was justified by the natural inferiority of non-Greeks (i.e., the barbarians). It must be stressed, however, that inferiority at the time was not equated with skin colour or any other physical trait. Indeed, members of the Greek city-states (*polis*) who founded cities along the shores of the Black Sea and the Mediterranean freely intermarried with the local population and easily accepted them as Greek citizens when the natives learned the Greek culture. In a similar vein, during the later Hellenistic experience under Alexander the Great, conscious efforts were made to assimilate the "barbarians" into Greek culture. It is known that Alexander himself married a Persian princess and encouraged his men to do likewise (Head 1985; Cox 1959).

Like the Greeks, the Roman Empire, the next great organization of human society in Europe following the fall of the Greek city-states, exhibited no racial antagonism.[7] As conquerors, the Romans captured several Greeks as slaves, and sometimes the enslaved Greek became the educator of his or her master. The basic social division among the Romans, like the Greeks, was not racial[8] but was based on a distinction between citizens and non-citizens. All non-Romans, regardless of their skin colour, were referred to as "barbarians" and considered inferior in learning and culture. Head (1985) writes that during the barbarian invasions of the fifth and sixth centuries, the Germanic people who conquered and later destroyed the Roman Empire were indeed considered inferior in culture.

Furthermore, in-depth analyses by Cox (1959) and Head (1985) suggest that there was no racial antagonism among medieval Europeans. The main division of people, according to these authors, was Christians versus non-Christians. The latter were considered heretic, infidel, and inferior. The fact is, around this time, Europeans knew very little about foreign lands. It was not until the first Crusade that Europe began to venture into "strange" lands. During the initial stages of the ensuing explorations, race was not a major factor, at least among the Spanish and the Portuguese, who made the initial skirmishes into Africa under such notables as King Henry the Navigator, Vasco da Gama, and Ferdinand

Magellan. Indeed, Africans who converted to Christianity were initially considered as equals. There are indications that upon initial contact, the Europeans were astonished by the wealth and civilization they saw in Africa (Rodney 1974). So, as Anton Allahar (1993: 41) queries, "When did Black people come to be worth less than others?"

Racial Antagonism and Capitalism: The Enduring Debate

Several Marxist analysts, following the pioneering works of Wakefield (1849), Cox (1959) Williams (1966), and others, argue that racial antagonism is a recent development limited to Western societies and rooted in capitalism. In the Canadian context, this viewpoint has been echoed by analysts such as Bolaria and Li (1988) and Head (1985). All of these authors situate the origins of racial antagonism in capitalism; more specifically, the capitalist search for cheap and submissive labour. Thus, to them, racial problems are inherently labour problems. Perhaps the most insistent and persistent voice in this school of thought belongs to Cox (1959: 322) who asserts:

> Our hypothesis is that racial exploitation and race prejudice developed among Europeans with the rise of capitalism and nationalism, and that because of the world-wide ramifications of capitalism, all racial antagonisms can be traced to the policies and attitudes of the leading capitalist people, the white people of Europe and North America.

Similarly, Head (1985: 645) notes that: "the evolution of racism, however, *began* with the rapid exploration and invasion of foreign nations by European merchants and explorers" (emphasis added).

Not surprisingly, these analysts contend that "slavery was not born by racism; rather, racism was the consequence of slavery" (Williams 1966: 7), and that slavery was more of an economic than a racial phenomenon. As Williams (1966: 19) characteristically puts it: "[Slavery] had to do not with the color of the labor, but with the cheapness of the labor." Bolaria and Li (1988: 186), drawing from the works of Wakefield (1849), Stampp (1956), and Williams (1966), suggest that the slave system was instituted "because a 'free' labour force, given the choice and opportunity, may not choose plantation labour." Thus, slavery was primarily an economic issue, which started as a rational choice of labour made by the plantation owners with a view to maximizing profit (Bolaria and Li 1988). In effect, the cause of slavery "relates not to vice or virtue, but to production" (Wakefield, 1849: 323).

While these arguments have some intuitive and emotional appeal to several social scientists, especially those of the Marxist persuasion, there are a number of conceptual and theoretical problems associated with them. First, there are indications that various people had independently discovered racism at different periods in history. For instance, studies by van den Berghe (1966, 1967) suggest that the Japanese looked down upon the Ainu of Hokkaido, and the Chinese compared the first Europeans to monkeys because of their hairiness. Also there is little doubt that the Indian caste system has significant racial undertones. In fact, Verna—the division of Hindus into four main castes (Brahman, Kshatriya, Vaisya, and Sudra)[9]— literally means "colour." Racism and racial prejudice were exhibited among ancient Africans also. The Bantus of central Africa regarded the pygmies who lived among them as an intermediary race between humans and chimpanzees; and the Fulani rulers of Zaire distinguished themselves from their Huasa subjects on the basis of their skin colour, hair, and facial form. Moreover, the Tutsi aristocracy of Burundi and Rwanda, who ruled over the Twa and the Hutu people, engaged in various forms of stratification on the basis of physical traits such as height and skin colour (van den Berghe 1966, 1967).

The fact that "the Western strain of the virus [of racism] has eclipsed all other forms in importance," however, remains indubitable; and "apart from its geographical spread, no other brand of racism has developed such a flourishing mythology and ideology" (van den Berghe 1967: 13). Western racism even had its theoreticians, such as Joseph Arthur de Gobineau and Houston Stewart Chamberlain (the so-called Nazi Prophet); its poets, such as Kipling; its theologians, such as Alfred Rosenberg; its pseudo-scientists, such as Madison Grant; and its politicians, such as Adolph Hitler. However, we must not forget that prior to Europe's scramble for Africa, Arabs were engaged in racial oppression and slave trade in East Africa, shipping Black Africans from Somalia, Kenya, and Sudan to Arabia, Persia, and India via the Indian Ocean (de Blij and Muller 1988). Chancellor Williams in his *Destruction of Black Civilization* (1971) estimates that Arab imperialism in Africa preceded that of Europeans by more than two thousand years. While industrial capitalism has benefited, and continues to profit immensely, from the labour exploitation inherent in racism, any supposition that racial antagonism was deliberately developed by the capitalist to procure cheap and submissive labour is contentious at the very least. Needless to say, racism has sometimes been counterproductive and dysfunctional for industrial capitalism. For one thing, racial hostilities often disrupt the workplace and cause damage to industrial property. Thus, if we even grant for the sake of argument that racism was consciously developed by the capitalist to enhance capital accumulation, we still have to admit that the strategy sometimes backfires.

Furthermore, the argument that racial antagonism derives from the cunning manipulations of the capitalist disregards the fact that the working class (or the proletariat) has also perpetrated some of the worst forms of racial exploitation in the workplace. The staunch Marxist may retort that the racial antagonism and exploitation carried out by the working class derive from the divide-and-rule tactics of the capitalist. But, as Satzewich (1999: 325) argues, this supposition is fallacious because it assumes that "the working class is like an empty vessel that can be filled with any rubbish that capitalists like."

The position that slavery was caused not by racism but by the capitalist's need for cheap labour, and therefore has nothing to do with vice, is equally difficult to sustain. It raises some critical questions. First, are we ready to assert that whenever the need for cheap labour arises, the capitalist can resort to coercion without infringing upon any moral imperatives? Second, and more importantly, why were Blacks the main target of slavery in North America? Bolaria and Li (1988: 186) argue that Blacks were the main target because, "of the three groups available at the time—Native Indians, White, and Blacks—the latter was the *most defenseless and powerless* vis-à-vis the White plantation owners" (emphasis added). Given that a slave is a person who has been rendered powerless and defenseless, this argument exhibits all of the characteristics of *petitio principii,* the logical fallacy of begging the question.[10] These writers are caught up in a helix: what they are really asserting is that Blacks were the main target of slavery because they were slaves.[11] Indeed, the real question of why Blacks were forcibly captured from their homeland and rendered powerless and defenseless in the New World in the first place remains unresolved.

In contributing to the debate, Elliott Skinner (1993), a Franz Boas Professor of Anthropology at Columbia University, has suggested that Black Africans were targeted partly because they did not have a nation-state structure at the time, and partly because they had achieved that level of agricultural and technical skill that was needed by the Europeans. Obviously, "nation-state" as used by Skinner here connotes Western-style nation-state; Africans had their own thriving nations, kingdoms, and empires prior to the era of slavery, something that should not be news to an anthropologist. While Skinner's argument has some merit, there is definitely more to the enslavement of Blacks in the New World than just their agricultural and technical know-how and their political set-up. Examined at very close range against the backdrop of the racial doctrines at the time, one can argue that the reasons for the enslavement of Blacks relate to race and vice and to racism and moral weakness. It is probably unnecessary to recall that, during that era, the human status was accorded *de jure* to Whites. In the words of De Gobineau (1853: 205–206):

> The Negroid variety is the lowest, and stands at the foot of the ladder.… We now come to the white peoples. These are gifted with reflective energy, or rather with an energetic intelligence. When they are cruel, they are conscious of their cruelty; it is very doubtful whether such a consciousness exists in the Negro.… I need hardly add that the word honor, together with all the civilizing influences connoted by it, is unknown to both the yellow and black man.

The ascendance of the supposed "superiority" of Caucasians had reached such a height during the era of slavery that any explanation of the slave system that disregards racism will, to paraphrase Jean-Paul Sartre (1963: 8), be caught up in its own contradictions. While the interplay between slavery, racism, and capitalism is tangled up in an indecipherable muddle, it is hard not to conclude that racism was a crucial component of slavery. The oppression of Blacks on racial grounds is indistinguishable from the oppression of Blacks for economic reasons (Rodney 1974). Before we examine the intricate links among racism, Christianity, and colonialism, it is apposite to profile the key racial doctrines that have emerged over the years. Only with this knowledge can we grasp the theoretical foundations of the dehumanization perpetrated upon Blacks and other indigenous people in Canada and across the globe.

Racial Doctrines

Concerns for racial differences between human groups antedate the birth of social science as an organized and self-conscious academic discipline in the nineteenth century (van den Berghe 1981). During the eighteenth century, racial and cultural differences were explained from the perspective of environmental determinism—the view that the physical environment determines human behaviour and culture to a greater extent than heredity. The basic tenet of environmental determinism is that people differ in custom, innovative capacity, and appearance because they live in different environments and pass on to their descendants the characteristics acquired in their respective habitats. This determinist thesis had a host of powerful sympathizers. For instance, Montesquieu, the famous French political philosopher, argued that humans progressed especially in areas of high winds and frequent storms. Similarly, the French philosopher and educational reformer Victor Cousin once observed:

> Yes, gentlemen, give me the map of a country, its configuration, its climate, its waters, its wind and its physical geography; give me its

natural productions, its flora, its zoology, and I pledge myself to tell you, *a priori*, what the man of this country will be, and what part this country will play in history, not by accident but by necessity, not at one epoch but at all epochs. (quoted in Febvre 1925: 10)

The high point of eighteenth-century environmental determinism, in its application to race relations, was the 1787 book by Samuel Stanhope Smith—*Essay on the Causes of the Variety of Complexion and Figure in the Human Species* (1965). In this book, Smith attempts to account for disparities in skin colour using geographical variables such as climate and topography. There is no denying the long-standing scholarly pedigree of the environmental determinist thesis. In fact, both Plato and Aristotle regarded Greece as having the ideal climate for government and intellectual work.

During the final quarter of the nineteenth century, European and U.S. social scientists embraced genetic determinism, and this gave rise to a version of racism couched in social Darwinism. Pioneered by writers such as Herbert Spencer, Walter Bagehot, Ludwig Gumplowicz, William Graham, and Benjamin Kidd, social Darwinism borrowed several biological concepts and propositions from Darwin's *Origin of Species* (1859) to justify overseas exploitation. With social Darwinism, disparities in human abilities, cultures, and behaviour were attributed to difference in genetic make-up. The social Darwinists saw the world "as a gladiatorial arena where populations were locked in mortal combat over scarce and valuable resources.... Those well adapted to compete in this ongoing struggle prospered; those poorly adapted lapsed into decline" (Elliott and Fleras 1992: 38). Under gurus such as Sir Francis Galton, Charles Darwin's cousin, social Darwinism entered the realm of eugenics—the pseudoscience of improving *homo sapiens* by purging the species of unwanted specimens. It is instructive to note that the eugenic movement gained considerable popularity not only in Nazi Germany, but also in several Western European countries, the United States, and Canada (particularly in Alberta). Now only scattered traces of eugenics remain due to the dearth of a receptive social and political climate (Elliott and Fleras 1992).

A related racial doctrine at the time was Lamarck(ian)ism, developed by the French naturalist Jean Baptiste de Larmark. The central theme of this doctrine was that changes in heredity occurred as people adapted to changes in the environment. Lamarckism was a powerful opposing force to Darwinism. It was reasoned that if variations in humans were attributable to environmental pressures, then natural selection needed to be relegated to a secondary role in human evolution (Gregory 1986). Lamarckism offered such a forceful critique to Darwinism that even

Charles Darwin was compelled to accept its veracity to some degree.

By the early 1900s, the intellectual currents in the social sciences had shifted once again to the environmentalist direction, and scholars such as Robert Park in sociology, Franz Boas in anthropology, and Ellen Semple in geography began to spread the environmental determinist thesis with renewed vigour. Semple's *Influences of Geographic Environment* (1911), which begins with the famous statement "Man is a product of the earth's surface," is replete with powerful environmental determinist sentiments. In describing the effect of mountain environment on human society, Semple (1911: 600–601) notes:

> The mountain-dweller is essentially conservative. There is little in his environment to stimulate him to change, and little reaches him from the outside world.... The bitter struggle for existence makes him industrious, frugal, provident.... He is peculiarly honest as a rule.... When the mountain-bred man comes down to the plain, he brings with him therefore certain qualities which make him a formidable competitor in the struggle for existence—the strong muscles, unjaded nerves, iron purpose and indifference to luxury bred in him by the hard conditions of his native environment.

A scholarly fact of major significance is that the existing racial ideology is not so much that indigenous people are inferior as that they must remain inferior (Cox 1959). Needless to say, no one can (or has) objectively proven the superiority of one human "race" over another. Given the obvious emotional undertones of racial discourse, it is hard to achieve any objectivity in matters of race. Notwithstanding the debates and misconceptions, there seems to be a growing consensus among contemporary social scientists that race is not so much a biological concept as a social construct; that differences in physical traits *within* racial groups are greater than differences *between* such groups; that it is impossible to regard any human group as superior or inferior due to skin colour or any other physical characteristics; and, finally, that racism is generally dysfunctional (Li 1999; Head 1985; van den Berghe 1981; UNESCO 1978).

Racism, Slavery, Colonialism, and Christianity: The Quadruple Web

It is impossible to comprehend the intricacies of modern race relations without examining their links with colonialism. As Cashmore (1988) reminds us, many contemporary race issues are the consequences of colonial conquest and exploitation. Colonialism involves the establishment and maintenance of rule by a sovereign power over other people who live in distant territories (Cashmore 1988; Lee 1986a). It is a policy by which the colonial power binds its colonies to itself through political ties with the primary aim of promoting its own economic interest. Through colonialism, Western racial ideologies and folklores spread like a wild fire in the harmattan[12] across Africa, Asia, and the Americas from the sixteenth century to the mid-twentieth century. The racial doctrines that were deployed generally portrayed Whites as superior without any objective attempt to prove the superiority of other racial groups.

Using their advanced technologies in navigation and warfare, the colonial powers, notably Spain, Portugal, Britain, France, the Netherlands, and, to a lesser extent, Denmark and Germany, conquered several traditional states in Africa, Asia, and the Americas and installed new systems of production, land tenure, and government. By the late nineteenth century, following the Treaty of Berlin in 1885,[13] nearly the entire continent of Africa was divided among the leading colonial powers. Only Ethiopia and Liberia were sovereign states in Africa at the beginning of the twentieth century.

A similar colonial scramble went on in the Far East and South East Asia, to the extent that by 1900 only Japan, China, and Thailand were outside direct colonial rule (Woddis 1967). The prevalence of names such as Portuguese Angola, Portuguese Guinea, Spanish Morocco, British Gold Coast, French West Africa, Belgian Congo, German East Africa, and Dutch East Indies attests to the level of domination exercised by imperial powers over their respective colonies.

In dealing with colonialism, we need to distinguish between *colonies de l'exploitation* and *colonies de peuplement*. The former refers to colonies exploited primarily for raw materials and cheap labour. The latter refers to those colonial dominions, such as Australia, New Zealand, Canada, and South Africa, that were the spatial extension of the imperialism and capitalism of the mother country, established to ease the pressure of population on European land (Nkrumah 1962). From the perspective of indigenous people, however, this distinction may be solely academic in the sense that, under both systems, native people were subjected to fairly similar patterns of exploitation, degradation, land robbery, and sometimes genocide.

Colonialism enabled the imperialist to secure cheap labour, cheap raw materials, and dumping grounds in Africa, Asia, and the New World. Inevitably, the colonial system evolved into a strong heartland–hinterland relationship, as Europe persistently determined the role to be played by the colonies. The uneven development between the colonies and the mother countries destroyed the capacity of the indigenous people to be self-sufficient. The colonies were totally dependent on what the imperialists were prepared to buy from them and sell to them. There is little doubt that from the standpoint of the Europeans, the colonies existed mainly for the enrichment of Europe through the human and natural resources they produced and the market they provided for the surplus manufactured commodities from Europe.

Racism was complementary to the colonial enterprise. Racial doctrines were often invoked to justify the exploitation of indigenous people. Characteristically, colonized people were seen as subhuman and were treated accordingly. The belief was that indigenous people were so "backward," "uncivilized," "primitive," and "untamed" that they could not be treated in any way similar to European settlers. As Joyce Green (1995) points out, under the colonial adventure, incommensurabilities between the Europeans and the natives were invoked to assert the "superiority" of the former and the inevitability of a new order of relationship grounded in race privilege.

The colonial ideology was predicated on a form of paternalistic, benevolent despotism (van den Berghe 1966, 1967). Yet, in the philippic words of Jean-Paul Sartre (1963: 25): "This was nothing but an ideology of lies, a perfect justification for pillage, its honeyed words, its affection of sensibility were only alibis for our aggression."

Through discriminatory laws, bureaucratic procedures, and military might, the colonial powers were able to create an insurmountable divide between the colonizer and the colonized populations in all spheres of life. In most cases, there existed separate and unequal communities (or townships) for the colonized people and the European settlers. The best description of the disparities that existed between these two spatial entities can be found in the bone-chilling words of Frantz Fanon (1963: 38–39):

> The two zones are opposed.... Obedient to the rules of pure Aristotelian logic, they both follow the principle of reciprocal exclusivity. No reconciliation is possible, for the two terms, one is superfluous. The settlers' town is a strongly built town, all made of stone and steel. It is a brightly lit town; the streets are covered with asphalt.... The settler's feet are never visible.... His feet are protected by strong shoes although the streets of his town are clean and even, with no holes and stones. The settler's town is a well-fed town, an easygoing town; its belly is always full of good things. The settlers' [sic] town is a town of white people, of foreigners.... [Conversely] the town belonging to the colonized people ... is a place of ill fame, peopled by men of evil repute. They are born there, it matters little where or how; they die there, it matters not

where, nor how. It is a world without spaciousness; men live there on top of each other, and their huts are built one on top of the other. The native town is a hungry town, starved of bread, of meat, of shoes, of coal, of light.

In colonial societies the law of the frontier was justice, as genuine ethics were generally abandoned. Native women were considered booty, hence miscegenation, in the form of institutionalized concubinage between indigenous women and White men, was common. Intermarriages were rare, however, not only because there was such vast disparity between the indigenous and the settler cultures that the common understanding necessary for marriage was unattainable, but, more importantly, because the miscegenation was generally seen by the dominant groups as "another of its legitimate prerogatives and forms of exploitation" (van den Berghe 1967: 27). With this attitude, it is not surprising that there emerged a large segment of people with mixed blood in all colonies.

The resulting "potpourri" of skin pigmentation further complicated race relations under colonialism. Depending on a variety of factors such as the race of the native population, the imperial power involved, and the level of exploitative zeal among the settlers, those of mixed blood may, or may not, be favoured by the colonizers. In the case of most Black African and Caribbean countries, especially those in which the number of European settlers was relatively small, the mixed-bloods (i.e., the mulattos or the so-called Native Whites) were favoured on the basis of their degrees of admixture: usually, the lighter the melanin, the greater the social and economic opportunities. Usually taxonomy of skin colour was devised, with recognized names and mythologies for the different shades of whiteness or blackness (Fanon 1963, 1967). In the case of South Africa, where racism had been a way of life, the spectrum of whiteness was not only socially acknowledged, but legally sanctioned as well.[14] In other colonial situations, especially in places such as the United States, Canada, and Australia where the number of settlers was relatively large, minimal melanin was not "so high prized" (Cox 1959: 364). Indeed, among people of colour, darker shades, especially in men, was preferred to increasing whiteness among the mixed-bloods; and lighter shades attracted no social or economic favours from Caucasians.

The use of gunpowder gave the Europeans an enormous edge over indigenous Africans in maintaining the colonial enterprise for as long as they did. The brute force with which the "superiority" of Europeans and European values was affirmed in the colonies still evokes suspicion when Western values are mentioned in front of people from former colonies. As Frantz Fanon (1963: 43) bluntly asserts: "It so happens that when the native hears a speech about Western culture, he pulls out his knife—or at least he makes sure it is within reach."

Despite the obvious significance of brute force and military might in sustaining systematic racial exploitation in the colonies, we must recognize the hypocritical role of missionaries in disseminating Christian ideas that were conducive to racial domination and colonialism. The Christians among the colonialists invoked and twisted a host of theological doctrines and Bible stories to rationalize their shameful deeds. One of the most enduring manipulations of Biblical stories involves the story of Noah's descendants, found in the book of Genesis. Genesis Chapter 9, Verse 20 begins the story of how Ham, one of Noah's three sons, saw his father drunk and naked in a tent. Ham went and told his other brothers, Shem and Ja'pheth, who took a piece of garment and covered Noah without looking at his naked body. Upon waking and learning that Ham saw him naked, Noah cursed Ham, saying that from now on he will be the lowest of slaves to his brothers. Even though the Bible does not say that Blacks descended from Ham, some White Christians were somehow able to ascertain, quite sanctimoniously, that Whites were the descendants of Ja'pheth, while Blacks hailed from Ham and, therefore, were destined to be servants to Whites.[15]

Christians routinely used Ham's link with sin and evil as a moral justification for the enslavement of Blacks during the colonial period. Additionally, the early Christians maintained a colour symbolism that invariably portrayed the colour black as inferior, sinful, and satanic (Bastide 1968). Indeed, one need only compare the pictures of Christ (or the Virgin Mary) to the popular depictions of Satan in Christian books of antiquity and modern times to appreciate how the chromatic politics of Christianity works. Jesus, a Jew, has been metamorphosed into an Anglo-Saxon. As Anton Allahar (1993: 46) puts it:

> Christ has become rather Aryanized. For his presumed Jewish origins are now quite difficult to detect phenotypically, owing to the deliberate whitening or bleaching effort that changed Christ from a Semitic to an Aryan person. Thus, the dark hair Christ is thought to have had is now rendered as sandy-brown or blonde, while his once-matching dark eyes have become blue.

Christians found themselves in an ironic situation: apparently "the old Christian belief that God made man in his own image and likeness has been reversed: man (White man) is now seen to have remade God in his own image and likeness" (Allahar 1993: 49). In their efforts to justify the racial oppression and enslavement of Blacks in the New World, both Protestants

Figure 2.2: Major Sources of Africa Slaves

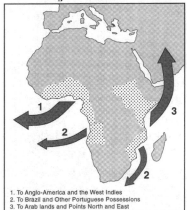

1. To Anglo-America and the West Indies
2. To Brazil and Other Portuguese Possessions
3. To Arab lands and Points North and East

Source: Modified from Fellows 1967: 121

and Catholics relied heavily on the claim that Blacks were evil, cursed by God, and therefore deserving of the punishment of enslavement. Some Christians even asserted that the enslavement of Blacks was a religious activity meant to redeem Blacks from their sins and prepare them for salvation and, ultimately, heaven (Omi and Winant 1998; Allahar 1993).

As Nkrumah (1962: 13) writes: "While the missionaries implored the colonial subject to lay up his treasures in Heaven where neither moth nor rust doth corrupt, the traders and administrators acquired his land and mineral resources." The hypocrisy here is apparent. In the caustic words of Walter Rodney (1974: 89): "How else can one explain the fact that the Christian church participated fully in the maintenance of slavery and still talked about saving souls!"

The dehumanization of colonialism in Africa reached its apogee in the late nineteenth century with the exportation of millions of Blacks to the New World. The vast majority of the slaves destined for the Americas were derived from the west coast of Africa, from areas such as Côte d'Ivoire, Ghana, Nigeria, Dahomey, Cameroon, Gabon, and Congo. Most of the slaves derived from Africa's east coast were natives of Mozambique (Figure 2.2). While our primary interest now is on the movement of slaves across the Atlantic to the New World, we must not overlook the fact that an equally significant wave of forced relocation of Africans occurred across the Indian Ocean and the Mediterranean Sea to the Arab world.

No one knows for certain the number of Africans shipped to the Americas. Generally accepted estimates place the number of African slaves anywhere from ten to fifteen million. The absence of data on Africa's population during the era of slavery makes it difficult to undertake any scientific assessment of the impact of the trade. In any case, as Rodney (1974: 96) rightly suggests, any estimate of the number of Blacks shipped to the Americas "which is narrowly based on the surviving records is bound to be low, because there were so many people at the time who had vested interest in smuggling slaves."

> [Furthermore] on any basic figure of Africans landed alive in the Americas, one would have to make several extensions—starting with a calculation to cover mortality in transshipment…. There were also numerous deaths in Africa between time of capture and time of embarkation, especially in cases where captives had to travel hundreds of miles to the coast…. Most important of all, it is necessary to make some estimate as to the number of people killed and injured so as to extract the millions who were taken alive and sound. (Rodney 1974: 96)

While the colonial system yielded some "benefits" including the diffusion of agricultural, educational, and medical innovations to the colonies, it is fair to concede that the system essentially served the interest of the colonialists. Indeed, radical Africanists such as Kwame Nkrumah, Frantz Fanon, and Walter Rodney insist that all the development projects undertaken in the colonies—railways, roads, bridges, schools, and hospitals—were merely accidental adjuncts to facilitate the economic exploitation of the colonies.

The colonial system took a hefty toll not only on human life but also on the cultural heritage of native populations throughout the world, not to mention the psychological deprivations it engendered. Millions of people were systematically and skillfully injected with fear and assertions of their inferiority. We thus find Frantz Fanon asserting in his *Black Skin, White Mask* (1967: 93) that "the feeling of inferiority of the colonized is the correlative to the European's feeling of superiority…. *It is the racist who creates his inferior*" (original emphasis).

Canada and the Black Societies of Africa and the Caribbean

So far, we have examined colonialism and its attendant race relations from the standpoint of African and other colonies in the developing world. The discussion clearly shows that the colonial enterprise actively created, intensified, and maintained racism for its own survival. Where does Canada fit in all this? What was the connection between Canada and the Black societies of Africa and the West Indies during the colonial era? To what extent were the socio-economic and racial dynamics of Canada different from, or similar to, those of Black African and Caribbean nations during the period of imperial domination? How did Canada's relationship with

Figure 2.3: Canada's Links with the Black Societies of Africa and the Caribbean during the Colonial Framework

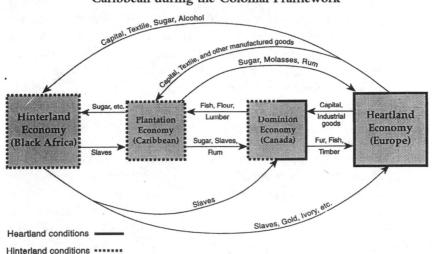

Heartland conditions ——
Hinterland conditions ·······

Europe (specifically, Britain and France) at the time of the trans-Atlantic slave trade compare with the Euro-Afric-Caribbean link? It is to these questions that we turn in the remainder of this chapter.

As noted, the colonial system created a heartland–hinterland relationship between the metropolis and the colonies. Europe functioned as the core of control and change, while the colonies remained dependent with limited social, economic, and political clout. The resulting asymmetrical relationship was manifested in patterns of investment, trade, migration, and exploitation. In nearly all colonial situations, the heartland dictated and controlled the level of inter-colony trade. The colonies shared direct trade links with their respective metropolis, and most inter-colony trade was mediated by the metropolis.

As depicted in Figure 2.3, being a colonial dominion, Canada exhibited some of the characteristics of the European heartland, together with some of the conditions of the Afric-Caribbean hinterland. For the most part, however, Canada was closer to Europe, in social and economic terms, than to the Black nations of Africa and the Caribbean. And between Africa and the Caribbean, Canada had far greater commodity exchange with the latter. Items such as flour, timber, and fish were shipped from Canada to maintain the plantations of the Caribbean; in turn the Caribbean islands supplied Canada with sugar, rum, molasses, and Black slaves.

Unlike the colonial situation that existed in Canada, private enterprise among Blacks and other indigenous people in Africa and the Caribbean was consciously restricted by imperial Europe. As Anderson (1993) rightly points out, during the colonial era, conditions and possibilities existed in Canada for small private enterprises to rise in response to the needs of communities. The activities of fishing, trapping, lumbering, and homesteading provided significant impetus for the emergence of a small domestic market in Canada. This was not the case in most African and Caribbean nations. Indeed, the Black colonies, unlike Canada, were primarily meant for exploitation, and Black people were treated as property to be disposed of or used for the benefit of Whites, especially under the plantation agriculture so prevalent during the era of slavery. In fact, few analysts will disagree with Anderson's (1993) assertion that the human degradation of plantation slavery is a phenomenon without parallel in the annals of human cruelty.

Notwithstanding these differences, there are some noteworthy similarities between the colonial past of Canada and that of Africa and the Caribbean. To begin with, they were all tied primarily to British and French imperialism. Second, both Canada and, in particular, the Caribbean experienced a massive influx of Black immigrants during the colonial era. With the notable exception of the free slaves who were sent from the Caribbean and Nova Scotia to Sierra Leone, large-scale migration was generally one-way: from Africa to the Americas (Figure 2.3).

Following the abolition of slavery, the Caribbean's source of immigrant labour shifted from Africa to places such as India, China, and the Middle East. These immigrants were used as indentured labour to replace the Black slaves. A fairly similar influx of East Indian, Chinese, and Japanese indentured labourers, as well as Black Loyalists, occurred in Canada during the late eighteenth and early nineteenth centuries. These immigration trends have left the indelible imprint of the plural society phenomenon and a concomitant racially based social and economic stratification system in both Canada and the Caribbean (Porter 1965; Anderson 1993). Thus we find in both Canada and the Caribbean a class pyramid with Blacks and indigenous people at the very bottom and Whites at the apex.[16] Finally, as we shall see in the next chapter, the enslavement of Black Africans took place not only in the Caribbean islands but also in Canada.

Conclusion

Before closing this chapter we need to take note of key implications of the preceding discussion for our understanding of the Black presence in contemporary Canada. First, while nothing is really gained by comparing the inhumanities endured by various visible minority groups at the hands of European settlers in Canada, it is pertinent to note that the Black experience in Canada is unique. As we shall see in Chapter 3, Blacks were the only people relocated into Canada through forced and impelled migration and subjected to slavery at the same time. Several historical and contemporary factors work in concert to accentuate the racial denigration and marginalization of Blacks in Canada, as in many other Western industrialized nations. The key factors include the high visibility of Blacks; the legacy of slavery and its attendant dehumanization; the innumerable negative connotations of the word "black" in social discourse; and the primacy of skin-colour racism in Canada. The fact is, much of the negative racial mythology and stereotypes developed under colonialism and slavery did not disappear with the abolishment of slavery. The symbolism of colour and race, for instance, is still prevalent in both the sacred and secular domains of Canadian society. Thus, the straitened circumstances of Blacks in contemporary Canada are not fortuitous; they correspond to the colonial ideologies of the past. Any contemporary study of the Black situation in Canada that ignores this, to use John Berger's (1974: 40) phrase, "acquires the oversimplified character of a fable." Without a doubt, it is because of the legacy of slavery that Blacks are frequently treated with utter condescension and discriminated against in nearly all spheres of Canadian life. We cannot reasonably expect a group to endure centuries of racial prejudice, concocted negative mythology, slavery, and other forms of dehumanization without facing long-term stigmatization afterwards. In a nutshell, the racism faced by Blacks today is an extension of the racism of the colonial era.

Second, it is important to note that, because racial prejudice and racism are ultimately reducible to a set of negative attitudes, they create among victims enormous psychological deprivation and disillusionment, such as inferiority complex and loss of self-esteem. As Cox (1959: 368) observes, racism tends to reduce the civic pride of its victims: "It keeps them spiritually on the move; it denies them the right to call their country home; it limits patriotism severely, thus making a genuine love of one's country virtually impossible."[17] In their extreme forms, these problems can render the victims ashamed of their skin colour and their cultural heritage. Naturally, Blacks are not affected equally by racism, neither do they respond in a uniform manner to racial problems. Rather, complex response mechanisms have emerged among Blacks. These vary based on age, sex, country of birth, period of immigration, educational background and a host of other factors. There are indications that higher-status visible minorities, including Blacks, tend to seek the acceptance of the dominant White group and, at the same time, try to prevent their privileges from being impinged upon; the lower-status group, on the other hand, tends to be more radical (Li 1988: 34). In the absence of any reliable scientific research on mulattos, one can only speculate on the psychological disillusionment that may follow the sudden realization that in Canada, unlike places such as the Caribbean, Latin America, and Africa, lighter skin colour is hardly rewarded with any socio-economic opportunities.

A third major implication worthy of note is the fact that under the colonial system, different Black nations came under the control of different imperial powers, most of which endeavoured to replace the indigenous language, religion, and culture, including food, entertainment, and sports preferences, with their own European versions. With time, these Black societies became so transformed that some shared more in common, especially in terms of religion, official language, and food preference, with their imperial powers than with other Black nations. As a consequence, it is not uncommon to find that Black immigrants from neighbouring countries in Africa with different colonial masters (e.g., British Ghana and French Ivory Coast) have virtually nothing in common, besides their humanity, skin colour, and, of course, their experience with racism in Canada. Li (1988: 31) went to the crux of this particular matter when he observed that "the ability of Asian, African, and Central American immigrants to speak English—long before they immigrated to North America— is more a result of the colonial legacy than of assimilation into the North American mosaic." Despite this diversity, Blacks, in particular, are often treated as a homogenous group in Canadian society. In many instances, skin colour is assumed to override all attributes of their human individuality. This is obviously a serious analytical blunder.

Finally, we must note that in addition to the cultural transformation engendered by colonialism, Black immigrants, like all other immigrants, inevitably make adjustments to accommodate and to reflect the Canadian socio-economic and geopolitical climate. Therefore, the Black cultures found in Canada are not a simple replication of cultures transferred from Caribbean or African societies to Canada. Some so-called Black cultural attributes are, indeed, social constructions improvised on Canadian soil to help the Black diasporic communities cope with life in Canada (Geschwender 1994; Li 1988).

The preceding paragraphs clearly show that Canada's relationship with Black societies goes back to the era of slavery. Blacks have been forcibly relocated, traded, and recruited from various African and Caribbean nations to Canada. By and large, due to their high visibility and to the legacy of slavery, Black immigrants, irrespective of their country of origin, face severe race-related problems in Canada. Along with Native Canadians, Blacks occupy the lowest level of social acceptability in Canadian society. In all this, it should be made abundantly clear that there is not and has never been, a Black problem in Canada. As Folarin Shyllon (1993: 244) points out: "When Whites, for example, object to Blacks moving into a particular street or district, it is those Whites who manifest such a poverty of respect for humanity who have a problem that cries aloud for solving" and not the powerless Blacks.

Notes
1. See Satzewich 1999: 315.
2. A phenotype is a classification based on the outwardly visible or physically expressed action of the genes; the actual genetic makeup that is not visible but is manifest in the phenotype is called a genotype.
3. Indeed, Vic Satzewich (1999) has recently echoed this call in the Canadian context.
4. The assertion that race is the most dangerous myth was made by Ashley Montagu (1964) (quoted in Satzewich 1999: 317).
5. Environmental perception geographers commonly make a homologous argument to the effect that "decision makers operating in an environment base their decision on the environment as they see it and not as it is [from the standpoint of objective science]. The action resulting from their action on the other hand is played out in real environment" (Brookfield 1969: 53).
6. This statement is from *The Reformer*, published by the former Reform Party of Canada, January 5, 1992, vol. 1, p. 2; quoted in Kirkham (1998: 252).
7. It is instructive to note that a somewhat different view has been presented by John Block Friedman (1984) in his *Staying Power: The History of Black People in Britain* (London: Pluto). Friedman's work suggests that beginning with the writings of Homer, as early as the ninth century BC, all the way through to the works of Virgil (70–19 BC), and even in the travel reports of Alexander the Great, one finds a virtual obsession with the "monstrous race" that supposedly lived on the margins of the Greco-Roman world.
8. That is not to say that there was no iota of racial/ethnic prejudice among the Greeks and Romans, Cicero, the Roman consul, orator, and writer, once told Atticus not to get his slaves from Britain "because they are so stupid and so utterly incapable of being taught that they are not fit to form a part of the household of Athens" (quoted in Cox 1959: 331).
9. In the Caste System, the Brahman means spiritual leaders or teachers; Kshatriya refers to a warrior a nobleman; Vaisya means merchant or craftsman; and Sudra is a farmer or a worker.
10. This is a fallacy committed if one assumes as a premise for his argument the very conclusion he intends to prove. A more complete version of this fallacy is called circular argument. An example of this fallacy is as follows: "One may argue that Shakespeare is a greater writer than Robbins because people with good taste in literature prefer Shakespeare. And if asked how one tells who has good taste in literature, one might reply that such persons are to be identified by their preferring Shakespeare to Robbins" (Copi 1978: 98).
11. Note that we are substituting the word "slave" for "a person who has been rendered powerless and defenseless" in line with our definition of "slave."
12. Harmattan is the name of the dry dusty winds that blow from the Sahara toward the West African coast.
13. The Berlin Conference, which lasted for nearly three months, began in No-

vember 1884. Otto von Bismarck, the architect of the German Empire, initiated it. The conference—attended by fourteen imperial powers—sought to settle the political segmentation of Africa. At the time of the conference, more than 80 percent of the African continent was under some form of traditional African rule. Nonetheless, the colonialists proceeded to partition the continent for their respective political and economic interests (De Blij and Muller 1988: 438).

14. Under the apartheid system, the South African population was legally divided into four races, which in a descending order of "superiority" were made up of Europeans or Whites, Indians, Coloured or mixed-bloods, and Africans. For a comprehensive treatment of race relations under the South African apartheid system readers may consult Chapter 5 of van den Berghe (1967).

15. The question then becomes "Who are the descendants of Shem?" Also, Genesis, Chapter 10, Verse 6 tells us that Cush, a descendant of Ham, became the father of Nim'rod, who, according to the Bible, was the first person on earth to become a mighty warrior. Apparently, Noah's curse on Ham was nothing more than the hollow grumbling of an intoxicated old man. It is instructive to note here that some Black theologians have also deployed the Bible to denigrate Whites in their struggle against racial domination. For instance, many Blacks have cited the story of Miriam, narrated in the book of Numbers, Chapter 12, to suggest that "whiteness" is a sign of God's displeasure. According to the story, Miriam changed colour to white when she objected to Moses's marriage to an Ethiopian woman (i.e., Cu'shite woman).

16. Undoubtedly, a similar pattern of stratification can be found in some African countries, especially South Africa, a country that is synonymous with racism and racial oppression in the minds of many people.

17. Although I would wish to be proven wrong on the relevance of Cox's assertion to the Black situation in Canada, I believe that careful research would reveal that many Blacks feel detached from the civil and political life of Canada. Even though Black Canadian citizens, like all others in Canada, have the right to vote, very few actually exercise this right.

Chapter Three

The History of Blacks in Canada

To be sold—A Black Woman, named Peggy, aged about forty years; and a Black boy her son, named Jupiter, aged about fifteen years, both of them the property of the Subscriber. The Woman is a tolerable Cook and washer woman and perfectly understands making Soap and Candles. The Boy is tall and strong for his age, and has been employed in Country business, but brought up principally as a House Servant.... The Price for the Woman is one hundred and fifty Dollars—for the Boy two hundred Dollars, payable in three years with Interest from the day of Sale to be properly secured by Bond &c—But one fourth less will be taken in ready Money. (An advertisement in the *Upper Canada Gazette*, quoted in Walker 1980: 21)

At the risk of arousing resentment, the above-quoted advertisement is a succinct encapsulation of the dehumanization that Blacks endured in Canada during the era of slavery. It provides an illuminating historical motif through which we can view the contemporary circumstances of Black Canadians. Due to the legacy of slavery, Blacks are stigmatized and subjected to an unfavourable ideological heritage in Canadian society (Boyko 1998; Bolaria and Li 1988). Yet, as Lampkin (1985) points out, some Canadians still believe that slavery did not exist in this country and that slavery was an entirely U.S. phenomenon. This is not surprising since Canadian historians have generally attempted to black out the Black experience in Canada. "A student of Canadian history," writes Walker (1980: 3), "can go right through our school system, university courses and even graduate school without ever being exposed to the history of Blacks in Canada." Right from early elementary school, Canadian students are taught histories that dwell on an endless glorification of Whites with few parenthetical references to Blacks and other visible minorities. Green (1995: 87) laments that "in Canada, 'conventional' history (history which underpins our social and political conventions) has distorted our collective consciousness, overstating certain contributions while making others invisible." What is surprising is how these histories are so successfully disseminated and accepted by many, including highly educated Blacks.

The exploitation of Black labour through slavery was such an essential element in the foundation of Canada that the neglect of Black history can hardly be accidental. Drawing on the works of Boyko (1998), Bolaria and Li (1988), Lampkin (1985), Walker (1980), Winks (1971) and other scholars, this chapter examines the history of Black Canadians. The intention here is not only to demonstrate that slavery was a real part of the Canadian labour system, but also to challenge the displacement of Black history by aeriform theories and self-serving mythologies and, ultimately, to help correct some of the misconceptions about the Black presence in Canada.

Slavery and the Early Settlement of Blacks in Canada

The forced relocation of Blacks from Africa to the New World started around the early 1600s. Initially, the Blacks were used as indentured servants, but within a few years of their arrival many were coerced into slavery. By 1670, slavery was accorded statutory backing in Virginia, Maryland, and other colonies in the New World (Wilson 1973). Because no large-scale plantation agriculture existed in Canada, many Canadians believe that slavery was not practised here. However, historical records show that slavery persisted in Canada, although it never assumed the level it did in the United States and the Caribbean (Walker 1980; Tulloch 1975; Winks 1971). The arrival of a Black man by the name Matthew Da Costa (or Mattieu da Costa) in Nova Scotia in 1606 has generally been considered the root of Black history in Canada (Lampkin 1985).[1] According-ing to Boyko (1998: 158), Da Costa arrived in Canada with explorer Pierre Du Gua De Monts, who, together with Champlain, founded Port Royal in the early 1600s. From the time of Da Costa's arrival to about the last quarter of the seventeenth century, Black slavery was insignificant in Canada. Most of the slaves then were Native Indians, referred to as *panis* (Winks 1971; Bolaria and Li 1988). It was towards the end of the seventeenth century that acute labour shortages prompted the importation of Blacks in significant numbers. And, as Walker (1980: 19) points out, "from then until the early nineteenth century, throughout the founding of the present Quebec, Nova Scotia, New Brunswick, and Ontario, there was never a time when Blacks were not held as slaves in Canada."

Settlement in Atlantic and Central Canada

Historians such as Walker (1980) and Tulloch (1975) believe that the prosperity of the New England colonies, which many attributed to the prevalence of Black slave labour led to a demand in New France for the importation of Blacks. Jean Talon, the first intendant of New France, successfully persuaded King Louis XIV to allow the importation of Black slaves from Africa, the Caribbean, and the United States, even though slavery had been abolished in France. In fact, slavery continued in Quebec even after the 1759 Conquest brought Quebec under British control. According to Boyko (1998: 158) "the article of capitulation, signed after the fall of Montreal in 1760, guaranteed the continuation of slavery in the colony." The demand for Black slaves was so high that, in 1763, when General James Murray, the first British governor of Quebec, sent a request to New York for a shipment of slaves, he pleaded:

> I must most earnestly entreat your assistance, without servants nothing can be done. Had I the inclination to employ soldiers which is not the case, they would disappoint me, and Canadians will work for nobody but themselves. Black slaves are certainly the only people to be depended upon. (quoted in Walker 1980: 23)

While some of the Black slaves around this time were used for agricultural, shipbuilding, and mining purposes, the vast majority performed domestic duties for the elite—the governors, doctors, prelates, and the merchant class. The status of slaves in New France was regulated by the *Code Noir,* which though never officially proclaimed in the colony was used as a customary law (Winks 1971). The *Code,* originally promulgated in 1685 to protect the slave owners of the West Indies from slave revolt, theft, and escape, extended some protection and privileges to the slaves in New France. For example, the *Code Noir* allowed slaves to serve as witnesses at religious ceremonies, marry with their masters' consent, and even petition against a free person (Winks 1971).

Some contemporary analysts contend that slavery was never institutionalized in New France and that it was merely "an unsystematic, spasmodic approach to solving labour problems" (Lampkin 1985: 654). Perhaps, those who articulate this view need to be reminded that the slave system was given full legal backing in New France by 1709, and nearly all respectable members of society, including bishops and governors, owned Black slaves. As a matter of fact, in 1734, the New France militia was used to assist a slave owner in retrieving an escaped slave, "thus bringing all the power of the state to bear in the enforcement of servitude" (Walker 1980: 24).

Slavery was also prevalent in the Maritimes. Black slaves were used to build Halifax, which latter became a leading centre for the public auction of Black slaves. The first group of Blacks to arrive in any considerable numbers in the Maritimes was made up of slaves brought to Nova Scotia (which then included New Brunswick) in the 1750s by former New

England residents after the expulsion of the Acadians (Krauter and Davis 1978). At the beginning of the American Revolution in 1776, there were already some five hundred Black slaves in Nova Scotia, and this figure tripled as White Loyalists, who supported the British, fled during and after the five-year Revolutionary War, taking their slaves with them (Clairmont and Magill 1970). Meanwhile some three thousand Blacks, emancipated in the American colonies in exchange for supporting the British, entered Canada with the assistance of General Washington and Sir Guy Carleton, commander of the British troops in North America. Most of these Black Loyalists settled in Nova Scotia, which became their main centre in Canada (Boyko 1998; Clairmont and Magill 1970; Krauter and Davis 1978). The only known public resistance to slavery at the time came from Halifax's small Quaker population, but it was mostly ignored (Boyko 1998: 158).

In the belief that they were fighting not only for their own freedom but for the ultimate abolition of slavery in North America, Blacks made an immense contribution to the British war effort. They served as soldiers, guides, spies, buglers, entertainers, and general labourers (Walker 1980; Tulloch 1975). For their services, the Black Loyalists were promised treatment equal to that of their White comrades-in-arms, but the British pledge of one hundred-acre land grants to each Black never materialized. Indeed, about 60 percent of the Blacks received no land whatsoever (Lampkin 1985). Only five hundred of them received land grants, but these were mainly one-acre lots[2] on the edge of White townships (Krauter and Davis 1978). Most land grants to Blacks were in the Annapolis Valley, with a few near Halifax, Shelburne, and Guysborough. It is important to note that the lot size of land granted to White Loyalists at the time ranged from fifteen to one hundred and fifty acres and that these Whites were given their choices of location. Boyko (1998: 159) points out that "if a White family wished to have a Black family's land they could take it without compensating its owner."

Far more disturbing, though, is the fact that when the first Black Loyalists arrived, there were suggestions that they should be used as ransom for the British prisoners held by the Americans (Walker 1980). In the midst of these betrayals, discrimination, and heightened vulnerability, Blacks became the source of cheap labour, scrambling to survive by any means possible. Some became tenant farmers, sharecroppers, and casual labourers, while others indentured themselves as domestic servants. It is therefore not surprising that, with the exception of a few large communities such as Birchtown and Brinley Town, most of the early Black settlements in Canada failed.

With the fear that Christianity would eventually enlighten slaves to believe in the equality of the races, slaves owners generally discouraged any contact between their slaves and Christian missionaries. Nonetheless, over time, the Blacks' desire for spiritual life intensified, and the church became their main rallying point. Several Black community activities were organized and defined by the church. Many preachers became community leaders, and vice versa. A striking irony is that Christianity, at the time, was somewhat compatible with slavery, and various Christian denominations condoned and actively participated in the slave system. Attempts were made to develop a religious rationale for slavery, and every vestige of class differentiation in the Holy Scripture was exploited to justify the system. For instance, in an attempt to deal with the inherent contradiction between Christianity and slavery, the Roman Catholic Church saw the slave-master relationship as a form of contract, and it craftily devised the argument that slave status was not "inherent in man but was a temporary condition arising from the accident of event" (Winks 1971: 12). Lo and behold, slaves were urged to uphold their morality in servitude, for their spiritual life transcended their slavery. The shallowness of this argument is too obvious to demand critical analysis.

Consistently caught up in the web of their own inconsistencies, several Christian churches permitted Black slaves to participate in sacraments, such as baptism and communion, and burial ceremonies. Some even urged the congregation to treat slaves more humanely. Despite this *ad hoc* benevolence, Blacks were naturally disillusioned with the slave enterprise from which they constantly tried to escape. In 1791, Thomas Peters, an emancipated Black man, risked a journey across the Atlantic to London to lodge a formal complaint about the injustice meted out to Blacks in Nova Scotia. While in London, Peters met liberal reformers such as Granville Sharp and Henry Thornton, the chairman of the famous Sierra Leone Company, which was chartered in July 1791. Following deliberations between Peters and these White philanthropists, the Sierra Leone Company agreed to send the Nova Scotian Blacks to Sierra Leone free of charge. The Blacks, in turn, were to assist in the settlement and development of Sierra Leone, which was mostly controlled by the company. After the necessary preparations, some twelve hundred Nova Scotian Blacks left for Sierra Leone in 1792 under the leadership of Lieutenant John Clarkson, a brother of Thomas Clarkson, one of the Sierra Leone Company's directors (Wyse 1993; Walker 1980).

These Black returnees, most of whom were literate, religious, and politically opinionated, founded Freetown, the capital of Sierra Leone. Not surprisingly, it did not take long for the Blacks to rise up against the Sierra Leone Company, which insisted on retaining ultimate control over the affairs of the emerging settlement in Sierra Leone. Several uprisings were staged against the company over taxation and other regulations without much success (Wyse 1993).

Nearly four years after the Sierra Leone exodus, some 550 Maroons were sent from Jamaica to Nova Scotia. The Maroons (a term from the Spanish-American language meaning "runaway") were the descendants of fugitive Jamaican slaves who engaged in a concatenation of battles against the British for their independence. Many believe that the Maroons were slaves from the famous Ashanti tribe of Ghana, noted for their fierce battles against British imperialism in Africa (Wyse 1993: 344). Constant fears that the Maroons would team up with the French to battle the British led to the Maroons' deportation to Nova Scotia, a safer location. John Wentworth, the Nova Scotia governor, and his military leaders, impressed with the physique and military prowess of the Maroons, enthusiastically welcomed them. With the impending danger of French attack, the British saw the Maroons as an important addition to their military fortification; the Maroons were eventually enrolled in a single battalion.

Over time, however, the self-confidence of the Maroons, together with their persistent refusal to be exploited by the Whites, was seen as arrogance, "a menace to society" (Lampkin 1985: 655). In 1800, with their usual divide and rule tactics, the British shipped the Maroons (under a military escort) to Sierra Leone to counteract the Nova Scotian Blacks in that country. With the reinforcement of the Maroons, the British were able to subdue the political uprisings of the Nova Scotian Blacks in Sierra Leone for some time. However, as time went on, these two Black groups coalesced with the common objective of total liberation from White domination (Wyse 1993). These Blacks frustrated the Sierra Leone Company to the extent that in 1806 the company asked the British government to take responsibility for the colony.

The next major wave of Black immigrants from the United States to Nova Scotia occurred around 1815 (Krauter and Davis 1978). During the War of 1812, the British encouraged Black slaves to desert their U.S. masters in return for settlers' status and land. Some 3,600 Black American slaves were brought to Canada, the majority of whom lived in Nova Scotia (Krauter and Davis 1978; Tulloch 1975). The well-known Black settlement of Africville was created in 1842 out of a Black refugee community planted near Halifax (Boyko 1998). As usual, these Black refugees were not given a title of ownership to the land. Rather, they were given plots on a license of occupation and so were not at liberty to sell their allotments. Bolaria and Li (1988) write that the size, tenure, and quality of the land given to the Blacks were such that many were impelled to survive on charity and public assistance. The high levels of unemployment further straitened the lamentable circumstances of these Black refugees. To worsen matters, mice destroyed numerous potato and grain fields in 1815, so-called the "year of the mice" in Canadian history (Krauter and Davis 1978). In 1816, "the year without summer," during which crops were massively destroyed by frost and snowfall, the condition of Blacks got so bad that some emigrated to Trinidad (Krauter and Davis 1978: 44).

The consequent poverty among the Canadian Black population at the time was blamed on psychological and motivational inadequacies such as laziness and lack of ambition. However, set against the words of General James Murray, cited earlier on in this section—namely, "Had I the inclination to employ soldiers which is not the case, they would disappoint me.... Black slaves are certainly the only people to be depended upon"— this explanation of Black poverty, still prevalent among White Canadians, becomes nothing more than a misguided attempt to devaluate Blacks. Of course, Blacks do not shy away from hard work any more than members of other races.

While the major concentrations of Blacks in Atlantic Canada have traditionally been in Nova Scotia, we must note for the sake of historical remembrance that, indeed, all Atlantic provinces were actively involved in the nasty business of the dehumanization of Blacks through slavery.[3] As the work of Jim Hornby (1991) shows, the Loyalists who settled in Prince Edward Island (the former Île Saint-Jean) came with their Black slaves, as they did in Nova Scotia, New Brunswick, and even Newfoundland (which was not yet a province of Canada). The main historical community of Blacks in Prince Edward Island was located in the West End of Charlottetown, known as "the Bog"; the history of this Black settlement parallels that of Africville, except the latter was larger and better known (Hornby 1991).

Another significant wave of Blacks to enter Canada during the early 1800s was comprised of the "fugitives" who came through the now famous Underground Railroad[4] with its mythical trains (Lampkin 1985). With the passage of the *Abolition Act* of 1793 in Upper Canada, runaway slaves entering the country were considered free; consequently, Upper Canada became a safe haven for them. Harriet Tubman, the Black woman dubbed "Black Moses" at the time, was very instrumental in the success of the Underground Railway. Risking arrest and possible death, she repeatedly plied the Underground Railway as a "conductor," assisting and escorting more than three hundred Blacks to relative freedom in Canada; she is known to have provided shelter for refugees in a rented house in St. Catharines (Macionis and Gerber 1999: 334; Boyko 1998: 160).

With the passage of the *Fugitive Slave Act* of 1850, which made northern U.S. states no longer safe for runaways, the flow of Blacks to Canada soared. Without enough funds, most of the Black fugitives could not venture deep into Canada and terminated their run in Ontario communities near the United States border. Soon Black settlements developed in places such as Amherstburg, Buxton, St. Catharines, Windsor, London, Chatham and later around Toronto. While no official data are available on the number of Black fugitives crossing into Canada during this era, it is estimated that about ten thousand fugitives were in Canada prior to 1850 and, between 1850 and 1860, perhaps twenty thousand Blacks entered Canada (Krauter and Davis 1978: 44).

The massive immigration of Black fugitives put a tremendous stress on the Ontario economy, and the level of discrimination against Blacks increased. As Lampkin (1985: 657) notes, "It got progressively worse until some Blacks complained of more prejudice in Canada than in the United States."[5] Blacks faced segregated schools, restaurants, theatres, and hotels in Canada, as in the United States. Boyko (1998: 160) notes that it was illegal for Blacks to run for public office or to sit on juries; it was even illegal for Blacks to purchase land or own a business license in some counties. Several charity, church organizations (e.g., the American Missionary Association and the Anti-Slavery Society), and individuals assisted the Blacks through donations and other forms of relief assistance. Yet, the number of Blacks in need was such that only a small number could benefit from these charities (Bolaria and Li 1988; Walker 1980). With the outbreak of the American Civil War and the *Lincoln Emancipation Proclamation* of 1863, many returned to the United States to fight on the Union side. By the end of the war, most Blacks had returned to the United States.

Settlement in Western Canada

While most Blacks settled in central and eastern Canada, especially Ontario, Quebec, and Nova Scotia, some from the western United States settled in the Prairie provinces and British Columbia. The first Black settlers in western Canada came mainly from California, towards the end of the 1850s. These Blacks were not fugitives; they were mostly skilled and literate people dissatisfied with the level of racial injustice that was developing in California. In 1850 the California legislature disqualified Blacks from giving evidence against Whites. And two years later, legislative attempts were made to permit newly arriving slave owners to retain their slaves despite the 1849 constitutional ban on slavery in California (Winks 1971).

Most of the Californian Blacks settled in Victoria on Vancouver Island, where they were accepted as settlers without any legal discrimination. Many of these Black pioneers went into business for themselves as carpenters, bakers, tailors, barbers, and traders, while others worked for the Hudson's Bay Company (Krauter and Davis 1978). Perhaps the most outstanding example of Black entrepreneurship at the time was that of the Lester and Gibbs trading enterprise, which provided the first known serious competition to the Hudson's Bay Company in the Victoria area (Lampkin 1985).

Victoria's elite, including Governor James Douglas, accepted the Blacks from the outset. There was a general feeling that the island needed all the settlers it could get if it was to be able to fight the Native Indians. Winks (1971: 274–75) propounds that Douglas' "knowledge that his mother was either a West Indian mulatto or a Creole obviously increased his concern [for the Blacks]." Lampkin (1985: 657) and Krauter and Davis (1978: 45) contend that the Black experience in British Columbia was the "closest approximation to equality for Canadian Blacks in the nineteenth century." Despite this, Blacks encountered some discrimination, especially around the 1860s when several White Americans migrated to Vancouver Island and began spreading their misguided assumptions about Blacks. For instance, a strong, racially motivated opposition led to the disbanding of the African Rifles, a Black military unit, in 1866 (Lampkin 1985). Also, there are indications that the Blacks who volunteered to join the Victoria Fire Brigade were turned down for homologous reasons (Winks 1971). Disturbingly, the church was one of the first major sources of racial division on Vancouver Island; when Blacks were invited to the Congregational Missions Church in Victoria, resentment of their presence created tensions within the church. Notwithstanding these racial incidents, British Columbian Blacks, by and large, fared better than their counterparts in central and eastern Canada. Blacks in British Columbia were neither barred from public schools nor from holding public office.

The Canadian Prairies were the last frontier to be ventured by Blacks. While there were some Blacks in the Prairie provinces during the 1870s, it was not until the early 1900s that they arrived there in large numbers. In 1909, some two hundred Blacks migrated from Oklahoma to Saskatch-ewan and another three hundred settled in Alberta a year later at the invitation of some railway companies and the provincial governments (Troper 1972). As usual, they were promised good farmlands but, upon arrival, were given poor land and had to create farms from dense bush and swamps with rudimentary implements. The work of Stewart Grow (1974) shows that the largest group of Black pioneers settled in the Northern Alberta community of Pine Creek (eventually named Amber Valley), 32 kilometres east of Athabasca. Others settled in Wildwood and Breton, while some stayed in major cities such as Edmonton, Saskatoon, and Regina. Grow (1974), who admirably documents the hardships endured by the Black pioneers of Amber Valley with comprehensive narratives and quotations from some of the original settlers and their descendants, writes that although Whites have bought up some of the land in Amber Valley, most of it is still run by the descendants of the original Black residents.

It is important to stress that while the Blacks somehow managed to survive, many of their settlements in the Prairies never grew mainly because the Prairie governments, business establishments, and many ordinary citizens did all they could to frustrate the existing Black communities and also to prevent the influx of additional Blacks into the region.

Many businesses and towns across the Prairies advocated the exclusion of Blacks from the Prairies, through petitions and town council resolutions. Boyko (1998: 164) notes that in 1901 and 1911, the boards of trade of almost all Prairies towns and cities passed resolutions demanding the curtailment of Black immigration. Some resolutions called for strict segregation or, worse still, deportation of Blacks back to the United States. In fact, in 1911, the Edmonton City Council passed a notorious resolution banning Blacks from the city altogether (Boyko 1998: 164). For their part, the Prairie governments attempted to restrict Black immigration by arguing that the climate[6] of the region was too harsh for the Blacks (Lampkin 1985). They also used stringent medical inspections to frustrate prospective Black immigrants. According to Boyko (1998: 166), immigration doctors were offered a bonus for every Black they turned away at the border. In fact, Winnipeg's Dominion Commissioner of Immigration Bruce Walker admitted that the Canadian government "was doing all in its power ... to keep Negroes out of Western Canada" (quoted in Winks 1971: 311). Major railroad companies supported the movement to restrict Blacks from the Prairies by either charging full fares for Black families or refusing to carry any Blacks at a time when the fares for White families settling the Prairies were routinely reduced or waived entirely (Boyko 1998: 167).

Government efforts to limit Black immigration to the Prairies waned with the outbreak of the First World War, when several Blacks began to emigrate to U.S. cities. Many of the Black men who wanted to demonstrate their patriotism during the enlistment for the war were turned away by the Canadian military. In fact, not a single Black person was admitted to the Canadian military in the fall of 1914 (Boyko 1998: 168). In 1915 Toronto's General Logie became the first to admit Blacks into a regiment, which he was having difficulty building. The hastily trained Blacks constituted the Number 2 Construction Battalion, responsible for building bridges, digging trenches, and clearing roads. Not surprisingly, the Black soldiers were segregated from their White comrades. Perhaps the worst act of racist denigration was perpetrated by the Canadian Red Cross, which was careful to segregate the "Black" blood from the "White" blood (Boyko 1998: 172).

Racial discrimination and segregation were facts of life for nearly all Blacks across Canada prior to the second half of the twentieth century.

Blacks faced segregation in schools, restaurants, and social clubs. Many real estate agents and landlords ensured that Black families were kept out of White residential areas. Some churches banned the burial of Black people in church-owned cemeteries (Boyko 1998: 176). As we shall see in Chapter 4, it was not until the 1960s that Canada witnessed another major immigration of Blacks, primarily from the Caribbean and, to a lesser extent, Tropical African countries, as a result of changes to Canada's immigration policy.

Table 3.1 shows the size of the Black population in Canada from 1921 to 1996. In 1921 there were 18,291 Black Canadians, a meager 0.20 percent of the national population. The relative size of the Black population remained fairly stable for the next five decades or so with some increases in 1971 and 1981. The first major jump in the size of Canada's Black population occurred as recently as 1991 when the number of Black Canadians exceeded 500,000 (or 2 percent) for the first time. According to the 1996 census—the most reliable data on Blacks to date—there are some 573,860 Black Canadians. This represents 2.01 percent of the 1996 population of Canada. Evidently, at no time in the history of Canada have Blacks constituted more than 3 percent of the nation's population. And, as Winks (1971) points out, Blacks have never been abundant enough, either in relative or absolute terms, to threaten any large segment of the Canadian working class. Indeed, with the exception of cities such as Toronto, Montreal, and Halifax, the Black presence has not been sufficiently organized to exert any significant political influence either. Nonetheless, we must note that "numbers do not determine historical significance"

Table 3.1 Black Canadians 1921–1996

Year	No. of Blacks	Total population of Canada	Blacks as % of Canadian Population
1921	18,291	8,787,949	0.20
1931	19,456	10,376,78	0.19
1941	22,174	11,506,655	0.19
1951	18,020	14,009,429	0.13
1961	32,127	18,238,247	0.17
1971	62,470	21,568,311	0.29
1981	144,500	24,343,181	0.59
1991	557,940	26,994,045	2.06
1996	573,860	28,528,125	2.01

Sources: a) The 1921–71 figures are from Bolaria and Li 1988 and Canada, Statistics Canada. b) The 1981 figures are from Bolaria and Li 1988. The Black population includes African, Caribbean, Haitian, and other Blacks. c) The 1996 figures are from Canada, Statistics Canada.

(Walker 1980: 3) and that Black history is an integral part of Canadian history.

Conclusion

The preceding paragraphs indicate that at one point in our history all of Canada, from the smallest province to the biggest, was implicated in the dehumanization of Blacks through slavery; evidently, not even tiny Prince Edward Island can claim innocence in this regard. Some Black pioneers entered Canada as slaves, while others came as indentured labourers, Loyalists, refugees, or voluntary settlers. Slaves were used for farming, construction, and mining, while others performed domestic duties for the Canadian elite. After the American Revolution, when some Black Canadians were given the right to farm for themselves, they were denied title to the land; the pledges of land grants for Blacks were broken over and over across Canada.

Although Blacks encountered relatively less racial oppression in British Columbia, harsh economic conditions and extreme racial discrimination forced most Black pioneers in Central and Eastern Canada, in particular, to rely on marginal jobs and charitable donations to survive. Indeed some of the Black Loyalists who settled in these areas alleged that racial oppression was more pervasive in Canada than in the United States, and, consequently, they returned there to settle. Arguably, it does not really matter whether this allegation was based on misplaced nostalgia or rooted in the reality of the Black experience in Canada, for the response in terms of returned migration was real. This allegation is still prevalent among some Black Canadians who are disillusioned by the subtle and sophisticated racism in this country; at least in the United States, Blacks generally know what they are up against.

Like Blacks, Aboriginal people were subjected to slavery in Canada, but the enslavement of Aboriginal people was quite short-lived; it ended with the importation of Blacks from Africa, the United States, and the Caribbean. In fact, there are indications that some Aboriginal leaders even participated in the enslavement of Blacks.[7] Without question, like Blacks, Aboriginal people remain victims of lingering racist stereotypes and denigration in Canada. However, what makes the situation of Blacks worse (or, at least, different) is the enduring primacy of skin colour racism in Canada, as in many Western industrialized nations. All things being equal, an Aboriginal person who wants to "pass" for White and so steer clear of the racially discriminatory barriers imposed by society, has a far better chance of doing so successfully than does a Black person, given the latter's high visibility. Also, unlike Blacks, Aboriginal people have a legitimate claim to special status in Canada with regard to self-government and land claims, due to their aboriginality. That is not all: the deplorable social, economic, and political conditions in several contemporary Black African and Caribbean countries feed into the stereotype of Black inferiority worldwide.[8] And, of course, because of the economic situation in these "Black homelands," many arrive in this country with virtually nothing, which places them at or near the very bottom of the Canadian socio-economic hierarchy.

Notes

1. We must note, however, that some historians, including Walker (1985), trace the history of Blacks to 1628 when a young Black boy, about eight years of age, from Madagascar landed on Canadian soil. While the circumstances surrounding the arrival of this boy, latter baptized and given the name Olivier Le Jeune, are not clear, some (e.g., Walker 1980, Lampkin 1985) believe he came with David Kirke and his brothers during their invasion of New France. Boyko (1998: 158) writes that Da Costa was the first Black slave to land on Canadian soil but Olivier Le Jeune was the first Black slave to settle in Canada.
2. Boyko (1998: 159) notes that the size of the land granted to Blacks was on average less than twenty acres—this estimate is higher than the one-acre suggested by authors such as Krauter and Davis (1978).
3. The need to stress this point was suggested by an anonymous reviewer of this book, for which the author is grateful.
4. The term "Underground Railroad" was coined around 1830 (when steam railroads were being built in America) to describe the secret passage of slaves through the free northern states. As Walker (1980: 48–49) suggests, it would be a mistake to regard the Underground Railroad only as an organized system for passing fugitive slaves from "station" to "station." The term embraces the series of overt and covert routes used by slaves as they passed through the northern states.
5. This view is still held by some Black Canadians, who argue that racism in Canada is far more hypocritical and damaging. A similar view is expressed by Stanley R. Barrett who asserts that "if racists as a category all wore horns, the battle against them would be a great deal easier. But this is not the case … the type that chilled me the most, in fact, was not the hard-nosed bully who wanted to kick somebody's teeth in, but rather the highly educated man, wealthy and sophisticated, who sat sipping his cognac while elaborating on the nobility of the white race" (quoted in Elliott and Fleras 1992: 49).
6. Consider that nearly a third of the labourers who constructed the Alcan Highway, from Dawson Creek, British Columbia, to Big Delta, Alaska, during the Second World War were U.S. Blacks (See Krauter and Davis 1978: 46).
7. Boyko (1998: 159), for instance, writes that the powerful Mohawk leader Thayedanegea (Joseph Brant) used Black slaves to build his impressive home near present-day Burlington, Ontario.
8. Mahamadu Bawumia (1995) argues that the high level of racism faced by Africans in the global context is attributable to the low level of economic development on the African continent.

Chapter Four

The Geography of Blacks in Canada

Immigration and Spatial Distribution

Prophecy now involves a geographical rather than historical projection; it is space not time that hides consequences from us. (John Berger 1974: 40)

The present epoch will perhaps be above all the epoch of space. We are in the epoch of simultaneity: we are in the epoch of juxtaposition, the epoch of the near and far, of the side-by-side, of the disperse. (Michel Foucault 1986: 22)

In the previous chapter it was argued that Canadian historians have attempted to black out Black history. A fairly similar argument can be made regarding the reaction of Canadian geographers to the Black presence in this country. Canadian geographers have long overlooked the racial and ethnic phenomena in general, and the Black experience in particular. Concerns about the acute dearth of attention to race and ethnic issues by Canadian geographers are not new. At a 1987 conference on *Canada 2000: Race Relations and Public Policy in Canada*,[1] Elliot Tepper, a Carleton University political scientist observed: "Another area where future research is required is the spatial dimension of ethnicity. Who lives where in Canada, in terms of ethnicity, is not currently known, nor is it likely to be known without some guided research" (1989: 27). As noted in the introductory chapter, social and historical analyses have so successfully occluded spatial discourse that, until quite recently, influential theoreticians have managed to project an image of ethnic Canada that seems to exist on the head of a pin, with virtually no spatial dimensions.

Yet geography matters. As Harney (1985: 6) points out, the "study of ethnicity in Canada as a North American process is best understood when integrated into a spatial ... frame." Ethnoracial relations occur in space: the facts of spatial segregation among ethnic and racial groups in various

Canadian cities; of rural-urban, inter- and intra-provincial variations in the distribution of ethnic and racial groups in Canada; and of immigrants originating from different geographical regions attest to the relevance of geography in this area of research. Indeed, many analysts now believe that the spatial distribution of ethnic and racial minorities has significant implications for their social and economic well-being (Musterd and Ostendorf 1998; Kazemipur and Halli 1997; Massey and Denton 1993). In this connection, it bears stressing, for didactic purposes, that space is a social product and that "spatiality is simultaneously the medium and outcome, presupposition and embodiment, of social action and relationship" (Soja 1985: 98). Thus, "just as there are no purely spatial processes, neither are there any non-spatial social processes" (Massey 1984: 52).

While it has taken some time for the spatial components of immigration, ethnic, and racial issues to be taken up in Canada, these matters are becoming increasingly popular among Canadian social geographers and geographically oriented sociologists, especially following the creation of centres of excellence for research in immigration and integration at leading universities in the late 1990s. At present, noteworthy works in this area include David Ley and Heather Smith's study on the geography of immigration and poverty in Canadian cities (1997); A. Kazemipur and S.S. Halli's examination of the spatial concentration of poverty among immigrants (1997); Dan Hiebert's work on immigration and the changing social geography of Vancouver (1999a) and on labour market segmentation among immigrants (1999b); Robert Murdie's probe into whether or not Blacks in Toronto live in near-ghettoes (1994); and Thomas Owusu's analysis of the residential patterns of Ghanaian immigrants in Toronto (1998, 1999). Other relevant works in this area are those of Konadu-Agyemang (1999); Murdie (1998); Lo and Wang (1997); Preston and Wenona (1997); and Teixeira and Murdie (1997).

Despite the growing interest in this line of inquiry, few Canadian spatial analysts have examined the specific case of Blacks. As Owusu (1998) recently noted, most of the available works focus mainly on the large and more established immigrant groups, such as Chinese and Indo-Canadians, and relegate Blacks to the background. In fact, of the two major sets of "Focus Essays on Immigration and Ethnicity in Canada," put together by the Canadian Association of Geographers in the *Canadian Geographer* (Hiebert 1994; Kobayashi 1988), none deals primarily with Blacks, and the peripheral references made to Blacks treat them as a homogenous group.

There are a number of potential reasons for the relative dearth of geographic analysis on Black in Canada. First, data on Blacks were both scarce and unreliable until quite recently. Second, in both relative and absolute terms, the Black population in Canada has been quite small until recently, thereby undermining its usefulness for geographic analysis. Third, with the exception of a few cities, such as Toronto, Montreal, and Halifax, the spatial concentrations of Blacks have not been enough to attract the attention of many analysts. Finally, the acute dearth of spatial analysis on Blacks may be a strategic move on the part of some geographers to avoid the contentious issues surrounding race and racism in Canada. Nonetheless, given the increasing significance of race in determining social and economic power in Canadian society (Stasiulis 1999), it is about time that Canadian spatial analysts paid more attention to the Black presence in this country.

As a contribution to the literature, this chapter explores the Black presence in Canada from a geographic perspective. More specifically, it examines the theoretical models of international migration and refugee movements, and it highlights the Canadian immigration policy amendments that have influenced the flow of Blacks into Canada over the years. This is followed by an overview of the geographic distribution of Blacks across Canadian provinces and territories as well as a discussion of the spatial pattern of Blacks in the metropolitan centres of Canada, with special emphasis on the Toronto, Montreal, and Vancouver Census Metropolitan Areas (CMAs). Since a geographic undertaking such as this inevitably requires empirical data, it is to the data difficulties inherent in the analysis of Black Canadians that we shall first attend.

Data Limitations

Until the 1996 census, data on Black Canadians were awfully unreliable. No one knew with any reasonable degree of steadfastness just how many Blacks there were in Canada, as no clear attempt had been made to officially measure race in Canada. Neither the Canadian census nor the immigration statistics provided a dependable base for the enumeration of Blacks. Even the 1996 census was not that clear on what is meant by the term "Blacks." Winks lamented decades ago in his *Blacks in Canada: A History* that the "terminology [Black] is frustratingly vague" (1971: 485). Unfortunately, not much has changed since Winks' observation.

Until 1996, ethnicity rather than race had been the main focus of the Canadian census in identifying population groups. Before the 1981 census, a single ethnic origin, traced through respondents' paternal ancestry, was reported. An allowance for multiple ethnic origins in the Canadian census came with the 1981 question "To which ethnic or cultural group did you or your ancestors belong on first coming to this country?" While this change enhanced the data on ethnicity, it in turn has created some statistical and methodological problems, as the multiple response count for each ethnic category does not usually match the sum of the responses for the component ethnic group.[2] The issue was further complicated in the 1991 and 1996 censuses when the 1981 census question on ethnic origin was changed slightly to read "To which ethnic or cultural group(s) did your ancestors belong?" It is also important to note that while the 1991 census question on ethnic origin included fifteen mark-in categories and two write-in spaces, the 1996 question required respondents to write in their ethnic origin(s) in four write-in spaces, guided by twenty-four examples of ethnic origins, which included "Canadian." Needless to say, these changes in question format have a bearing on the comparability of census data for different years. As Statistics Canada (Canada, Statistics Canada 1998: 9) illustrates, "some respondents who checked the mark-in 'Black' in 1991 may have written-in 'Haitian' or 'Jamaican' in 1996.

Three major ethnic origin categories in the 1991 census—African Origins, Caribbean Origins, and Black Origins—are particularly relevant for the estimation of Black Canadians on the basis of that census. Although one can reasonably speculate that the majority of the people captured by these three categories were Blacks, there is still no denying that only a rough estimate of the actual number of Black Canadians can be ascertained from these categories. Without a direct question on race, no one can know for sure whether a person who specified any of the groups under the broad categories of African Origins or Caribbean Origins was Black or not, given the sizeable number of non-Blacks living in various African and Caribbean countries. It is instructive to note that unlike the previous censuses, the 1996 one asked respondents to specify their race, with the aid of the following eleven mark-in categories: White, Chinese, South Asian, Black, Arab/West Asian, Filipino, South East Asian, Latin American, Japanese, Korean, and Other-specify. This has certainly improved the reliability of the available census data on Canadian Blacks.

The immigration and refugee statistics commonly used for the empirical analysis of Black Canadians pose similar problems. This database, compiled by Citizenship and Immigration Canada, generally classifies immigrants according to either their "country of birth" or their "country of last permanent residence." Consequently, one can only speculate on the race of the immigrants involved. For instance, while most of the immigrants from Western African countries such as Ghana, Nigeria, and Côte d'Ivoire are likely to be Blacks, the same cannot be inferred about immigrants from Northern, Southern, and Eastern African countries. North Africans, including Moroccans, Libyans, Algerians, Tunisians, and Egyptians, usually consider themselves, and are best described, as Arabs. Also, immigrants from South Africa are just as likely to be White, Indian, or Coloured as they are to be Black. The situation among Eastern Africans is equally complicated by the large number of Europeans, Arabs, and Asians, particularly East Indians, in that part of Africa.

The task of deciphering the race of immigrants from the place of last permanent residence or place of birth is doubly difficult with regard to people from Caribbean countries such as Jamaica, the Dominican Republic, and Trinidad-Tobago, where centuries of "blood mixing" have stripped the notion of race of any possible empirical measurement and pushed it into the realm of mythology. Due to these problems of definition, measurement, and historical comparability, caution should always be used in interpreting data on Canadian Blacks. Indeed, any empirically based categorical statements about Black Canadians, including those made in this book, are debatable.

Theories of International Migration

Since the 1960s, many immigrant-receiving nations in the West (e.g., Canada, Australia, and the United States) have witnessed a dramatic increase in the flow of international immigrants from visible minority regions such as Asia, Africa, and Latin America. This trend has changed the basic socio-economic structure of these Western nations, transforming them into multi-ethnic societies. The emergence of international migration as a fundamental feature of nearly all contemporary Western nations testifies to the potency and coherence of the underlying forces (Massey et al. 1997). Yet, the theoretical base for understanding international migration remains woefully inadequate. In the words of Massey et al. (1997: 258): "At present, there is not a single, coherent theory of international migration, only a fragmented set of theories that have developed largely in isolation from one another, sometimes but not always segmented by disciplinary boundaries."

One of the first noteworthy attempts at migration theory was by the British demographer Ernst G. Ravenstein, who studied internal migration in England in 1885. Ravenstein (1885) formulated from his data several generalizations or what he called "laws of migration." Some of Ravenstein's generalizations, including the fact that "the majority of migrants go only a short distance" and that "each current of migration produces a compensating counter-current," have stood the test of time. Others, such as his hypotheses that "natives of towns are less migratory than those of rural areas" and that "females are more migratory than males within their country of birth, but males more frequently venture beyond" have lost their power, especially in the context of contemporary industrialized nations (Richmond 1994: 49).

The American sociologist, S.A. Stouffer, in 1940 introduced the concept of intervening opportunities to explain the spatial pattern of human migration. Stouffer's notion of intervening opportunities posits that the number of movements or flows between an origin and a destination is directly proportional to the number of opportunities at that destination and inversely proportional to the number of intervening opportunities. Thus, intervening opportunities are the attractions that serve to reduce the spatial interaction, or the migration, that otherwise might develop between two complementary areas (or an origin and a destination).[3] To account for the interaction and migration patterns between pairs of places George K. Zipf (1949) developed what he called the gravity model, a crude analogue of Newton's law of universal gravitation. In its simplest formulation, the gravity model states that the migration between any pairs of places is a positive function of their populations and inversely proportional to the distance between them.[4] In contributing to the literature, the prolific Nigerian geographer Akin Mabogunje (1970) used the systems approach to examine the relationships and interdependence between economic, social, technological, environmental factors, and migration. For Mabogunje, migration is best conceptualized as a circular, intricately intertwined, self-modifying system. While most geographers and spatial interactionists have focused on the dynamics of internal migration, other analysts—notably, economists, sociologists, and political economists—have generally focused on international migration theory.

Theories of international migration are routinely classified as macro or micro, depending on the level of analysis. The macro theories deal with large-scale migration, focusing on the socio-economic and demographic characteristics of migrants in aggregate terms. They typically examine the broader societal causes, consequences, and ramifications of international migration. The micro theories, on the other hand, are concerned with the socio-economic and behavioural factors that differentiate between movers and non-movers. More often than not, these theories examine the thought process that goes into the decision to migrate (Richmond 1994: 48). Much of the work in this area has been done by social psychologists, many of whom see the decision to migrate as an individual choice, with or without consultation with family members. The basic assumption behind a good number of micro analyses is the concept of economic rationality: the supposition that migration decisions are made by people with access to adequate information on which to base an economically rational decision to migrate or not to migrate, after subjectively weighing all conceivable "push" and "pull" factors.

The push factors in migration theory are the negative attributes of the prospective migrant's present location, while the pull factors are the perceived positive attractions of the planned destination. The push factors are more likely to be accurately perceived than the pull ones, which are only vaguely known to potential migrants because of distance decay.[5] Often migrants base the decision to migrate on inflated positive images and expectations of their destinations—the proverbial greener grass on the other side of the fence.

Another insightful classification recently deployed by Massey et al. (1997) categorizes international migration theories into migration initiation and migration perpetuation theories. The major initiation theories identified by Massey et al. (1997: 258–63) include: (a) the neoclassical economics theory, which attributes international migration to wage differentials among nations; (b) the "new economics of migration," which sees international migration primarily as an attempt by households, or any culturally defined economic unit, to reduce or diversify the risks to their incomes; and (c) the world systems theory, which dwells on Immanuel Wallerstein's "world-system," and attributes international migration to the displacement of peasant labour by the penetration of the capitalist market into peripheral regions of the world.

Massey et al. (1997) identify three main international migration perpetration models: network theory, institutional theory, and the theory of cumulative causation. To the network theorist, international migration essentially is perpetuated through interpersonal connections among migrants, former migrants, and non-migrants in both origin and destination areas. These ties constitute a form of social capital, which migrants and non-migrants rely on to gain useful insights into foreign labour markets. Institutional theorists, on the other hand, give primacy to the activities of private and non-profit immigration organizations that aim to "satisfy the demand created by an imbalance between the large number of people who seek entry into capital-rich countries and the limited number of immigrant visas these countries typically offer" (Massey et al. 1997: 265). Complementing both the network and institutional theories is the notion of cumulative causation, originally developed by Swedish social theoretician Gunnar Myrdal, in 1957.[6] As used here, cumulative causation posits that each migration flow changes the social and economic context in which subsequent migration decisions are made. For the most part, the impact of these changes is positive, as they make it easier and less costly for new immigrants to make the move (Massey et al. 1997: 266). Also, the social labeling of some jobs as "immigrant jobs" in receiving nations makes these jobs unattractive to natives; this also intensifies the process of cumulative causation.

Figure 4.1 summarizes the connections between the international migration initiation and perpetuation theories through the reinforcing

Figure 4.1 A Model of International Migration

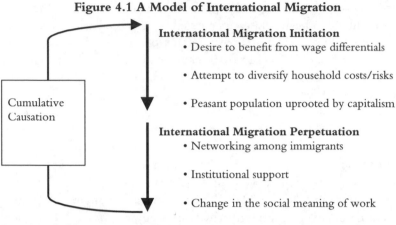

International Migration Initiation
- Desire to benefit from wage differentials

- Attempt to diversify household costs/risks

- Peasant population uprooted by capitalism

International Migration Perpetuation
- Networking among immigrants

- Institutional support

- Change in the social meaning of work

Cumulative
Causation

Source: Crafted from Massey et al. 1997

effects of cumulative causation. As the figure shows, the dynamics of the international migration initiation and perpetuation are not independent; rather, they are mutually supportive and inseparably connected to the process of cumulative causation from the outset to the outcome.

International Refugee Movements

It should be noted that all of the migration models identified so far deal mainly with voluntary migration and have virtually no relevance to our understanding of refugee movements. Who is a refugee? What factors initiate refugee movements? As inadequate as the existing theories on voluntary migration are, there is in the available literature an even greater paucity of theoretical foundation for refugee movements.

While voluntary migrants usually have a choice of where and when to migrate, by definition the opposite is true of all forced and impelled migrants. Admittedly, migration decisions of all kinds are made under some pressure. But in the case of forced migration, the pressure is so intense that the prospective migrants often are impelled to move with a sense of loss of control over their own fate (Richmond 1994; Lam 1983).

Following the lead of the 1951 United Nations Convention for Refugees, several Western nations, including Canada, now define a refugee as a person who flees his or her country for well-founded fear of persecution for reasons of "race, religion, nationality, membership of a particular social group or political opinion."[7] The label "refugee" or what the United Nation calls "convention refugee," in particular, comes with several internationally guaranteed benefits and protections. Among other things, host countries, such as Canada, that are signatories to the U.N.

Convention cannot return refugees against their will without first allowing them entry and assessing the merit of their refugee claim, and they are obliged to offer protection and basic social assistance (i.e., food, shelter, and clothing). Needless to say, not all of the implications of the "refugee" label are positive. Labeling usually leads to stereotyping and ecological fallacy in which individual identities are subsumed under group identities (Boyle et al. 1998: 180).

The notion of pull factors routinely used in the analysis of voluntary migration has little relevance in the case of refugee movements. Push factors—notably, armed conflicts, geopolitical struggles, environmental hazards, and straitened economic circumstances—dominate as causes of refugee movements (de Blij 1993). While internal environmental hazard and geopolitical and religious conflicts are commonly and visibly behind many refugee movements, "it is no longer possible to treat refugee movements as completely independent of the state of the global economy" (Richmond 1994: 51). Internal and external social, economic, political, and environmental factors combine in different permutations to produce refugee situations. At times the so-called economic migrants are responding as much to political conflicts and repression as to material deprivation (Richmond 1994). Conversely, it is not hard to find "political refugees" who are responding as much to economic and material circumstances as to political repression (Dowty 1987). While the distinction between political refugees and economic migrants is often blurred, most political refugees face limited options and excruciating choices (Richmond 1994).

The refugee experience is generally traumatic. Studies show that some refugees harbour extreme fatalistic attitudes; others exhibit symptoms of paranoia, hypochondria, anxiety, and depression (Lam 1983; Tyhurst 1977). Furthermore, as de Blij (1993: 135) points out, unlike voluntary migrants, most refugees move with little or no tangible property, and the vast majority move without any official documents.

Following Boyle et al. (1998: 191–93), the model presented in Figure 4.2 summarizes the major stages of the refugee experience and highlights the state of mind of refugees as they pass through the different phases. As the model suggests, during Stages I and II, the refugee goes through fear, uncertainty, and anxiety over the likelihood of being detected and of leaving relatives and friends behind. Such emotions may persist until the refugee reaches a safe destination (Stage III), where feelings of euphoria for having escaped and survived and optimism about the future set in.

At Stage IV, arrival at a receptive camp, the refugee experiences a variety of emotions including depression, uncertainty, and guilt over leaving loved ones behind. The refugee may exhibit signs of apathy and even aggression toward other refugees at the camp, as they all compete for

Figure 4.2 The Refugee Experience with Special Emphasis
on State of Mind

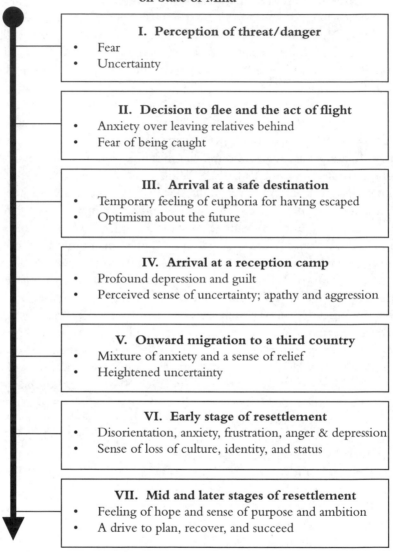

I. Perception of threat/danger
- Fear
- Uncertainty

II. Decision to flee and the act of flight
- Anxiety over leaving relatives behind
- Fear of being caught

III. Arrival at a safe destination
- Temporary feeling of euphoria for having escaped
- Optimism about the future

IV. Arrival at a reception camp
- Profound depression and guilt
- Perceived sense of uncertainty; apathy and aggression

V. Onward migration to a third country
- Mixture of anxiety and a sense of relief
- Heightened uncertainty

VI. Early stage of resettlement
- Disorientation, anxiety, frustration, anger & depression
- Sense of loss of culture, identity, and status

VII. Mid and later stages of resettlement
- Feeling of hope and sense of purpose and ambition
- A drive to plan, recover, and succeed

Source: Crafted from Boyle et al. 1998: 191–93

scarce resources. Confronted with the possibility of an onward migration to a third country (Stage V) the refugee may be filled with mixed emotions: uncertainty, anxiety, and a sense of relief over the possibility of going to a country such as Canada.

Stage VI, the earlier of the two resettlement stages identified by Boyle et al. (1998: 191–93), is full of disorientation, anxiety, frustration, anger, and a sense of loss of culture, identity, and status. Not until the mid and later stage of resettlement (Stage VII) does the refugee attain a sense of purpose and the urge to recover and succeed in the new country. As Boyle et al. (1998: 191–93) and some earlier writers (i.e., Hitch 1983; Stein 1981), point out, not every refugee passes through all of the stages set out in the model. Similarly, one cannot expect a single theoretical model to capture all possible stages and mental outlooks implicated in refugee movements worldwide.

Blacks Immigration to Canada: Underlying Factors

What motivates Blacks to come to Canada? What circumstances cause Blacks to leave their homelands and place themselves in situations entailing the drastic change in lifestyle required by immigration to a country like Canada? The hazards and frustrations that many Black immigrants face en route to Canada testify to the strong lure of this country and the desperate socio-economic and political conditions in the homeland. There are no simple answers to why people migrate. However, for most Blacks from Africa and the Caribbean, the move to Canada can reasonably be attributed to economics and politics: the yearnings for a higher standard of living and political freedom. Black African and Caribbean countries have not had many viable alternatives in their efforts to develop economically. Their economic situations are so harsh that international migration provides a rare opportunity for improvement of living conditions.

While there have been various attempts at economic diversification in many Black African and Caribbean nations, agriculture remains the predominant activity, employing more than 70 percent of the people in Black Africa (Fornos 1992) and slightly less in the Caribbean. In spite of this, many of these nations suffer from chronic food shortages. In African countries such as Somalia, Ethiopia, Chad, Mali, Angola, and Mozambique, nutrition is woefully inadequate and ill-balanced. Similar dietary conditions can be found in Caribbean nations such as Haiti. Farming tools often are primitive, agricultural techniques have not changed much, and farm yields per unit area remain abysmally low. Furthermore, due to the acute dearth of agricultural credit, the spectre of debt constantly hangs over most farmers in these societies. Faced with these hardships, many farmers pay minimal attention to soil conservation techniques, and not surprisingly, all available evidence points to a widespread deterioration of the natural environment (Ghai 2000).

Additionally, civil wars and political unrest have devastated the economies of several African countries in the past two decades or so. Angola, Burundi, Chad, the Democratic Republic of Congo, Eritrea, Ethiopia, Liberia, Mozambique, Namibia, Rwanda, Sierra Leone, Somalia, Sudan, Uganda, and Zimbabwe are among the countries most seriously affected by civil strife and geopolitical conflicts (Ghai 2000; Mensah and Adjibolosoo 1998).

As Frances Stewart (2000) points out, the economic performance of these African nations has been adversely impacted not only by the inevitable diversion of scarce resources to military expenditure, but also by the destruction of the available socio-economic infrastructure. Moreover, the climate of instability, insecurity, and lawlessness created by these conflicts intensifies refugee movements; reduces both domestic and foreign investment; and promotes the flight of capital and skilled labour to other countries. Undoubtedly, other regions of the world, including Latin America, South East Asia, and Eastern Europe, have experienced their fair share of civil wars and geopolitical conflicts, but as Ghai (2000: 7) argues, "the conflicts in African countries have often been more prolonged and more destructive of human life and physical and social infrastructure, in some cases such as Somalia, Liberia, Sierra Leone, and Zaire, resulting in virtual collapse of state structures."

Amidst all of these economic and political problems is the simultaneous, and apparently contradictory, threat of population "explosion" and the HIV-AIDS epidemic on the continent of Africa. The continuing surge of human population in Black African countries such as Nigeria throws out of kilter the intricate ecological balance that sustains life. Black Africa was once a grain exporter but, since the early 1980s, its food production has grown only half as much as its population (Fornos 1992). Drought and excessive population pressure on rural agricultural land have intensified rural-urban migration throughout Black Africa and some parts of the Caribbean. The cities of both regions are well known for their overcrowding, poor infrastructure, inadequate sanitation, and high unemployment, yet living conditions in the rural areas are such that many people, especially the youth, consider a city-ward migration as the only feasible alternative for improving their quality of life. Meanwhile, 60 percent of the twenty-four million HIV-infected people around the world live in Black Africa, and an even higher share of the total AIDS mortality is estimated to have occurred there (Cornia and Mwabu 2000: 44). With this profile, it comes as no surprise that many Black Africans and Caribbeans would like to emigrate to a country like Canada.

Clearly, the underlying factors behind Black immigration to Canada are not much different from those for other immigrants. Blacks come to Canada in search of better wages and a favourable social and political milieu in which basic human rights and freedom are upheld. Simply put, they come for a better standard of living. Furthermore anecdotal evidence from Konadu-Agyemang (1999) and Owusu (1999, 1998) suggests that, as with other immigrants, the influx of Blacks is perpetuated by a host of network, institutional, and cumulative causation factors, to borrow Massey et al.'s (1997) terms. Additionally, Opoku-Dapaah's (1995) work on Somali immigrants in Toronto, and Adjibolosoo and Mensah's (1998) work on African immigrants in Vancouver, indicate that most Black refugees have been through the migration patterns, mental outlooks, and settlement problems unraveled by Boyle et al. (1998: 191–93).

Blacks and Canada's Immigration Policy

Historically, Canadian immigration policy has been racist, to put it bluntly (Stafford 1992; Taylor 1991). Until the 1960s, various Canadian governments sought to maintain a White society by giving preferential treatment to White immigrants from places such as the United Kingdom, Western Europe, and the United States. Blacks and other visible minorities were generally considered "undesirable elements," and access to Canada was restricted through a variety of exclusionary regulations (Stafford 1992; Seward and Tremblay 1989).[8] The conventional wisdom in pre-1960s Canada was that Blacks, in particular, were so physically, mentally and morally inferior to Whites that the influx of Blacks would inevitably create racial problems in this country.

The *Immigration Act of 1906* prohibited the landing on Canadian soil of the "feeble-minded," the "destitute," "paupers," "beggars," and anyone "likely to become a public charge."[9] And whenever these exclusions failed, the government could "prohibit the landing in Canada of any specified class of immigrants" (Canada 1906: ch. 93, s. 26–30). In the years following the 1906 Act, ethnocentrism and racism against immigrants became rampant among Canadian politicians. For instance, in a speech in 1908, Robert Borden, then opposition leader, asserted that his "Conservative Party stands for a white Canada" (quoted in Walker 1984: 9). Not to be outperformed, the Liberal government, under Sir Wilfrid Laurier, quickly introduced more restrictive immigration guidelines including the Continuous Journey Stipulation of 1908 (D'Costa 1989; Walker 1984). Two years later, the Laurier government passed the *Immigration Act of 1910,* which empowered the governor-in-council to prohibit the entry of immigrants belonging to "any race deemed unsuited to the climate or requirements of Canada, or of immigrants of any specified class, occupation or character" (quoted in Calliste 1993/94: 133).

Despite these tight controls, Canadian authorities always found ways to admit Blacks and other "undesirables" whenever the economic situation warranted. This was exactly the case in the early 1900s, when Blacks were recruited from the Caribbean, especially from the Island of Barbados, to work in the steel mills and coal mines of Sydney, Nova Scotia. Also, as we shall see in Chapter 6, starting from the early 1900s, Black domestic workers were recruited from several Caribbean islands to work in all parts of Canada. And, during the First World War, hundreds of West Indian Blacks were brought in to work for the Cape Breton mines (Calliste 1993/1994; Walker 1984: 8–9). These Black immigrants were used as a cheap reserve army of labour employed in a split labour market where they were paid less than their White counterparts for performing similar or even more tedious tasks. In 1910, Black domestic workers in Quebec were paid less than half the monthly wage received by Whites, even though several employers commended the performance of their Black domestic workers (Calliste 1993/94). Also, at the Sydney steel plants, Blacks were by and large restricted to working around the coke ovens and blast furnaces, under the cruel and misguided assumption that "Blacks could withstand the heat better than Whites" (Calliste 1993/94: 135). As a *bona fide* industrial reserve army, these Black pioneers were the last to be hired and the first to be fired by most employers, especially during economic recessions. Clearly, during this early period, Blacks and other visible minorities were considered good enough to resolve temporary labour shortages in Canada but not to take up permanent residence or citizenship.

Much of Canada's postwar immigration regulations, up until the sixties, were based on the principles declared by William Lyon Mackenzie King in his renowned May 1, 1947, policy statement on immigration. Among other things, King stated his intention to encourage immigration based on Canada's "absorptive capacity" and to "remove from our legislation what may appear to be objectionable discrimination" (Canada, House of Commons 1947: 2646). It is not surprising, therefore, that some analysts, including Anderson (1993), see King as instrumental in moving Canada toward a colour-blind immigration policy. Nonetheless, it is difficult to ascertain King's position on racial discrimination in immigration. In the same speech, the prime minister declared:

> There will, I am sure, be general agreement with the view that the people of Canada do not wish, as a result of mass immigration, to make a fundamental alteration in the character of our population. Large-scale immigration from the orient would change the fundamental composition of the Canadian population. Any considerable oriental immigration would, moreover, be certain to give rise to social and economic problems of a character that might lead to serious difficulties in the field of international relations. The government, therefore, has no thought of making any change in immigration regulations which would have consequences of the kind. (Canada, House of Commons 1947, 2646)

While the above statement zeros in on Orientals, when one digs deeper into the implicit it becomes clear that King was against the influx of non-Whites into Canada. King's landmark speech had something for both critics and sympathizers. The speech was deliberately vague. Beneath the common-sense veneer was a hidden terrain of ambiguity, resulting from his calculated attempt to appease members of both sides of the debate. Arguably, King's inclination towards a colour-blind immigration was nothing more than a crafty attempt at window dressing.

It was not until 1962 that Canada formally revoked the preferential treatment given to White immigrants. For the first time, emphasis was placed on education and professional skills and not on race or ethnicity. Further changes to the immigration regulations in 1967 resulted in the point system under which prospective immigrants are evaluated on the basis of variables such as age, education, and occupational demand irrespective of their racial and ethnic background (D'Costa 1989; Li 1988). Also, the 1967 regulations provided for the creation of the Immigration Appeals Board to deal with problems arising from the implementation of the policy amendments. For the first time in Canadian immigration history, applicants from all countries were treated equally, and skilled and professional Blacks from the Caribbean and Africa were able to come to Canada on their own merits. The opening of Canadian immigration offices in Jamaica and Trinidad–Tobago in 1967, and later in other Black nations such as Haiti, Barbados, Kenya, and Côte d'Ivoire (Serge 1993) was another significant impetus for the immigration of Blacks to Canada (Walker 1984).

Adding to these developments was the 1973 policy initiative that allowed for the immigration of temporary workers under an employment visa program. This program, later incorporated into the 1976 *Immigration Act*, permits the use of foreign workers for short-term jobs, especially in agricultural and domestic activities, for which no Canadian citizens or landed immigrants are available (Stafford 1992; Bolaria and Li 1988). The 1976 Act also established an inland refugee determination system for the processing of claims submitted within the borders of Canada. For the first time, the Canadian refugee program covered not only refugees who were screened abroad, but also United Nations Convention refugees who arrived on Canadian soil spontaneously, without any prior evaluation.

Unlike the point system, which focused primarily on the skills and educational qualifications of immigrants, the 1976 Act placed emphasis on family unification and settlement of refugees (Creese 1992; D'Costa 1989). Two years later, the 1978 immigration regulations revised the point system of 1967 by placing emphasis on occupational experience at the expense of educational attainment and by enhancing the business immigrant program

Table 4.1 Immigration to Canada by Region of Last Permanent Residence for Selected Years

Region	1961 #	1961 %	1971 #	1971 %	1981 #	1981 %	1994 #	1994 %
Africa	1,088	1.5	2,841	2.3	4,887	3.8	13,706	6.1
Asia	2,901	4.0	22,459	18.4	48,830	38.0	141,587	63.2
S. America*	2,738	3.8	16,687	13.6	15,760	12.3	21,402	9.6
Europe	51,937	72.4	51,743	42.4	46,295	36.0	38,641	17.3
Australia	1,432	2.0	2,902	2.4	1,317	1.0	1,108	0.5
U.S.	11,516	16.1	24,366	20.1	10,559	8.2	6,234	2.8
Others	77	0.1	902	0.7	970	0.7	1,197	0.5
Total	71,689	100.0	121,900	100.0	128,618	100.0	223,875	100.0

This includes Caribbean and Central American countries.
Source: Citizenship and Immigration Canada, Immigration Statistics (Ottawa: Ministry of Supply and Services, various years).

Figure 4.3 Top Ten Countries of Birth for Immigrants to Canada 1991–1996

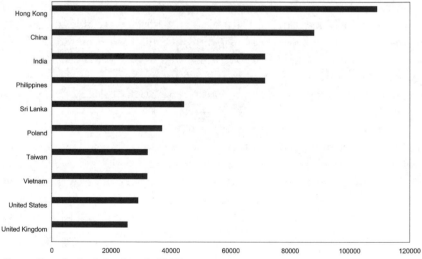

Source: Canada, Statistics Canada 1999b.

under which entrepreneurs are encouraged to establish and create employment opportunities in Canada.

The new regulations have broadened the sources of immigrants to include Blacks and other visible minorities from Africa, the Caribbean, Asia, and South America. As can be seen from Table 4.1, while the proportion of immigrants from the traditional sources such as Europe and the United States have generally declined in recent decades, the comparable figures for Africa, Asia, and South America have increased. For instance, the proportion of European immigrants, which stood at an overwhelming 72.4 percent of the total number of immigrants in 1961, plummeted to 17.3 percent by 1996. In contrast, the relative share of African immigrants increased from a meager 1.5 percent in 1961 to a sizeable 6.1 percent in 1996. Estimates by Frideres (1992) suggest that during the late 1970s, Canada received more immigrants from the developing world, relative to its own population, than any other developed nation. Figure 4.3 shows the top ten sources of immigrants to Canada as of the 1996 census. Leading the list is Hong Kong,[10] followed by other Asian nations, such as China, India, the Philippines, and Sri Lanka, in that order. The only non-Asian countries among the top ten are Poland, the United States, and the United Kingdom.

Since the 1980s, escalating ethnopolitical conflicts in a number of developing countries and favourable refugee policies in Canada have fostered an influx of refugees from such regions as Africa and the Caribbean. Table 4.2 shows the distribution of Canada's refugee population by source regions for 1980 1986, and 1990. It is useful to note that the percentage of African refugees, out of the Canadian total, increased from a scanty 0.4 percent in 1980 to 6.5 percent in 1986, and it jumped again to 10.3 percent in 1990. While the refugee data are not broken down by

Table 4.2 Refugees to Canada by World Regions,* for 1980, 1986, and 1990

World Region	1980		1986		1990	
	#	%	#	%	#	%
Africa	191	0.4	1,249	6.5	4,048	10.3
Ethiopia	72	–	905	–	2,173	–
Ghana	0	–	38	–	145	–
Nigeria	2	–	5		28	–
Somalia	6	–	35	–	1,069	–
S. Africa	16	–	53	–	50	–
Sudan	9	–	19	–	171	–
Uganda	3	–	54	–	71	–
Other Africa	83	–	140	–	341	–
Eastern Europe	4,062	10.1	5,388	28.1	15,381	39.2
Indochina	34,637	85.8	6,065	31.7	6,547	16.7
Middle East	37	0.1	1,139	5.9	3,515	8.9
Central America**	308	0.8	3,934	20.5	5,393	13.7
South America	396	0.9	407	2.1	811	2.1
Other Regions	717	1.7	965	5.0	3,483	8.9
Total	40,348	100.0	19,147	100.0	39,178	100.0

* Based on the country of last permanent residence.
** Includes the Caribbean and Mexico.
Source: Canada, Citizenship and Immigration Canada 1991.

race, there are good reasons to believe that most of the African refugees in Canada are Blacks, as the leading sources of African refugees include predominantly Black nations such as Ethiopia, Ghana, Nigeria, Somalia, Sudan, South Africa, and Uganda (Table 4.2).

Despite the recent increases in the number of refugees from Africa and Latin America, some analysts (e.g., Nash 1994) contend that the Canadian refugee and humanitarian programs still have some racist undertones. It is alleged that Canada tends to focus on non-visible minority regions that are not major sources of refugees and that it gives little attention to the visible minorities regions where nearly nine-tenths of the world's refugees are located (Nash 1994). There seems to be some truth to this allegation. Estimates on the number of refugees across the globe vary, but from all accounts the refugee crisis is far more acute in Africa (Weiner 1999; Boyle et al. 1998; United Nations High Commission for Refugees [UNHCR] 1995; Richmond 1994). The UNHCR (1995) estimates indicate that there were about 14.5 million refugees worldwide at the beginning of 1995, of which Africa accounted for 6.8 million or 47 percent. In the words of Boyle et al. (1998: 187), "Africa is the epicenter of the global refugee crisis." Thus, it is not unreasonable to suggest that the Canadian government has exercised some subtle political bias or even racism in the selection of its refugees. As Nash (1994: 260) observes: "The bias in humanitarian programs towards, say, Poland rather than Haiti, illustrates these concerns." More recently, there has been a shift on the part of the government to reduce the flow of refugees into Canada (Nash 1994). This move is due partly to the need to reduce the uncontrollable flow of "false" refugee claimants (Creese 1992) and partly to the Canadian government's inclination to use immigration as an economic tool rather than a humanitarian instrument (Nash 1994). Based on the preceding analysis it may be wise for those who praise the colour-blindness of the Canadian refugee program to do so with a dose of cynicism.

Table 4.3 shows the periods of immigration for Blacks and other immigrants to Canada as of 1996. The restrictions imposed on the immigration of Blacks and other visible minorities prior to the 1960s are empirically evident. Of the 312,870 Black immigrants in Canada by the 1996 census, only 1.52 percent came prior to 1961; the corresponding figures for the decades of 1971–1980 and 1981–1990, and the five-year period of 1991–1996 were slightly greater than 28 percent respectively (Table 4.3). While mortality must have taken its inevitable toll on the pre-1960 Black immigrant population, the preceding discussion clearly shows that, before the 1960s, voluntary Black immigration into Canada was highly restricted.

As admirable as the above amendments to Canada's immigration

Table 4.3 Canada: Black and Other Immigrants by Period of Immigration

Periods of Immigration	Black Immigrants		All Other Visible Minorities		All Other Immigrants to Canada	
	#	%*	#	%*	#	%*
Before 1961	4,745	1.52	26,465	1.42	1,054,930	21.22
1961–1970	39,635	12.67	113,350	6.08	788,580	15.86
1971–1980	89,680	28.66	421,220	22.61	996,160	20.09
1981–1990	89,675	28.66	621,540	33.36	1,092,400	21.98
1991–1996	89,135	28.49	680,500	36.53	1,038,995	20.90
Total	312,870	100.0	1,863075	100.0	4,971,065	100.0

These are column percentages.
Source: Canada, Statistics Canada 1999b.

policy may be, one might still wonder why the racially selective immigration regulations were changed? Interior to this question lies another: Why did the changes start in the early 1960s? To answer these questions with any steadfastness demands a hard look at the demographic and labour market realities of Canada in the global context just before the 1960s.

By the early 1960s, it was apparent that the quality of European immigrants had been "diluted" by a large number of unskilled workers, who had immigrated mainly as relatives of earlier immigrants (Li 1988). While Canadian politicians engaged in endless debate over which ethnic group was desirable for immigration, all appreciated the urgent need to boost Canada's skilled labour base through immigration. Compounding the labour shortages was the massive emigration of Canadian skilled labour and professionals to the United States between the early fifties and sixties. Estimates by Parai (1965: 47–57) point to a net outflow of 79,626 professionals and skilled workers from Canada to the United States from 1953 to 1963.

Moreover, in 1965, the United States replaced the *McCarran-Walter Act of 1952*[11] with an Act that facilitated the immigration of skilled labour. Some Canadian analysts (e.g., D'Costa 1989; Li 1988; Parai 1965) believe that the 1967 amendment to the Canadian immigration policy was an attempt to compete with the United States for scarce skilled labour from around the world. Also, the rebuilding of Europe after the Second World War enhanced job opportunities there, making some Europeans hesitant to move across the Atlantic. Indeed, there are indications that entry level jobs in Europe paid better than comparable ones in Canada (Frideres 1992). Decreasing birth rate among the traditional source countries in Europe was yet another impetus for the changes in Canada's immigration policy. By the late 1950s several Western European nations were entering the fourth stage, or low stationary phase, of their demographic transition,[12] and their citizens were consciously reducing their fertility levels and family sizes. Canada, like many advanced countries, saw the need to use immigration policy to siphon off skilled and professional people from the developing world.

Mention must also be made of the impact of Canada's participation in international organizations on its post-1960 immigration regulations. Towards the end of the 1960s, some newly independent nations (e.g., Jamaica, Ghana, and Nigeria) began to mount a vehement attack on international racism at various international forums, such as those of the United Nations and the Commonwealth. The obvious inconsistency between Canada's discriminatory immigration policy and its rising leadership role in these multi-racial organizations, especially in the Commonwealth, compelled the Canadian government to be racially sensitive (Taylor 1991; D'Costa 1989). At home, spirited protests, legal challenges, and lobbying by minority groups within Canada against the racist immigration regulations, as well as the potential power of the "ethnic vote," forced politicians to change their positions (Taylor 1991; Walker 1984).

Clearly, the transition from European to visible minority immigration was not caused by a sudden liking or altruism for Blacks and other visible minorities. Rather it was engendered by a combination of political expediency, international pressure, humanitarian concerns, and internal economic requirements. As Elliott and Fleras (1992) point out, it was not until the traditional sources of immigrants were exhausted that admittance was extended to Blacks and other visible minorities. Indeed, some still contend that amendments to the Canadian immigration policy are mostly cosmetic and that the changes in the law removed the explicit racist language but not the racist intent.[13] It is fair, though, to assert that the current Canadian immigration policy reflects a commitment to a balance between humanitarian and economic concerns.

The Spatial Distribution of Blacks in Canada

The impact of recent Black immigration is felt differently across the various provinces and territories of Canada. According to the 1996 census, some 573,855 Blacks live in Canada, making Black the third-largest visible minority group after Chinese and then South Asians (Table 4.4). In fact the number of Black Canadians now is slightly more than that of Latin Americans, Filipinos, Japanese, and Koreans combined (Table 4.4).

Table 4.7 and Figure 4.4 present data on the spatial distribution of Blacks across Canada. Column 3 of the table shows that in terms of absolute numbers, the highest populations of Blacks reside in Ontario, Quebec, Alberta, British Columbia, Manitoba, and Saskatchewan, in that order. The

Table 4.4 Canada: Composition of Visible Minority Groups, 1996

Group	Number	Percent*
1. Chinese	860,150	29.90
2. South Asian	670,585	20.97
3. Black	573,860	17.95
4. Arab/West Asian	244,665	7.65
5. Filipino	234,200	7.32
6. Latin American	176,975	5.53
7. Southeast Asian	172,765	5.40
8. Japanese	68,135	2.13
9. Korean	64,835	2.03
Visible minority n.i.e.**	69,745	2.18
Multiple visible***	61,570	1.93
Total visible minority	3,197,485	100.00

* Percent out of total visible minority population. ** Includes Pacific Islanders and other visible minority groups. n.i.e. = not included elsewhere. *** Includes respondents who reported more than one visible minority group.
Source: Canada, Statistics Canada 1999b.

Table 4.5 Canada: Distribution of Blacks by Provinces and Territories, 1996

Rank*	Province/ Territory	Total Population #	Total Population %	Black Population #	Black Population %	Rate of Over-/ Under-represent- ation of Blacks**
1	Ontario	10,642,790	37.31	356,215	62.07	1.66
2	Nova Scotia	899,970	3.15	18,105	3.15	1.00
3	Quebec	7,045,085	24.70	131,970	23.00	0.93
4	Manitoba	1,100,290	3.86	10,775	1.88	0.49
5	Alberta	2,669,195	9.36	24,915	4.34	0.46
6	BC	3,689,75	12.93	23,275	4.06	0.31
7	Saskatchewan	976,615	3.42	4,265	0.74	0.22
8	N. Brunswick	729,625	2.56	3,120	0.54	0.21
9	Yukon	30,650	0.11	125	0.02	0.20
10	NWT	64,125	0.22	225	0.04	0.17
11	PEI	132,855	0.47	265	0.05	0.10
12	Newfoundland/ Labrador	547,160	1.92	600	0.10	0.05
	Canada	28,528,115	100.0	573,855	100.0	–

* Ranking is in descending order of the rates of over-/under-representation of Blacks.
** The rate of over-/under-representation is calculated by dividing the percentage of Canadian Blacks living in a province/territory by the percentage of the total Canadian population living in that same province/territory. A rate of 1.0 shows neither over- nor under-representation of Blacks. Rates higher than 1.0 show over-representation, while those lower than 1.0 indicate under-representation. In the geographic literature this rate is called the location quotient (LQ).
Source: Canada, Statistics Canada 1999b.

Figure 4.4 Number of Blacks by Provinces and Territories, 1996

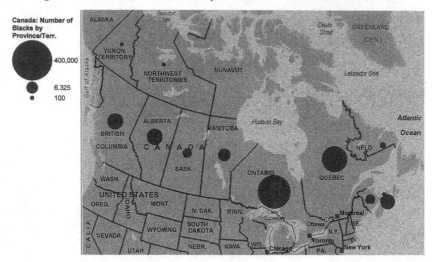

lowest numbers are in the Yukon and the Northwest Territories, with the four Atlantic provinces sandwiched somewhere between these two extremes. However, as column 5 of the table shows, in relative terms Blacks are under-represented in all Canadian provinces and territories excepting Ontario and Nova Scotia. Quebec ranks third in this regard with an under-representation rate (or location quotient) of 0.93, while Newfoundland and Labrador and Prince Edward Island have the lowest rates of 0.1 and 0.05, respectively, being surpassed even by the Yukon and the Northwest Territories.

Despite the obvious significance of historical factors in accounting for the high concentrations of Blacks in provinces such as Ontario, Quebec, and Nova Scotia, as we saw in Chapter 3 one must not lose sight of other factors, such as the proximity of these provinces to the Black nations of Africa and the Caribbean; the cumulative effects of earlier immigration; the recruitment of Haitians into Quebec during the province's Quiet Revolution; the time-honoured lure of Ontario and Quebec's economy to immigrants; and the propensity of recent immigrants to settle in large metropolitan centres, most of which are in Ontario and Quebec.

While earlier European immigrants had been more spatially dispersed, with many settling in rural agricultural communities, a salient feature of the Black presence in Canada is their high concentration in large cities. Table 4.6 and Figure 4.5 provide data on the spatial distribution of Blacks across Canada's twenty-five census metropolitan areas (CMAs).[14] Note that almost 48 percent of all Black Canadians live in the Toronto CMA; Montreal comes in second with 21.3 percent. Ottawa-Hull, Vancouver, and Halifax also have sizeable proportions of Blacks, according to Table 4.6 and Figure

Table 4.6 Population of Blacks in Canadian Census Metropolitan Areas, 1996

CMA* Rank	CMA Population	BLACKS #	% of national Black pop**	% of CMA pop***	Rate of Over-/Under-representation of Blacks
1. Toronto	4,232,905	274,935	47.91	6.50	3.23
2. Montreal	3,287,645	122,320	21.31	3.72	1.85
3. Halifax	329,745	12,000	2.09	3.64	1.81
4. Ottawa-Hull	1,000,935	30,805	5.36	3.08	1.53
5. Windsor	275,745	6,295	1.09	2.28	1.13
6. Oshawa	266,580	5,760	1.0	2.16	1.06
7. Hamilton	617,815	10,060	1.75	1.63	0.81
8. Winnipeg	660,055	10,025	1.74	1.52	0.76
8. Kitchener	393,905	5,990	1.04	1.52	0.76
9. London	379,345	5,740	1.0	1.51	0.75
10. Edmonton	854,225	11,275	1.96	1.32	0.66
11. Calgary	815,985	10,580	1.84	1.30	0.64
12. Saint John	124,215	1,340	0.23	1.08	0.54
13. Regina	191,485	1,805	0.31	0.94	0.47
14. St. Catharines	367,790	3,415	0.59	0.93	0.46
15. Vancouver	1,813,935	16,400	2.85	0.90	0.45
16. Victoria	300,035	2,085	0.36	0.69	0.35
17. Saskatoon	216,445	1,490	0.25	0.69	0.34
18. Sudbury	158,935	980	0.17	0.62	0.31
19. Sherbrooke	144,575	685	0.11	0.47	0.24
20. Quebec City	663,885	3,065	0.53	0.46	0.23
21. Trois-Rivières	137,700	590	0.10	0.42	0.21
22. Thunder Bay	124,325	430	0.07	0.35	0.17
23. St. John's	172,090	320	0.05	0.19	0.09
24. Chicoutimi****	158,865	240	0.04	0.15	0.08
All CMAs	17,689,165	538,630	100.0	3.04	–

* Census metropolitan areas of Canada in a descending order of their rates of over-/under-representation of Blacks (or location quotients).
** These percentages are computed out of the national figure of 573,855.
*** These percentages are computed out of the respective CMA populations.
**** Refers to Chicoutimi-Jonquière in the Province of Quebec.
Source: Canada, Statistics Canada 1999b.

4.5. Of the top ten CMAs, only Quebec City is home to less than 1 percent of the total Black population in Canada. The last column of Table 4.6 shows the rates of over-/under-representation (or location quotients) of Blacks across the various CMAs. The data suggest that only six CMAs, including Toronto, Montreal, Halifax, Windsor, Ottawa-Hull, and Oshawa, exhibit over-representations of Blacks. The remaining nineteen CMAs, including

Figure 4.5: Population of Blacks In CMAs, 1996

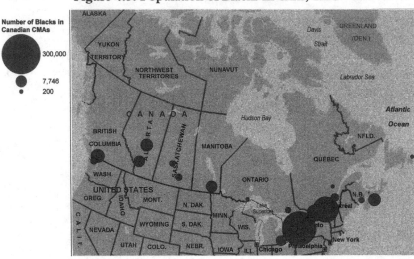

big centres such as Vancouver, Edmonton, and Calgary, have under-representations of Blacks.

Table 4.7 summarizes the relative size of the various visible minority groups in the three largest CMAs of Canada. Blacks are the third largest visible minority group in Toronto after Chinese and South Asians, in that order. While the number of Blacks in Montreal, in absolute terms, is less than half of the comparable figure in Toronto, it is worth noting that Blacks are the leading visible minority group in Montreal. Blacks constitute close to a third of all visible minorities in Montreal, with Arab/West Asians and Latin Americans placing a distant second and third, respectively. Of Canada's top three metropolitan centres, Vancouver has the least proportion of Blacks among its population; notice from Table 4.7 that Blacks rank eighth out of the nine visible minority groups listed. While the distribution of Blacks and other visible minorities across Canada is difficult to explain, we cannot discount the impact of geographic distance between the various origins and destinations of these visible minority immigrants. Not surprisingly, Vancouver's proximity to Asia and the Pacific Rim nations means that it attracts the bulk of immigrants from that part of the world, just as many Africans and Caribbeans end up in Toronto and Montreal. This also explains the popularity of Toronto and Montreal (as compared to Vancouver) among the former residents of most African and Caribbean cities (Mensah and Adjibolosoo 1998). Also, it is intuitively appealing to expect that most of the French-speaking African and Caribbean Blacks settle in Montreal and that their English-speaking counterparts choose Toronto as their preferred destination, given the propensity of Black immigrants, like many visible minority groups, to settle in major cities.

Table 4.7 Percentage Composition of Visible Minority Groups in Toronto, Montreal, and Vancouver, 1996

	Toronto (N = 1,338,090)*		Montreal (N = 401,410)		Vancouver (N= 564,610)	
	%	Rank	%	Rank	%	Rank
1. Chinese	25.05	1st	11.49	5th	49.42	1st
2. South Asian	24.65	2nd	11.50	4th	21.28	2nd
3. Black	20.55	3rd	30.47	1st	2.90	8th
4. Filipino	7.41	4th	3.58	7th	7.21	3rd
5. Arab/West Asian	5.39	5th	18.42	2nd	3.22	6th
6. Latin American	4.61	6th	11.63	3rd	2.45	9th
7. Southeast Asian	3.48	7th	9.37	6th	3.61	5th
8. Korean	2.13	8th	0.87	8th	3.03	7th
9. Japanese	1.27	9th	0.58	9th	3.88	4th
10. Visible minority n.i.e.**	3.41	–	0.87	–	1.20	–
11. Multiple visible***	2.05	–	1.21	–	1.81	–
Total visible minority	100.00	–	100.0	–	100.0	–

* N = the total number of visible minorities in the respective CMAs; the percentages are based on the N in each case.
** Includes Pacific Islanders and other visible minority groups; n.i.e. = not included elsewhere.
*** Includes respondents who reported more than one visible minority group.
Source: Canada, Statistics Canada 1999b

What is the residential pattern of Blacks in major Canadian cities? Do Canadian Blacks usually reside in inner city or suburban areas? What is the extent of spatial concentration or spatial distance between Blacks and other ethnic groups in these cities? Traditionally, North American urban sociologists and urban geographers, following the works of the Chicago School of Urban Ecology,[15] have taken for granted a situation in which immigrants and socially marginalized groups reside in low-cost housing areas of the inner city, close to industries employing cheap labour, and later move outward to the suburbs. Ernest Burgess, a leading proponent of this hypothesis, depicts the city as a series of concentric zones in which affluence, assimilation, and social acceptability increase with distance from the central business district (CBD). Burgess and his followers postulate that as the city grows, the established and wealthy people build their homes on the vacant land on the periphery, leaving the old houses near the city centre to the urban poor, immigrants, and other disadvantaged groups. According to Burgess's model, this sequence of invasion and succession yields a residential pattern in which Blacks and other disadvantaged groups are almost always found in the downtown areas of cast-off housing, the only type of housing they can afford (Yeates 1990; Cadwallader 1985). To what extent does Burgess's model fit the spatial distribution of Blacks in Canadian cities? In what follows, we examine this and related questions with special reference to the top three metropolitan areas of Canada: Toronto, Montreal, and Vancouver.

Unlike the case in the United States, Black Canadians are, arguably, among the least segregated groups, despite the existence of some easily identifiable Black enclaves in places such as Toronto and Montreal. In their 1987 study *Segregation of Visible Minorities in Montreal, Toronto, and Vancouver,* Balakrishnan and Kralt conclude that, of the three visible minority groups studied—i.e., Indo-Pakistanis, Chinese, and Blacks—the latter was the least segregated. Among other things, they found that 50 percent of Blacks in Montreal lived in 11.4 percent of Montreal's 665 census tracts, compared with only 7.4 percent of Indo-Pakistanis and 7.2 percent of Chinese. Similar patterns of spatial concentration were found among these groups in both Vancouver and Toronto. The indices of dissimilarity (ID)[16] for Blacks in Montreal, Toronto, and Vancouver were estimated at 46, 37, and 32 respectively. The comparable figures for Indo-Pakistanis stood at 57, 40, and 37 respectively, and those for Chinese were 59 for Montreal, 44 for Toronto, and 50 for Vancouver (Balakrishnan and Kralt 1987). Fairly similar findings have been reported by Ray (1994), Davies and Murdie (1993), Richmond (1989), and Bourne et al. (1985).

In fact, there are indications that Blacks are even far less spatially concentrated than non-visible minority groups, such as Jews, Greeks, and Portuguese, in Canadian cities (Davies and Murdie 1993). Thus, the long-standing supposition that spatial segregation increases with social distance (Balakrishnan 1982; Massey 1981) is not readily applicable to the case of Black Canadians, considering that Blacks are less segregated in spatial terms despite their relatively low "social acceptability" in Canadian society (Moghaddam et al. 1994; Pineo 1977).

A recent study by Ley and Smith (1997) notes that, of the top three Canadian CMAs—Toronto, Montreal, and Vancouver—the latter follows the more conventional American model in which urban poverty is heavily concentrated in inner city census tracks; Toronto shows evidence of suburbanized poverty; and the situation in Montreal falls somewhere between the two. Moreover, they note that, unlike the American case where poverty areas are heavily concentrated and tend to persist for decades, such areas in Canadian cities are not only more dispersed, but they also tend to dwindle over time (Ley and Smith 1997). Nonetheless, research suggests that Blacks in Canadian cities are increasingly being relegated to poor neighbourhoods. For instance, Kazemipur and Halli (1997) found that 18.7 percent of Blacks in Montreal live in census tracts with extreme poverty rates (i.e., 40 percent or more), making Blacks the fifth largest group (out of the twenty-seven studied) living in such areas, following Vietnamese, Greeks, Filipinos, and East Indians. Even though only 4.7 and 3.9 percent of Blacks live in such extreme poverty areas in Vancouver and Toronto respectively, the position of Blacks does not fare any better in these two centres than in Montreal, as Blacks ranked second in Toronto and fifth in Vancouver with regard to their concentration in extreme poverty areas (Kazemipur and Halli 1997, Table 5).

Not surprisingly, some observers, especially members of the Reference Group—a Black advocacy organization in Toronto—have charged that Toronto "Blacks live in near ghettoes"[17] (Owusu 1999; Murdie 1994). The Reference Group alleges that the Metro Toronto Housing Authority (MTHA) tends to place Blacks in specific derelict, high-rise buildings, leaving the most desirable, low-rise housing complexes for White applicants. For its part, the MTHA contends that there is no deliberate attempt to segregate or discriminate against Blacks in public housing, but it so happens that Blacks usually prefer complexes with a relatively high proportion of Blacks, while, at the same time, Whites have the tendency to move out of such buildings.

After a comprehensive, empirical examination of this allegation, Murdie (1994) found that the share of Blacks in MTHA housing increased from 4.2 percent in 1971 to as high as 27.4 percent by 1986. He also found some level of spatial concentration of Blacks within MTHA housing, especially in suburban high-rise projects such as the Firgrove, Yorkwoods, and Jane/Milo projects in North York; the Galloway/Lawrence and Kingston Road complexes in Scarborough; and the Islington/St. Andrews project in Etobicoke. More substantively, Murdie (1994) noted that the spatial concentration of Blacks in Toronto's public housing has more to do with "constrained choice"[18] than any "racial grading" by the housing authority to steer Blacks toward undesirable projects. In a more recent study, Owusu (1999) found that Ghanaians in Toronto exhibit intense local concentration in specific suburban neighbourhoods, notably along the Jane-Finch corridor in North York, primarily because of their desire to live among other Ghanaians.

Evidently, the residential pattern of Blacks is far more complicated than "the taken-for-granted notion of initial location in the inner city and subsequent diffusion to the suburbs" (Ray 1994: 263). The spatial pattern of Blacks in Canadian cities defies the conventional explanations offered in most of the existing literature. It is about time we followed the lead of Goldberg and Mercer (1986) by ridding ourselves of the theoretical straitjacket and avoiding the dogmatic application of U.S.-based urban models to Canadian cities. Goldberg and Mercer (1986) have long demonstrated that the notion of the "North American city" is a myth and that Canadian cities are different from their United States counterparts.

How then do we account for the spatial pattern of Blacks in Canadian cities? Why do Black Canadians, unlike their counterparts in the U.S., tend to cluster in suburban, as opposed to inner-city, areas? And how do we explain the fact that Blacks are among the least segregated groups in Canadian cities?

There are several possible explanations, but, by far, the most dominant relates to the spatial distribution of public housing and low-end private rental units in the two countries. Until recently, nearly all affordable public housing projects in American cities were not only massive in scale, but were also heavily concentrated in inner-city areas. The Canadian versions have generally been different in terms of both scale and geographic distribution. Canadian cities tend to build small-scale social housing projects, most of which are spatially dispersed, with considerable stocks in suburban communities (Murdie 1998; Mensah 1995; Ray 1994). As Ray (1994: 264) vividly points out in his analysis of the residential pattern of immigrants in Toronto:

> The settlement of immigrants in Toronto, with its distinctive suburban character, becomes easier to understand when one considers the type of housing occupied and tenure. Immigrants of some financial means who wish to own a home and prefer single-family housing are much more likely to fulfill their housing aspirations in the suburbs. Similarly, Afro-Caribbean immigrants in the public and private rental markets, contrary to many North American cities, are also more likely to find affordable housing in Toronto's suburbs.

Thus, the suburban character of Blacks is mainly attributable to the way Canadian cities have been planned over the years, or, more specifically, to the geographic distribution of private and public rental accommodation in Canadian cities.

Other plausible explanations for the relative concentration of Blacks in suburbs have to do with network and migration factors, such as the channeling effects of chain migration; the desire of Blacks to live among fellow Blacks for social and psychological support, and, indeed, to limit the impacts of discrimination; and the reliance of Blacks on friends and relatives for information on housing (Owusu 1998, 1999; Konadu-Agyemang 1999; Murdie 1994, 1998; Ray 1994; Henry 1994). Undoubtedly, ethnoracial segregation in cities is a two-edged sword. Just as the phenomenon can provide important social and psychological support for immigrant groups, it can also foster social exclusion and discrimination among groups. While there are no U.S.-style ghettoes in Canada, there are indications that some Blacks are experiencing considerable social exclusion and discrimination in education, employment, and housing in places such as Toronto (Opoku-Dapaah 1995; Henry 1994), Montreal (Hamilton 1990/91), and Vancouver (Adjibolosoo and Mensah 1998). In fact Henry's (1994) work points to the emergence of a Black youth underclass in Toronto. It bears stressing that such exclusions tend to compel Blacks to cluster in familiar places for social, economic, and psychological support. And, based on the preceding analysis, one can reasonably contend that, in the Canadian context, such areas of Black topophilia[19] are in the suburbs, where there are already large concentrations of Blacks. That Canadian Blacks are relatively less segregated than their counterparts in the United States, other visible minorities in Canada (e.g., Chinese and Indo-Pakistanis), and other non-visible minorities (e.g., Greeks and Jews) can be explained by the relative smallness of the Black population in most Canadian cities. It is likely that as the proportions of Blacks in these cities grow, their level of segregation also will increase either voluntarily or otherwise.

Conclusion

This chapter explored the geography of Black Canadians from the standpoint of their immigration and spatial distribution. The analysis shows that it was only after the early 1960s that Canada revoked its race-based immigration policy and allowed Blacks to enter this country in significant numbers. For most Black immigrants, the move to Canada is attributable to the yearning for political freedom and economic security. Political repression, ethnic conflicts, and civil wars have combined perilously with harsh environmental and economic circumstances to push many Black Africans and Caribbeans to seek better livelihoods in overseas countries such as Canada. The empirical data provided in the chapter clearly show that Ontario, Quebec, and Nova Scotia are home to the vast majority of Black Canadians. We also noted that the Black presence in Canada is an urban phenomenon, with the overwhelming majority living in metropolitan centres such as Toronto, Montreal, Halifax, and Ottawa–Hull. Unlike the situation in the United States, where Blacks live in extremely segregated inner-city neighbourhoods, we found that Canadian Blacks are suburbanized. While recognizable spatial concentrations of Blacks occur in some neighbourhoods in Toronto, Montreal, and Halifax, for example, the extent of segregation among Canadian Blacks certainly pales in comparison with what persists in American cities.

It is asserted that the invasion-succession model commonly used to account for the settlement pattern of immigrants and minorities in North American cities has limited applicability to the spatial pattern of Blacks in Canadian cities. By describing the social, economic, and geopolitical situation in Africa and the Caribbean, this chapter sets the stage for the next, which uses the case study approach to profile the major Black groups in Canada, with the intent of stressing the heterogeneity within the Canadian Black population.

Notes

1. Of the fifty-two active participants and observers at this conference, none was a geographer. For a full list of those present consult Dwivedi et al. 1989.
2. For example, a respondent giving the ethnic origin of Jamaican and Haitian will be counted in both the Jamaican and Haitian multiple responses; however, this respondent will be counted only once in the ethnic category for Caribbean origins.
3. For instance, Toronto could act as an intervening opportunity for a migrant from Lagos, Nigeria, who plans to settle in Los Angeles, California. He or she may stop over at Toronto and decide to settle there for good.
4. Newton's law of universal gravitation states that any two bodies attract each other with a force, which is directly proportional to gravitational constant and to the product of their masses and inversely proportional to the square of the distance between them. Newton's gravity equations is:
$G_{ij} = g (M_i M_j) / d_{ij}^2$
Where: G_{ij} = Gravitational force between places i and j
   M_i = Mass of i, and M_j = Mass of j
   d_{ij} = Distance between i and j
   g = Gravitational constant
Following Newton, a more sophisticated formulation of Zipf's gravity model is as follows:
$F_{ij} = g (P_iP_j) / d_{ij}^2$
Where F_{ij} = The flow of migrants between i and j
P_i = Population of place i, and P_j is the population of place j
d_{ij} = Distance between places i and j
g = a constant, which is empirically determined by simple arithmetic
5. Distance decay is the principle that states that the intensity of many spatial phenomena and processes tends to decline with increasing distance from its point of origin.
6. Myrdal in his *Rich Lands and Poor* (New York: Harper and Row, 1957) defines cumulative causation as the forces in economic growth that support change and encourage cumulative growth.
7. Quoted in de Blij (1993: 135).
8. For instance, Black Americans were turned back at the border on several occasions; special head taxes were imposed on Chinese immigrants; quotas were instituted for Japanese; and East Indian immigration was curtailed by the Continuous Journey Stipulation, which prohibited immigrants "from landing or coming to Canada unless they come from the country of their birth, or citizenship, by continuous journey" (see D'Costa 1989: 47).

9. Arguably, these are just code words for Blacks and other visible minorities.
10. Note that Hong Kong is currently part of China.
11. Under this U.S. Act, immigrant selection was based on national origin quotas.
12. This model, based on the demographic experience of developed nations, describes the changing levels of fertility and mortality over time. Starting from around the eleventh century, the model divides population changes into four stages: Stage I, the high stationary phase, was the period of high birth and death rates; Stage II, the early expanding phase, was the period of high birth rate and low death rate; Stage III, the late expanding phase, experienced a declining birth rate with a much faster decrease in death rate; Stage IV, the low stationary phase, was the time of very low birth and death rates. For a comprehensive treatment of the model, refer to any introductory human geography textbook (e.g., de Blij 1993).
13. Refer to Taylor (1991) for a comprehensive treatment of the ongoing debate between the conventional and racist theorists on Canada's immigration; the former argue that the policy changes of the 1960s removed the racist intent, while the latter disagree. A National Film Board video documentary entitled "Who Gets In" lends some support to the allegation of racism in Canada's immigration.
14. Census metropolitan area (CMA) is a geographic term used by Statistics Canada in the Canadian census. It is defined as a very large urbanized core, together with adjacent urban and rural areas, which have a high degree of economic and social integration with the core; to qualify as a CMA, an urban area should have a population of at least 100,000, based on the previous census.
15. The Chicago School refers to members of the University of Chicago's sociology department whose studies of the city, based mainly on the concepts of human ecology, were carried out around the 1920s but have greatly influenced later research in the fields of urban sociology, urban geography, and criminology. The key members of the Chicago School included Ernest Burgess, Robert Park, and R.D. McKenzie.
16. The index of dissimilarity (ID) measures the percentage of a group (in this case Blacks) that has to be relocated to make the group's distribution similar to that of the general population. The ID value ranges from 0 to 100. An ID value close to 0 implies that the two populations have similar spatial distribution, the closer the value is to 100 the more dissimilar the two spatial distributions, and hence the greater the degree of residential segregation. (Note that ID value can be divided by 100; in that case the index will range from 0 to 1). The ID is calculated by the following formula:

$$IDxy = \frac{\sum (Xi - Yi)}{2}$$

Where: Xi = the percentage of the X population in the ith area
Yi = the percentage of the Y population in the ith area
$IDxy$ = the index of dissimilarity between groups x and y
Notice that one needs to sum up the *absolute* difference between percentages of each group in all the areas before dividing by 2.
17. A phrase used by Bob Murdie in his 1994 paper on Blacks in Toronto's social housing.
18. The constrained choice argument posits that those who are desperately in

need of affordable housings, as a result of limited income and choice, may be compelled to take up any first offer, whereas those who are not as desperate may decide to wait longer and probably end up in better complexes (Murdie 1994).

19. The term "topophilia" refers to people's affective or emotional ties to a place.

Chapter 5

Profiles of Selected Black Groups in Canada

Notwithstanding the insights provided by Chapters 3 and 4, both covered the Black presence in Canada at a highly aggregated or general level, with virtually no attention to the differences within the Black population. This chapter complements the two preceding ones by profiling the "indigenous" Black population in Nova Scotia, together with four selected Black immigrant groups, including Jamaicans, Haitians, Ghanaians, and Somalis. More specifically, the chapter examines the contemporary circumstance of the indigenous Blacks in Nova Scotia and unravels the immigration trends and settlement patterns of the selected Black immigrant groups in Canada. Obviously, the vast majority of Black immigrants in Canada come from the Caribbean and Africa, each of which is represented by two of the selected groups (Jamaicans and Haitians for the Caribbean, and Ghanaians and Somalis for Africa). The justifications for the selection of these specific immigrant groups will be provided in due course.

The ethnocultural and geopolitical background of Black Canadians, perhaps even more than any other group, is highly varied, with virtually infinite diversity in native dialects, religion, and other cultural attributes. The account given here is necessarily selective in highlighting the features and trends considered relevant to our understanding of the Black diasporic communities in Canada. Furthermore, as noted in Chapter 1, the bulk of the available work on Black Canadians deals with Caribbeans, relegating the presence of Africans and indigenous Blacks to the background. By profiling all these groups here, the chapter acknowledges and, indeed, underscores the heterogeneity of the Canadian Black population.

Blacks in Contemporary Nova Scotia

As we saw in Chapter 3, the Black presence in Nova Scotia is the longest-standing among all Canadian provinces and territories. It goes back to the mid-eighteenth century when the first major group of Black slaves was brought by former New England residents, after the expulsion of the

Acadians. The Black population in the region rose with the arrival of Black Loyalists during the 1770s, and later with the arrival of the Maroons from Jamaica. These Black pioneers tilled the land, worked the mines, and built roads and structures that exist even now. The racism and dehumanization they endured over the years have been documented in Chapter 3, and they deserve no reiteration. In this section we profile the demographic and spatial characteristics of Blacks in contemporary Nova Scotia and compare their economic circumstances with those of "all visible minorities" and "all Nova Scotians," using empirical data from the 1996 census.

Some Demographic and Spatial Characteristics

The 1996 census of Canada puts Nova Scotia's population at 899,990 people, of which some 31,320 (or 3.5 percent) are visible minorities. Not surprisingly, Blacks are by far the largest visible minority group in the province, with a population of 18,105; this represents 57.8 percent of the visible minority population in Nova Scotia. The sex ratio of Blacks in Nova Scotia, calculated as the number of males per 100 females, is 86, which is lower than the comparable ratios for "all visible minorities" and the general Nova Scotian population, as can be discerned from Table 5.1 below.

A sizeable proportion of Nova Scotian Blacks, compared to "all visible minorities" and "all Nova Scotians," was born in that province (Table 5.1). In fact, unlike other visible minorities, the overwhelming majority of Blacks in Nova Scotia are non-immigrants. This and other census data authenticate the thesis that Nova Scotian Blacks are far more "indigenous" than Blacks elsewhere. For instance, while as high as 94 percent of Nova Scotian Blacks are non-immigrants, the corresponding figure for the entire Canadian Black population is only 41.9 percent. In a similar vein, the Canadian citizenship status of Nova Scotian Blacks and the entire Canadian Black population are estimated at 97.6 and 80 percent, respectively.

Table 5.1 Selected Demographic Characteristics of Blacks, All Visible Minorities and All Nova Scotians

Variables	Blacks	All Visible Minorities	All Nova Scotians
Sex Ratio★	86	96	95
Born in Nova Scotia (%)	87.2	61.9	79.0
Canadian Citizenship (%)	97.6	85.9	98.4
Non-immigrant population (%)	94.0	68.7	95.1
Speaks neither English nor French (%)	0.1	2.2	0.1
Total Population	18,105	31,320	899,970

★ Calculated as the number of males per 100 females.
Source: Canada, Statistics Canada 1999b.

Another indication of the high indigenousness of Nova Scotian Blacks, compared to other Black Canadians, is the fact that only 0.1 percent of the former, as opposed to 1.3 percent of the latter, have neither English nor French speaking ability. Indeed, the proportion of non-immigrants among Nova Scotian Blacks is also far higher than comparable figures for all other visible minority groups in Canada. Estimates by Kazemipur and Halli (1997: 21) suggest that the relative share of non-immigrants among visible minority groups in Canada generally ranges from 18 to 40 percent, compared to the whopping 94 percent for Nova Scotian Blacks.

Blacks constitute the most visible (in both physical and numerical sense) of the visible minorities in Halifax, the provincial capital, where the majority (66.3 percent) of Blacks live. Of the city's 329,750[1] residents, some 22,320 are visible minorities, out of which 12,000 (or more than half) are Blacks. Blacks in Halifax tend to be concentrated in high poverty areas. Out of the twenty-seven ethnic groups in Halifax examined by Kazemipur and Halli (1997: Table 5), Blacks were second only to Vietnamese in their concentration in census tracts with high poverty rates—i.e., 40 percent or more. In fact, only four Canadian cities, including Saint John, Quebec City, Sherbrooke, and Montreal, exhibit a higher spatial concentration of poverty among Blacks (Kazemipur and Halli 1997). Unlike the situation in other provinces, there are sizeable numbers of Blacks in several Nova Scotian cities and small towns including Sydney, New Glasgow, Kentville, Truro, Antigonish, Amherst, and Digby.

Educational, Income, and Labour Market Disparities

Like all four Atlantic provinces, Nova Scotia has been economically depressed for some time now. The question is "How are Blacks faring economically?" Are they bearing a disproportionate brunt of the economic malaise in that province? Is there any evidence that anti-Black discrimination persists in the Nova Scotian labour market? Are Blacks faring any worse than other visible minorities in that province? We examine these questions in what follows, using snapshot data from the 1996 census.

The data presented in Table 5.2 clearly show that Blacks are over-represented among people with less than Grade 9 education and acutely under-represented in the category of those with a bachelor's or higher degree in Nova Scotia. Other visible minorities in the province have higher educational levels than both Blacks and the general provincial population. Quite expectedly, the 1996 census data suggest that Blacks are not doing well in the province's labour market. For instance, only a meagre 0.2 percent of the Blacks in the province's work force hold senior management positions, compared to 1.2 and 0.6 percent among "all visible

Table 5.2 Selected Labour Market Characteristics of Blacks, All Visible Minorities, and All Nova Scotians

Variable	Blacks	All Visible Minorities	All Nova Scotians
Education			
Less than grade 9 education (%)	15.1	11.1	11.0
Trade certificate/diploma	3.7	2.7	3.9
With bachelor's or higher (%)	7.3	20.9	12.2
Employment			
In senior management positions	0.2	1.2	0.6
Professionals	8.7	16.5	12.6
Supervisors	5.9	6.0	5.8
Intermediate sales and service positions	15.5	14.1	14.1
Semi-skilled manual workers	11.3	7.3	11.3
Unemployment rate (%)	20.0	15.7	13.3
Labour force participation rate (%)	57.2	59.2	61.0
Income			
With annual under $5,000 (%)	25.7	25.6	17.1
With annual income of $60,000 or more	1.5	4.0	3.9
Average income ($)	16,007	19,136	21,552
Median income ($)	12.257	12,675	16,000
Income from gov't transfer payment (%)	24.7	16.8	19.1
Total population	18,105	31,320	899,970

Note: Education, employment, and income data are based on population 15 years and over.
Source: Canada, Statistics Canada 1999b.

minorities" and "all Nova Scotians," respectively. The situation of Blacks in professional jobs and supervisory positions is not much different, according to Table 5.2. Blacks are, however, slightly over-represented in low-level jobs, such as intermediate sales and service positions and semi-skilled manual work; although the size of the Black population in the latter employment category is equal to that of the general population, it is far higher than that of "all visible minorities."

Perhaps the greatest indicator of the straitened circumstances of Blacks in the Nova Scotian labour market is their high unemployment rate. Whereas the unemployment rate for the province as a whole stood at 13 percent in 1996, the rate for Blacks was as high as 20 percent, which is five percentage points higher than the rate for "all visible minorities" in the province. One can also infer higher seasonal unemployment among Blacks from Table 5.2, based on the high proportion of Blacks depending on government transfer payments. We also find in Table 5.2 that Blacks have considerable income shortfall, compared to "all visible minorities" and "all Nova Scotians." The table also shows that, like "all visible minorities in the province," a quarter of Blacks have annual incomes of under $5000.

However, unlike "all visible minorities," Blacks have far smaller representation among those with annual incomes of $60,000 or more. Given the low levels of formal education among Nova Scotian Blacks, it is not surprising that they have employment and income deficits, compared to the general population. At the same time we cannot discount the fact that their low educational levels—and, consequently, their appalling employment and income characteristics—have something to do with the racism that they continue to endure in Nova Scotia (*Globe and Mail* 1991; *Toronto Star* 1991).

Black Immigrant Groups in Canada

Until the early 1960s, Britain, and to some extent the United States, was the main destination for Black migrants from Africa and the Caribbean. Britain had an open-door policy towards her colonial dependents, and most African and Caribbean migrants did not need a visa to visit, work, or even settle in Britain.[2] In the years following the Second World War, the number of Blacks in Britain increased sharply as some of the Blacks who assisted the British war efforts settled in Britain. And, as Shyllon (1993) points out, it did not take long for racial tensions to surface in British urban and industrial centres, where most Blacks lived. For instance, in 1948, Blacks were terrorized in Liverpool; similar attacks occurred in London's Deptford and Camden Town in 1949 and 1954, respectively. Two years later came the Notting Hill Riots, followed by the notorious Nottingham Riot of 1958 (Shyllon 1993).

As the number of Black immigrants rose and racial tensions and riots became rampant so did political demands to control the influx of Blacks to Britain. These demands culminated in the passage of the first *Commonwealth Immigrants Act of 1962,* which severely curtailed the right of Commonwealth members to come to Britain. The second and third Acts were passed in 1968 and 1971, respectively, each with additional restrictions on the entry of Blacks into Britain. Just as the British immigration doors were being shut for Blacks, the opposite was happening in Canada, as we saw in Chapter 4. This explains the persistence of double lap[3] and step-wise[4] migrations among Caribbean and some African immigrants in Canada (Konadu-Agyemang 1999; Henry 1994).

In what follows we first examine the leading sources of Caribbean immigrants in Canada and explicate the reasoning behind the selection of the Jamaicans and Haitians for our close-up view. This is followed by their respective profiles. A similar outline is used to examine the selected African groups—i.e., Ghanaians and Somalis—in the subsequent sections. It is important to note at this juncture that the immigration statistics upon

Table 5.3 Top Ten Sources of Caribbean-born
Immigrants in Canada, 1996

Rank	County	Immigrants	
		Number	Percent
1	Jamaica	115,800	41.44
2	Trinidad–Tobago	62,020	22.19
3	Haiti	49,395	17.67
4	Barbados	15,225	5.45
5	St. Vincent and the Grenadines	7,170	2.56
6	Granada	7,095	2.53
7	Dominican Republic	4,560	1.63
8	Cuba	3,100	1.10
9	St. Kitts and Nevis	2,465	0.88
10	Saint Lucia	2,360	0.84
	Others	10,215	3.65
	Total	279,405	100.0*

* The total percentage is less than 100 due to rounding.
Source: Canada, Statistics Canada 1999b.

which the empirical analyses in the next sections are based do not identify
the race of immigrants. Immigrants are commonly categorized on the basis
of their country of permanent residence or their country of birth.
Consequently, generalizations about Black Canadians based on the immigration statistics need to be interpreted with caution. Additionally, the
pervasiveness of double lap and step-wise migrations among Caribbeans
and Africans demands some level of caution in interpreting the immigration statistics of these groups.

Caribbean Immigrants to Canada: Leading Sources

Since the immigration policy amendments of the early 1960s the number
of Black immigrants from the two principal sources—Africa and the
Caribbean—has increased substantially. The Caribbean, despite its relatively small size, played a crucial role in the transatlantic slave trade and in
the struggles of the imperial powers to gain a foothold in the New World
(Henry 1994). The present cultural characteristics of the Caribbean derive
from the legacy of European conquest and slavery. While the region has a
wide variety of ethnic groups, the overwhelming majority of the people
are of African descent. As a consequence, several cultural attributes and
landscapes in the Caribbean—e.g., the style of village dwellings, the
operation of village markets, and the prevailing gender roles and artistic and
linguistic expressions—bear close resemblance to those of Black Africa.

The largest contingent of Caribbeans in Canada comes from Jamaica,
followed by Trinidad-Tobago, Haiti, and Barbados, in that order (Table

Table 5.4 Cultural Characteristics of the Major Countries of Caribbean Immigrants

Country	Major Ethnic Group	Principal Languages*	Major Religions	Colonial Power**
Jamaica	76% African; 15% Afro-European; 3% East-Indian; 3% White; 1% Chinese; 2% Others	*English* Patois	Mostly Anglican; some Rastafarians	Britain (1962)***
Trinidad–Tobago	41% Black; 41% East Indian; 16% Mixed; 2% White, Chinese & Others	*English* Hindi French Creole Spanish	60% Christian; 25% Hindu; 6% Moslem; 9% Other	Britain (1962)
Haiti	95% Black; 5% Mulatto, White, and others	*French* (spoken by about 10% of the people) Creole	80% Catholic (many of whom practise Voodoo); 10% Protestant; 10% Other	France (1804)
Barbados	80% Black; 16% mixed; 4% European	*English*	70% Anglican; 9% Methodist; 4% Catholic; 17% others	Britain (1966)
Grenada	Mainly Black African descent	*English* some French patois	Largely Catholic; Anglican; and other Protestants	Britain (1974)
St. Vincent and The Grenadines	Mainly Black African descent; the rest are Mixed; Whites; East Indians; and Caribbean Indians	*English* French patois	Mostly Anglican Methodist Catholics, and Seventh-Day Adventist	Britain (1979)
Dominican Republic	73% Mixed; 16% White; 11% Black	*Spanish*	95% Catholic; 5% Other	Spain (1844)
Cuba	51% Mulatto; 37% White; 11% Black; 1% Chinese	*Spanish*	Majority Roman Catholic	Spain (1902)
St. Kitts and Nevis	94% Black African; 3% Mixed; 1% White	*English*	33% Anglican; 29% Methodist; 9% Moravian; 7% Catholic	Britain (1983)
Saint Lucia	90% Black; Mixed 6%; East Indian 3%	*English* French patois	90% Catholic; 7% Protestant; 3% Anglican	Britain (1979)

*Official language in italics. **Reference is to the last colonial power. ***Year of Independence.
Sources: (i) Rand McNally (1998), *World Facts and Maps* (ii) John Robert Colombo (1994), *The Canadian Global Almanac*.

5.3). These four areas accounted for more than 85 percent of the Caribbean-born immigrants in Canada as of 1996. While the Canadian immigration statistics do not specify the race of people, available surveys and interviews suggest that well over 80 percent of the Caribbean immigrants in Canada are Blacks and mulattos (Henry 1994; Hamilton 1990/91; Walker 1984).

Table 5.4 summarizes the cultural characteristics of the leading sources of Caribbean immigrants to Canada. Clearly, people of Black African descent feature prominently in all the countries listed. In fact, in countries such as Haiti, Jamaica, Barbados, and Grenada, Blacks and mulattos are the vast majority. Still, it is important to note that the Caribbean region "contains a microcosm of the world's major population groups" (Walker 1984: 3). After slavery was abolished in the early 1800s, several Chinese and East Indian indentured labourers were brought to the region to work on the sugar plantations. Many of these labourers brought their families with them and remained in the Caribbean after their contracts were fulfilled. Over the years, sexual liaison among the various ethnic and racial groups, including Europeans, Black Africans, Chinese, and East Indians, yielded sizable proportions of mixed population throughout the Caribbean (Walker 1984).

Due to the legacies of slavery and White domination, a colour continuum, which associates blackness with disadvantage and whiteness with power and prestige, persists in almost all Caribbean nations. For example, in Haiti, where 95 percent of the population is Black and 5 percent mulatto, it is the mulatto minority that holds the lion's share of the nation's social, economic, and political power. Similarly, in the neighbouring Dominican Republic, the pyramid of socio-economic and political power puts the 16 percent of Whites on top of the 73 percent of mixed and the 11 percent of Blacks. And, in Jamaica, the 15 percent mulatto population plays a role of prominence that far outweighs their proportionate share of the island's population (Table 5.4).

During the colonial era, Europeans of many nationalities inhabited the Caribbean. Quite expectedly, several European languages—including English, French, and Spanish, together with their respective patois or Creole[5] versions—are spoken throughout the region. Of the two Canadian official languages, English is the most prevalent among the leading countries of Caribbean immigrants. With the notable exceptions of Haiti, Cuba, and the Dominican Republic, all of the leading Caribbean source countries have English as their official language (Table 5.4). In fact, Haiti is the only country among the top ten with French as its official language, hence the affinity of Haitian immigrants for Quebec in the Canadian context.

Before proceeding any further, it is important to understand the logic behind selecting Jamaicans and Haitians for a close-up view. Jamaicans were selected not only because they represent the largest Caribbean group in Canada, but also because of their long-standing ties with Canada, which go back to the eighteenth century with the immigration of Maroons to Halifax, Nova Scotia, and more recently with the recruitment of Jamaican women under the West Indian Domestic Scheme of 1955 (Calliste 1996). Additionally, as we just learned, the overwhelming majority of Jamaicans in Canada, as in their homeland, are Blacks or mulattos. The second largest Caribbean group in Canada comes from Trinidad-Tobago, but Haiti was selected, instead of the former, for three main reasons. First, unlike Trinidad-Tobago, the overwhelming majority of Haitians are Black. Second, Haitians constitute the largest francophone Black community in Canada, and their inclusion allows us to examine the French dimension of the Black diaspora in Canada. Finally, Haiti has had stronger and longer-standing immigration ties with Canada than Trinidad and Tobago.

Jamaican Immigrants in Canada

Background

Jamaica is the third largest island of the Greater Antilles and the largest island of Commonwealth Caribbean. Christopher Columbus claimed the island for Spain in 1494. As the native Arawak Indian population died out from overwork and European diseases to which they had no immunity, Blacks were brought from Africa to work the plantations. Britain gained control of Jamaica in the seventeenth century, and for a time the island was one of the most important sugar and slave centres of the New World. In that early period, and even after the end of the slave trade in 1808 and of slavery in 1834, Jamaica was governed by an assembly dominated by a planters' oligarchy, even though ultimate authority rested with the crown and British Parliament (Kaplan et al. 1976). During the mid-nineteenth century, economic decline and political turmoil compelled the British government to step in and assume full control over the island. A crown colonial government was instituted in 1866.

Local political control of Jamaica began in the 1930s, but the nation became fully independent in 1962. Since then, the country has been governed by two main political parties—the Jamaica Labour Party and the People's National Party—under a parliamentary democracy. As in several countries of the developing world, politics in Jamaica is full of corruption, embezzlement, and intimidation. Violent clashes between armed gangs of political parties over the control of specific localities and urban neighbourhoods are commonplace, especially during elections. In addition, illicit drug activities have given rise to high levels of violent crime, creating fear and a heightened state of anxiety among Jamaicans. Yet, because many of the criminal activities have strong political ties, a nonpartisan assault on crime has so far proven elusive (Kaplan et al. 1976).

The Jamaican economy, although productive by the standards of the developing world, is constantly faced with serious unemployment, under-employment, and inflation. While there has been some economic diversification, agriculture, mining, and tourism remain Jamaica's mainstay. Historically, the Jamaican economy was one in which absentee landlords held much of the good farmland. Since independence, the government has tried to resolve the inequities in land ownership through land reallocation and mandatory formation of cooperatives. Yet, landlessness among peasant farmers persists to the extent that a large number of peasants now earn their living not from their own farms, but by working for other farmers or landlords. To survive economically, many in rural Jamaica leave the agricultural labour force and migrate to urban areas, swelling the ranks of shantytown dwellers, particularly in Kingston, the national capital. Although the production of bauxite (aluminum ore) has been one of the main sources of government revenue, it has not supported any significant employment and industrialization within Jamaica, as much of the processing activities are done outside the country, in such places as Kitimat, British Columbia.

As with most people in developing countries, Jamaicans are trapped in an international economic order in which they have little control. Their good agricultural land is under export crop; their flourishing tourist industry is largely controlled by multinational corporations and foreigners; even their import substitution industries depend substantially on imported raw materials, capital, and technology. With such an economic structure and mounting unemployment and inflation, it is not surprising that many Jamaicans have emigrated overseas to countries such as Canada.

Immigration to Canada

The history of Jamaican immigration in Canada is a long-standing one. As we learned in Chapter 3, one of the first large groups of Blacks to enter Canada was the Maroons of Jamaica, who landed in Halifax in 1796. Also, during the First World War, Jamaican Blacks were among those recruited to work in the coal mines of Sydney and the shipyards of Halifax and Collingwood (Ontario). However, until the immigration policy amendments of the 1960s, Jamaicans, like other Blacks, were allowed into this country only to fill a labour market need. For instance, in 1955 when it became increasingly difficult to meet the demand for domestic workers in

Canada, due to intense competition from Britain and other western European nations, Canada initiated the West Indian Domestic Scheme. Jamaicans and Barbadians were the first to be recruited. Until the 1960s, the domestic scheme was one of the very few legal avenues by which Jamaicans could enter Canada, and several Jamaican nurses, teachers, secretaries, and clerks took advantage of the program to gain a foothold in this country (Calliste 1996).

Another large group of Jamaicans to enter Canada prior to the immigration policy changes of the 1960s consisted of students. Jamaican and other Caribbean students had been coming to Canada on temporary visas since the 1920s. After the end of the Second World War, their numbers increased substantially, and by the early 1960s there were sufficient concentrations of Jamaican and other Caribbean students in major Canadian universities to establish their own student clubs (Lampkin 1985; Walker 1984).

Despite the favourable immigration policy changes of 1962, harsh economic realities in Canada discouraged any immediate increase in immigration from Jamaica (and other parts of the Caribbean), as can be seen from Table 5.5 and Figure 5.1 below. The high point of Jamaican immigration to Canada was between 1973 and 1977, peaking in 1974 with as high as 11,286 immigrants (Figure 5.1). Towards the end of the 1970s, however, renewed restrictions on immigration reduced the number of Jamaican immigrants.

The new restrictions, first tabled in 1976 and proclaimed in 1978, revised the 1967 point system by shifting the emphasis away from educational qualification onto occupational and employment experience of prospective immigrants. In addition, the revision placed more weight on independent immigrants and refugees at the expense of family-class immigrants. The impact of these changes on Jamaican immigration was quick, direct, and drastic, as can be seen from Figure 5.1. With these changes, most of the young university graduates from Jamaica, lacking employment experience, were restricted from entering Canada. Furthermore, the family-class immigration, which traditionally had been used—and, arguably, abused by several Jamaicans and other Caribbean nationals, due to the lack of a precise definition of "relatives" eligible under the system—decidedly was curtailed (Anderson 1993).

Moreover, the political situation in Jamaica at the time did not lend itself easily to a refugee claim in Canada. Unlike places such as Haiti and Cuba where intense political persecution and suppression have forced many of their citizens to seek political asylum elsewhere, Jamaica has had a relatively stable democratic structure, and very few Jamaicans have been forced to leave the island for reasons of political persecution. However, by

Table 5.5 Jamaican Immigrants, Arrivals 1973–1994*

Year	Total	Male	Female	Sex Ratio**
1973	9,363	4,080	5,283	129
1974	11,286	4,947	6,339	128
1975	8,211	4,030	4,181	104
1976	7,282	3,630	3,652	101
1977	6,291	3,091	3,200	103
1978	3,858	1,798	2,060	114
1979	3,213	1,496	1,717	115
1980	3,161	1,460	1,701	116
1981	2,553	1,144	1,409	123
1982	2,593	1,244	1,349	108
1983	2,423	1,022	1,401	137
1984	2,479	987	1,492	151
1985	2,922	1,185	1,737	146
1986	4,652	1,742	2,910	167
1987	5,422	2,277	3,145	138
1988	3,923	1,809	2,114	117
1989	3,896	1,910	1,986	104
1990	2,387	1,067	1,320	124
1991	4,997	2,324	2,673	115
1992	5,921	2,640	3,281	124
1993	5,990	2,736	3,254	119
1994	3,930	1,820	2,110	116

* The figures represent immigrants for whom Jamaica is the country of last permanent residence. ** Defined as the number of females per 100 males.
Source: Canada, Citizenship and Immigration Canada, Various Years [1993–1995].

Figure 5.1: Jamaican Immigrants, Arrivals, 1973–1997

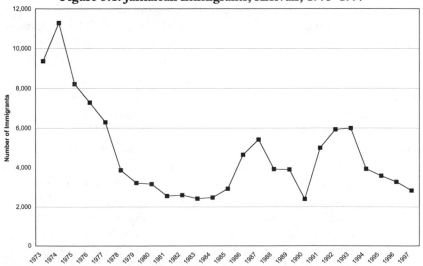

Source: Canada, Department of Citizenship and Immigration (various years).

Table 5.6 Persons of Jamaican Ethnic Origin★
by Provinces and Territories, 1996★★

Province/ Territory	Jamaican Population		Percent Prov./Terr. Pop. Jamaican	Percent Prov./Terr. Visible Minority Pop. Jamaican
	#	%		
Newfoundland /Labrador	90	0.047	0.016	2.360
PEI	80	0.042	0.059	5.263
Nova Scotia	800	0.423	0.087	2.554
New Brunswick	460	0.243	0.062	5.757
Quebec	10,075	5.337	0.141	2.321
Ontario	159,470	84.478	1.482	9.480
Manitoba	2,920	1.547	0.262	3.774
Saskatchewan	940	0.497	0.094	3.487
Alberta	7,815	4.139	0.289	2.902
British Columbia	6,030	3.194	0.162	0.913
Yukon	30	0.015	0.097	3.000
NWT	55	0.029	0.085	3.293
Canada	188,770	100★★★	0.654	5.903

★ This includes the number of people who provided both single and multiple responses for Jamaican ethnic origin.
★★ Note that the data in this and other tables derived from the 1996 census are rounded up or down to the nearest multiple of 5. Consequently there may be some variations and inconsistencies in some of the table totals.
★★★ Percentage figures do not add up to 100 due to rounding up.
Source: Canada, Statistics Canada 1999b.

the late 1970s, when the new immigration restrictions caused the number of Jamaican immigrants to decrease, the Jamaican presence in Canada had been fully established, especially in Ontario cities such as Toronto, Mississauga, Scarborough, London, Hamilton, Kichener-Waterloo, and Windsor. Indeed, Jamaica has always been a major source of Black immigrants to Canada. Estimates by Serge (1993) indicate that Jamaica was among the top ten sources of immigrants into Canada from 1969 to 1979 and from 1984 to 1988.

As the sex ratios provided in Table 5.5 clearly indicate, there have been more female than male immigrants from Jamaica over the years. Similar sex ratios are common among other Caribbean groups in Canada, including Haitians. The opposite tends to be the case for African immigrants, according to a recent study by Mensah and Adjibolosoo (1998). Later in this chapter we will explore possible explanations for this disparity.

What is the geographic distribution pattern of Jamaican immigrants in Canada? Which provinces and cities are the leading centres of Jamaican

Table 5.7 Persons of Jamaican Ethnic Origin★ by Census Metropolitan Area (CMA), 1996

Census Metropolitan Area★★	Number of Jamaicans	Percent
Toronto	133,690	74.08
Montreal	9,610	5.32
Vancouver	4,105	2.27
Ottawa-Hull	6,340	3.51
Edmonton	3,240	1.80
Calgary	3,910	2.17
Quebec City	40	0.22
Winnipeg	2,770	1.53
Hamilton	4,905	2.72
London	1,860	1.03
Kitchener	2,545	1.41
St. Catharines-Niagara	1,065	0.60
Halifax	495	0.27
Victoria	570	0.31
Windsor	935	0.52
Oshawa	2,960	1.64
Saskatoon	200	0.11
Regina	555	0.31
St John's	40	0.02
Sudbury	280	0.15
Chicoutimi-Jonquière	0★★★	0
Sherbrooke	30	0.16
Trois-Rivières	10	0.01
Saint John	165	0.09
Thunder Bay	145	0.08
Total	180,465	100★★★★

★ This includes the number of people who provided both single and multiple responses for Jamaican ethnic origin.
★★ The CMAs are listed in ranked order.
★★★ Note that due to confidentiality, data cells containing counts of less than 5 are undisclosed and represented by a zero instead of the actual data. Also, note that the data in this and other tables based on the census are rounded up or down to the nearest multiple of 5. Consequently there may be variations and inconsistencies in some the table totals.
★★★★ Percentage figures do not add up to 100 due to rounding up.
Source: Canada, Statistics Canada 1999b.

settlement in Canada? The data presented in Table 5.6 show that the vast majority (84.5 percent) of Jamaicans live in Ontario, where they account for 1.5 percent of the provincial population and nearly one-tenth of the visible minority population. Outside of Ontario, the major concentrations of Jamaicans occur in Quebec, Manitoba, Alberta, and, to some extent, British Columbia. The least numbers of Jamaicans are found in the Atlantic

Provinces and the two territories, as can be seen Table 5.6; indeed none of these areas had a thousand or more Jamaican residents as of 1996. Nonetheless, it is important to note that as a percentage of the total provincial or visible minority population, these areas are not much different from the other Canadian provinces, with the notable exception of Ontario, which dominates by all accounts.

Table 5.7 depicts the distribution of Jamaicans across the twenty-five census metropolitan areas (CMAs) of Canada. It clearly buttresses the fact that the Jamaican presence in Canada, like that of other visible minorities, is an urban phenomenon. A whopping 180,465, or 95 percent, of the total 188,770 Jamaicans living in Canada by 1996 resided in the twenty-five largest cities or CMAs. By far, the largest concentration of Jamaicans is found in the Toronto CMA, especially in and around the Bathurst, Jane-Finch, Eglington, and Danforth corridors, where Jamaicans have established a variety of social and cultural associations and are served by countless grocery shops, nightclubs, and beauty salons. The Montreal and Ottawa-Hull CMAs, as well as most of the metropolitan centres of Western Canada, are also home to sizeable numbers of Jamaicans. With the notable exception of Halifax, where indigenous Blacks have long-standing settlement ties, only a small number of Jamaicans live in the cities of Atlantic Canada.

Haitian Immigrants in Canada

Background

Haiti occupies the western third of the island of Hispaniola. Spanish colonization of Haiti began with the very first trip of Columbus to the New World. By 1505, the Native Indian population had been decimated through ruthless exploitation and diseases. It was not until 1697 that the French gained control of what is now Haiti (English 1984). The French greatly expanded the African slave population, and by 1800 there were an estimated 700,000 Black slaves and some 28,000 mulattos controlled by a mere 40,000 French (Jackson and Hudman 1990). The slaves were used above all for the production of sugar cane, coffee, and other cash crops on plantations. Haiti yielded such a rich supply of these commodities that the French referred to the island as the "Pearl of the Antilles."

Taking advantage of the French Revolution of the late eighteenth century, the Haitian slaves, led by notables such as Toussaint L'Ouverture, Jean Jacques Dessalines, and Henry Christophe, revolted in 1791. By 1804, the independence of Haiti from France was firmly secured, setting up the world's first Black republic (Hamilton 1990/91). Since independence,

however, Haiti has been politically unstable, socially fragile, and economically depressed. Few capable leaders have ruled Haiti since independence.
Power struggles, *coups d'état*, and foreign occupation[6] have become the
hallmark of Haitian politics. Estimates by English (1984) suggest that, from
1804 to 1911, only four of Haiti's nineteen political leaders actually
completed a term of office or died peacefully in office. Political power in
Haiti is usually sought for self-aggrandizement. Until quite recently, no
generally accepted and workable procedure for succession had been
established.

During the reign of François Duvalier, in particular, Haiti witnessed
a dictatorship, whose level of corruption, repression, suppression, and utter
lack of social conscience and economic direction has been surpassed
perhaps by no other nation in the Western Hemisphere. By the time of his
death in 1971, François Duvalier had altered the nation's constitution to
enable his nineteen-year-old son, Jean-Claude, to succeed him as the
president for life. With the help of his equally power-drunk mother and
other trusted members of his father's government, Jean-Claude Duvalier
managed to survive a rather rocky beginning. To maintain the status quo,
the ruling class in Haiti actively violated human rights by cracking down
on and terrorizing political dissidents. Hamilton (1990/91: 34) writes that
"anyone who was against the Duvalier regime had to leave or die," as the
government consistently hunted down its opponents. The climate of
collective insecurity among the populace drove several young academicians and technicians into the ranks of political exiles (Jean-Baptiste 1979).
The Duvalier dictatorial dynasty ended in 1986, when Jean-Claude fled
the country. However, continued political unrest and *coups d'état* resulted
in six different governments in the three-year period between 1987 and
1990. There were high hopes that the internationally monitored election
that brought Jean-Bertrand Aristide into power in 1990 would stabilize the
country. However, a coup in 1991 returned Haiti to military government
until 1994 when a U.S.-sponsored initiative ousted the military junta and
returned Aristide to power.

In addition to their current political problems, Haitians find themselves in one of the most rugged physical landscapes in the Western
Hemisphere. In fact, the name Haiti means "land of mountains." Highlands
constitute about 80 percent of the country's topography, and more than
half of the country has slopes exceeding 40 degrees (English 1984; Jean-
Baptiste 1979). On this unsympathetic landscape, half the size of Nova
Scotia, some 7.2 million people eke out a precarious subsistence. Furthermore, like most Caribbean islands, Haiti is frequently in the path of
hurricanes; a bad one destroyed much of the harvest in 1980. Political and
economic mismanagement and environmental degradation has plunged

Haiti into an advanced state of poverty. The erstwhile Pearl of the Antilles is now the undisputed pauper of the Antilles, with a 1997 GNP per capita of U.S.$250, an adult literacy rate of 43 percent, and an average life expectancy of fifty years (Fellmann, et al. 1999: 539).[7]

Since the beginning of the twentieth century, many Haitians have migrated to the neighbouring Dominican Republic even though the border between the two nations has been officially closed most of the time (Lundahl 1983). Other Caribbean islands, notably Jamaica and the Bahamas, continue to receive large numbers of Haitian legal and illegal immigrants. Some estimates suggest that about a fifth of the present Bahamian population is of Haitian origin (English 1984). As these Caribbean destinations approach saturation and tighten their immigration regulations, more and more Haitian "boat people" have turned to Canada and the United States in search of a better life.

Immigration to Canada

The available literature divides Haitian immigration to Canada into two major waves: the first, from 1967 to around 1972; and the second from 1972 onward (Hamilton 1990/91; Lampkin 1985). The first wave was made up mostly of political exiles, scholarship students, and professionals working in health services, education, and social services. These pioneers, numbering some few hundred per year, were from the privileged class of the Haitian society (Hamilton 1990/91; Lampkin 1985). Quite expectedly, the vast majority of them settled in the province of Quebec where they had the least linguistic difficulty, as most of them spoke both French and French-based Creole. Worsening economic and political conditions in Haiti and the relaxation of Canada's immigration restrictions toward Blacks in the 1960s were the main push-pull factors for this initial influx.

During the early 1960s, Quebec initiated extensive educational reforms under its Quiet Revolution,[8] and many of these early Haitians—most of whom had completed their studies beyond Haiti—found teaching positions throughout Quebec. Haitian nurses, laboratory technicians, and physicians also were accepted in Quebec hospitals. However, like other immigrant groups in Canada, Haitian physicians, dentists, engineers, planners, and other professionals had to clear various employment hurdles such as entrance examinations, upgrading, professional certification, and professional membership before they were allowed to work in Canada. In the case of physicians, there was the additional requirement of Canadian citizenship. Because many Haitian professionals were in the state of waiting, hoping for an improvement in Haiti's political situation so that they could return home, some abandoned their professions and accepted lower level jobs in Quebec's semi-skilled and unskilled labour market.

Table 5.8 Haitian Immigrants, Arrivals, 1973–1994★

Year	Total	Male	Female	Sex Ratio★★
1973	2,178	1,072	1,106	103
1974	4,857	2,475	2,382	96
1975	3,431	1,603	1,828	114
1976	3,061	1,476	1,585	107
1977	2,026	950	1,076	113
1978	1,702	770	932	121
1979	1,268	567	701	123
1980	1,633	716	917	128
1981	3,667	1,586	2,081	131
1982	3,468	1,552	1,916	123
1983	2,827	1,322	1,505	114
1984	1,397	658	739	112
1985	1,297	562	735	131
1986	1,727	763	964	126
1987	2,121	968	1,153	119
1988	1,815	830	985	119
1989	2,369	1,103	1,266	115
1990	2,387	1,067	1,320	124
1991	2,793	1,288	1,505	117
1992	2,365	1,025	1,340	131
1993	3,629	1,618	2,011	124
1994	2,121	984	1,137	116

★ The figures represent immigrants for whom Haiti is the country of last permanent residence.
★★ Defined as the number of females per 100 males.
Source: Canada, Citizenship and Immigration Canada, Various Years [1973–1995].

The second major wave of Haitian immigration was much larger. Of these thousands of artisans, skilled and unskilled workers, most went to work in Quebec's plastic and textiles industries, as well as in the service sector, especially as domestic workers. Unlike the first-wave immigrants, this group had more problems adjusting to life in Canada due to their low educational and socio-economic backgrounds; many were illiterate and spoke only Creole. In 1973, the government of Canada, under Bill C-197, offered persons who had entered Canada illegally or as tourists the right to apply for landed immigrant status. And, for the first time, the number of Haitian immigrants to Canada exceeded one thousand, peaking in 1974 with close to five thousand immigrants (Table 5.8 and Figure 5.2). Since 1973, the annual number of Haitian immigrants to Canada has always been more than a thousand.

Estimates by Hamilton (1990/91) suggest that by 1971, Haiti was not among the top twenty nations from which Quebec immigrants originated. However, by 1981, Haiti was ranked sixth. Between 1980 and 1988, over

Table 5.9 Persons of Haitian Ethnic Origin* by Provinces and Territories, 1996

Province/ Territory	Haitian Population		Percent Prov./Terr. Pop. Haitian	Percent Prov/Terr. Visible Minority Pop. Haitian
	#	%		
Newfoundland /Labrador	60	0.071	0.011	1.572
PEI	10	0.012	0.007	0.657
Nova Scotia	240	0.286	0.026	0.766
New Brunswick	190	0.227	0.026	2.377
Quebec	75,705	90.469	1.060	17.444
Ontario	6,180	7.385	0.057	0.367
Manitoba	275	0.328	0.024	0.355
Saskatchewan	80	0.095	0.008	0.296
Alberta	455	0.543	0.016	0.168
British Columbia	470	0.562	0.012	0.071
Yukon	0	0	0	0
NWT	10	0.012	0.015	0.598
Canada	83,680	100**	0.029	2.617

* This includes the number of people who provided both single and multiple responses for Haitian ethnic origin. ** Percentage figures do not add up to 100 due to rounding up. *Source:* Canada, Statistics Canada 1999b.

Figure 5.2: Haitian Immigrants, Arrivals, 1968–1997

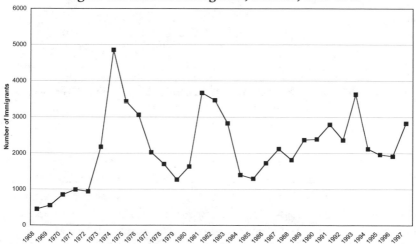

Source: Canada, Department of Citizenship and Immigration (various years).

nineteen thousand Haitians immigrated to Quebec, making Haiti one of the primary homelands of the province's immigrants. The Quebec government has traditionally used immigration as a means of compensating for the province's low birth rate. However, studies (e.g., Hamilton 1990/91;

Table 5.10 Persons of Haitian Ethnic Origin*
by Census Metropolitan Area (CMA), 1996

Census Metropolitan Area**	Number	Percent
Toronto	1,380	1.72
Montreal	71,055	88.67
Vancouver	190	0.24
Ottawa–Hull	4,670	5.82
Edmonton	105	0.13
Calgary	205	0.26
Quebec City	1,210	1.51
Winnipeg	240	0.29
Hamilton	140	0.17
London	55	0.06
Kitchener	35	0.04
St. Catharines–Niagara	35	0.04
Halifax	65	0.08
Victoria	10	0.01
Windsor	40	0.05
Oshawa	25	0.03
Saskatoon	10	0.01
Regina	0	0
St John's	10	0.12
Sudbury	60	0.07
Chicoutimi–Jonquière	95	0.12
Sherbrooke	235	0.29
Trois-Rivières	215	0.26
Saint John	35	0.04
Thunder Bay	10	0.01
Total	80,130	100***

* This includes the number of people who provided both single and multiple responses for Haitian ethnic origin. ** The CMAs are listed in ranked order. *** Percentage figures do not add up to 100 due to rounding up.
Source: Canada, Statistics Canada 1999b.

Lampkin 1985) suggest that Quebecers were not prepared for the presence of Blacks in their midst. Some felt invaded while others were afraid of, or uncomfortable with, Blacks. It was just a matter of time before racial problems surfaced. Incidences of racism and racial prejudice against the Haitian population in Quebec have been reported in many studies, including Anderson (1993), Hamilton (1990/91), and Lampkin (1985). Haitian taxi drivers, in particular, have experienced intense discrimination from members of the Quebec public who refuse to ride taxis driven by Haitians and from dispatchers who decline to send Haitian drivers to customers (Hamilton 1990/91; Lampkin 1985).

The overwhelming majority of Haitians in Canada live in Quebec.

Table 5.11 Top Ten Sources of African-born
Immigrants in Canada, 1996

Rank	Country	Immigrants	
		#	%
1	Egypt	33,930	14.79
2	Republic of South Africa	28,465	12.41
3	Morocco	20,435	8.91
4	Tanzania	18,130	7.90
5	Kenya	18,005	7.85
6	Somalia	16,740	7.30
7	Ethiopia	13,925	6.07
8	Ghana	13,080	5.70
9	Uganda	10,750	4.68
10	Algeria	8,005	3.49
	Others	47,830	20.86
	Total	229,295	100.00

Source: Canada, Statistics Canada 1999b.

Figure 5.3: African Immigrants in Canada by Region of Birth, 1996

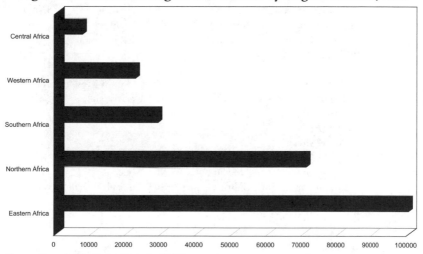

Source: Canada, Statistics Canada 1999b.

Indeed, as Table 5.9 shows, only in Quebec do Haitians constitute more than one percent of the provincial population, and the high proportion of Haitians among Quebec's visible minority population is equally discernible. Haitian populations in all other Canadian provinces and territories, with the exception of Ontario, are in the tenths and hundredths. The data provided in Table 5.10 reinforce the overwhelming concentration of Haitians in Quebec, especially in the Montreal CMA where as high as 88.67

Table 5.12 Cultural Characteristics of the Major Countries of Black African Immigrants

Country	Major Ethnic Groups	Principal Languages*	Major Religions	Colonial Power**
Egypt	90% Egyptian (Eastern Hamitic); 10% Others: Greek, Italian, Syro-Lebanese	Arabic, English; French	80% Moslem; 20% Christian	Britain (1922)
Republic of S. Africa	70% Black; 16% White; 10% Mulatto; 3% Indian	Afrikaans; English; Xhosa; Zulu; Swasi	19% Black Independent; 14% Dutch Reform; 10% Catholic	Britain (1910)***
Morocco	99.1% Arab–Berber; 0.7% non-Moroccan; 0.2% Jewish	Arabic; Berber dialects; French	98% Moslem; 1.2 % Christian; 0.8% Jewish and others	France (1956)
Tanzania	99% Black African (consisting of over 100 tribes); 1% Asian, White, and Arab	English; Swahili;	33% Christian; 33%Moslem; 33% African 1% Others	Britain (1961)****
Kenya	99% Black African (major tribes: Kikuyu, Luhyu, Luo, Kakenji, Kamba); 1% Others	English; Swahili; Kikuyu; Luo	25% Christian; 6% Moslem; 69% African	Britain (1963)
Somalia	85% Somali; the rest are mostly Bantus and some 30,000 Arabs; 3,000 Whites; and 800 Asians	Somali; Arabic; Italian; English	Mostly Sunni Moslems; Small Christian Community	Italy and Britain (1960)
Ethiopia	40% Oromo; 32% Amhara and Tigrean; 6% Somali; 4% Afar; 2% Gurage; 1% Asian, White, and Arab	Amharic; Tigrinya; Orominga; Arabic; English	45% Moslem; 40% Ethiopian Orthodox; 15% Others	None*****
Ghana	99% Black African (major tribes: Akan, Ewe, Ga, Moshi-Dagomba); 1% Others	English; Akan; Ewe; Ga;	40% Christian; 30% Moslem; 30% African Moshi-Dagomba	Britain (1957)
Uganda	99% Black African; 1% Asian, Whites, and Arabs	English; Luganda; Swahili	33% Catholic; 33% Protestant; 16% Moslem; 18% African******	Britain (1962)

| Algeria | 99% Arab–Berber; 1% Others | Arabic; Berber; French | 99% Moslem; 1% Christian | France (1962) |

* Official language in italics.

** Reference is to the last colonial power.

*** The apartheid regime was dismantled in 1990s following the release of Nelson Mandela in 1990 and his subsequent presidential electoral victory in 1994.

**** Year of Independence

***** Ethiopia was never colonized. However, between the 1930s and 1941, Italy invaded and occupied it.

****** This religion combines Christian and Traditional African beliefs.

Sources: (i) Rand McNally (1998), *World Facts and Maps*. (ii) John Robert Colombo (1994), *The Canadian Global Almanac*.

percent of the total number of Haitians in Canada's CMAs reside. The second most popular CMA is Ottawa-Hull—not surprising, given the francophone background of Hull. Toronto, as a home to some 1,380 Haitians, comes in a distant third. Evidently, of the two Caribbean groups profiled, Haitians are far more spatially concentrated than Jamaicans, due to the limited spatial extent of the francophone isogloss in Canada.

African Immigrants in Canada: Leading Sources

Table 5.11 presents data on the leading sources of African immigrants in Canada. Egypt tops the list, followed by the Republic of South Africa, Morocco, and a host of Eastern African nations including Tanzania, Kenya, and Somalia, in that order. The only Western African nation that made the top ten list is Ghana. Figure 5.3 depicts the relative size of immigrant groups from the various subregions of Africa. Notice that the smallest numbers come from the predominantly Black regions of Western and Central Africa. The Arab region of Northern Africa tops the list, followed by Eastern Africa, which has a sizeable East Indian population, as we observed in Chapter 4. Note also that while Southern African countries generally have high proportions of Blacks, most of the immigrants from that subregion come from the Republic of South Africa, which obviously has a large White population.

The cultural characteristics of the leading sources of African immigrants to Canada are summarized in Table 5.12. While the countries listed, like most African nations, are predominantly Black, there exists a great deal of cultural diversity within and between most of them. Africa exhibits a great degree of linguistic diversity, perhaps more so than any other major region of the world. In fact, estimates by de Blij (1993) and Jackson and Hudman (1990) suggest that Africa contains as many as six hundred to one thousand different languages. Tanzania, the fourth ranked homeland of

African immigrants to Canada has more than one hundred ethnic groups, most of whom speak different languages. Also, Kenya, the fifth ranked nation, has an estimated forty different ethnic groups, each with its own language; and Ghana, the highest-ranking Western African nation among the top ten, has approximately fifty languages and dialects (de Blij 1993). Perhaps the only atypical country in this respect is Somalia, which is remarkably homogeneous in cultural identity. The overwhelming majority of Somalis speak both Arabic and Somali (the two official languages) with some English and Italian. Despite the inter- and intranational linguistic diversity in Africa, we must note that as a reflection of their colonial past, many African countries have English or French as their official language.

Another important source of cultural diversity in Africa is religion. While membership in such universalizing religions as Christianity and Islam is widespread in the region, many Africans belong to various traditional African religions, most of which are tied closely to nature and a belief in animism. Due to the influence of the Islamic faith from northern African countries such as Libya, Algeria, Tunisia, Morocco, and Egypt, several Eastern and Western African nations (including Ghana, Nigeria, Sudan, Somalia, and Ethiopia) have a north-south regional split in religion, with Islam to the north and a mixture of Christianity and traditional African religion to the south. And, as de Blij (1993) rightly points out, "Few cultural boundaries are as consequential as the trans-African interfaith border."

What are the justifications for the selection of Somalis and Ghanaians, given that these groups rank sixth and eighth, respectively, among the leading African immigrant sources as of 1996? While there is some element of arbitrariness in the selection of Ghanaians[9] and Somalis, there is little doubt that Ghana and Somalia are among the leading sources, if not *the* leading sources, of Black Africans in Canada. As we learned from the preceding paragraphs, by all accounts the vast majority of immigrants from the other leading African sources (including Egypt, the Republic of South Africa, Morocco, Tanzania, Uganda, and Ethiopia) are not Blacks but rather Whites, Arabs, or East Indians.[10] Indeed, available data from Citizenship and Immigration Canada and the national censuses indicate that Ghanaians are among the few Black African immigrants to come to Canada in large numbers since the introduction of the point system in the 1960s.[11] And, although Somali immigration to Canada is a recent phenomenon, the increasing presence of Somalis in nearly all of the major Canadian cities since the early 1990s can hardly escape the keen social observer. Additionally, the selection of Somalis allows us to have some glimpse into Canada's contribution to the settlement of African refugees.

Ghanaian Immigrants in Canada

Background

In 1470, the Portuguese became the first Europeans to venture along the coast of Ghana, West Africa, which they named the Gold Coast. The area's rich gold deposits inspired a competition among several imperial powers that lasted until 1874, when Ghana formally became a British colony (McNally 1998). The British administration ended on March 6, 1957, when the Gold Coast became the first Black African nation to attain independence. The country changed its name to Ghana in the same year.

As of 1998, Ghana had an estimated population of 17.9 million (McNally 1998: 121), 44 percent of which belongs to the Akan ethnic group. Other large ethnic groups are the Ewes and Gas in the south, and the Moshi-Dagomba in the north. More than one hundred indigenous languages and dialects are spoken in Ghana: Twi-Fante, Ga, and Ewe dominate the southern half; while Dagbane, Grushi, and Gurma are the most popular languages in the north. The official language of Ghana is English, which is used extensively in government, business, and educational institutions. Islam and Christianity are the main non-African religions in northern and southern Ghana, respectively.

Like many African countries, Ghana's economy is dominated by primary resources, with cocoa, timber, and gold as the main exports. Despite a strong natural resource base, a reasonably well-educated labour pool, and various attempts at economic diversification, the secondary and tertiary sectors of the Ghanaian economy remain woefully underdeveloped. At the time of its independence, Ghana was heralded as Africa's shining star. The Ghanaian economy, arguably, was more advanced than those of all sub-Saharan African countries at the time. But since the early 1970s, the production of cocoa, the main cash crop, has declined due to poor management, transportation and storage problems, smuggling, and price fluctuation in the world market. Excessive budgetary deficits, hyperinflation, fraud, corruption, and embezzlement have also resulted in serious structural imbalance in the Ghanaian economy (McNally 1998).

The precarious economic situation in the country, particularly during the 1980s, was exacerbated by the return of nearly one million Ghanaian deportees from Nigeria in 1983. In the mid-1980s, the government of Jerry Rawlings embarked on several economic recovery programs under the auspices of the International Monetary Fund (IMF), with mixed results. Austerity measures such as the elimination of government subsidies on utilities and petroleum products; introduction of school fees at the nation's universities; and retrenchment of civil services placed an enormous economic burden on many Ghanaians, culminating in social unrest and international emigration. The National Union of Ghanaian Students (NUGS) has provided the most vocal opposition to the various governments of Ghana over the years. No wonder university closures have become part and parcel of tertiary education in the country (Immigration and Refugee Board Documentation Centre 1990).

Immigration to Canada

Ghanaian immigration to Canada can be divided into two broad waves. The first spans from the early 1970s to 1986, and the second from about 1990 to the present, with the four-year period from 1987 to 1990 serving as a transition phase. Unlike Caribbean Blacks (notably Jamaicans and Haitians), who were able to gain access to Canada through short- and long-term employment schemes prior to the 1960s, the first wave of Ghanaians (and other Black Africans) came to Canada after the introduction of the point system.

Deteriorating economic and political conditions in Ghana, immigration restrictions in Britain and other European countries, and relatively favourable immigration policies in Canada fueled this first wave. It involved a few hundred immigrants per annum and was made up mostly of scholarship students; professionals working in education, health, and social services; and a few political dissidents escaping persecution. Some came from Britain, where thousands of Ghanaians had settled since the early 1950s. The majority of these pioneers made their home in Ontario, especially in Toronto, which continues to be the hub of Ghanaian settlement in Canada.

Following the 1976 *Immigration Act*, which incorporated the U.N. Convention's definition of a refugee into Canadian law, more Ghanaian political refugees fled to Canada, although the overall number of Ghanaian immigrants to Canada did not increase much during this time. At the beginning of the 1970s and the early 1980s, Canada was hit with economic difficulties that understandably restricted the number of immigrants selected through the refugee and the point system in favour of business-class immigrants.

By 1987, Ghanaian immigration had entered its transition period and was preparing to launch its second major wave. As seen in Figure 5.4, for the years between 1973 and 1990 the number of Ghanaian immigrants approached one thousand only in 1987. The Canadian recession of the early 1980s was over by the mid-1980s, and the government had re-intensified its commitment to refugees and family-class immigration with pressure from humanitarian and ethnic lobby groups. Meanwhile the political situation in Ghana was rapidly deteriorating.[12] Increased resentment among the general Ghanaian population over continued political

Figure 5.4: Ghanaian Immigrants, Arrivals, 1993–1997

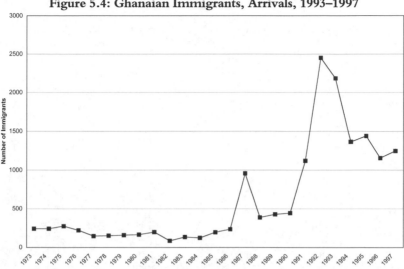

Source: Canada, Department of Citizenship and Immigration (various years).

and economic mismanagement led in June 1987 to a series of university student demonstrations that culminated in the closure of all three university campuses until August and September of that year. Political uncertainties and economic hardships coupled with intense human rights abuses compelled several Ghanaians (mostly students and the relatively well-off) to emigrate abroad. However, for better or for worse, the momentum gathered during the mid-1980s stalled in the late 1980s as Canada plunged into another economic recession, delaying the start of the second wave of immigration.

The Canadian recession was over by early 1991. And it was around this time that the Ghanaian immigration entered its second major wave, as political dissidents, students and skilled and unskilled workers pushed the annual number of Ghanaian immigrants beyond one thousand (Figure 5.4 and Table 5.13). Data from Citizenship and Immigration Canada show that of the 9,607 African refugees that came to Canada in 1992, some 1,262 (or 13 percent) were from Ghana. In fact, by 1991 the Ghanaian immigrant population in Canada was big enough to benefit from the cumulative effects of Canada's family unification program in particular and international migration in general. Unlike the pioneers, members of the second wave are less educated, as many of them have come under the refugee and family unification classes in which educational and employment backgrounds are not key determining factors. It is, therefore, not surprising that settlement problems relating to employment and language proficiency are worsening among the Ghanaian immigrant community (Owusu 1998; Adjibolosoo and Mensah 1998). Unlike immigrants from the Caribbean,

Table 5.13 Ghanaian Immigrants, Arrivals, 1973–1994*

Year	Male	Female	Total	Sex Ratio**
1973	173	69	242	40
1974	149	93	242	62
1975	161	113	274	70
1976	121	99	220	82
1977	68	77	145	113
1978	73	77	150	105
1979	66	71	157	107
1980	81	84	165	104
1981	109	89	198	82
1982	49	36	85	73
1983	69	65	134	94
1984	74	48	122	65
1985	100	94	194	94
1986	151	83	234	55
1987	688	268	956	39
1988	177	210	387	119
1989	217	211	428	97
1990	244	200	444	82
1991	703	415	1,118	59
1992	1,584	867	2,451	55
1993	1,246	939	2,185	75
1994	630	733	1,363	116

* The figures represent immigrants for whom Ghana is the country of last permanent residence. ** Defined as the number of females per 100 males.
Source: Canada, Citizenship and Immigration Canada, Various Years [1973–1995].

notably Jamaica and Haiti, the sex ratio of Ghanaian immigrants (and, indeed, African immigrants in general) has been in favour of males (Table 5.13). The possible explanations for this include, but are not restricted to, the points identified in Box 5.1.

Since 1993 the annual number of Ghanaians entering Canada has been declining steadily. This is to be expected, given the immigration restrictions introduced through Bill C-86, which came into effect in January 1993. Among other initiatives, Bill C-86 has tightened the requirements of immigration medical examinations; increased immigration processing and landing fees; introduced the fingerprinting of asylum seekers; and empowered immigration officials to refuse a refugee claim if the applicant traveled to Canada through a safe country or through any country in which the applicant could have applied for a refugee claim.

Tables 5.14 and 5.15 provide data on the geographic distributions of Ghanaians across Canadian province/territories and CMAs, respectively. Quite like their Jamaican counterparts and unlike Haitians, the Ghanaian diasporic community in Canada is heavily concentrated in Ontario, where

Box 5.1
Why are there more males than females among Black African immigrants in Canada?

The following are some of the possible explanations as to why the sex ratio of African immigrants in Canada, unlike their Caribbean counterparts, is generally in favour of males:

a) Women from Africa have not traditionally benefited from Canada's Domestic Work Scheme, under which many Caribbean women have gained entry into Canada.

b) While men have greater socio-economic and political power than women across the globe, this power imbalance is far more entrenched in Africa. Consequently, in most African families it is only the men who have the resources and the power to embark on such a long-distance, life-altering migration process.

c) Obviously, with Canada's point system, the higher one's education and occupational background, the better one's chances of being accepted. Given the bias in favour of male education in nearly all African countries, one can expect that more African men, than women, would gain access to Canada. Indeed, a similar male-female differential can be expected among African students who attend various Canadian colleges and universities, following the same line of thought.

d) Even discounting the imbalance in education, African males would still gain greater access to Canada than their female counterparts through the refugee system, as African men (like men elsewhere) usually take more leadership responsibilities in civil and political conflicts, thereby elevating their eligibility for a refugee status.

e) Finally we must recall that one of E.G. Ravenstein's (1885) "laws of migration" posits that females are more migratory within their native country while males more often venture beyond. While this "law" may not apply in many advanced societies now, it is still relevant in the African context due to the extreme patriarchy in African culture.

Source: Mensah and Adjibolosoo 1998.

some 11,105, or nearly 75 percent, live. Only small numbers of Ghanaians, numbering in the tenth percentile, live in the Atlantic Provinces and two territories. Again, like their Jamaican counterparts, Ghanaians have settled in sizeable numbers across the Prairies and in British Columbia. However,

Table 5.14 Persons of Ghanaian Ethnic Origin★
by Provinces and Territories, 1996

Province/ Territory	Ghanaian Population		Percent Prov./ Terr. Pop. Ghanaian	Percent Prov./Terr. Visible Minority Pop. Ghanaian
	#	%		
Newfoundland/ Labrador	10	0.066	0.002	0.262
PEI	0	0	0	0
Nova Scotia	45	0.301	0.005	0.144
New Brunswick	35	0.234	0.004	0.438
Quebec	1,755	11.751	0.024	0.404
Ontario	11,105	74.355	0.103	0.660
Manitoba	215	1.439	0.019	0.277
Saskatchewan	375	2.510	0.037	1.391
Alberta	635	4.251	0.023	0.235
British Columbia	750	5.021	0.020	0.113
Yukon	0	0	0	0
NWT	10	0.067	0.015	0.598
Canada	14,935	100★★	0.052	0.467

★ This includes the number of people who provided both single and multiple responses for Ghanaian ethnic origin. ★★ Percentage figures do not add up to 100 due to rounding up. *Source:* Canada, Statistics Canada 1999b.

the population of no Canadian province nor territory is near one percent Ghanaian, as can be seen from Table 5.14. Data in Table 5.15 show that of the 14,530 Ghanaians living in Canada's twenty-five CMAs, the vast majority (68.99 percent) calls Toronto home. Montreal comes in a distance second with a total of 1,720 Ghanaians among its residents as of 1996.

Other centres of reasonable Ghanaian concentrations include Vancouver, Ottawa-Hull, and Edmonton, in that order. Owusu (1999) found in his recent analysis of the residential pattern of Ghanaians in Toronto that most of them are concentrated in older and newer suburban districts such as North York, Etobicoke, and Mississauga, primarily because of their need for affordable public and private rental accommodations (most of which are in the suburbs) and their desire to live close to other Ghanaians. In an earlier study, Owusu (1998) observed that Ghanaian immigrants in Toronto have a low home-ownership rate compared to the Canadian-born population. Among other things, he attributes this disparity to the recency of Ghanaian immigration; the relative smallness of Ghanaian households in Canada; and, more importantly, the desire of most Ghanaian immigrants for home-ownership back home, as well as the intention of many Ghanaians to return home permanently.

Table 5.15 Persons of Ghanaian Ethnic Origin*
by Census Metropolitan Area (CMA), 1996

Census Metropolitan Area**	Number	Percent
Toronto	10,025	68.99
Montreal	1,720	11.84
Vancouver	610	4.19
Ottawa-Hull	390	2.68
Edmonton	335	2.30
Calgary	265	1.82
Quebec City	25	0.17
Winnipeg	195	1.34
Hamilton	125	0.86
London	45	0.30
Kitchener	70	0.48
St Catharines-Niagara	65	0.44
Halifax	45	0.31
Victoria	70	0.48
Windsor	85	0.30
Oshawa	100	0.68
Saskatoon	130	0.89
Regina	185	1.27
St John's	0	0
Sudbury	15	0.10
Chicoutimi-Jonquière	0	0
Sherbrooke	0	0
Trois-Rivières	0	0
Saint John	10	0.07
Thunder Bay	20	0.13
Total	14,530	100***

*This includes the number of people who provided both single and multiple responses for Ghanaian ethnic origin.
** The CMAs are listed in ranked-order.
*** Percentage figures do not add up to 100 due to rounding up.
Source: Canada: Statistics Canada 1999b.

Somali Immigrants in Canada

Background

Unlike the people of many other African countries, the estimated 9.8 million people who make up the East African country of Somalia are remarkably homogenous in terms of language, religion, and other cultural attributes. Somalis are mostly nomadic and semi-nomadic herders of camel, sheep, goat, and cattle. The history of the Somalis goes back to the ninth century when Arabs from the Arabian Peninsula converted the ancestors of Somalis into Islam. With time, the Arabs and Persians

Box 5.2
The Canadian Peacekeeping Fiasco in Somalia

Following an invitation by then U.S. president George Bush (Senior) for Canada to join the U.S.-led relief mission to war-torn Somalia, the Mulroney government dispatched the Canadian Airborne Regiment from CFB Petawawa to Somalia, with little tactical and logistical preparation: the soldiers had leather boots, thick sweaters, and steel helmets made for colder climates. As the Somalia Commission of Inquiry found out, even the rules of engagement were not clear to the soldiers. With the penetrating insights of hindsight, many now question whether the Airborne Regiment, which was basically a combat unit, was the best choice for a peacekeeping mission in such a markedly different cultural environment as that of Somalia. The Somali Inquiry's report asserts that certain members of the Airborne Regiment had behaviours that were worrisome to some military leaders even before their departure. A notorious group within this regiment, dubbed "the Rebels," routinely and against military orders raised the Confederate flag, the infamous symbol of U.S. racism, in its barracks at Camp Petawawa. And Canadians saw with utter disgust and bewilderment the amateur video depicting members of this same regiment using racist slurs and engaging in offensive hazing rituals.

The crux of the Somali debacle lies in the shooting of two Somalis who infiltrated a Canadian base, apparently to steal food, on March 4, 1993, and the torture-killing of a sixteen-year-old Somali, Shidane Arone, on March 16, 1993. The truth regarding who knew what and when, among the Canadian military chain of command and politicians, may never be known due to allegations of high-level cover-up, lies, shredding of documents, alterations of military computer logs, and, of course, the untimely shut-down of the Somali Commission of Inquiry by Doug Young, then minister of defence.

Evidence from the Somalia Commission's report suggests that the Canadian soldiers increasingly were frustrated by some desperate Somali youths who had been sneaking into the Canadian camp to steal food and anything else that they could scavenge. John DeMont, Luke Fisher, and Anthony Wilson-Smith (1997: 3) write, with evidence from the inquiry, that the shooting incident of March 4, 1993 was highly calculated: "Using food and water as bait, a team of Canadian soldiers, including a sniper, lay waiting in the dark. Two Somalis crawled through a fence and grabbed the food. The soldiers ordered them to halt. When the Somalis turned and ran, the Canadian soldiers, equipped with night goggles, shot both of them in the back, killing one." This incident, as well as the torture-killing of Shidane Arone, somehow took place with Canadian military officers standing some eighty feet away. Perhaps more disturbing was the military police revelation that some members of the Canadian Airborne regiment in Somalia sent home trophy photos of several Somalis, tied up and put on public display; obviously they were proud of their misdeeds. No wonder the commissioners of the Somalia Inquiry concluded that Canada's military system is "rotten to the core."

Surprisingly, despite the obvious racial undertones of the Somali brutalities—judging from the prevalence of racial slurs among the Airborne regiment, the routine posing of the Confederate flag, the encouragement by some military leaders "to get the Somalis" with offers of champagne, and the taking of trophy photos—few Canadian analysts, if any, have been bold enough to admit that racism was a crucial factor. The unfortunate thing is that the actions of these soldiers have stained Canada indelibly in the minds and souls of the Somali people. Quite disturbingly, in a futile bid to stop his three-hour ordeal at the hands of the Canadian soldiers, all Shidane Arone could say was "Canada, Canada, Canada."

Sources: DeMont et al. 1997; Fisher 1996, 1997

established several trading posts along the Somali coastline in such places as Zeila in the north and Merca, Brava, and Mogadishu (the capital) in the south (Lewis 1981).

During the notorious scramble for Africa in the late nineteenth century, Britain was the first to lay claim to Somalia by signing a protectorate agreement with some clan leaders in the north. The strategic location of Somalia as a vital connecting point to India and the Middle East enticed the French and, later, the Italians to join the feast at the Horn of Africa. By 1890 the French managed to claim as French Somaliland that part which is now Djibouti, while Italian settlers established themselves in southern Somalia, which they formally colonized in 1893 (Makinda 1993; Lewis 1981). Meanwhile, Ethiopia, the local superpower at the time, engaged in its own imperial expansion under Emperor Menilek and took control of the Somali-inhabited Ogaden region in the west.

These colonial powers so successfully exploited the clan system, through the usual divide and rule tactics, that by 1960, when British- and Italian-Somaliland joined to form the independent Republic of Somalia, the traditional, community-oriented, social and economic system had been markedly diluted. At present, despite their common identity, clan loyalty often undermines the sense of shared nationhood among many Somalis (Makinda 1993).

Since independence in 1960, Somalia has witnessed numerous internal conflicts and border clashes with neighbouring Ethiopia and Kenya over the treatment of Somalis living in these countries. But, without question, the greatest Somali tragedy to date occurred in the early 1990s when the country became totally dysfunctional as a result of a civil war, and the world community was confronted with shocking, dramatic images of thousands of Somalis dead from starvation and many more who were mere "walking skeletons." The collapse of Somalia resulted from an incremental degeneration of the moral, social, economic, and political base of the country, which has been ongoing since independence.

President Siad Barré, who took power in a military coup in October 1969 and then ruled until he was ousted[13] in January 1991, maintained power by suppressing critics, detaining opponents, and pitting one clan against another for political gains (Makinda 1993). By 1991, when Siad Barré was overthrown, Somalia was a country in complete anarchy. There was no law, no police force, no army, no civil service, no banks, no schools, no functioning hospitals, nor any formal institution, for that matter, to regulate relations among individuals and groups (Makinda 1993: 11). Unfortunately, the various opposition groups failed to develop any plan beyond their composite efforts to remove Siad Barré from office. Consequently, as Lyons and Samatar (1995: 24) rightly point out, when the detested Barré was finally toppled, the only thing left behind was the wreckage of distorted traditions and dysfunctional institutions, "a vacuum that the most ruthless elements in society soon filled" (McNally 1998: 10).

When Barré's government was overthrown in January 1991 and Somalia was plunged into rioting, looting, and revenge-seeking rage, there was virtually no coverage of this in the Western press. The main news item at the time was the Iraqi invasion of Kuwait; obviously, something that threatened the West-imposed new world order. It was only when the crisis peaked in 1992 and the body count reached the tens of thousands that many Western leaders and international bodies (e.g., the United Nations, the Organization of African Unity, the League of Arab States, and the Islamic Conference) were compelled to intervene.

In the fall of 1992, the U.N., the U.S., and other countries including Canada sent troops to Somalia to restore order and to facilitate worldwide relief efforts to save Somalis from total annihilation. While the U.S.-led U.N. mission was successful in providing relief to thousands of starving Somalis and, consequently, saving them from perishing, it failed to restore peace among the feuding clans. The late General Mohammed Farah Aidid in particular thwarted the efforts of the U.N. to the extent that he was eventually declared a fugitive and hunted by the U.N. and U.S. troops. Aidid eluded capture time and again. He eventually declared himself president of Somalia, following the withdrawal of U.S. troops in 1994 and U.N. troops in 1995. As part of the U.N. mission in Somalia, Canadian troops performed diligently. Unfortunately, their work was tainted severely by the racist conduct of some members of the force, which culminated in a national inquiry upon their return home (Box 5.2). Beside the dramatic images of human suffering, few things caused such utter bewilderment among observers as the massive amount of guns and heavy military machinery available in an impoverished country like Somalia. In a curiously roundabout way, the U.S., in particular, was forced to face its own guns and ammunitions, which were supplied to Somalia during the Cold War.

Immigration to Canada

Until the late 1980s, the number of Somali immigrants to Canada was minuscule—less than ten persons per annum for several years (Table 5.16; Figure 5.5). In 1987, following the intense human rights abuses of the Siad Barré government, the number of Somali immigrants to Canada, for the first time, got into the hundreds. As one might expect from the Somali profile presented earlier (together with the relatively flexible refugee policy in Canada, at the time), the number of Somali immigrants increased substantially in subsequent years, peaking at as high as 5,456 in 1992. In fact, figures from Citizenship and Immigration Canada indicate that by 1988, Somalia had become the leading African source of refugee claimants in Canada. While the annual flow of Somali immigrants has been in the thousands since 1990, it appears from the data in Table 5.16 and Figure 5.5 that the immigration and refugee restrictions initiated under Bill C-86, which came into force in January 1993, is having some constraining effects.

The sex ratios for Somali immigrants, as with immigrants from other Black African countries, have for the most part been in favour of males (see Box 5.1). Like many African immigrants in Canada, the major settlement problems facing Somali immigrants relate to language, affordable housing, and racial discrimination—especially in the labour market. Perhaps far more disturbing is the extent of labour market discrimination faced by Somali women, most of whom have to wear a veil as part of their Islamic practice (Adjibolosoo and Mensah 1998).

A pilot study of the health and social needs of Somalis in Toronto (Kendall 1992) found that because of their traumatic background, many Somali immigrants suffer from a host of psychological problems that are typical of torture victims. Depression, anxiety, nightmares, severe head-

Table 5.16 Somali Immigrants, Arrivals 1973–1994*

Year	Male	Female	Total	Sex Ratio**
1973	3	–	3	–
1974	3	4	7	133
1975	1	2	3	200
1976	3	5	8	167
1977	3	1	4	33
1978	1	2	3	200
1979	2	–	2	–
1980	7	–	7	–
1981	4	–	4	–
1982	4	2	6	50
1983	10	8	18	80
1984	11	12	23	109
1985	19	11	30	58
1986	38	14	52	37
1987	164	26	190	16
1988	165	65	230	39
1989	307	132	439	43
1990	758	390	1,148	51
1991	2,010	1,211	3,221	60
1992	3,047	2,409	5,456	79
1993	1,515	1,559	3,074	103
1994	859	869	1,728	101

* The figures represent immigrants for whom Somalia is the country of last permanent residence.
** Defined as the number of females per 100 males.
Source: Canada, Citizenship and Immigration Canada, Various Years [1973-1995].

Figure 5.5: Somali Immigrants Arrivals, 1973–1997

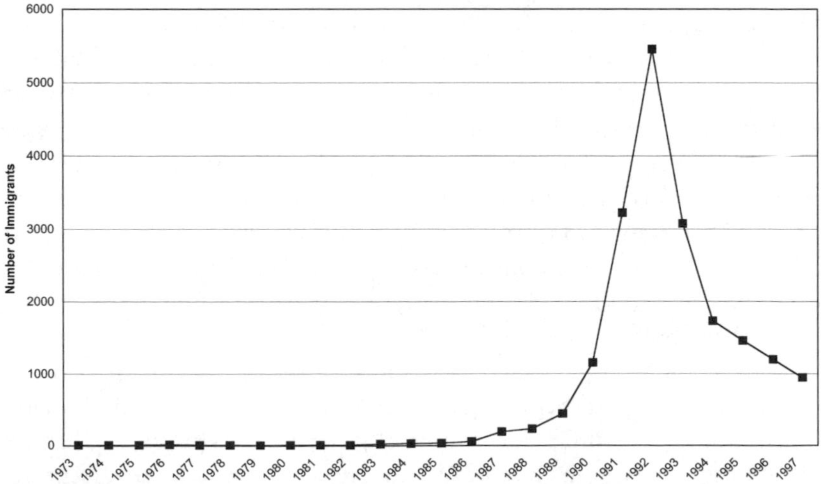

Source: Canada, Department of Citizenship and Immigration (various years).

Table 5.17 Persons of Somali Ethnic Origin*
by Census Metropolitan Area (CMA), 1996

Census Metropolitan Area**	Number	Percent
Toronto	16,915	56.55
Montreal	1,293	4.32
Vancouver	1,130	3.77
Ottawa-Hull	7,350	24.57
Edmonton	415	1.38
Calgary	210	0.70
Quebec City	65	0.22
Winnipeg	160	0.53
Hamilton	285	0.95
London	530	1.77
Kitchener	840	2.80
St Catharines-Niagara	265	0.09
Halifax	40	0.13
Victoria	55	0.18
Windsor	250	0.83
Oshawa	25	0.08
Saskatoon	40	0.13
Regina	0	0
St John's	10	0.03
Sudbury	10	0.03
Chicoutimi-Jonquière	0	0
Sherbrooke	10	0.03
Trois-Rivières	0	0
Saint John	0	0
Thunder Bay	10	0.03
Total	29,908	100[3]

* This includes the number of people who provided both single and multiple responses for Somali ethnic origin. ** The CMAs are listed in ranked-order.
*** Percentage figures do not add up to 100 due to rounding up.
Source: Canada, Statistics Canada 1999b.

aches, memory loss, and lack of concentration are commonplace among Somalis in Canada (Kendall 1992). Many analysts agree that to successfully treat these illnesses Canadian hospitals and community health centres need to use culturally-sensitive approaches to bridge the linguistic and other cultural gaps between the health care providers and the Somali community (Adjibolosoo and Mensah 1998; Kendall 1992; and Opoku-Dapaah 1995).

It is worth noting that unlike any of the other countries profiled in this chapter, Somalia does not have either English or French as its official language. The official languages of Somalia are Arabic and Somali. Consequently, Somalis face far greater language-related problems in their attempt to settle in Canada. It is encouraging to note that many Somalis are enrolled in English as a Second Language (ESL) courses across Canada. Nonetheless, as Richmond (1994: 144) points out, ESL programs have not been very effective due to massive government cutbacks, which have resulted in restricted entry conditions and shorter courses.

According to the 1996 census, the overwhelming majority of Somali immigrants live in Central Canada. Ontario alone is home to some 26,585, out of the 30,193 (or 88 percent) of the Somali population in Canada. Quebec is in second place with a total of 1,440. Outside of Central Canada, only British Columbia has more than a thousand Somalis (1,265) by the 1996 census. This is followed by Alberta (635), Manitoba (160), Nova Scotia (40), Saskatchewan (35), and the Northwest Territories (25), in that order.

One can both see in Table 5.17 and infer from the above provincial distribution that the Toronto CMA hosts by far the greatest number of Somalis in Canada—16,915 in total—which is more than half of the 29,908 Somalis who live in Canada's twenty-five CMAs. Like their Ghanaian counterparts, sizeable concentrations of Somalis can be found in centres such as Ottawa, Montreal, and Vancouver, with acute under-representation in the metropolitan centres of Atlantic Canada (Table 5.17).

Conclusion

This chapter has examined the socio-economic circumstances of Blacks in Nova Scotia and the immigration patterns of four selected Black immigrant groups, including Jamaicans, Haitians, Ghanaians, and Somalis. We noted that Nova Scotian Blacks are far more "indigenous" than their counterparts elsewhere. For instance, they are more likely than Blacks in other provinces and territories to be Canadian-born, to have Canadian citizenship, and to be proficient in at least one of Canada's official languages. However, like other Blacks, they are still subjected to high levels of racial discrimination, especially in employment.

With regard to the immigrant groups, their influx has been influenced not only by the evolution of Canada's immigration from a racist to a non-racist stance, but also by the socio-economic and geopolitical dynamics of their respective homelands. The chapter has revealed some interesting similarities and differences between Caribbean and African immigrants in Canada. For instance, by and large, African immigrants are generally more heterogeneous than their Caribbean counterparts in terms of cultural attributes such as native language and religion (with the notable exception of Somalis). Thus Adjibolosoo and Mensah (1998: 43) assert:

> For the most part, African immigrants from the same country may not speak the same native language. Wisdom born of experience

suggests that what tends to link many Africans with regards to language is mostly their ability to speak English or French.

Needless to say, the extent of cultural diversity and intra-group conflicts among African immigrants, in particular, undermines any serious movement towards Black unity in this country. Unfortunately, there is evidence that some of the ethnic and tribal conflicts in various African homelands have been carried over to Canada (Adjibolosoo and Mensah 1998). Furthermore, the preceding analysis suggests that whereas females outnumber males significantly among Caribbean immigrants in Canada, the opposite is generally true for Africans. The limited number of women among African immigrants is attributable not only to the high level of patriarchy in African societies, but also to the fact that African women, unlike their Caribbean counterparts, have not benefited much from Canada's immigrant employment schemes over the years. Moreover, Caribbean countries were found to have far longer-standing voluntary immigration ties with Canada than their African counterparts.

Despite these differences, African and Caribbean immigrants in this country have some important commonalities. First, many among both groups have been involved in double lap and step-wise migrations. Second, both Caribbean and African immigrants tend to settle in urban areas, especially in the large cities of Central Canada, with Toronto and Montreal acting as the leading settlement hubs for anglophones and francophones, respectively. Third, as people of colour, most African and Caribbean immigrants in Canada do not fit readily into what is primarily a White society. By and large, as predominantly Black people, members of these groups are markedly marginalized in terms of income, employment, and occupational status, as we shall see in the next chapter. One final point: it is fair to assert, on the basis of the data presented in this chapter, that Canada has made remarkable contributions to the settlement of Black African refugees, notably from Somalia, over the years, despite allegations of racism in Canada's refugee program.

Notes

1. Note that in 1995, Halifax, Dartmouth, Bedford, and all of Halifax County formed a single city unit.
2. Since the nineteenth century, a number of prominent African and Caribbean Blacks have been educated in Britain. Many of these educated Blacks used Britain as their intellectual battleground for the emancipation of their homelands from the shackles of imperialism and colonialism. By the early 1900s a forceful Black leadership had emerged in Britain including eminent West Indians such as George Padmore and C.L.R. James and notable Africans such as Kwame Nkrumah and J.B. Danquah of Ghana, Jomo Kenyatta of Kenya,

and Obafemi Awolowo and Adetokunbo Ademola of Nigeria.

3. That is, moving first to, say, the U.K. and then on to Canada.

4. Step-wise immigration is fairly common among African immigrants in Canada, notably Ghanaians. It usually starts from the hometown and proceeds to the regional capital, the national capital, and later across neighbouring countries to some European countries before arriving in Canada (see Konadu-Agyemang 1999).

5. Patois or Creole is a language that has its origin in extended contact between two or more language communities, one of which is usually European. Creole or patois incorporates features from each of the contributing languages to constitute the mother tongue of the emerging community.

6. Haiti was occupied by U.S. marines from 1915 to 1934.

7. Fellmann et al. (1999) derived these data primarily from the 1997 World Population Data Sheet published by the Population Reference Bureau.

8. With the election of the Jean Lesage's Liberal government in 1960, Quebec moved in a new direction, commonly referred to as the Quiet Revolution. As part of this revolution the government of Quebec took a more (ethnic) nationalist stance and created a more powerful civil service that allowed francophones access to the middle and senior positions often denied them in the private sector.

9. Admittedly, and quite naturally, the fact that the author is a Ghanaian-Canadian also weighed into the decision to select Ghanaians here.

10. Between 1971 and 1979 when Uganda was ruled by the notorious Idi Amin, a large number of Asians in the country were driven out, most of whom ended up in Canada. Similarly, when Julius Nyerere introduced his African socialism, the Ujamaa, in Tanzania, many East Indian businessmen there were compelled to migrate, and most of them came to Canada.

11. It is no wonder that Ghanaians have been one of the very few African groups listed consistently in various census data over the years.

12. For instance, in October 1985 the Goka-Djan brothers, led by Major Boakye-Djan, conspired unsuccessfully to overthrow the government of Jerry Rawlings. J.H. Mensah, chairman of the London-based Ghanaian Democratic Movement, was arrested in the U.S. that same year and was accused of conspiracy to purchase weapons for shipment to dissidents in Ghana (Immigration and Refugee Board Documentation Centre 1990). The political situation from 1986 to 1988 was even more volatile. In March 1986, police in Rio de Janeiro, Brazil, intercepted an arms and ammunitions shipment bought by mercenary dissidents heading to Ghana to overthrow the Jerry Rawlings government. In May of the same year, a coup attempt by Captain Edward Adjei Ampofo was foiled in Madina, a suburb of Accra. The Rawlings government was defeated in a general election in December 2000.

13. This is not surprising, for those who use force to control usually lose control by force.

Chapter 6

Blacks and the Canadian Labour Market

If there is any one key to the systematic privilege that undergirds a racial capitalist society, it is the special advantage of the white population in the labour market.
(Robert Blauner, Racial Oppression in America, *1972; quoted in Steinberg 1995: 179)*

Any critical analysis of the dynamics of racial oppression from the standpoint of Blacks would quickly reveal that the real issue is not the misguided myths, malicious stereotypes, and racist predilections that many people have about Blacks. Rather, it is the colour line in the job market that relegates most Blacks to low–paying, dead-end jobs or excludes them from some segments of the labour market altogether. The unabashed racial discrimination in the job market impacts Blacks more than any other form of bigotry.[1] Obviously, without jobs, nuclear families (Black or White) cannot survive; without jobs, parents cannot afford better education for their children; without jobs, people resort to crime, drugs, and other illicit activities for their livelihood; without jobs, people become dependent on the welfare system (Steinberg 1995: 199). It stands to reason that much of the racial stereotypes and discrimination faced by Blacks in such areas as housing, education, sports, and entertainment have definite labour market implications.

This chapter focuses on the characteristics of Blacks in the Canadian job market. It provides an overview of the major theoretical paradigms used to explain inequalities in the labour market and appraises their respective applicability to the circumstances of Black Canadians. We examine the labour market characteristics of Black Canadians and explore how gender and race interlock to accentuate the employment inequities of Black women in Canada. We critically assess the leading arguments used to explain the plight of Blacks in the labour market and analyze the extent of individual and institutionalized discrimination faced by Blacks in the

Canadian labour market. The chapter concludes with some provocative thoughts on why racism persists in the Canadian job market.

Theoretical Framework

Labour market analysts have adopted several, usually overlapping and sometimes conflicting, theoretical standpoints in their analysis of ethnic and racial inequalities in the capitalist labour market. In this section, we review four such perspectives—the human capital theory, the Marxist perspective, labour market segmentation theories, and the vertical mosaic thesis—deemed apposite for our understanding of the subordination of Black labour in Canada. The review pursued here is neither comprehensive nor exhaustive. It is meant to introduce the main concepts and theoretical positions adopted by previous analysts to help set the conceptual stage for this chapter. While many of the racial problems faced by Blacks in the job market are similar to those experienced by other visible minorities, such as Chinese and Filipinos, it will be demonstrated that, for one reason or another, the situation is far worse among Blacks.

The Human Capital Theory

Economists use the term "human capital" to imply the "accumulated education and training workers receive that increase their productivity" (Taylor and Johnson 1997: 761). As with the accumulation of physical capital, such as factory equipment, the accumulation of human capital invariably requires investment of time, money, and other resources. Furthermore, as Taylor and Johnson (1997) point out, the decision to invest in human capital is influenced by considerations similar to those that motivate firms to invest in physical capital: the weighing of the present cost of investment against possible future returns.

The human capital theory of labour posits that, all things being equal, better educated job seekers are more likely to get well-paying and higher-status jobs and are less likely to be unemployed than their less educated counterparts. The theory assumes that the economic contributions that different jobs make to society determine their respective remuneration in the job market. The theory also predicts that unhealthy and dangerous jobs pay more to compensate for their greater risk (Krahn and Lowe 1998). Like most economic theories, the human capital approach to labour is based on the assumption of perfect competition—the supposition that there is a single, open market for labour in which employers and job seekers have perfect knowledge of job openings, employment conditions, and wages; that employers always make rational hiring decisions based on merit; and that all job seekers with the necessary qualifications have an equal chance of being hired. Naturally, the human capital theory of labour attributes unemployment and underemployment of Blacks, or any other group for that matter, to human capital lapses.

The basic logic of the human capital argument is certainly intuitively appealing, given that well educated people tend to have higher-paying jobs. However it is difficult to ignore the mounting evidence to the contrary. As we shall soon see, some minority groups in Canada, including Blacks, do not benefit as they should from their human capital in the Canadian labour market due to the prevalence of racial exploitation in the labour market. Also, many are those who are in high-status employment positions not because of their qualifications, but because of their family backgrounds and their personal connections in the labour market. Evidently, while there is some truth to the human capital argument, it certainly downplays the issues of class and unequal power relations in society. The theory also ignores the adverse impacts of the exclusionary tactics of trade unions and professional organizations on the employment chances of Blacks and other visible minorities. "To understand who gets the good jobs," write Krahn and Lowe (1998: 112–13), "we must look beyond the labour market to families, schools, and other institutions that shape labour market outcomes."

The Marxist Perspective

To some western analysts, to invoke Marx and Engels in this post-Soviet Union era "is to touch sacred things, expose oneself to the lightnings of orthodoxies both novel and venerable" (MacRae 1988: 111). However, it does not take much theoretical sophistication to envisage a Marxist interpretation of the conditions of Blacks in the Canadian labour market. In Canada, the relationship between race and class is such that only an artful manipulation of objective facts can enable one to downplay the relevance of Marxist thought to the discourse on racial exploitation in the job market. Admittedly, Marxist theory is full of ambiguities, and, indeed, contradictions. But, paradoxically, therein lies the unique power of Marxist thought: it is these ambiguities and contradictions that give Marxist analysis its strength, malleability, and applicability to a plethora of socio-economic issues. In this section, we identify the key tenets of Marxist thought on labour under capitalism to shed light on the plight of Blacks in the Canadian labour market.

As the main alternative paradigm to neoclassical economics, Marxist theory seeks to lay bare the hidden mechanisms and contradictions of industrial capitalism. Marxist labour economics posits that, to sustain itself under capitalism, free labour (as opposed to slave labour) has to offer its services to those who own capital (i.e., the capitalists) for wages. This labour power is then used to produce goods and services that are sold at a greater price than the cost of labour, as reflected in wages. Ultimately, this yields a surplus value, which is then appropriated by the capitalist as profit. To the Marxist, therefore, it is the ownership of capital that enables the capitalist to exploit the working class or proletariat. The appropriation of surplus value from labour is the starting point of capital accumulation under capitalism in Marxist thought.[2]

Marxists argue that to maximize the appropriation of surplus value from labour, it is in the interest of the capitalist to have free, as opposed to enslaved, labour. Why? Because with free labour, the capitalist can reduce his or her overhead cost by laying off workers whenever market conditions warrant—as in periods of economic recession—and pass the maintenance cost of these workers over to the public welfare system, something that a slave owner cannot easily do (Li 1988: 44). The ability of the capitalist to employ workers at any time and lay them off with little or no notice, in response to the boom-bust cycles of capitalism, invariably leads to the formation of what Marx and Engels call the industrial reserve army, which is made up of workers who find work only as long as their labour increases capital formation. Members of this army are highly exploited; they are exposed to all the vagaries and volatility of the capitalist market just like any other commodity.[3]

MacRae (1988: 115) writes that Marx has the uncanny ability to stress the unapparent; and this is exactly what Marx does with the concepts of historical materialism and alienation. Marx, in Volume 1 of *Capital,* asserts that the economic base of society is the most crucial structural determinant of the overall direction of society through time. Put differently, the mode of production, or the economic substructure, is connected to the super-structures of religion, law, ethics, and institutions in a recursive relationship, with the economic base playing a far more crucial role in the process. This realization—dubbed "historical materialism" by Marx—places an ex-planatory premium on underlying historical laws that guide the evolution of economic substructure and, consequently, determine the overall direc-tion of society. This is where Marxist thought overlaps with structuralism, that is, the doctrine that explanations do not arise from observable facts and events, but rather from the existence and functioning of underlying structures. Marxists insist that it is our material conditions that most clearly affect what we are able to do in our lives and that a person's economic standing determines his or her overall position in society. While this is not always true, it offers valuable insight into why racial oppression and exploitation tend to be far more intense, frequent and, indeed, damaging in the economic arena.

There are several versions of alienation in Marxist thought, three of which—thing, self, and human alienation (Marx 1983)—are relevant in our present context. Marx uses the concept of thing alienation to demonstrate how members of the working class become increasingly separated (or alienated) from the commodities (or things) they help to produce with their labour. Marx's well-crafted argument in this context bears quoting:

> The more objects the worker produces the fewer he can possess and the more he falls under the domination of his product; the more value he creates the more worthless he becomes; the more refined his product the more crude the worker ... the more powerful the work the more feeble the worker; the more the work manifests intelligence the more the worker declines in intelligence and becomes a slave of nature. (Marx 1983: 307–308)

Marx also uses the concept of alienation in exploring the relationship between the proletariat and the production process. It is not the product made by labour that is alien to workers, but rather the production process or the workers' activity itself. Here Marx conceptualizes the workers' own activity as something alien and not belonging to them. Workers endure work and see it as an activity directed against themselves, independent of them and not belonging to them—this is what Marx calls self-alienation. According to Marx, this is why "the worker feels himself at home only during his leisure time, whereas at work he feels homeless. His work is not voluntary but imposed" (Marx 1983: 308–309).

Marx's concept of human alienation shows how the economic order of society is able to isolate and drive a wedge between humans, especially between members of different economic classes. Marx argues that the relationship between the working class and the capitalist class is asymmetrical and antagonistic, even though they need each other to exist. Marx (1983: 311) contends that, under industrial capitalism, "every man regards other men according to the standards and relationships in which he finds himself placed as a worker." Engels was even more acerbic in his description of human alienation under industrial capitalism.[4] Consider the following statement from his Conditions of the Working Class in England (1958: 30–31):

> Hundreds and thousands of men and women drawn from all classes and ranks of society pack the streets of London. Are they not all human beings?... Are they not all equally interested in the pursuit of happiness?... Yet they rush past each other as if they had nothing in common. They are tacitly agreed on one thing only, that everyone should keep to the right of the pavement so as not

to collide with the stream of people moving in the opposite direction. No one even thinks of sparing a glance for his neighbours in the streets. The more Londoners are packed into a tiny space the more repulsive and disgraceful becomes the brutal indifference with which they ignore their neighbours and selfishly concentrate upon their private affairs.

The preceding exposition has a number of compelling implications for our understanding of the straitened circumstances of Blacks in the Canadian labour market. For instance, the consistent and insistent Marxist probe into underlying structures and historical events suggests that only a limited insight can be gained into the plight of contemporary Blacks without a shrewd understanding of the racial and colonial ideologies of the past. As we saw in Chapter 3, during the era of slavery in particular, Blacks were considered subhuman and were, therefore, subjected to a host of atrocities and demeaning stereotypes. And life and history give eloquent testimony to the fact that racial stereotypes die hard; no wonder Blacks continue to face racial stigmatization and discrimination in nearly all vestiges of Canadian life (Henry 1994; Henry and Ginzberg 1985a, 1985b). Also, by all accounts, African and Caribbean immigrants, most of whom are Blacks, constitute only a small proportion of immigrants who enter Canada as business-class immigrants. Implicitly, from the outset only a handful of them have the financial resources to join the capitalist class in Canada. Indeed, as we shall soon see, Blacks have such a diminutive control over the socio-economic and political resources of this country that few analysts, if any, will disagree that Blacks are generally part of Canada's proletariat.

In their attempt to augment their surplus value, many Canadian employers use various race-based tactics such as scapegoating and segregation of work to coerce, oppress, and exploit Blacks and other people of colour in the work force (Das Gupta 1996). Racism in employment is, therefore, not an aberration nor a historical accident. Rather it is a deliberate attempt to maintain the vulnerability and powerlessness of Blacks and other visible minorities and, consequently, preserve cheap labour to maximize the appropriation of surplus value and enhance capital accumulation (Das Gupta 1996; Li 1988).

Unlike in the United States, where both Blacks and Whites seem to be conversant with the prevailing colour lines, racism in Canada is so clandestine, so sophisticated, and indeed so high-tech that even many of those adversely impacted remain unaware of the racial undertone of their circumstances. Despite this subtlety, the dividing lines, especially regarding occupational and residential segregation, increasingly are becoming visible in cities such as Toronto and Montreal. Often, as the proportion of Blacks in a particular city neighbourhood increases, there is the tendency for Whites and some other racial/ethnic groups to move out, taking with them their businesses and investments. While this trend is well documented as a major source of Black unemployment and underemployment in the United States,[5] as yet it has not received much research attention in Canada. Clearly, several of the themes and concepts developed within the Marxist perspective (e.g., alienation, historical materialism, surplus value, and industrial reserve army) have some bearing on our understanding of the circumstance of Blacks in the Canadian labour market.

Despite the obvious relevance of the Marxist perspective to the analysis of racial exploitation in the capitalist job market, some Marxists analysts (e.g., Li 1988; Cox 1959) habitually subsume issues of race under class. In fact some even contend that social class factors are at the root of all forms of racial exploitation and, therefore, that any attempt to resolve the latter without overhauling the former is bound to fail. However, as we shall see in this chapter, the reduction of racial issues to class dynamics is problematic. For one thing, it downplays the fact that members of the working class and their unions are also implicated in the racial oppression of Blacks in the workplace. Undoubtedly, the race-based hierarchical systems that segment and reserve desirable jobs for the White rank-and-file and relegate Blacks to less desirable jobs are to be blamed equally for the plight of Blacks in the Canadian labour market. Thus, there is more to the plight of Blacks in the job market than just class. As Steinberg (1995: 53) argues, race is an autonomous force to be reckoned with on its own terms, and by shifting the focus of racial oppression to class dynamic, these leftists are inadvertently undermining the existing anti-racist programs.

Labour Market Segmentation Theories

Some analysts, including Hiebert (1999b), Gordon et al. (1982), and Edwards (1979), account for ethnic and racial inequalities in employment from the standpoint of labour market segmentation theories. These theories posit that capitalist economies generally are composed of two separate labour markets: the primary and the secondary. The primary labour market, according to these theorists, is made up of jobs with specialized skills, higher pay, better promotions, greater unionization, generous pensions, and other fringe benefits. Conversely, the secondary labour market—made up mostly of Blacks and other visible minorities and disadvantaged groups—is characterized by low-paying, dead-end jobs with little or no career development prospects. Beck et al. (1978) and O'Connor (1973) envisage a corresponding duality in the economic structure of industrial capitalist countries. In their view, these economies consist of two sectors: a monopolistic or core industrial sector and a competitive or peripheral sector. The monopolistic sector, according to this perspective, consists of oligopolistic and unionized industries with high productivity, high profits, and high capital to labour ratios. The competitive sector, on the other hand, is characterized by smaller, non-unionized industries with low productivity, low profits, and high labour to capital ratios (Beck et al. 1978; O'Connor 1973).

Another version of the segmentation perspective—the "split labour market theory"—introduced and popularized by Edna Bonacich (1972, 1975, 1976, 1979), demonstrates how race is often used to differentiate the price of labour in a way that benefits employers and majority workers at the expense Blacks and other minorities. Bonacich points out that in a split labour market, it is not uncommon to find White workers using their racial privileges to monopolize the better paying positions or to receive higher wages for doing the same work as their non-White counterparts.

With the notable exception of Edna Bonacich, few labour market segmentation theorists have been sufficiently explicit on issues of ethnic and racial inequalities in the job market. However, implicit in their general argument is the thesis that discrimination against Blacks and other minority groups invariably forces them into jobs in the secondary or peripheral markets.

Several criticisms have been leveled against segmentation theories over the years. For instance, Charlene Gannage in her *Double Day, Double Bind* (1986) contends that the labeling of smaller, more labour-intensive industries as peripheral is not totally accurate. Writing from a knife-edged feminist standpoint, Gannage argues that the distinction between peripheral and core industries has some in-built bias in favour of industries that employ more men than women. She alleges, for instance, that the Canadian garment industry—which in her estimate is the third-largest manufacturing sector in this country, has been unionized since the early 1900s, and now employs a large number of skilled workers—is routinely categorized as peripheral, mainly because it is a major employer of women.

Gordon et al. (1982) have also expressed serious concerns about the fact that many segmentation theorists do not attempt to explain why Blacks and other disadvantaged groups end up in the secondary labour market. As they rightly point out, in the absence of such explanations, we are left with the erroneous impression that, perhaps, members of these groups are deficient and, therefore, suited only to the peripheral economies. Das Gupta (1996) has criticized the common practice, among segmentation theorists, of treating members of the secondary labour market as though they are homogenous, with little regard for pertinent intra-group differences.

Despite these criticisms, the relevance of the labour market segmentation approach to our understanding of the condition of Blacks in the Canadian job market is quite obvious. For one thing, unlike their neoconservative and human capital counterparts (e.g., Polachek 1979, 1985), who quite naively assume open competition and dwell so much on the importance of self-effort, the segmentation theorists, like the Marxists, acknowledge the effects of structural impediments upon the employment chances of Blacks and other disadvantaged groups. It is clear from the segmentation theories that higher educational and occupational attainments do not necessarily translate into larger returns in income and other rewards for many minorities. Thus, race and ethnicity are not mute variables in determining these returns (Hiebert 1999b).

The Vertical Mosaic Thesis

In 1965, John Porter, a Carleton University sociologist, initiated a period of intense academic discourse on ethnic and racial stratification in Canada with the publication of his seminal book *The Vertical Mosaic: An Analysis of Social Class and Power in Canada*. The empirical data for Porter's work were derived from the 1931, 1951, and 1961 censuses. Porter's main argument was that ethnic and racial affiliations were critical determinants of occupational roles and, consequently, class formation in Canada. Thus, Canada is not a classless society with no perceptible income and occupational lines between racial and ethnic groups. It is important to note that Porter's vertical mosaic is not a scientific theory with a universal application, but rather a thesis consisting of several loosely connected suppositions about the nature of ethnic stratification in Canadian society.

Among other things, Porter makes an important distinction between "charter status" and "entrance status" in his analysis of ethnic stratification in Canada. Charter status refers to the many privileges and prerogatives enjoyed by the British and French who constitute the founding groups of modern Canada. Porter argues that as founders of this nation, these two groups lay down the ground rules for the admission of other ethnic groups into Canada. He notes that of the two charter groups, the British are far more dominant, as they constitute the majority of Canada's economic and corporate elite, and they rank higher in occupation and income than their French counterparts. Porter uses the term "entrance status" to connote the class positions at which other immigrant groups join the Canadian society. His basic point is that the British and French, with their charter status, determine which ethnic groups to admit into Canada and what types of jobs, or entrance statuses, are to be given to the new ethnic groups (Porter 1965: 62). The concept of entrance status therefore implies lower occupational status even though, as Porter points out, some ethnic groups might be able to improve upon their entrance status in time.

According to Porter, the socioeconomic achievements of various ethnic groups in Canada are contingent upon their respective entrance statuses. He notes that the entrance status of ethnic groups may persist over time, as initial cultural barriers evolve into more or less permanent barriers (Porter 1965: 88). Furthermore, Porter argues that with time, strong ethnic affiliations may restrain the status aspirations of members of various ethnic groups and, ultimately, stultify their motivation for higher education and better employment. Porter was convinced that some groups were restricted to lower occupational status primarily because of their ethnic affiliations—this realization is what he dubbed the ethnically blocked mobility thesis. As a fervent assimilationist, Porter was concerned that efforts by ethnic groups to perpetuate their distinctiveness could create barriers to their own vertical mobility within the Canadian social hierarchy.

Porter found that, for the most part, people of White Anglo-Saxon Protestant ancestry prevail at the top of the Canadian vertical mosaic, while Aboriginal people occupy the very bottom. Other ethnic and racial groups are usually found somewhere between these extremes. Porter had very little to say about Blacks in his treatise. One can scour the pages of his *Vertical Mosaic* and find only a handful of references to Black Canadians. Arguably, he saw Blacks as nonentities in Canadian society—this last barb is perhaps unfair, as the number of Black Canadians at the time was too small, in both relative and absolute terms, for any meaningful synthesis.

Porter's vertical mosaic suggests that race/ethnicity is a crucial factor in the assignment of occupational roles and, consequently, the formation of social class in Canada. But, are race and ethnicity really as powerful factors in occupational stratification as Porter wants us to believe? And do British and French people enjoy any exclusive privileges and prerogatives in the present-day labour market? These are some of the issues that Porter's vertical mosaic thesis raises in the context of contemporary Canada.

Over the years, Porter's thesis has been appraised, disputed, and subjected to so many different interpretations that it is now even difficult to decipher the veracity of his thesis without reading his original work. After re-analyzing Porter's data, Darroch (1979) found that while the rank-order of ethnic groups has been rather stable over time, ethnic occupational dissimilarity (measured by the index of dissimilarity) decreased between 1931 and 1971. Consequently, Darroch (1979) concludes that ethnicity is far less important in stratifying the Canadian labour market than Porter asserts. A fairly similar conclusion was reached by Reitz (1980), who found a decline in labour market inequalities among ethnic groups. Several analysts, including Isajiw et al., (1993), Agocs and Boyd (1993), and

Ogmundson and McLaughlin (1992), also have questioned whether ethnicity is still as potent a determinant of occupational status and social class as it used to be. Tepperman (1975) takes issue with Porter's basic assumptions on charter status. In his view, other European immigrant groups in Canada are increasingly undermining the privileged position that the British and French have enjoyed in the labour market. In fact, a 1985 work by Pineo and Porter lends some support to Tepperman's position.

On the pro side, Lautard and Loree (1984: 342), using 1931, 1951, 1961, and 1971 census data, found that though ethnic inequality in the job market is decreasing, Porter's vertical mosaic "remains a durable feature of Canadian society." In fact, they found ethnic inequalities in occupation to be four times greater than gender inequalities, thereby confirming the persistence of Porter's vertical mosaic in Canadian society. Satzewich and Li (1987) observe that non-White groups suffer occupational status and income differentials that are attributable to ethnicity. In addition, they found that in cases where occupational inequalities have declined over time, income inequalities have persisted. Many other studies, including Hou and Balakrishnan (1996), Geschwender (1994), Boyd (1992), Herberg (1990), Rajagobal (1990), Li (1988), and the Abella Commission Report (Abella 1985), suggest that non-Whites in Canada still face discrimination and other negative consequences in the Canadian labour market. Some of these works are examined in some detail from the standpoint of Blacks later in this chapter.

Several cautionary remarks and conclusions can be synthesized from the preceding analysis of Porter's vertical mosaic thesis, three of which are noteworthy:

- First, it is virtually impossible to discount categorically the effects of ethnicity and race on occupational stratification in Canada. Indeed, this is not peculiar to Canada; studies[6] from Britain, the United States, and Australia suggest that ethnic- and race-based stratification in the labour market is a recurrent feature of industrial capitalism, although, as Hale (1995: 423) rightly points out, the specific nature of stratification varies from country to country.
- Second, subtle biases are inherent in all vertical mosaic studies, as the number and types of ethnic/racial groups included in any of these analyses have considerable impact on the ultimate results. The only non-White ethnic groups included in the works of Porter (1965), Darroch (1979) and Lautard and Loree (1984) were Asians and Aboriginals. Consequently, the debate among these writers on whether there is a vertical mosaic in Canada or not is open to a wide range of interpretation, depending on the groups involved in each case. As Satzewich and

Li (1987: 231) point out, the limited number of non-White groups covered in most of these studies invariably masks the real nature of ethnic/racial inequalities in the labour market. Arguably, any recent study on the vertical mosaic that does not include a reasonable number of visible minority groups is seriously flawed, considering that the flow of visible minorities into Canada has increased substantially since the early 1970s.

• Third, contemporary analysts need to pay more attention to race, as opposed to ethnicity, in examining the vertical mosaic thesis. Several studies, including Reitz (1990) and Li (1988), suggest that race is becoming far more important than ethnicity in stratifying labour in Canada. Also, intra- and inter-visible minority variations need to be given more analytical attention. Almost any ethnic and racial stratification in the labour market is bound to affect most seriously those groups that rank lowest in the hierarchy of acceptance. It is therefore important to identify these groups if we are to make any meaningful contribution to the vertical mosaic debate.

Despite its limitations and criticisms, Porter's work is remarkable for its forthright and uncompromising empirical analysis. Later in this chapter we will have a closer look at some of the empirical evidence in support of the vertical mosaic thesis from the standpoint of Blacks. Before then, it is appropriate to have some insight into the labour market characteristics of Black Canadians.

Labour Market Characteristics of Blacks in Canada: A Comparative Overview

Using empirical data from the 1996 census, this section examines the labour market characteristics of Black Canadians as a prelude to our understanding of the employment problems facing Black Canadians. The specific variables examined include educational qualifications, official language proficiency, labour force participation, unemployment rates, types of occupation, industries of employment, and income levels. It is important to note that the analysis does not deal with the case of Blacks in isolation. Rather, it compares the characteristics of Blacks with those of "all visible minorities" and "all Canadians." Additionally, the chapter sheds light on the gender disparities in employment within the Black population by comparing the relevant variables of Black women with those of non-Black women and Black men.

Before proceeding any further, we need to clarify how Statistics Canada officially defines two key concepts—unemployment rate and labour force participation rate—in the national census. Labour force participation rate is the main measure of economic activity among those in paid employment. Statistics Canada bases its calculation of this indicator on the number of people, fifteen years of age or older, who are working for pay or are actively looking for work. Thus, those who are unemployed but have been looking actively for a job for the past four weeks are also counted as part of the labour force. However, those who perform unpaid household duties are excluded from the labour force, despite the essential contributions they make to our social and economic well-being.

Statistics Canada defines unemployment rate as the percentage of the labour force participants who are not employed at a particular point in time but are looking actively for work (or have looked actively for work in the past four weeks). Thus, the official unemployment rate invariably under-estimates the actual level of unemployment, as it takes into consideration only people who are out of work and actively seeking work. The so-called discouraged workers, those who stop their job search for reasons of frustration or otherwise, are not officially considered unemployed. Also, people who settle for jobs of a lower level than those for which they are actually qualified, because it is difficult to find jobs that match their level of qualifications—that is, the underemployed—are all considered employed. In what follows we compare the relevant labour market indicators of Blacks with those of other Canadians.

While higher educational qualifications do not always translate into better job opportunities or higher incomes, the positive effect of education on labour force involvement remains indisputable. As in most advanced industrial nations, many employment activities in Canada require some form of specialized training and nearly all jobs demand basic literacy. Consequently, people who are not functionally literate or numerate and cannot analyze information in at least one of Canada's official languages face enormous challenges in the job market.

Table 6.1 shows that, overall, the educational attainment of Blacks is not much different from that of the average Canadian. For instance, whereas 22.97 per cent of all Canadians have some university education, the comparable figure for Blacks is 22.11 percent. Indeed, the percentage differences between Blacks and "all Canadians" in nearly all of the educational categories listed in Table 6.1 are minuscule, with the notable exception of the "less than Grade 9" and "other non-university only" categories, where Blacks even fared better than "all Canadians." Compared with "all visible minorities" Blacks have a smaller proportion of university-educated people and a smaller proportion of individuals with less than Grade 9 education. After a comprehensive analysis of the 1991 census data, Macionis and Gerber (1999) conclude that "overall the Asian and Black

Table 6.1 Total Population 15 Years of Age and Over by Highest Level of Schooling for Blacks, All Visible Minorities and All Canadians, 1996*

	Blacks N= 402,985		All Visible Minorities N = 2,419,140		All Canadians N=22,628,925	
	#	%	#	%	#	%
Less than Grade 9	33,445	8.29	276,905	11.45	2,727,210	12.05
Grades 9 to 13	146,395	36.32	807,965	33.39	8,379,380	37.02
Without graduation	92,495		493,685		51,40,795	
With graduation	53,900		314,285		3,238,590	
Trades Certificate/Diploma	13,220	3.28	49,165	2.03	837,160	3.70
Other non–University only	120,795	29.95	487,565	20.15	5,487,505	24.25
Without certificate/diploma	39,940		160,820		1,474,925	
With certificate/diploma	80,860		326,745		4,012,580	
University	89,130	22.11	797,540	32.97	5,197,665	22.97
Without degree	46,590		328,895		219,890	
Without cert/diploma	19,505		161,270		967,305	
With cert/diploma	27,085		167,625		1,229,580	
With bachelor's or higher	42,540		468,635		3,000,780	

* Note that the data in this and other tables derived from the 1996 census are rounded up or down to the nearest multiples of 5. Consequently, there may be variations and inconsistencies in the table totals.
Source: Canada, Statistics Canada 1999b.

communities in Canada actually have higher levels of educational attainment than either the British or French." We must note, however, that the high levels of education usually recorded among Asians and Blacks are "not necessarily characteristic of members of those minorities who are born or schooled in Canada"; rather they are due to the immigration of relatively well-educated Asian and Black immigrants (Macionis and Gerber 1999: 492).

Table 6.2 presents information on the major fields of study for Blacks, "all visible minorities" and "all Canadians" with respect to post-secondary education. There is a striking contrast among the three groups in the area of mathematics and physical sciences, where Blacks and "all Canadians" are surpassed by "all visible minorities" by almost a two-to-one margin. In engineering and applied science the proportion of Blacks and "all Canadians" also are relatively high compared to that of "all visible minorities." In addition, Blacks and "all visible minorities" lag behind "all Canadians" in the category of educational, recreational, and counseling services. Another remarkable feature of Table 6.2 is that Blacks are more involved in social science and related studies than "all visible minorities" and "all Canadians."

Figure 6.1 compares the official language ability of Blacks with those

Table 6.2 Total Population 15 Years of Age and Over with Post-secondary Qualification by Major Field of Study for Blacks, All Visible Minorities, and All Canadians, 1996

	Blacks N = 163,710 (%)	All Visible Minorities N = 1,012,170 (%)	All Canadians N = 9,080,105 (%)
Educational, recreational and counseling services	6.72	6.81	10.57
Fine and applied arts	5.48	4.32	5.61
Humanities and related fields	5.31	6.29	6.30
Social science and related fields	11.25	9.56	9.58
Commerce, management and business administration	23.30	24.95	22.19
Agriculture and biological sciences/technologies	4.69	4.78	4.71
Engineering and applied science	2.85	8.72	4.11
Engineering and applied science technologies and trades	20.72	15.25	22.02
Health professions, sciences and technologies	15.97	12.03	11.31
Mathematics and physical science	3.39	7.04	3.37
No specialization and other specializations n.i.e.*	0.28	0.20	0.18

* Not included elsewhere.
Source: Canada, Statistics Canada 1999b.

of other Canadians. Like "all visible minorities" and "all Canadians," English is the main official language spoken by the vast majority of Blacks. Indeed, only 10.75 percent of Black Canadians speak French only, compared to 73.79 percent, who speak English only. It is clear from Figure 6.1 that Blacks fare far better than "all visible minorities" in terms of official language ability; whereas only 1.36 percent of Blacks speak neither English nor French, the comparable figure for "all visible minorities" is 9.35 percent.

According to Table 6.3, there was a total of 402,990 Blacks aged fifteen years and over by the 1996 census; some 270,495 of these were in the labour force, giving Blacks a labour participation rate of 67.1 percent. The participation rates for "all Canadians" and "all visible minorities" were slightly lower, estimated at 65.5 and 63.6 percent, respectively. As can be seen from the table, however, the unemployment rate for Blacks, as of 1996,

**Figure 6.1: Official Language Abilities of Blacks,
All Visible Minorities, and All Canadians**

Legend:
- ☐ English Only
- ■ French Only
- ■ English & French
- ☐ Neither English nor French

Categories (x-axis): Blacks, All Visible Minorities, All Canadians

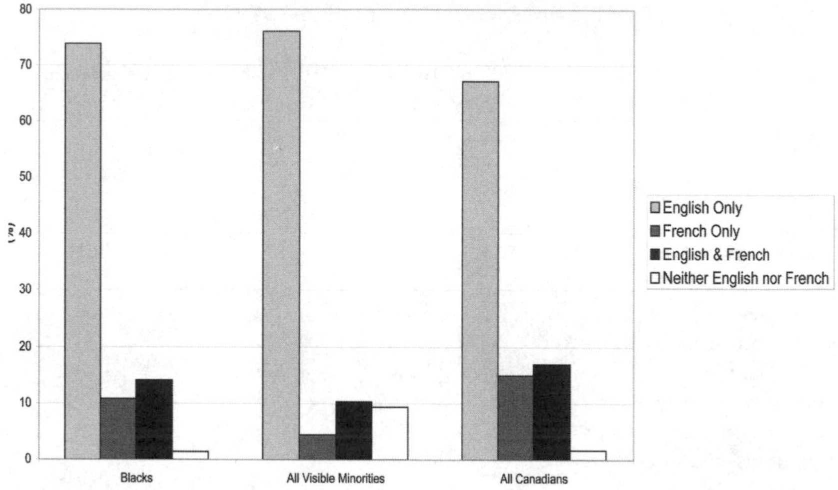

Source: Canada, Statistics Canada, 1999b.

**Table 6.3 Total Population 15 Years of Age and Over by Labour Force
Activities for Blacks, All Visible Minorities, and All Canadians, 1996***

	Blacks N = 402,990	All Visible Minorities N = 2,419,140	All Canadians N =22,628,925
Total labour force	270,495	1,538,760	14,812,700
Employed	218,330	1,320,870	13,318,740
Unemployed	52,160	217,890	1,493,960
Not in the labour force	132,495	880,380	7,816,225
Participation rate	67.1%	63.6%	65.5%
Employment-population ratio	54.2%	54.6%	58.9%
Unemployment rate	19.3%	14.2%	10.1%

* Note that the data in this and other tables derived from the 1996 census are rounded up or down to the nearest multiples of 5. Consequently, there may be variations and inconsistencies in the table totals.
Source: Canada, Statistics Canada 1999b.

was almost twice as high as the comparable figure for "all Canadians" and some five percentage points higher than that for "all visible minorities." Obviously, the assertion that Blacks face higher unemployment in Canada is substantiated by reliable empirical evidence.

Table 6.4 presents data from the 1996 census on the industrial categories in which Blacks, "all visible minorities" and "all Canadians" worked. Statistics Canada adopted the *1980 Standard Industrial Classification* scheme, which is based on the general nature of the business carried

Table 6.4 Total Population 15 Years of Age and Over Who Worked since January 1 1995, by Industry Divisions for Blacks, All Visible Minorities, and All Canadians

Employment Industry Divisions	Blacks N = 269,065	All Visible Minorities N = 1,593,635	All Canadians N=15,547,115
	(%)	(%)	(%)
Primary industries	1.18	1.81	5.68
Manufacturing industries	17.09	19.28	14.05
Construction industries	2.68	2.53	5.71
Transportation and storage	3.92	3.01	4.09
Communications and other utilities	3.51	2.61	3.03
Wholesale trades	4.34	5.14	4.86
Retail trades	11.29	12.92	12.55
Finance and insurance	4.06	4.79	3.54
Real estate	1.25	1.89	1.84
Business service	7.81	7.94	6.46
Government service	4.85	3.40	6.19
Educational service	4.98	4.90	6.98
Health and social service	15.53	9.72	9.72
Accommodation, food and beverage	8.18	11.26	7.23
Other service industries	9.26	8.73	7.99

Source: Canada, Statistics Canada 1999b.

out by the employer for whom the respondent works. Despite the apparent symmetry in the percentage distributions of Blacks, "all visible minorities" and "all Canadians" among the various industries, a closer look at the table points to a higher concentration of "all Canadians" in the four categories of primary industries, construction, government services, and educational services. The percentage distributions of Blacks across the various industries are fairly similar to those of "all visible minorities" with the notable exception of health and social services, where the former is relatively more concentrated.

Table 6.5 depicts the employment equity occupational categories in which Blacks and other Canadians worked during the reference year of 1995.[7] Perhaps the most striking, albeit unsurprising, feature of the table is the under-representation of Blacks in the top occupations. Notice, for instance, that whereas the percentage of "all Canadians" in the senior manager category stood at 0.97, the parallel figure for Blacks was only 0.27—three and a half times smaller. The proportion of Blacks in middle and other management positions was also small compared to the figures for "all visible minorities" and "all Canadians." Conversely, relatively higher

Table 6.5 Total Population 15 Years of Age and Over Who Worked Since January 1 1995, by Employment Equity Groups for Blacks, All Visible Minorities, and All Canadians, 1996

Occupation	Blacks	All Visible Minorities	All Canadians
	N = 269,065	N = 1,593,635	N =15,547,120
	(%)	(%)	(%)
Senior managers	0.27	0.69	0.97
Middle and other managers	3.81	7.04	7.67
Professionals	12.71	14.14	13.92
Semi-professionals/technicians	6.06	5.42	6.13
Supervisors	1.28	1.16	1.21
Supervisor: Crafts and trades	1.10	1.22	3.48
Administrative and senior clerical	3.43	3.85	5.41
Skilled sales and services	4.14	5.48	4.59
Skilled crafts and trades	5.45	4.92	7.45
Clerical personnel	14.52	12.52	11.07
Intermediate sales and service	13.84	12.68	12.33
Semi-skilled manual workers	13.80	13.33	11.48
Other sales and service personnel	14.45	13.04	10.16
Other manual workers	5.03	4.45	4.06

Source: Canada, Statistics Canada 1999b.

proportions of Blacks were found in the lower occupational echelons, such as clerical personnel, intermediate sales and service, semi-skilled manual personnel, and other manual workers.

Given the high unemployment rate for Canadian Blacks together with their acute under-representation in high-status occupations, it is hardly surprising that they have relatively lower employment incomes for both full- and part-time workers and lower average annual income (Table 6.6 and Figure 6.2). Moreover, as can be discerned from Table 6.7, excepting the province of Quebec and the Northwest Territories, Blacks have higher unemployment rates than the average person in all Canadian provinces and territories. For instance, Ontario's provincial unemployment rate for 1996 stood at 9.1 percent, but the comparable figure for Blacks was 18.3 percent or twice as high as the provincial rate. And in Newfoundland and Labrador where a quarter of the provincial population was unemployed in 1996, close to a third of the Black population was in that situation during the same year.

Fairly similar disparities emerge between Blacks and their non–Black counterparts in nearly all Canadian provinces and territories regarding average income. In Ontario where the average annual income of $27,309 is the highest in the country, the corresponding figure for Blacks is $20,144,

Table 6.6 Income Levels of Blacks, All Visible Minorities, and All Canadians, 1996

	Blacks N = 355,225 (%)	Total Minority N = 2,092,820 (%)	All Canadians N = 20,916,760 (%)
Under $5,000	22.51	23.18	15.09
$5,000–$9,999	14.29	14.13	12.74
$10,000–$19,999	24.47	23.78	23.91
$20,000–$29,999	16.40	15.51	16.17
$30,000–$39,999	11.03	10.24	12.38
$40,000–$49,999	5.52	5.66	7.96
$50,000–$59,999	2.89	3.26	5.03
$60,000 and over	2.89	4.25	6.72
Average income ($)	$19,033	$20,158	$25,196
Median income ($)	$14,430	$14,438	$18,891

Source: Canada, Statistics Canada 1999b.

Table 6.7 Key Labour Market Indicators for Blacks, All Visible Minorities, and All Canadians, by Provinces and Territories, 1996

Province/ Territory	Unemployment rate		Univ. Education		Average Income	
	Blacks %	Prov./Terr. %	Blacks %	Prov./Terr. %	Blacks $	Prov./Terr. $
Newfoundland/ Labrador	32.6	25.1	44.15	18.78	16,526	19,710
P.E.I.	*	13.8	48.71	22.10	*	20,527
Nova Scotia	20	13.3	17.65	23.46	16,007	21,552
New Brunswick	19.9	15.5	21.43	20.08	18,039	20,755
Quebec	11.8	26.3	24.46	20.19	15,483	23,198
Ontario	18.3	9.1	20.11	24.32	20,144	27,309
Manitoba	10.4	7.9	33.03	23.11	19,931	22,667
Saskatchewan	11.2	7.2	36.39	21.61	21,331	22,541
Alberta	11	7.2	25.86	23.52	20,383	26,138
B.C.	16	9.6	29.82	25.48	21,310	26,295
Yukon	*	11	33.33	26.47	*	29,079
N.W.T.	6.9	12.9	39.39	18.08	*	29,011

* No data available.
Source: Canada, Statistics Canada 1999b.

creating a deficit of $7,165 for the province's Black population. By far, the highest income deficit for Blacks is recorded in Quebec where the provincial average stood at $23,198 and the comparable figure for Blacks was a mere $15,483—a deficit ratio of 66 cents for every dollar. Ironically,

Figure 6.2: Average Employment Incomes ... Canadians

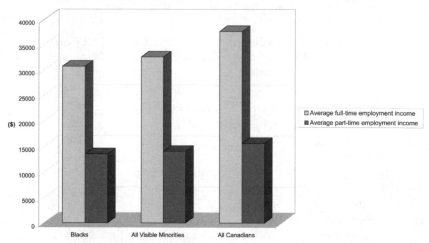

Source: Canada, Statistics Canada, 1999b.

the provincial unemployment rate in Quebec is more than two times higher than the unemployment rate for Blacks in that province.

Pooled together, the preceding evidence suggests that the high unemployment rate and low average income for Blacks have little to do with the educational background of Blacks. On average, Blacks have higher proportions of people with some university education in all provinces and territories with the exception of Nova Scotia and Ontario. It is important to note that Blacks are generally better off (at least based on the three variables summarized in Table 6.7) in the Western and Prairie Provinces of Manitoba, Saskatchewan, Alberta, and British Columbia. The circumstances of Blacks in the Atlantic Provinces of Nova Scotia, Newfoundland and Labrador, and New Brunswick are also better compared to the situation in Central Canada.

Table 6.8 shows how the various visible minority groups in Canada fare regarding the key labour market variables discussed above. While Blacks fare better than some groups, such as Latin Americans, there is no denying that Blacks are among the worst groups in terms of unemployment rate, average income, and incidence of low income,[8] even though their education and official language ability are better than many visible minority groups.

Having said that, one should refrain from jumping to any conclusions of higher anti–Black racism in the labour market, based on the preceding data alone. For one thing, without statistically controlling for relevant variables (i.e., education, age, province of residence, and immigration status) in a multivariate fashion, we cannot reasonably conclude that Blacks

**Table 6.8 Selected Educational, Employment, and Income
Characteristics of Blacks, Visible Minorities, and All Canadians, 1996**

	Neither English nor French (%)	% with University Education (%)	Unemployment Rate (%)	Incidence of Low Income (%)	Average Income ($)
Black	1.36	22.11	19.3	44.9	19,033
South Asian	8.60	33.45	15.3	29.0	21,477
Chinese	17.98	33.96	10.2	32.4	20,490
Korean	13.61	53.57	9.9	44.5	16,934
Japanese	4.86	40.63	6.6	18.4	29,815
Southeast Asian	13.19	22.69	16.7	42.2	18,114
Filipino	1.26	52.07	8.1	23.9	20,025
Arab/West Asian	7.43	41.17	18.5	51.4	19,347
Latin America	10.36	24.97	19.5	49.5	16,316
Visible minority n.i.e.*	0.74	18.61	12.9	24.9	21,468
Multiple Visible Minority	6.40	33.44	12.6	28.3	20,658
Total Visible Minority	9.35	32.97	14.2	35.9	20,158
All Others	0.69	21.77	9.6	17.6	25,756
Total Canada	1.66	22.96	10.1	19.7	25,196

* Not included elsewhere.
Source: Canada, Statistics Canada 1999b.

have lower income and higher unemployment because of racism, no matter how intuitively appealing such a claim may appear on a *prima facie* basis. In subsequent sections of this chapter we shall have a closer look at some of the few studies that have controlled for these intervening variables, in an attempt to shed some light on the dynamics of racial disparities in income in Canada.

Black Women and the Canadian Labour Market

One of the most dramatic trends in Canada since the early 1960s has been the increase in the number of women in the workplace (Ghalam 1994; Hiller 1991). However, Canadian women are still concentrated in traditional female jobs such as nursing, retail, clerical and other business services, and they still earn incomes that are lower than those of men (Preston and Giles 1997; Hiller 1991). While the existence of gender inequities in the Canadian labour market is indisputable, we must note that every woman experiences life not only through the prism of gender, but also through that of race, ethnicity, class, and other such variables (Sandoval 1984). Race, like gender, carries connotations of power in society (Billson 1991). Therefore, viewing gender as unidimensional has serious implications for theoretical discourse; it leads to distortions and facile generalizations based on the experiences and world-views of dominant groups (Billson 1991). In this section we examine how gender and race intersect to intensify the employment inequities of Black women in Canada.

It is widely believed, at least among members of the Black community, that Black women (like their male counterparts) encounter severe discrimination not only in nursing and domestic work, where many have traditionally gained employment (Box 6.1), but, indeed, in nearly all levels and sectors of the economy. This is despite growing public awareness and acceptance of democratic principles, such as equal rights and justice, and despite the feminist pontifications about women's rights in Canada. Is there any empirical evidence even to suggest that Black women are accorded unequal market worth, or are treated any differently than other women, in the contemporary Canadian labour market? To what extent are the employment characteristics of Black women different from those of other Canadian women? And how do Black women fare relative to their male counterparts in the Canadian job market?

Table 6.9 compares the education, employment, and income characteristics of Black women to those of "all visible minority women" and "all Canadian women." The data show that there is not much difference between the education and official language abilities of Black women, and those of "all Canadian women." For instance, the fraction of women with neither English nor French ability in each group is less than 2 percent.

Table 6.9 Selected Educational, Employment, and Income Indicators for Black Women, All Visible Minority Women, and All Canadian Women, 1996

Variable	Black Women	All Visible Minority Women	All Canadian Women
Education and Language Characteristics			
% with neither English nor French ability	1.70	11.19	1.97
% with less than Grade 9 education	9.45	14.00	12.38
% with university education	19.9	29.90	22.28
Employment and Income Characteristics			
Labour force participation rate (%)	62.6	57.6	58.6
Unemployment rate (%)	19.8	15.3	10.0
% in senior management positions	0.19	0.29	0.44
% in middle and other management positions	3.05	4.87	5.55
Average full-time employment income	$27,561	$27,465	$30,130
Average part-time employment income	$12,461	$12,244	$12,727
Average annual income	$16,959	$16,621	$19,208
% of income from government transfer payment	22.1	15.9	11.8

Source: Canada, Statistics Canada 1999b.

Box 6.1
The Case of Black Domestic Women from the Caribbean

Since the early 1990s, Canada has instituted two main Caribbean domestic schemes. The first scheme, which occurred in 1910–1911, involved about a hundred Guadeloupian women, who were recruited by J.M. Authier, a former American counsellor in Guadeloupe, on behalf of some middle-class residents of Quebec. Due to the racism characteristic of the early 1900s, these Black women were recruited with extreme caution. Available reviews of the job performance of these Black women suggest that their performance exceeded the expectations of many employers, even though they received lower wages than their White counterparts. Despite their favourable work evaluations and lower wages, the scheme was terminated by August 1911, due to fierce criticisms by those who feared it would ultimately lead to an increase in Black immigration in Canada.

During the 1950s, intense competition for domestic workers was sparked by high increases in the participation of women in the work force, the affluence that accompanied the rebuilding efforts of the postwar period, and the baby boom. This compelled the Canadian government to institute the second domestic scheme in 1955. The women recruited were mainly from Jamaica and Barbados; the initial group was made up of only one hundred women. Eligible recruits had to be single, 18 to 35 years of age, in good health, and with a minimum of Grade 8 education. After working in domestic service with a contractually designated employer for a year, the women were granted landed immigrant status and were eligible for citizenship after five years in Canada. These basic requirements were, indeed, applied to all domestic immigrants to Canada at the time. However, as could be expected, there were additional requirements concocted to satisfy the racist whims and caprices of the Canadian public. For instance, unlike that of their European counterparts, the final medical screening of the Black women was controlled exclusively by Canadian authorities. Also, as part of the agreement, Caribbean governments were required to pay the return fare of any of their domestic workers deported within the first year of arrival in Canada.

Most of the women who came under the second scheme had not been domestic servants at the time of their application. Nurses, secretaries, clerks, and teachers took advantage of the scheme to establish a foothold in Canada, as that was virtually the only means by which they, as Black women, could enter Canada at the time. Like those of their first-wave counterparts, the job evaluations of most of the women in the second domestic scheme were satisfactory. As a result, in the following years the Canadian government increased the annual quota for the scheme to 280 people, drawn from a wider range of Caribbean nations, including Trinidad, Antigua, British Guyana, St. Vincent, Dominica, Grenada, Montserrat, St. Lucia, and St. Kitts, with the largest numbers still from Jamaica and Barbados. While the vast majority of the women worked in Toronto and Montreal, it is important to stress that these Black women worked in all parts of Canada. It is estimated that by 1965 Canada had admitted some 2,690 Caribbean women under the second domestic scheme. This figure exceeded the number of all Caribbean immigrants to Canada before 1945. Like their first-wave counterparts, the women in the second scheme endured severe loneliness, isolation, racial oppression and exploitation at the hands of Canadians. The Caribbean Domestic Scheme was cancelled in 1967, following the introduction of the "point system."

Since 1967, women from the Caribbean and other developing countries have been admitted into Canada under the "point system." However, domestic workers seldom gain admission, given the gender biases of this system and the fact that domestic workers usually gain no points for occupational demand, despite the perennial shortage of domestic labour in Canada.

Following a thorough review of the domestic situation in Canada, the government introduced a new Live-In Caregiver Program in 1992. Under this program—which is still in existence—a foreign domestic worker needs a Grade 12 equivalency, a working knowledge of either English or French, and at least six months' full-time training in care-related services. Also, a domestic worker is expected to live with her (or his) employer for at least two years, after which she (he) qualifies for landed immigrant status. Generally, Canadian households rely on private domestic placement agencies to assist them in their search for foreign domestic workers. As gatekeepers, these placement agencies play a pivotal role with regard to who gets accepted into Canada and under what conditions. Available statistics indicate that during the last decade or so, the Philippines has been the largest source of live-in domestic workers in Canada, followed by Europe and the Caribbean. The shift from the Caribbean to the Philippines as the major source of domestic workers is due to several factors, including the growing preference of Canadian households for Filipino domestic workers, the compliance of placement agencies with the racial preferences of employers, and the racial biases of immigration officers against Black women from the Caribbean.

Admittedly, many Black women have benefited, at least economically, from Canada's foreign domestic programs over the years. However, we cannot deny that Canada's domestic programs have reinforced the demeaning images and stereotypes of Black women, contributed to brain drain, and perpetuated the dependency syndrome in the developing world. The mistress-servant relationship in domestic work and the inherent exploitation of minority women by White upper- and middle-class women shore up some of the disingenuousness of the Canadian feminist project.

Sources: Arat-Koc 1989; Bakan and Stasiulis 1995; Barber 1991; Calliste 1993/94; 1996; and Walker 1984.

Similarly, less than three percentage points separate Black women and "all Canadian women" regarding their respective proportions with less than Grade 9 education and those with university education. Compared with "all visible minority women," however, Black women have better official language ability, but they fall behind the former in terms of the percentage of people with university education.

Despite the close symmetry between the education and official language ability of Black women and the average Canadian woman, the former have far worse employment and income characteristics than the latter. According to Table 6.9, the unemployment rate for Black women, which stands at 19.8 percent, is nearly twice as high as the rate for the average Canadian woman, which is 10.0 percent. Likewise, only 0.19 percent of Black women hold senior management employment positions compared to 0.44 percent for "all Canadian women"—a ratio of over two to one in favour of the latter. Moreover, the average annual income for Black women is $2,249 below the $19,208 national average for women. Also, there is a marked income difference between the two groups for full-time workers. The average income for Black women who worked full-time was $27,561, whereas the corresponding figure for the average Canadian woman was $30,130. The income disparity between part-time workers in the two groups was negligible, however.

It is revealing that while some of the labour market characteristics of Black women are similar to those of "all visible minority women," Black women have a higher labour force participation rate and a higher unemployment rate, and they derive a higher percentage of their income from government transfer payments. A fairly similar finding was reported by Geschwender (1994), who studied the ethnic disparities in income and labour force participation among married women in Canada, using the 1986 Canadian Census Public Use Sample Tape. Among other things, Geschwender (1994) found that married Black women have a higher labour force participation rate than married women of other ethnic groups covered in that study.[9] He also observed that whereas 42.6 percent of married Black women worked full time, the corresponding figures for Asians and Chinese, also visible minority groups, were 36.8 and 38.3 percent, respectively. The labour market participation gaps between married Black women and married women of European ancestry were even greater: only 22.7 percent of married Dutch women, 24.5 percent of married French women, and 27.1 percent of married German women were employed full time (Geschwender 1994: 61).

Intriguingly, Geschwender found that Black wives make a far greater contribution to their family income than the married women of any other ethnic group in his study. While the earnings of Black wives increased total family income by as much as 32.2 percent, the comparable figures for other groups ranged from a low of 16.2 percent for Dutch wives to a high of 24.4 percent for Asian wives. Based on these findings, one can reasonably postulate, as does Agnew (1996: 36), that a large percentage of women of colour are married to low-income men and, therefore, cannot afford the luxury of being full-time housewives. Clearly, the traditional feminist struggle to limit women's economic dependence on men is problematic, at least from the standpoint of Black feminism.

Before we bring this section to a close, let us see how Black women compare with Black men on the various education and labour market indicators examined above. Table 6.10 provides the necessary data for such a comparison. Clearly, Black men fare better than Black women in all of the eleven variables presented. They have better education and language ability, lower unemployment rates, and higher income levels for both part-time and full-time workers. And, not surprisingly, Black men derive a fairly small share of their income from government transfer payments when compared to Black women.

The preceding paragraphs suggest that even though Black women have education and official language abilities that are fairly similar to those of the average Canadian woman, the former tend to have higher unemployment, lower incomes, and higher dependence on government transfer payments. Also, when compared to the average visible minority woman, Black women have higher unemployment rates and, understandably, higher dependence on government transfer payments. The average annual income and average employment income of Black women were not much different from those of the average visible minority woman, however. The

Table 6.10 Blacks in Canada: Male–Female Differentials in Selected Educational, Employment, and Income Indicators, 1996

Variable	Black Women	Black Men
Education and Language Characteristics		
% with neither English nor French ability	1.7	0.99
% with less than Grade 9 education	9.45	6.96
% with university education	19.9	24.67
Employment and Income Characteristics		
Labour force participation rate (%)	62.6	72.4
Unemployment rate (%)	19.8	18.8
% in senior management positions	0.19	0.34
% in middle and other management positions	3.05	4.58
Average full-time employment income	$27,561	$33,264
Average part-time employment income	$12,461	$14,556
Average annual income	$16,959	$21,378
% of income from government transfer payments	22.1	12.8

Source: Canada, Statistics Canada 1999b.

above analysis suggests that, contrary to popular belief, Black men in Canada generally do better than Black women when it comes to income and employment, even though this may not hold true for all Black groups in Canada.[10]

Understanding the Plight of Blacks in the Canadian Labour Market

It is not uncommon for Blacks and other visible minorities to make allegations of racism and unfair treatment in the Canadian labour market, but is there any empirical evidence to support these allegations? Can we say Blacks are treated more unfairly than other visible minorities in Canada? To what extent is the income deficit among Black Canadians, as observed in the previous section, attributable to racial discrimination in the labour market? As in the United States, discussions on the plight of Blacks in the Canadian labour market tend to divide into several camps, with varying degrees of explanatory weight given to culture, class, race, and ethnicity. In this section we discuss the arguments of these camps in some detail, and we examine the individual and institutionalized discrimination faced by Blacks in the Canadian labour market.

The Class Argument

To some analysts, especially those of a Marxist persuasion, including Li (1988), Rex (1983), and Cox (1959), the inequalities faced by Blacks and other people of colour in the job market are ultimately reducible to class dynamics in industrial capitalism. To them, racial oppression is a mere epiphenomenon of class exploitation. While this position can be traced to the writings of Marx and Engels, its popularity soared following the publication of *The Declining Significance of Race* in 1978 by William Julius Wilson, a renowned African-American sociologist. Wilson forcefully argued that the predicaments of Blacks in the U.S. job market are rooted in their working-class status rather than in their race. In his view, the endemic employment problems of Blacks are not caused by deliberate racial exclusions. Rather, they are the consequence of class relations in a changing global economy that has wiped out many industrial jobs in advanced capitalist societies.

The plight of Blacks, Wilson argues, is exacerbated by their lack of education and skills to compete in the emerging knowledge-class jobs. Wilson does not refute the fact that race is important but, in his view, the explanatory primacy belongs to class rather than race. Consistent with his position, Wilson does not support race-specific policies in addressing Black unemployment and underemployment. To him, the best policies are those that target the working class as a whole, regardless of race. Wilson reinforced his position on class-based policies in his 1987 book *The Truly Disadvantaged*, arguing that while the previous race-based policies have enhanced the socio-economic status of better-placed and better-trained Black professionals (the Black middle class), they have done little to improve the employment situation of the Black underclass—"the truly disadvantaged," to use Wilson's term.

> [Consequently] if policies of preferential treatment ... are conceived not in terms of the actual disadvantages suffered by individuals but rather in terms of race or ethnic group membership, then these policies will further enhance the opportunities of the more advantaged without addressing the problems of the truly disadvantaged. (Wilson 1987: 115)

As Steinberg (1995) aptly points out, Wilson and his apologists place too much emphasis on de-industrialization, and they assume that low-income Blacks would have better job chances if not for the "collapse" of the manufacturing sector, despite the enormous evidence of racism in this and other sectors of the economy. Also, Wilson and his supporters assume that affirmative action has been beneficial to only middle- and upper-income Blacks, even though research shows that it has enhanced the employment opportunities and upward mobility of Blacks in several areas, such as law enforcement, fire fighting, construction, and manufacturing, not only in the United States but also in Canada and other western nations (Steinberg 1995; Nelson and Fleras 1995; Elliott and Fleras 1992). As we shall soon see, the evidence of racial

discrimination against Blacks in the Canadian labour market is so overwhelming that one cannot candidly attribute the Black unemployment and
underemployment to class dynamics, devoid of the race factor.

The Culture Argument

Other analysts, notably conservative behaviouralists,[11] shift the blame away
from class and onto Blacks themselves. As Cornel West (1993: 11–15)
points out, they argue that the plight of Blacks in the job market is caused
primarily by the antisocial behaviour and cultural defects of Blacks, which
allegedly prevent them from upholding the canons of mainstream work
ethics, including hard work, punctuality, personal responsibility, and
perseverance. This mode of explanation is not new; it goes back to the
Moynihan Report of 1965, entitled *The Negro Family*.[12] The author of this
United States national report, Daniel Patrick Moynihan, argued that,
during the 1960s, the United States government removed many of the
structural impediments to Black employment through antidiscrimination
legislation, and that the disintegration of the Black family and the antisocial
behaviour among Blacks are the root causes of the problems facing Blacks
in the job market. In a 1987 article on the "American underclass,"[13] Myron
Magnet espoused a similar view: "What primarily defines them [the
underclass] is not so much their poverty or race as their behaviour—their
chronic lawlessness, drug use, out-of-wedlock births, nonwork, welfare
dependency, and school failure" (130).

Obviously this analysis is not much different from Oscar Lewis's
"culture of poverty." Lewis (1966), an anthropologist, argued that in
Western societies poverty is a subculture, a way of life handed down from
one generation to another. By the time children living in this culture reach
the age of five or six, they have usually acquired the basic attitudes and
values of the subculture, which is characterized by a low level of social
organization and a heightened sense of hopelessness and inferiority, among
other things. According to Lewis, because of the self-perpetuating nature
of this culture, the people involved become psychologically unready to
participate fully in mainstream society. In consonance with their assessment of the issue, these conservative and neoconservative behaviouralists
believe that nothing short of a revival of work ethics among Blacks will
improve their employment situation. They endorse only those policy
initiatives that target the alleged antisocial behaviour of Blacks. Simply put,
change the victims but leave the underlying socio-economic structures
intact.

Can we really blame the victims? Are we not confusing cause with
effect by assuming that the alleged cultural defects of Blacks are independent of the past and present material circumstances of Blacks? Can we claim

forthrightly that the underlying socio-economic structure has no causal bearing on the employment plight of Blacks? Several analysts have criticized this neoconservative explanation. William Ryan (1980), the U.S. psychologist who coined the phrase "blaming the victim," argues that this mode of explanation individualizes the problem by giving causal priority to factors relating to the victims themselves. Unlike the old-fashioned conservative racial ideology (which simply dismisses Blacks as inferior) victim-blaming is often very subtle. It is "cloaked in kindness and concern ... [it] bears all the trappings and statistical furbelows of scientism, it is obscured by a perfumed haze of humanitarianism" (Ryan 1980: 466). Arguably, this position is ideological to the extent that it involves distortions and misconceptions that seek to maintain the status quo in the interest of a particular group in society (Mannheim 1936; Ryan 1980; and Reiman 1990). As Ryan (1980: 467) aptly points out:

> All this happens so smoothly that it seems downright rational. First, identify the social problem. Second, study those affected by the problem and discover in what ways they are different from the rest of us as a consequence of deprivation and injustice. Third, define the differences as the cause of the social problem itself. Finally, of course, assign a government bureaucrat to invent a humanitarian action program to correct the difference.

By concentrating on Blacks, the culture argument diverts attention away from the social order. By concentrating on Blacks, it forgets that the competition for jobs in a society like ours is rigged in favour of non-Blacks. And, finally, by concentrating on Blacks, this explanation closes one's eyes to social injustices and seals one's ears to the question of whether social institutions historically have exploited Blacks (Reiman 1990: 124). Thus Cornel West (1993: 14) notes: "What is particularly naive and peculiarly vicious about the conservative behavioural outlook is that it tends to deny the lingering effect of Black history—a history inseparable from though not reducible to victimization." Stephen Steinberg's (1995: 142) renunciation of the conservative behaviouralists position could not be more explicit: "Why social scientists think they have *discovered* something when they find that an indigent and marginalized population lives according to 'different rules' from the middle class is itself perplexing" (original emphasis). Such claims and counterclaims are nothing new.[14] What is perhaps surprising is that they are getting more and more vitriolic.

The contention that the employment problems of Blacks are attributable to their alleged antisocial behaviour, notably their criminal activities and their lack of work ethics, is far more prevalent in the U.S. literature than in that of Canada. Even though many ordinary Canadians and social commentators hold this view, as is attested by public polls, media reports, and police accounts (Nelson and Fleras 1995; Lewis 1992), it has not been articulated forcefully in academic circles. Black youths are routinely stereotyped by the Canadian police as criminals, hustlers, drug-pushers, and pimps, however, and they are subjected to harassment, verbal abuse, strip searches, and physical assaults in cities such as Montreal and Toronto (Nelson and Fleras 1995; Andrew 1993; Elliott and Fleras 1992; Lewis 1992). Nelson and Fleras (1995: 253) note that "between 1988 and 1993, the police in Metro Toronto and surrounding regions wounded or killed a total of 10 African-Canadians, compared with only 12 Whites, even though the former comprise only a small proportion of the city's population." In comparing Blacks to Whites and Asians, Philippe Rushton, a psychologist at the University of Western Ontario in London, asserts that Blacks are not only more inclined to commit crime but are less intelligent as well (1990, 1988).[15] Indeed, many Canadians in positions of high repute believe that Blacks lack what it takes to succeed in the workplace. For instance, Henry and Ginzberg (1985a) note in *No Discrimination Here* that 28 percent of management of 199 large companies (i.e., companies with more than 50 employees) believed that Blacks do not have the ability to meet job performance requirements. Prevalent biases, ethnocentrism, and sensationalism in Canadian mass media add to these negative images of Blacks. Time and again, Blacks and other visible minorities are portrayed as being responsible for social problems in Canada (Nelson and Fleras 1995).

The Race and Ethnicity Argument: Its Primacy

Without question, racial discrimination is hard to prove under any circumstance, not only because of the intrinsic lack of empirical data in discrimination cases, but also because of the wide variety of interpretation that can be accorded to any available empirical data. Drawing theoretical and empirical insights from the works of Li (1988, 1998), Hou and Balakrishnan (1996), Das Gupta (1996), Henry and Ginzberg (1985a, 1985b) and others, this section provides evidence of racial discrimination in the Canadian labour market. Contrary to the class and culture arguments, the plight of Blacks in the Canadian labour market does have a lot more to do with race, and the alleged antisocial behaviours of Blacks are mere byproducts of the powerlessness and marginalization of Blacks in Canadian society (Henry and Ginzberg 1985a, 1985b). There is a monetary cost to being Black or non-White in the Canadian labour market, and this cost is hardly a phenomenon of the past, as the evidence will show.

Peter Li, in his 1988 book *Ethnic Inequality in a Class Society*, systematically examines the impact of ethnic/racial origin on income in Canada. The basic question he addresses is whether or not different ethnic and racial groups in this country are rewarded differently, despite having similar human capital characteristics. Li's central assumption was that in the absence of pronounced racial and ethnic discrimination in the labour market, income differences among individuals should simply reflect variables such as education, age, gender, occupation, and other achieved human capital characteristics. Consequently, after controlling for the relevant confounding variables, any observed ethnic or racial disparities in income can be a plausible indicator of job market discrimination. Using the 1981 Public Use Sample Tapes (PUST), produced by Statistics Canada, Li measured the effects of ethnic origin on income, after statistically controlling for age, education, gender, nativity, social class, sector of employment, and the number of weeks worked.

His findings suggest that, all things being equal, Blacks and Chinese suffer the most regarding income inequality in the Canadian job market. In 1981 members of these two groups earned $1,627 and $821 below the national average, respectively, even when they possessed human capital attributes that were fairly similar to those of their counterparts in other ethnic/racial groups (Li 1988: 116–17). It is important to note that the income deficit suffered by Blacks was almost twice as much as that of Chinese-Canadians (Table 6.11).

Obviously Peter Li's work, which is based on the 1981 census, is slightly out-of-date now. What empirical data do we have to suggest that this situation persisted beyond the 1980s? Can we maintain that there is a hidden monetary cost for being Black or non-White in the Canadian labour market of the nineties? Such were the issues explored in a 1996 paper by two University of Western Ontario sociologists, Feng Hou and T.R. Balakrishnan, using Statistic Canada's 1991 Public Use Sample Tapes. The methodology used by these two authors was fairly similar to that of Peter Li except that they included South Asians and other visible minorities, and also made slight changes to the control variables.

Like Li (1988), Hou and Balakrishnan (1996) found indications of racial and ethnic differences in monetary reward after controlling for immigration status, schooling, home language, gender, province of residence, and age. Once again, Blacks were among those who suffered the most regarding income inequality, with an estimated deficit of -$3,039. Other racial and ethnic groups with high income deficits included Greeks (-$3,195) and South Asians (-$1,956). While the income inequalities reported by Hou and Balakrishnan do not follow a strict colour line (as Greeks are among the lower ranks), the fact still remains that "visible minorities are generally at a disadvantage in this regard" (Hou and

Table 6.11 Rank-Order of Income Differences
among Selected Ethnic Groups, 1981 and 1991

Ethnic Group	1991 Income Difference		1981 Income Difference		Average Rank for 1981 and 1991
	Amount ($)	Rank	Amount ($)	Rank	
Portuguese	1,812	1	1,421	1	1
Italian	1,203	2	542	2	2
British	798	3	-20	3	3
Polish	781	4	-252	6	5
French	-22	5	-113	4	4.5
Chinese	-245	6	-821	8	7
Others	-246	7	-226	5	6
BLACKS	-3,039	8	-1,627	9	8.5
Greeks	-3195	9	-661	7	8
Standard Deviation	1,769		856	–	–

1. Average Rank represents the arithmetic mean of the ranking for 1981 and 1991.
2. Spearman's Rho =0.85 (Sig. at the 0.1 level; 2 tailed).
Sources: Computer from Li (1988: 117–17) and Hou and Balakrishnan (1996: 320) and used with permission from the publishers.

Balakrishnan 1996: 321).

Table 6.11 pools the income differentials of the nine ethnic and racial groups covered by both Li (1988) and Hou and Balakrishnan (1996). The computed standard deviations for the 1981 and 1991 income dispersions, which stood at $856 and $1,769, respectively, suggest that the situation is not getting any better. Indeed, income differences among the various ethnic and racial groups in the Canadian labour market are becoming more erratic and extreme. The monetary cost of being non-White in the Canadian labour market seems to be increasing. The estimated rank-order correlation coefficient (or Rho) between the 1981 and 1991 income differences stood at 0.85, suggesting that the rankings have not changed much since the early 1980s. Furthermore, the average rankings for 1981 and 1991 (shown in the last column of Table 6.11) suggest that Blacks have suffered the most in terms of income deficit during the periods under study, with the average rank of 8.5.

Admittedly, both Li (1988) and Hou and Balakrishnan's (1996) works are widely open to different interpretations. Neither provides categorical proof of racial and ethnic discrimination in the Canadian job market— something very difficult to prove, anyway. However, that they point to such a possibility is indubitable. As Hou and Balakrishnan (1996: 319) carefully put it:

Equality of opportunity in society implies that personal attributes and efforts basically determine an individual's accomplishments. Earnings are the rewards of an individual's investment in human capital. Therefore, income differentials among individuals should simply reflect their differences in education, occupation, age, and other achieved social and economic characteristics. The ascribed status of individuals, such as ethnicity and race, should not enter into the equation. In this sense any ethnic [and racial] differences in income may be an important indication of discrimination.

It is worth noting that in a 1998 follow-up article entitled "The Market Value and Social Value of Race," Peter Li arrived at a fairly similar conclusion on race-based disparities in income in Canada after controlling for variations in years of education, age, nativity, full- and part-time employment, gender, industry of work, occupation, and number of weeks worked. While Blacks fared better than visible minority groups such as Latin Americans, Arabs, and West Asians, the fact that visible minorities as a group continue to suffer income disparities remained unchanged and indeed indubitable based on Li's recent study. In fact, Li could not have put it any better when he observed:

Throughout the nineteenth and twentieth centuries, White people, mainly of European origin, were socially accepted in Canadian society as more desirable than non-White minorities. There is substantial evidence to indicate that this is the case today. Canadian society continues to attribute unequal social value to people of different origins.... Data from the 1991 Census confirm that ... a hierarchy of market value exists in accordance to White and non-White racial origins, and that non-White groups suffer an income penalty while most White Canadians receive an income premium as a result of their racial origin. (1998: 128)

Without question, the issue of whether there is anti-Black discrimination in Canada's labour market can be resolved only with studies that directly measure racial discrimination in employment. In the next section, we examine some of these studies to show the extent of racial discrimination faced by Blacks in the Canadian job market.

Evidence of Racial Discrimination in Hiring

The discrimination faced by Blacks and other people of colour in the job market can take different shapes. Some take the form of blatant bigotry. Others are submerged under the dynamics of the dual labour market. Some are systemic or institutional and, therefore, inherent in the operations of the Canadian labour market. Others are perpetrated skillfully by unions, rank-and-file workers, and management. Regardless of what form discrimination takes, Blacks and other visible minority immigrants have long come to the painful realization that, in Canada, they have to have superior performance in exams or in work to be treated as "equally" as their White counterparts. As one woman of colour remarked in a study by Ralston (1996: 412): "You have to be first among the first to succeed as well as Canadians"; another notes, "It's hard to be a foreigner; I have to get 100 percent to get a job."

Without question the observed income shortfalls for Blacks and other minorities could be the result of the split labour market in which members of these groups usually find themselves. Unlike Blacks and other people of colour, many White groups are firmly entrenched in the core sectors of the economy, and this may be partly responsible for their higher incomes. Notwithstanding the veracity of this argument, any attempt to explain the observed income disparities on grounds of the split labour market, *per se*, begs the question of why the race- and ethnic-based duality exists in the first place.

Several Canadian studies, including Henry and Ginzberg (1985a 1985b), Abella (1985), and the Ontario Human Rights Commission (1983), have documented credible evidence of individual and systemic racism in the recruitment and interview of Blacks and other visible minorities in the Canadian labour market. In *Who Gets the Work?* Henry and Ginzberg (1985b) present the results of a job search experiment in which four teams, each consisting of a Black and a White candidate with similar employment qualifications, were sent out to respond to job advertisements with virtually the same résumés. The advertisements were mostly related to jobs in low-rank occupations, such as the food industry, retail sales, unskilled labour, and some junior managerial positions. The results were painfully predictable, at least to many Black Canadians. The number of jobs offered at the end of the experiment was in the ratio of three-to-one in favour of the White applicants. Henry and Ginzberg (1985b) also noted that the White applicants in their experiment received more application forms and more helpful tips from employers than their Black counterparts.

A fairly similar finding emerged out of a study conducted by the Ontario Human Rights Commission (1983), which found that, among other things, Blacks and other visible minorities make more job applications and appear in far more job interviews, yet receive fewer job offers. While the hiring disparities between Blacks and Whites reported by these studies are remarkable, they still understate the situation. Why? Because it does not take much reflection to envisage that employers who harbour misguided racial prejudice against Blacks and other minorities are not likely even to advertise their job openings in newspapers; rather, they are likely to rely on word-of-mouth or, better still, use employment agencies to do their "dirty work" for them. And evidence from three consecutive studies conducted by the Canadian Civil Liberty Association in 1975 1980, and 1991[16] suggests that racial discrimination is routinely practised by employment agencies in Toronto on behalf of employers.

Manifestations of Racism by Management

In its most fundamental sense, racial exploitation is about asymmetric power relations between minority and majority groups. In the absence of any power imbalance the negative racial attitudes and stereotypes of the privileged group become nothing more than the barking of a toothless bulldog. It is only when the majority has the power, the authority, and the resources to ensure compliance with race-based practices that the minority group really feels the pinch of racism. Indeed, this is why Elliott and Fleras (1992: 58) question the recursive nature of racism. Can it be a "two-way street"? As they astutely point out, minority group members have an acute dearth of power to "exclude, exploit, persecute, dominate, or undermine the collective self-respect of the dominant group," making it highly problematic to attribute racism to them (Elliott and Fleras 1992: 58).

In almost all workplaces power rests in the hands of management. Indeed, the level of racism among rank-and-file workers is usually contingent upon the way in which they perceive management vis-à-vis race sensitivity. Vulgar-name-calling and other subtle and not-so-subtle forms of racism that are perpetrated by workers in the workplace derive primarily from their assessment of what they can, or cannot, get away with in the eyes of management. Discriminatory practices used by management to exploit, dominate, control, or otherwise peripheralize Blacks and other minorities ultimately affect and infest the rank-and-file and, indeed, the entire work environment.

Das Gupta (1996) exposes the common forms of racism practised by management. As she rightly points out, these race-based practices are usually founded on the misguided assumptions and rapacious hidden agendas of management. Some are based on "management's perception of what constitutes a 'threat' from workers of colour and management's effort to preserve their own power" (Das Gupta 1996: 35). Others derive from management's attempt to undermine the solidarity and, consequently, the bargaining power of rank-and-file workers by playing one racial group against the other. Still others are predicated on long-standing stereotypes about Blacks. The prevalent manifestations of racism on the part of management include targeting, scapegoating, marginalization, excessive monitoring, segregation of workers, and tokenism (Das Gupta 1996: 35–40).

Systemic and Institutionalized Forms of Racial Discrimination in the Job Market

Far more subtle, more hidden, and, arguably, more devastating than interpersonal or individual racism is the systemic or institutionalized racism that Blacks and other people of colour constantly encounter in the job market (Bolaria 1991; Elliott and Fleras 1992). Stokely Carmichael and Charles Hamilton, the *Black Power* authors who coined the term "institutionalized racism," point out further that, because these forms of racism are perpetrated by established and respected forces of society, they tend to attract far less, if any, public outcry and condemnation (1967: 4). While institutionalized racism may not necessarily derive from racial animus, they perpetuate employment and income inequalities all the same (Steinberg 1995: 76).

Instances of institutionalized racism abound in the history of Canada's treatment of Black people. Slavery was institutionalized in the sense that it had both legal authority and papal blessing. Of course, this is why it received minimal public condemnation. A similar case can be made regarding Canada's exclusionary immigration policy against Blacks and other minorities prior to the 1960s. Furthermore, as we learned in Chapter 3, Blacks who were recruited from the Caribbean to serve as domestic and farm workers in Canada were exploited and denied landed immigrant status based on a racist immigration policy that remained in effect until the 1960s. Bolaria (1991: 100) notes another form of institutionalized racism in which Black domestic workers from the Caribbean were subjected to gynecological testing for syphilis, because Canadian officials regarded Black women as promiscuous.

Moreover, there is evidence to suggest that, during the early 1900s, Blacks and other visible minorities, notably Chinese, were systematically excluded from trade union membership, especially in British Columbia (Bolaria 1991: 101). Also, until quite recently, Canadian police officers, fire fighters, nurses, airline and public transit employees had to meet weight and height (and to some extent skin colour) qualifications that were consciously or unconsciously skewed in favour of White applicants. These are good historical examples of the institutionalized racism to which Blacks and other visible minorities have been subjected.

Institutionalized and systemic racism is not a thing of the past, though. Blacks continue to face these forms of racism in the Canadian labour market, despite (or maybe because of) government antidiscrimination and employment equity initiatives. The contemporary forms of institutionalized racism are far more sophisticated and subtle. Examples of such practices in the Canadian labour market include the unbridled requisition for Canadian work experience; alleged shortfalls in foreign professional and educational qualifications; hiring by personal connections; seniority privileges; and the use of such vague and subjective standards as "fitting in" and "personality" for hiring and promotion purposes.

Richmond (1994: 144) notes in *Global Apartheid* that the systemic lack of recognition of skills and professional qualifications is one of the leading problems facing Blacks and other Third World immigrants in Canada. Several government reports have called for the establishment of a nation-wide body to assess and establish reasonable equivalence for foreign educational and employment qualifications, but so far no concrete action has been taken because of resistance from vested interest groups, such as professional associations and labour unions (Cumming et al. 1989; Adjibolosoo and Mensah 1998). This systemic racism undergirds the ironic, if not contradictory, situation in which well-educated immigrants from the developing world, whose skills are in limited supply in Canada, are recruited via the point system only to be told upon arrival that their qualifications are inadequate.

A fairly homologous form of systemic discrimination relates to the vicious cycle in which Blacks and other visible minorities are refused employment for the lack of "Canadian work experience." One wonders how they are ever going to obtain this one-of-a-kind experience without being hired in the first place. While the lack of Canadian experience may be a legitimate concern in some occupations, if the truth were to be told, we would have to admit that some employers use this as an excuse to discriminate against Blacks and other people of colour. At least, that is the perception among many people of colour (Adjibolosoo and Mensah 1998; Ralston 1996). The pervasiveness of this discriminatory excuse is so taken for granted that few analysts, if any, have actually pondered over its unethical, and, arguably, illogical foundations.

Let us have a closer look at this excuse. The preeminent eighteenth-century philosopher Immanuel Kant points out in his categorical impera-tive[17] that we ought to act only according to those maxims that can be consistently willed as a universal law.

> [Thus] the subjective, personal intention of the agent be such that it could be willed by the agent not only as his own intention in his particular case but also as the intention of all rational agents in similar circumstances; the subjective maxim must be *universalizable*. (Kant 1983: 56 emphasis added)

The issue then is: Is the employer who refuses to hire the Black person, or any visible minority immigrant for that matter, due to lack of Canadian experience really prepared to have this as a universal yardstick or maxim for hiring people in Canada? If so, consider some of the consequences. First, no foreigner could ever be hired in the Canadian labour market, unless the foreigner first enters into self-employment to gain this unique experience. Second, taken to its logical extreme, nobody, be he or she foreign- or Canadian-born, would ever get a first job (i.e., be hired by somebody else) unless, again, the person first becomes self-employed. Indeed, as Canada is a land of immigrants, it is likely that our hypothetical employer secured his or her first employment without any Canadian experience. Faced with these inconsistent and certainly uncomfortable scenarios, our hypothetical employer then would wish that this subjective maxim not become a universal yardstick for hiring people in Canada. The employer so defines him- or herself as a typical ethical egoist[18] but, either way, ends up tangled in his or her own inconsistencies. The potential for disaster, at least of a logical nature, seems high. Of course, a critic may argue that people get into business for profit and not for ethical imperatives. Fair enough, but one can assert plausibly that the whole Canadian economy and, consequently, all profit-making capabilities stand to suffer if we overlook such pertinent ethical issues.

The excuse (or, more charitably, the explanation) of not hiring Blacks and other visible minorities for their lack of Canadian experience can be looked at in a radically different way. Perhaps it is just another subtle, yet powerful, way to discriminate against people of colour—separating them out, redefining them or making them appear "different" in ways other than their skin pigmentation or physical appearance. Of course we all know that a clear-cut discrimination based on physical appearance is now illegal in Canada. What if that same form of discrimination is masked under the "Canadian experience" sophistry? Certainly nobody can prove these subtle and sophisticated forms of racism with any degree of certainty. Such excuses have become a good cover for employers who, blinded by racism and xenophobic frenzy, choose to discriminate and then never worry about having to face employment discrimination allegations.

Although there is no strong empirical evidence to support the belief that "difference" or "lack of experience" makes a job candidate inadequate and less apposite, this perception is very common among employers, regardless of the particular employment position at stake. The art of discovering "difference" is one of the oldest tricks used by members of a privileged group against minorities. Centuries ago, the Greeks deduced from a single characteristic—a difference in language—that the so-called barbarians were uncivilized, dangerous, wild, and scarcely more than animals. As William Ryan points out (1980: 468), all aspiring victim blamers (or discriminators, in this case), first must learn how to demonstrate that the group being blamed (or discriminated against) is different, regardless of what the difference may be in most cases. Another, fairly similar, excuse systematically used to disqualify Blacks and other immigrants from the developing world is to designate them as "overqualified." These people can never win: they either lack Canadian experience or have too much qualification for comfort. The irony is that in most cases these minorities are prepared to work for exactly what the prospective job pays and nothing more, even though they may truly be overqualified.

On the surface, hiring new employees on the basis of personal connections may seem race-neutral but, as Gertrude Ezorsky (1991: 14) states, this practice has a "powerful racist impact." The transmission of job information via family, friends, and neighbours by word of mouth is, undoubtedly, one of the most widely used recruitment methods in the labour market (Boros and Parkinson: 1980). Indeed, all segments or colours of the Canadian labour market, from blue to white, hire sizeable portions of their workers through personal connections—hence the cliché "It's not *what* you know, but *who* you know." Like most forms of institutional discrimination, the employers involved may not necessary harbour any racist intention; some may not even be aware of the racist implications of their actions. In actual fact, some employers may use these personal connections or referrals as a means of reducing the cost of job advertisement or as a way of finding a "reliable" employee in a short time. But, of course, there are those who will consciously use personal connections to mask their racist intentions.

Increasingly Blacks and Whites are living in two separate societies (at least in spatial terms) in Canadian cities such as Toronto, Montreal, and Halifax. With only minimal ties to high- or White society—as friends, neighbours, club members, co-workers, and acquaintances—many Blacks effectively are disconnected from the personal networks through which job information, especially on the most desirable and well-paid positions, is disseminated. And, since individuals often hear about job openings in their own kind of work, the practice of hiring via personal connections, word-of-mouth, and the old-boys and new-girls networks reinforces occupational segregation, leading more and more Blacks into the dead-end, low-paying jobs. An extended racist ramification of this practice is the perpetuation of the racist stereotype that invariably situates Blacks in hot, dirty, dusty, and menial jobs. Gertrude Ezorsky (1991: 16) notes in her analysis of institutionalized racism in the U.S. that "because whites disproportionately occupy elected government office, especially the more powerful positions, blacks suffer from the widespread use of political patronage to distribute government jobs." The veracity of this argument can certainly be extrapolated to cover the Canadian socio-political landscape.

Like recruitment through personal connections, the use of seniority to determine promotions, pay, job privileges, and layoffs seems race-neutral, at least on a *prima facie* basis. But in the current situation where, due to entrenched racism, Blacks in particular are usually the last to be hired in the workplace, the racist implications of this seemingly innocent practice become quite glaring to even the superficial analyst. As less senior in most Canadian workplaces, Blacks are less likely to be promoted and more likely to be laid off in times of economic recession. One may wonder whether there is any "fair" or better way around this. Gertrude Ezorsky (1991) discusses some innovative ideas on how to reduce the racial impact of seniority-based layoffs and advancement in the workplace. Some of her proposed remedies include the equitable distribution of the burden of layoff; a four-day week, work-sharing scheme in which the burden of a layoff is distributed across the entire work force, with the government compensating for the fifth day; and a proposal for keeping some minorities who should have been laid off by reason of seniority, and compensating Whites workers who are let go as a result of the race-based retention. While we do not have to agree with any of these proposals, one thing remains quite certain: seniority-based layoffs and promotions have serious racial implications.

Moreover, given that racism is widespread in the workplace, is it not reasonable to infer, as did Ezorsky (1991: 23), that the practice of hiring, evaluating, and promoting workers through such vague and subjective concepts as "fitting in," "personality," and "vigour" opens the door for racial biases? Having said that, it is only fair to acknowledge that Blacks in positions of power also can use these same subjective indicators to further their personal biases not only against Whites, but also against other Blacks in the workplace.[19] But, when all is said and done, the relative impact of this practice would be far more devastating on Blacks than on Whites, given the power imbalance between the two groups in a typical Canadian work environment.

All these forms of racism are by no means limited to the private sector of the labour market. In a recent comprehensive study of the hiring practices of fourteen government departments and agencies across Canada, John Samuel and Associates Inc. (1997) came to the conclusion that racial discrimination against visible minorities is common in the Canadian public service. Indeed, the prevalence of racism in the public service was noted not only by the visible minorities interviewed, but also by management, executives (i.e. assistant deputy ministers and directors general), and a control group made up of non-visible minority public service workers.[20]

Conclusion

Any candid interpretation of the census data and the theoretical arguments presented in this chapter would suggest that Blacks and other visible minorities face some level of racial discrimination in the Canadian labour market. As to whether Blacks are subjected to higher levels of racial discrimination than other visible minorities is contentious. While the bulk of the data points to severer employment problems and higher levels of racial discrimination against Blacks, there are instances in which the circumstances of other visible minorities, such are Arabs and Latin Americans seem to be worse than those of Blacks. All things considered, however, the plight of Blacks in the Canadian labour market is among the worst, no matter how one interprets the available empirical data presented in this chapter.[21]

What is to be made of all this? At the risk of being branded a cynic, or even a radical, one can conclude that Canadian society, like most industrial capitalist societies, secretly wants racism and gains some benefits by not forthrightly addressing it. How else can one explain a situation in which the federal government, for instance, is now among the worst violators of its own employment equity policies? In a society like Canada, racism offers some hidden "benefits" and performs some "functions," telling examples of which include the following four:

- First, racism produces cheap and oppressed labour that can be used to perform the menial tasks of society. In addition it ensures that the supply of cheap, oppressed labour is constant, as the proletariat (or the class of victims) ends up producing its replacement. This argument is certainly not new, it can be easily synthesized from the Marxist perspective on labour under capitalism.
- Second, racism creates avenues for charitable activities and opportunities for self-righteous finger-pointing in the form of public demonstration and protest over incidences of overt racism against racial minorities. The public outcry and anger emanating from such acts help cement society at large. Indeed a homologous argument was made by Emile Durkheim in his assessment of crime: "Crime (and by extension other forms of deviation) may actually perform a needed service to society by drawing people together in a common posture of anger and indignation" (quoted in Reiman 1990: 34).
- Third, racism allows the privileged class to exaggerate in its favour the income differential inherent in the skills hierarchy. This can be done by monopolizing and artificially restricting the labour supply and thereby raising the wages of those privileged and high status employments. As Li

(1988: 54) astutely puts it: "In a capitalist labour market, ethnicity can be seen as a liability for those who suffer discrimination, but an asset for others who control privileged positions. In the latter case, ethnicity can be used as a means of exclusion to safeguard one's privileges and to prevent others from encroaching on them."

• Fourth, racism can be manipulated by employers to undermine trade unions and ultimately reduce the price of both Black and White labour. It is not hard to envisage that in situations of extreme racism, where Blacks are compelled and willing to accept lower wages and adverse working conditions, the bargaining power of the entire work force suffers.

Given these hidden "benefits" it is not surprising that racism persists in Canada and, indeed, in all industrial capitalist societies with significant visible minority populations. The argument here is not that Whites in Canada intentionally make the work environment racist so as to derive these "benefits." Rather, it is reasoned that those who are in a position to make profound changes to alleviate racism in the job market (i.e., the various levels of government and the White society at large) are a bit complacent. It appears they are not in any rush to change the status quo. The critical silence of many Whites on these issues is very revealing to the sophisticated analyst. Meanwhile, and quite naturally, Blacks and other minorities who are most victimized and peripheralized by the system do not have the wherewithal to effect any meaningful emancipatory change.

Notes

1. As a Black colleague bluntly puts it: "As long as I can feed my family what do I care about the KKK?" This colleague is highly critical of anti-racist demonstrations against such groups as the KKK and White supremacists. To him such demonstrations are nothing more than a cover for people to engage in self-righteous finger-pointing while they continue to engage in far more damaging acts of racial discrimination in their own workplaces. Indeed, many Blacks are of this belief; and, arguably, this is why many Blacks do not participate in such public displays.
2. See Karl Marx's *Capital* (1977), vols. I and III, in particular, for a comprehensive discussion of surplus value and the accumulation of capital.
3. Refer to Marx and Engels' *Communist Manifesto* (1955) and Engels' *The Conditions of the Working Class in England* (1958) for a detailed exposition of the deplorable circumstances of the proletariat.
4. In fact both Marx and Engels discuss the concept of alienation in several of their writings, but perhaps their most forceful arguments can be found in Engels' *The Condition of the Working Class in England* (1958); Marx and Engels' (1976) *The German Ideology;* and Marx's "Alienated Labour" (1983).
5. Spatial mismatch theorists, such as Kain (1968), Kasarda (1989), and More and

Laramore (1990), argue that as the White flight to the suburbs intensifies, so do the employment problems of inner-city Blacks, most of whom depend on the jobs that are moved to the suburbs as a result of this flight. This flight, termed "suburbanization" in the urban geographic literature, is responsible for what George Clinton calls "chocolate cities and vanilla suburbs" in the United States (cited in West 1993: 5).

6. Rex and Tomlinson (1979); Miles (1982); and Boncich (1972) are good examples of international studies on the vertical mosaic.

7. The year preceding the year in which the census is held, in this case 1995 for the 1996 census.

8. The incidence of low income is defined by Statistics Canada as the "proportion of economic families or unattached individuals in a given classification below the low income cut-offs" (Canada, Statistics Canada 1999a). The low income cut-offs (LICOs) represent income levels below which a Canadian family is considered a low-income family, depending on where that family lives (i.e., the degree of urbanization) and the family size. The LICOs are updated annually by changes in the consumer price index. For a complete list of the LICOs matrix used for the 1996 census, consult Canada, Statistics Canada 1999a.

9. Ethnic categories covered by James Geschwender in this study include British, French, First Nations, Dutch, German, Other Europeans, Asian, Black, Other Non-Europeans, and Multiple ancestries.

10. Writing on the specific case of Jamaican women in Canada, Billson (1991: 51) observed: "As in Jamaica, many [women] are heads of households... The position of Jamaican women in Canadian society is generally quite different from Jamaican men, who are often less educated and less well employed." Whether this assertion can be supported by empirical evidence or not is hard to tell, though.

11. The term used by Cornel West in *Race Matters* (1993: 11).

12. Cited in Steinberg 1995.

13. This is a code word for Blacks in most cases.

14. The nineteenth-century French poet, novelist, and dramatist Victor Hugo espoused a similar position when he observed: "If the soul is left in darkness, sins will be committed. The guilty one is not he who commits the sin, but he who causes the darkness." (Quoted by Martin Luther King Jr. in his *Conscience for Change* 1967: 4).

15. The work of Rushton is discussed in Chapter 7.

16. These studies are cited in Das Gupta (1996: 12).

17. The Kantian categorical imperative is the command of reason that conduct ought to follow universal moral principles (see Kant 1983).

18. Ethical egoism is the view that people ought to do what is in their own self-interest. Thus, whether person *A* has done what is morally right or wrong depends solely on how good or bad the consequences of *A*'s action are for *A*. How others are affected is irrelevant (see Barry: 1978: 126–34). Of particular interest here is individual egoism, the view that the egoist is going to look after him- or herself and no one else. Moral philosophers have long revealed the inconsistencies in the different versions of ethical egoism. Brian Medlin (1967: 234) argues that ethical egoism is as illogical as asserting "I want ... to

be happy; and I want Tom to be happy; and I want ... not to care about Tom."

19. Here is a real-life observation by a Black professional whose identity must remain anonymous: "Given the choice, I prefer to be interviewed or evaluated by a White person. From what I have seen over the years, some of the few Blacks in positions of authority tend to be power-drunk; they somehow feel threatened when another Black person comes to the scene. In fact, some even use their positions to foster their nationalistic, tribal, ethnic, and egocentric agendas."

20. The study (John Samuels and Associates Inc. 1997) was sponsored by the Canadian Human Rights Commission; more than 2,000 public service employees participated in this study.

21. Native Canadians—arguably, the group most impacted by racial discrimination in the Canadian labour market—are not covered here, as they are officially excluded from the category of "visible minorities," due to their special status as Aboriginals.

Chapter 7

Blacks in Canadian Sport

Issues, Controversies, and Paradigm Shifts

Sport is one of the few areas in which Black Canadians have outperformed their White counterparts.[1] Indeed, the virtual takeover of elite-level track, boxing, soccer, basketball, and baseball by Black athletes is a global phenomenon that continues to intrigue both Black and White scientists and social observers. Given the persistent racism in the job market, it is hardly surprising that Blacks generally approach sport—perhaps the only level playing field they have—with passion. In fact, as the sociologist Ellis Cashmore (1990) points out, by the time Black youths are ready to make the transition from school to work, many have already taken sport as a career of first priority.

In this chapter, we examine the contribution of Blacks to Canadian sport and explore how this has evolved in light of the systemic racism that Blacks have endured in this country over the years. We examine the extent to which both stacking[2] and Canada's Athlete Assistant Program affect Blacks in Canadian sport. In addition, the contentious issues surrounding the apparent dominance or "superiority" of Blacks in sport are discussed with an inclination towards the separation of genuine scientific theories from their pseudo or folkloric counterparts. It is important to stress from the outset that while the focus remains on Canadian Blacks, the cross-border and international nature of elite sport and its athletes, competitions, organizations, and ideas making it virtually impossible to limit the discussion to Canada. The most authoritative and trend-setting studies on Blacks in sport, including John Hoberman's *Darwin's Athletes* (1997) and Jon Entine's *Taboo* (2000), emanate from the United States. Also, the Black dominance in sport—and the related racial myths and public infatuation— is now a global spectacle.

Blacks' Involvement in Canadian Sport: Historical Background

Many ethnic and racial groups have been involved in Canadian sport since the nineteenth century, but few, if any, have faced more systemic discrimination and dehumanization and yet been more successful than Blacks.

Historically an ethnoracial hierarchy in sport relegated Blacks, and to some extent Aboriginals, to the bottom of the ladder. Also, the colonial mentality that prevailed during the early days of sport encouraged Whites-only participation through ethnoracial and class-based exclusions and competitions. Generally, the closer one was to being White, Anglo-Saxon and protestant, the more likely one was to be part of organized sport in Canada (Cosentino 1998: 4). Even though Asians and Aboriginals also were considered inferior at the time, they occupied a higher rung than did Blacks, and the barriers that restricted members of these minority groups applied doubly and openly to Blacks. Notwithstanding these exclusions, sport somehow "gained a reputation as an egalitarian and apolitical agency which alone transcended the normal sectional divisions of the colonial social order" (Stoddard 1988: 651).

As in the U.S., boxing, horseracing, and rowing were among the first sports in Canada in which Blacks were allowed to compete against (or with) Whites. Even in these sports, explicit prohibitions against Blacks were not uncommon in many Canadian clubs during the nineteenth century. For instance, when the Niagara Turf Club was formed in 1835, its policy stated that "no Black shall be permitted to ride on any pretext whatsoever" (Cosentino 1998: 6). Also, when William Berry, a Black man, entered the 1863 championship race at the Toronto Regatta, the two White competitors refused to race with him (Cosentino 1998: 6).

Even though the glass ceiling was broken earlier in boxing, Blacks were virtually shut out of most world championship fights; they fought White opponents only in lesser bouts. As Entine (2000) points out, the heavyweight title, which came to symbolize the Anglo-Saxon ideal of White supremacy, for a long time was reserved for Whites only. For reasons of prejudice or fear (most likely the latter), the American Jim Jeffries, world heavyweight champion in 1904, declared that he would never fight a Black man. Not even the barrage of verbal punches from Jack Johnson, the Black U.S. contender, was enough to compel Jeffries to abdicate his self-imposed prohibition.

Johnson, whom Entine (2000: 156) likens to "an earlier-day Dennis Rodman," continued his in-your-face taunting of the White boxing establishment until he was finally allowed to fight Tommy Burns, the Ontario-born White Canadian who held the heavyweight title, on December 26, 1908 in Australia. Burns vowed to "battle [his] life to defend the laurels against Africa" (Cosentino 2000: 10), but he agreed to fight on the condition that his own manager be allowed to referee the bout.[3] By all accounts, even this laughable condition could not help Burns much, as Johnson peppered him with punches almost at will from the first to the fourteenth round when the Australian police finally stopped the bout (Entine, 2000; Cosentino 1998).

It is interesting to note that Jim Jeffries came out of retirement, renounced his self-imposed prohibition, and fought Johnson in 1910, but lost. Quite predictably, White America's resentment over Johnson's victory spilled over into Canada. As the search for the "Great White Hope" became elusive and frustration mounted, so did the use of racially loaded insults by sport commentators against Black boxers on both sides of the border. In Canada derogatory terms such as "nigger," "husky darky," and "coon" were frequently deployed to describe Black boxers in the leading newspapers, including the *Toronto Star* and the *Toronto Daily News* (Cosentino 1998: 10–13). Later that year, in a move that will not surprise any keen observer of race dynamics in the U.S., Jack Johnson was charged with having sex with a White woman—the biggest social taboo then—across a state line (Shropshire 1996). Johnson ran away to Canada in 1913 but, ironically, in that same year the Amateur Athletic Union of Canada banned Blacks from competing in Canadian championships, and in the following year, the Ontario government made Black-White bouts illegal (Cosentino 1998: 13).

The admixture of official and unofficial restrictions was imposed on Blacks in team sports such as baseball, football, and hockey as well. Black pioneer athletes—including Fredericton's William O'Ree, the first Black player in the NHL; Bill Galloway and Charles Lightfoot, two of the first Blacks to play in the Ontario Hockey Association League; and Gordon Simpson, one of the first Blacks to play in the Canadian amateur football league—had to deal with racial derision, not only from members of the opposing teams and their fans, but also from their own teammates and home crowd. Cosentino (1998: 9) describes instances in which players refused to compete on the same field with Blacks or be photographed with their Black teammates. At the same time, cries of "Kill the nigger!" "Kill the coon!" and "Tackle the nigger!" were common among both Canadian and U.S. spectators (Cosentino 1998; Wiggins 1997; Shropshire 1996). With such intense racial animosity, it is no surprise that all-Black barnstorming and sport teams became the norm across Canada during the late nineteenth and early twentieth centuries. Classic examples include baseball teams such as the London Goodwills, the Coloured Diamond of Halifax, and the Amber Valley All-Blacks of Alberta (Alexander and Glaze 1996).

Professional sport organizations in both Canada and the U.S. were compelled by the events surrounding the Second World War to re-evaluate and, indeed, tone down their racial attitudes in the post-war period. After playing for the minor-league Montreal Royals in 1947, Jackie Robinson broke the major-league colour barrier that same year by playing for the Brooklyn Dodgers (Tygiel 1983; Shropshire 1996). Notwithstanding this breakthrough, more than a decade passed before, in 1958, Willie O'Ree became the first Black to play in the NHL (Cosentino 1998: 9). Unlike in team sports such as baseball, football, and basketball, however, only a handful of Blacks—Grant Fuhr and Herb Carnegie and, more recently, Donald Brashear, Mark Grier, Jerome Iginla, Anson Carter, and George Laraque—have followed O'Ree into the NHL.

The civil rights movements of the 1960s and the revolt of African-American athletes during the 1968 Mexico Olympics[4] drew more attention to the plight of Blacks in North American sport. Furthermore, with the success of Black pioneers such as Jackie Robinson, the White teams realized that the inclusion of Blacks would boost their clubs' athletic success and, consequently, their revenues (McPherson et al. 1989).

The work of Consentino (1989) in *A Concise History of Sport in Canada* shows that professional football was a relative latecomer in Canadian sport history. College and other amateur football (more appropriately called rugby football) had been played in Canada since the nineteenth century, beginning with the formation of the Toronto Argonauts in 1874, the Winnipeg Rugby Football Club in 1880, and the Ottawa Rough Riders and Hamilton Tigers in 1883. The professional football league, as we know it now, was constituted in 1956 following the formation of the Canadian Football Council, which was renamed the Canadian Football League (CFL) in 1958 (Cosentino 1989). Since then the influx of U.S. players, mostly African-Americans, into the CFL has always been a source of confusion and tension among both players and league officials as they struggle to find ways of improving the quality of the sport with imported U.S. players without unduly infringing upon the niche of Canadian-born players. Cosentino (1989: 161) writes that by 1965 the import rules and manoeuvres had gotten so convoluted that there were as many as four categories of Canadians in the CFL—"the naturalized Canadian; the university-trained Canadian, the non-university-trained Canadian, and the Canadian-American"—each with their allowable cuts and quotas. Whether or not the import rules are good for the spirit and survival of the CFL is certainly anyone's guess. One thing is certain, though: Canadian professional football is now dominated by Black players, most of whom are from the U.S.

Undoubtedly no other team sport in both Canada and the U.S. has received the stamp of Black dominance more than basketball, a game invented in 1891 by Canadian James Naismith at the YMCA college in Springfield, Massachusetts (Crystal 1998: 680). As with football, Canadian Blacks have played amateur basketball in various universities, clubs, and international championships since the game was first introduced into Canada in 1892 (Keyes 1989). In fact, basketball seems to have had far less history of racial segregation in both Canada and the U.S., considering that

Blacks have played in the NBA since its formation in 1949. Bill Russell, an African-American, secured his coaching position in the NBA with the Boston Celtics as early as 1966 (Shropshire 1996).

In the Canadian context, the first major triumph by a Black athlete in basketball came in 1979 when Sylvia Sweeney became the most valuable player (MVP) in the world basketball championship in Seoul, South Korea. This high performance was recently emulated by Sue Steward, another Black woman who led the Canadian women's basketball team in the 1996 Atlanta Olympics. The inclusion of the Toronto Raptors and the erstwhile Vancouver Grizzlies in the NBA since the 1990s[5] has not only elevated the status of the game and increased the Canada-wide popularity of Black athletes such as Vince Carter, it has also heightened the public discourse on the Black dominance in professional basketball.

The increasing darkening of Olympic track and field athletes in Canada is also discernible to even the most cursory observer. In fact, since the Berlin Olympics of 1936, when Toronto's Sammy Richardson, the lone Black on Canada's Olympic team, placed second to Jesse Owens[6] in the 200-metre sprint (Alexander and Glaze 1996), the Black presence in Canadian Olympics has increased progressively. Throughout the 1960s, Harry Winston Jerome, a Black Canadian born in 1940 at Prince Albert, Saskatchewan, was undoubtedly the nation's premier sprinter. He was the first man to share the world 100-yard and 100-metre records with the time of 9.2 and 10.0 seconds, respectively; he represented Canada in three consecutive Olympics in the sixties—i.e., 1960, 1964, 1968 (Barris 1998).

Monumental performances by Donovan Bailey in the 100-metre dash, and the Canadian 4 x 100-metre relay team in the 1996 Atlantic Olympics, as well as Donovan Bailey and Michael Johnson's competition for "the fastest man on earth" at Toronto's Skydome are difficult to match in recent memory. Still, it is important to note that there are other Black (and of course non-Black) athletes who have and continue to make significant contributions to Canada's Olympic project. Notable Blacks include Charmaine Crooks, who still holds the Canadian women's 400-metre record (1.58 minutes) set in 1990 at Zurich; Angela Bailey, who set the Canadian women's record in 100-metre (10.98 seconds) in Budapest in 1987; Daniel Igali, who won a gold medal in wrestling at the Sydney Olympics in 2000; and Mark Boswell and Kwaku Boateng who hold the first and second places, respectively, in Canadian high jump; Curtis Herbert, the former Canadian Olympic gymnast; and Bruny Surin, one of the only two Canadian athletes to ever run the 100-metre dash under 10 seconds.[7] Also, anyone who follows Canadian women's soccer will readily recognized the face of Charmaine Hooper, the Black Canadian striker who has represented the nation in more than seventy international matches and scored over forty-five goals; she currently holds the record in both categories.

The point to stress here is that these athletic triumphs, and their related failures, are as much a part of the Black history as they are of the Canadian history. Most of these Black athletes are recent immigrants and refugees, who have in one way or another enjoyed the freedom of this country and the generosity and support of its citizens to attain these laurels. As with any human endeavour, not all Blacks in Canadian sport have demonstrated positive or praiseworthy conduct, as the Ben Johnson saga at the Seoul Olympics of 1988 clearly shows.[8]

The major sports that have attracted Blacks over the years (e.g., track, boxing, basketball, baseball, and football) are the ones that demand little in the way of special equipment and formal training. As Cashmore (1990: 86) puts it: "A strong pair of legs, fast hands, sharp reflexes, and a desire to compete" are the basic requisites of most of these sports. Much more economic resources are required in sport disciplines such as ice-hockey, golf, tennis, and swimming. These are mostly accessible to people from middle- and upper-income brackets, to which a relatively small proportion of Canadian Blacks belongs.

Stacking and Other Racial Manoeuvres in Sport

The accomplishment of Blacks in Canadian sport is remarkable. But how does this success measure up when one considers the high numbers of Black youths entering sport? Are Blacks really getting equal opportunities for equal abilities in organized sport in Canada? Put differently, are Blacks still subjected to racial manoeuvres in Canadian sport?

Short of outright prohibition and segregation, the main discriminatory tactic against Blacks in Canadian (and U.S.) sport has been stacking—the disproportionate concentration of Blacks in non-central, as opposed to central, positions in team sport. Central positions require a high level of interaction with other teammates and an ability "to read the game." Such positions are normally reserved for athletes with leadership and decision-making abilities—qualities hardly attributed to Black athletes in North American leagues, until quite recently.

Obviously, much has changed in North American sport since the 1960s, but some studies suggest that in football, for instance, Blacks still tend to be over-represented in the positions of running back and wide receiver and not in the central and prestigious quarterback position. Similarly, in baseball, Blacks are normally stacked in outfield positions and not in the starting pitcher, catcher, or second base positions (McPherson, et al. 1989; Jiobu 1988). Also, until recently, the position of point guard, or the "floor general," in basketball was reserved for Whites (Coakley 1978). Today, though, given the overwhelming dominance of Blacks in basketball, anti-Black stacking is virtually non-existent (Vogler and Schwartz 1993). Indeed, one can argue that, if anything, stacking in basketball now is against Whites, who have to overachieve to be accepted.

Stacking is not limited to North America. It is routinely practised in nearly all Western nations with sizeable racial minority athletes (Cashmore 1990; O'Donnell 1994; Hoberman 1997; Kew 1997). In European soccer, for instance, until quite recently, the midfield, often called the "engine room" because it controls most of the tactical decision of the game, almost always was reserved for Whites. As Hoberman (1997: 127–28) succinctly puts it:

> Keeping dark-skinned men out of the "engine room" was one of the classic racist caveats of the nineteenth century.... For the Western imagination, an African [or a Black] who combines technological skill and a capacity for leadership is unthinkable. In the world of sport, which does not require engineering skills, even the burdens of leadership have been considered too much for black men to bear until very recent times.

A similar dichotomy of central versus non-central positions and the attendant stereotypes is discernible in Australia and New Zealand sport, where the dark/brown-skinned Native, Maori, and other Polynesian athletes have traditionally been stacked in "non-White" positions in sports such as rugby and basketball (Phillips 1987).

O'Donnell (1994) has demonstrated, quite shrewdly, that in the global context racial stereotypes of athleticism commingle with images of different nations not only in sport but also in military and economic development. Among the kaleidoscope of images that have emerged are those of the efficient Japanese worker; the cool, rational, and clinical Swedish tennis player; the surgical precision of the Swiss worker or player. Others include the hard-working, disciplined, efficient German engineer or soccer player; the committed and courageous English sport team or soldier; the flamboyant, stylish, and inspirational French athlete; the temperamental or emotional Italian team and its fans; the creative and artistic, but undisciplined, Latin/Brazilian soccer player; and, of course, the reckless, irrational, and black magical African soccer player (O'Donnell 1994: 345). These sportive images and stereotypes constitute a worldwide "discursive network" that expresses and accentuates the racial hierarchy created by colonial relationships and contemporary industrial competition (O'Donnell 1994).

While empirical studies on the extent of stacking in Canadian sport are lacking, it appears the practice generally has been less pervasive here, at least compared with the U.S. Black Canadians frequently hold or play central positions in sport. For instance, several Blacks including Damon Allen (B.C. Lions), Marcus Crandell (Calgary Stampeders), Khari Jones (Winnipeg Blue Bombers) and Marvin Graves (Saskatchewan Roughriders) play quarterback positions for their respective CFL teams. In fact Black players and coaches, most of whom are Americans, dominate the CFL now. In the short span of the Canadian NBA establishment, both the Toronto Raptors and the erstwhile Vancouver Grizzlies have been dominated by Blacks not only as players in nearly all positions but also in coaching and management positions—Stu Jackson, Sydney Lowe, and Isiah Thomas, all have held coaching and top management positions. Also in baseball, Cito Gaston managed the Toronto Blue Jays to two World Series, while Felipe Alou successfully directed the affairs of the Montreal Expos.

Stacking invariably is based on the racist stereotype that Blacks have more physical, as opposed to mental, abilities, while the opposite is purportedly true for Whites. Not surprisingly, representatives of the White sport establishment—coaches, trainers, managers, and sportswriters—frequently depict Black athletes as having speed and strength. Whites, on the other hand, are said to exhibit leadership ability, intelligence, tactical insight, and mental toughness. Some analysts contend that Blacks have different physiological and psychological attributes that make them naturally suitable for specific positions and sports, and, therefore, stacking is not necessarily an anti–Black manoeuvre in sport. For instance, Worthy and Markle (1970) argued decades ago that Blacks do relatively better in reactive, as opposed to self-paced, activities than Whites, and vice versa. Self-paced activities, to these authors, are those in which the player responds, when he or she so chooses, to "a relatively static or unchanging stimulus" (Worthy and Markle 1970: 439). Examples of self-paced activities include pitching in baseball, free throws in basketball, and golf; obviously, Tiger Woods and his worldwide fans will agree to disagree with Worthy and Markle's dichotomy.

According to Worthy and Markle (1970: 439), reactive activities are those in which the player "must respond appropriately and at the right time to changes in the stimulus situation"; outfielders, running backs, wide receivers and cornerbacks all hold reactive positions. As McPherson et al. (1989) aptly questioned, how then do we account for the acute under-representation of Blacks in reactive sports such as autoracing, tennis, and squash? Furthermore, aren't Worthy and Markle (1970: 440–43) committing a logical fallacy of begging the question when they use as supporting evidence of their hypothesis the fact that, at the time of their research, only

7 percent of major league baseball pitchers were Black while 24 percent of the non-pitchers were Blacks? Clearly, the issue at stake is "Why are there so few Black pitchers?" By offering these percentages, Worthy and Markle merely are rephrasing the question as the answer—a classic case of *petitio principii*.[9]

Other sport analysts argue that, for the most part, stacking is self-initiated and, therefore, has little to do with racism. A version of this argument espoused by Jones and Hochner (1973) contends that Black athletes generally are socialized to prefer sports and positions that emphasize individual work and expressive or stylish performance rather than those that stress teamwork and technical thinking, hence the need and justification for stacking. Another version of this argument suggests that Black youths normally aspire to play the same positions that successful Black athletes (or role models) play, thereby perpetuating the phenomenon of stacking (McPherson 1975). Whatever the reasons for stacking, recent evidence of Black success in a variety of non-traditional sports and positions across the globe proves that the supposition that Blacks are not intelligent enough for any position is absurd, to put it mildly.

Stacking has subtle implications and residual effects that go beyond the playing field. For one thing, central-position players are more likely be appointed as coaches, managers, and televisions analysts when they retire from active sport (Vogler and Schwartz 1993). Moreover, stacking limits its victims' chances of getting sponsorship and being selected for commercial endorsements. Unlike in the U.S., television commercials and corporate sponsorships for athletes are fairly difficult to come by in Canada. The situation is doubly tough for Black athletes, who, by all accounts, have been under-represented when it comes to sport-based television commercials, public recognitions, and awards in Canada. In the next section we examine the Canadian Athlete Assistance Program (AAP) and its impacts on equity in sports, giving special attention to Blacks.

The Canadian Athlete Assistance Program (AAP) and Equity in Sport

To what extent is Canadian sport egalitarian? Earlier studies, including Gruneau (1976) and Kenyon (1977), found that most of Canada's high-performance athletes were White middle- and upper-income-class males. Like many nations, Canada is now committed to equity in sport. Sport Canada is quite explicit about this; its *1998–2001 Strategic Direction* states:

> [The agency seeks] to provide leadership and support to increase access and equity in sport for athletes with disability; to provide leadership and support to achieve equitable opportunities for

> female athletes, coaches, officials and leaders ... to promote
> participation in sport among Aboriginal people [and] to foster the
> inclusion of visible minority Canadians in sport.[10]

The federal government—both directly and through partnerships with
provincial/territorial governments, sport organizations, and the private
sector—provides financial support to athletes, coaches, and sport clubs to
enhance accessibility. For the most part, though, the federal funding for
athletes through the nation's Athlete Assistance Program (AAP) focuses on
elite or high-performance athletes—those who are or who have the
potential to be among the top sixteen in the world.[11] The financial
assistance provided to these athletes comes in the form a monthly stipend
and some post-secondary tuition allowance where applicable. The 1,263
athletes currently under the AAP's sponsorship are categorized, or carded,
into eight levels, with varying degrees of financial support. The present
monthly stipend ranges from $185 per month for the lowest category of
athletes, to $810 per month for the highest-level athletes. Sport Canada is
in the process of condensing the eight categories into two and is increasing
the stipend to a range of $500 to $1,100 per month.[12]

The pertinent question for our purpose here is whether the AAP is
reconcilable with Sport Canada's objective of making sport equitable and
accessible to all Canadians. Is the focus on high performance in concur-
rence, or inherently at odds, with the notion of equity in sport? It is
indisputable that the AAP has helped Canadians from a variety of socio-
economic backgrounds to pursue their sport careers and to compete in
high-level games such as the Olympics and the Commonwealth Games.
However, as Macintosh and Whitson (1990: 84–85) point out:

> It appears doubtful whether the assistance provided by the
> Canadian government, directly to individuals through the AAP and
> indirectly through Sport Canada contributions to facilities and
> programs oriented towards the elite is enough to keep many
> poorer young men and women in high-performance sport.

Given the high cost of resources (e.g., training, equipment, and club
membership costs) needed in sports such as hockey, figure skating,
swimming, tennis, and golf—not to mention the sheer elitist and country-
club outlook of some of them—it is doubtful whether people from poor
families stand a chance of even starting in these disciplines, let alone
reaching the performance level required to qualify for AAP support. The
situation is certainly different in sports such as track and field, boxing, and
basketball, where equipment, coaching, and other facilities are relatively

cheap and sometimes available for free in public institutions. Here even athletes with nominal resources have a reasonable chance of qualifying for AAP funds, as long as they have the potential and the self-discipline to persevere. No wonder Blacks, many of whom are from poor families, have found a niche in such sports.

The under-representation of people from the working-classes in the nation's AAP is exacerbated by the concentration of top-level sport training facilities on university campuses (and in wealthy neighbourhoods). This spatial distribution pattern has invariably skewed the rate of high-level sport participation and, consequently, AAP qualification in favour of university students and alumni. Not surprisingly, Mackintosh and Whitson (1990: 86) estimated that nearly two-thirds of AAP athletes of university age had attended university.

Gruneau (1976) found that Canada's high-performance athletes in winter sports, as of 1971, were predominantly White males from middle- and upper-income families; another study conducted in the eighties (i.e., Mackintosh and Albinson 1985) substantiated this finding. Thus we find Mackintosh and Whitson (1990: 81) contending that "although Sport Canada remains committed to the democratization of Canadian sport, its Athlete Assistance Program has not succeeded in altering significantly the socio-economic profile of Canadian athletes in Olympic sports." The basic argument here is not that the AAP is discriminatory against Blacks or working-class athletes, but that the program has inadvertently created, or at least reinforced, a class-based bifurcation of sport in Canada—one segment for the rich, the other for the poor. And for Black Canadians, as in the global context, this schism feeds directly into the myth of Blacks being inherently good in some sports but not in others, as we shall see in the next section.

The Apparent Dominance of Blacks in Sport: Are Blacks Naturally Superior in Sport?

"In rummaging through old magazines," writes Earl Smith, professor of American Ethnic Studies at Wake Forest University, "I came across a *Sports Illustrated* that pictures the start of an Olympic 100-metre dash. It showed only the athletes' feet, wearing Nike, Adidas, and Puma running shoes. I often wonder: 'Why are all the feet black?'"[13] It is hard to bring any discussion of Blacks in sport to a close without touching on the sensitive issues surrounding their real or perceived athletic superiority. Why do Blacks perform better in sports than Whites? This is the main question we must address in the rest of this chapter. Others that arise from this are: Does the infamous phrase "White men can't jump" have any empirical foundation? Do Blacks have different muscles that react in different ways than those of Whites? Does the athletic "superiority" of Blacks point to any substantial difference between Blacks and Whites? More importantly, what are the relative roles of environmental and socio-cultural factors, as opposed to biological or anatomical variables, in the making of the Black superathlete?

For more than a century now, coaches, athletes, physicians, physical educators, academicians, journalists, and laypersons have put forth their own theories regarding the athletic abilities of Blacks. In what follows we examine some of the paradigm shifts and controversies surrounding this issue. As one would expect, the literature in this field is highly internationalized with the bulk of it coming from the U.S., but attempts will be made to highlight the Canadian content, for obvious reasons.

The growing sense of Black athletic superiority among Westerners constitutes a dramatic paradigm shift, indeed "a historic reversal of roles in the racial encounter between Africans and the West" (Hoberman 1997: 100). Prior to the late nineteenth century, Blacks were never seen as potential athletes, as Europeans' self-serving sense of intellectual and cultural superiority presumed their physical and athletic superiority over Blacks. As Hoberman (1997: 100) puts it:

> Anglo-Saxon racial self-confidence was built on an athleticism of both physique and temperament, and the conquered or submissive inferior played a role in confirming the masculinity of the explorer or colonist, whose toughness and self-confidence made him a charismatic and athletic figure who was in most cases contemptuous of Africans and Asians as well as the whites who could not keep up with him.

During the colonial era, sport was used to reinforce the subordination and "inferiority" of Blacks and other colonized people. Among Europeans, sport symbolized "education, intelligence, and wealth in a society increasingly marked by class distinction" (Entine 2000: 139)—hence the notion of the Anglo-Saxon scholar-athlete (Stoddart 1988). And, given the close connection between education and the church, it is not surprising that the notion of "muscular Christianity"[14] became popular not only in Europe but also in the colonies. Similarly, Europeans scarcely conferred any capacity for courage on Blacks during the colonial era, notwithstanding the bravery and the sheer tenacity of will-power exhibited by Africans in colonial encounters such as the Ashanti-British Wars of 1824 and 1874, the Zulu War of 1879, and the Mau Mau insurrection in Kenya in the 1950s.[15]

However, faced with the overwhelming dominance of Black athletes in contemporary sport, Whites have no choice but to retreat and abrogate their groundless claims to physical vitality and athletic superiority. At the same time, they have managed to simultaneously downgrade sport from being a symbol of education, intelligence and wealth to a symbol of Black retardation, as we shall soon see. The point here is not to uphold any notion of Black superiority in sports, but to bring to light the intellectual imperialism and hypocrisy exhibited by many Whites in their dealings with Blacks over the years.

Empirical Evidence of Black Dominance in Sport
The evidence of Blacks' domination of global sport is so impressive that assertions regarding the "extinction" or "demise" of the White athlete are now widespread. In the cut-to-the-chase words of Entine (2000: 19):

> Becoming a professional athlete is still a long-shot for aspiring teenagers, but it's a lot longer for whites.... Check the NBA statistics: not one white player has finished among the top scorers or rebounders in recent years. White running backs, cornerbacks, or wide receivers in the NFL? Count them on one hand. Roll the calendar back decades, to the 1950s, to find the last time any white led baseball steals. A white male toeing the line at an Olympic 100-metre final? Not in decades.

Hoberman (1997: XXXV) also writes that the emergence of Blacks "as the most spectacular stars of the summer Olympic Games has also led to White fatalism and fears that the twilight of the Caucasian athlete has at last arrived." Similar concerns have been raised in major European centres where the lucrative and popular sports of soccer, track, and boxing are increasingly being taken over by Blacks (Kew 1997; Cashmore 1990). It is estimated that by the late 1980s, "over half of the British boxing champions were Blacks as were more than 40 percent of the Olympic squad of 1988 and virtually every football [i.e., soccer] league club had two or more Black players in its books" (Cashmore 1990: 85–86). And this is how Helmut Digel, the president of the German Track and Field Federation sums up his frustration:

> In the developed countries, track and field is caught in a deep crisis: the athletes see the superiority of the Africans in distance races [and the sprints] and many simply give up. No young person is going to train for the title of the "world's fastest white man."[16]

While the trend in Canada is not as pervasive yet, due primarily to the smallness of the Black population here, the information presented in preceding sections suggests that the accomplishment of Canadian Blacks in sport is impressive. The Canadian outdoor all-time rankings for track and field, compiled by Andy Buchstein and Cecil Smith, show that all of the top times recorded by men in Canadian sprints and jumps, including 100-metre, 200-metre, and high jump, have been set by Blacks; the statistics for women are not much different either.[17]

While the dominance of Black athletes cuts across many sport disciplines, it is doubly overwhelming in elite track and field. Analysis by Entine (2000) indicates that Blacks hold the world running records from the 100-metre dash through the 400 metres, together with their corresponding relays and hurdles, to the 10,000-metre race and the marathon. In fact, all of the athletes who have ever run the 100-metre dash under 10 seconds are Black: Frankie Frederick of Namibia; Maurice Green, Dennis Mitchell, and Carl Lewis of the U.S.; Alto Boldon of Trinidad and Tobago; Linford Christie of the U.K.; and our own Bruny Surin, Ben Johnson and Donovan Bailey (Entine 2000: 35). The fastest time ever recorded by a White athlete in the 100-metre sprint is 10.15 seconds, set by the Austrian Andreas Berger in 1993. Unfortunately, like many athletes in contemporary sport, Berger's career fell victim to doping scandals.

Until the 1960s, the general belief was that Blacks were good only in sprints and not in long-distance events—hence the cliché "great speed but little stamina" (Wiggins 1997: 9). As with the earlier myth about Whites' physical vitality and athletic superiority, few will now stand by this racist fairy tale, given the performance of East African long-distance runners in the Olympics and world championships. This particular pseudo-theory started to crumble in 1968, when East African runners won gold medals in long-distance events, and in 1978 when the Kenyan Henry Rono set world records for the 3,000-, 5,000-, and 10,000-metre runs (Vogler and Schwartz 1993: 111). Now the Kenyan hegemony in mid- and long-distance runs hardly can escape any observer of the international sport scene.

According to Entine (2000: 36), Kenyans now hold "more than half of the top times at 5,000 and 10,000 metres [and] hold the top 60-plus times in the 3,000-metre steeplechase." Also, Kenyan men have won the prestigious Boston Marathon every year since 1991; they have won world cross-country championships every year since 1986; and they have captured almost every world junior road-racing championship imaginable (Entine 2000). As one runner puts it, after finishing behind several Kenyan runners in the 1998 Cherry Blossom race in Washington: "They are not only slaughtering the Americans, they are slaughtering everybody" (Bloom 1998: C24). Indeed, some athletes and sport authorities have shown publicly their resentment towards the Kenyan hegemony and have initiated "conspiracy plans" to limit Kenyan entries in their meets (Bloom 1998: A1).

How do we account for the Black dominance in sport? Explanations have come from two main schools of thought. On the one hand are those who attribute the phenomenon to the biological make-up, or the "natural" advantages, of Blacks; on the other are those who attribute it to environmental and socio-cultural factors—i.e., nurture. In addition to these two extremes are those who situate themselves somewhere in the middle, with varying degrees of tilting, depending on factors such as the nature/level of discourse and the targeted audience.

Before we delve into the hydra-headed nature-nurture debate, two clarifications are in order. First, the notion of Black dominance in sport as used here connotes the excellence achieved by Blacks, relative to Whites, in sports such as boxing, track and field, basketball, soccer, football, and baseball, which have attracted significant number of Blacks for one reason or another. Implicitly, there are several other sports, including swimming, fencing, curling, tennis, ice-hockey and, until quite recently, golf and many others, in which Whites dominate. Second, Black dominance in sport does not go beyond the playing fields to the sidelines and boardrooms where the coaching and other key management decisions concerning trades, contracts, advertising, reporting, and team ownership are made. It is difficult to say whether or not the athletic success of Blacks has created only the illusion of Black dominance in the face of a modern-day plantation-like situation where Blacks sweat on the playing fields, albeit for sky-high incomes, while Whites control the boardrooms

The Nature-versus-Nurture Debate on Black Athletic Aptitude

Are Blacks naturally superior athletes? Is their ascendancy in sport biologically grounded? More importantly, does it provide evidence of substantial racial difference and, if so, what are the implications? Proponents of the nature argument (notably Martin Kane 1971) generally contend that Blacks are imbued with superior physiology, and this explains their dominance in the playing field. "Why has there never been a White Michael Jordan" is a common playful query from this camp. As the thought-provoking work of John Hoberman notes, some further assert that Blacks are substantially different from Whites and that the two groups "are distinct racial subspecies which have evolved special traits and capacities" (1997: 147). Not only that, some nature advocates believe in a racial hierarchy in which Blacks, the "bottom dwellers," are the racial antithesis of Whites. Extreme versions of the nature argument, including those espoused by the notorious Canadian psychologist Philippe Rushton

(1988, 1990, 1995), interpret racial difference as being synonymous with Black deficiency or retardation.

Conversely, ardent supporters of the nurture camp, including Ellis Cashmore (1990), Jonathan Marks (1995), Harry Edwards (1970, 1973), and W.M. Cobb (1934, 1936), attribute the athletic excellence of Blacks primarily to socio-cultural factors. To these analysts, Blacks do better in sport because they are forced by racism, and its attendant socio-economic deprivation and poverty, to approach sport with greater zeal and dedication, as their entire future may depend on it. Thus, while White athletes may have other career paths, Blacks tend to have little or nothing else to fall back on. Furthermore, as with all ethnoracial groups, Black youths identify with, idolize, and emulate successful Blacks—and more often than not, these successful Blacks are in sports and entertainment. Thus, the Black involvement in sport is somewhat self-perpetuating. As to why there has not been a White Michael Jordan, the simple, yet potent, answer from the nurture camp is that "until quite recently, there was no Black Michael Jordan either" (Marks 1995: 237).

Many in the nurture camp argue that the nature advocates' growing fixation with Black physiology is nothing more than an underhanded attempt to dehumanize Blacks by projecting an image of them as primitive and physical with limited mental capabilities (Cashmore 1990; Edwards 1970, 1973). Critics in the nurture camp say that this explains why the nature advocates hesitate to attribute White dominance in sports such as tennis or ice hockey to genes and muscles. Is there some form of cultural chauvinism or biological apartheid at play here?

The nature-nurture debate has gotten so vitriolic that some commentators are now calling it a civil war. For instance, Jon Entine (2000: 332), in his masterpiece *Taboo: Why Black Athletes Dominate Sports and Why We Are Afraid to Talk About It,* observed: "This debate resonates not of civil discourse but of civil war." Entine's title itself speaks loudly about the storm surrounding this topic. A striking feature of the debate so far is that most of the strong nature advocates (e.g., Martin Kane and Jimmy Snyder) are White, while the leading proponents of the nurture side are Black (e.g., W.M. Cobb and Harry Edwards). One wonders whether the debate is inherently racist. In any case, it is fair to say that while Whites have been the main promoters of the biological thesis and its tilt towards the confirmation of racial difference, some Blacks have adopted similar positions when it is convenient to do so.

Hoberman (1997) notes that the available literature on Black athleticism falls into two broad categories. The first is made up of scientific publications that compare "the anatomical features and physiological processes that may be relevant to athletic performance"; the second "presents a credulous and incongruous mixture of folklore and brief account of what is assumed to be scientific progress in unravelling the mysteries of racial biology" (Hoberman 1997: 190). In a nutshell, the literature involves materials from both genuine science and "tabloid" or pseudo-science.

The arguments of Martin Kane fall into the latter category. In, a 1971 jargon-soaked article entitled "An Assessment of 'Black is Best,'" this senior editor for *Sports Illustrated* argues that Blacks are endowed with a natural ability that gives them advantage in sport. He argues that an increasing body of scientific opinion suggests that physical differences between Blacks and Whites may enhance the athletic abilities of the former. Quoting a wide variety of sources and interviews with coaches, physicians, and athletes, Kane presents a litany of anatomical features that give Blacks an advantage over Whites in sport: a denser skeletal structure, longer legs, narrower hips, wider calf bones, and a more elongated body. Kane also believes in the folkloric "Middle Passage theory," which posits that Black hardiness is due to the fact that slavery weeded out the weak leaving only the toughest to survive the trans-Atlantic shipment. As Cashmore (1990: 88) points out, aren't mental abilities—i.e., intelligence, ingenuity, and anticipation—equally, if not more, important in matters of survival than physical abilities? And, isn't the time frame here too short in biological evolutionary terms?

Jimmy "the Greek" Snyder, a twelve-year veteran on the CBS show *The NFL Today*, lost his job for espousing fairly similar views. On January 15, 1988, he told a TV interviewer in Washington DC that Blacks do better in sport because "they were bred to be that way since the days of slavery" (quoted in Wiggins 1997: 194). Jimmy Snyder traced the beginning of Black athleticism to the period of the civil war when "the slave owner would breed his big black man with this big woman so that he could have a big black kid" (quoted in Wiggins 1997: 194). He was concerned about Blacks becoming coaches, saying that there would not be anything left for Whites in sport if the trend caught on (Wiggins 1997: 194).

The abundance of biological evidence concocted over the centuries to account for Black athleticism and to reinforce a sense of racial difference is simply astounding. The superior performance of Black athletes in sprinting and jumping has long been attributed to Blacks having longer heel bones and stronger Achilles tendons than Whites (Wiggins 1997: 194), even though there is no evidence that all, or even many, Black athletes exhibit these physiological characteristics. Indeed, after conducting a comprehensive anthropometric measurement of Jesse Owens, the renowned African-American anthropologist William Montague Cobb (1936) concluded that Owens did not possess the type of calf, foot, and heel bones commonly and speciously associated with Blacks, and that Owens' features were more of a Caucasoid type rather than a Negroid type.

More than three decades earlier a similar finding emerged in France. In 1901 Marshall "Major" Taylor, the famous African-American bicycle racer from Indianapolis, was examined by French physicians at the Academy of Science in Bordeaux to see whether he was anatomically different. After examining Taylor's heart, bones, and muscles, and after taking the necessary anthropometric measurements, they concluded that he "could be said to be absolutely perfect were it not for the fact that because of his bicycle racing, which has exaggerated the size of certain of his leg muscles, his thighs were a little over developed" (Ritchie 1988: 174). The 1941 work of the Jewish physiologist Ernst Jokl in South Africa is equally remarkable in this context. After comparing the physical strength, skills, and endurance of people from a wide variety of ethnoracial backgrounds, including Afrikaners, Jews, Bantus, Indians, Cape Coloured, and Chinese, Jokl and his colleagues concluded that "with the similarity between the standards of physical performance found in the different racial groups, no more impressive evidence of the basic equality of man has ever been reported" (quoted in Hoberman 1997: 146). Evidently, not even the shackles of apartheid were enough to undermine the open-mindedness of Jokl and his colleagues.

As noted earlier, until recently the general belief in Western sport circles was that Blacks do not have stamina. Now, thanks to Kenyans, Western sport theoreticians have been found back-peddling to the extent that some are now shamelessly, and quite patronizingly, dubbing the best White distance runners as "White-Kenyans."[18] The prevalent explanation now is that Kenyans do well in endurance races because the high-altitude environment in which they live and train makes them more efficient at metabolizing oxygen, as though Kenya is the only country with mountains.[19] Of course, there are some indications that altitude influences human aerobics. For instance, Bengt Saltin and his colleagues found in their analysis of Kenyan, South African, and Scandinavian athletes that they all tend to generate lower fatigue producing lactate toxins in their blood, and that they perform relatively better than athletes from other regions of the world; Saltin and his colleagues attributed this finding to the mountainous environments in which the athletes live (quoted in Hoberman 1997: 206–07). At the same time, it does not take much analytical savvy to realize that there is more to successful endurance running than acclimating oneself to living in high altitudes, else the Nepalese and Tibetans would be the best distance runners in the world, given the topography of their land.

As to why there are few Black swimmers, the textbook answer has been that Blacks have denser bones and water-absorbing skin, which reduce their buoyancy. Yet this often invoked, but seldom examined, no-buoyancy theory could not stand in the way of the young Black woman from the small Caribbean island of Curaçao, who became the world's fastest female swimmer in 1974 (Hoberman 1997: 139), and the Black swimmer from Surinam, Anthony Nesty, who won the Olympic gold medal in the 100-metre butterfly in 1988 (Entine 2000: 282–83).

No less a gentleman and sport icon than Jack Nicklaus could not avoid the temptation, or the misfortune, of being sucked into the vortex of this contentious debate. Blacks "have different muscles that react in different ways," was Nicklaus' response when a Canadian sports writer asked him in a 1994 interview to account for the minuscule number of Blacks in elite golf (quoted in Shapiro 1994: C6). One wonders what the Golden Bear's answer would be now, given Tiger Woods' performance. Like many other non-Blacks who have ventured recklessly into this debate, Nicklaus was subjected to harsh criticism until he took the infamous "I was misquoted/misinterpreted" escape route (Shapiro 1994: C6). A year later, Sir Roger Bannister, a retired Oxford dean, was embroiled in a similar situation across the Atlantic. Speaking at a conference organized by the British Association for the Advancement of Science on September 13, 1995, Bannister, who is a trained neurologist, observed: "I am prepared to risk political incorrectness by drawing attention to the seemingly obvious but under stressed fact that black sprinters and black athletes in general all seem to have certain *natural* anatomical advantages" (quoted in Entine 2000: 11, emphasis added). As Hoberman (1997: 144) points out, what Dr. Bannister overlooks in his carefully worded observation is that "what is obvious is Black performance rather than Black anatomy." Like Nicklaus, Bannister was severely chastised by the (British) Black community.

The sheer depth of the urge among many Whites to explain nearly all facets of Black athleticism from the standpoint of Black anatomy is simply astonishing. Even more astounding, though, is the fact that some of the physical attributes assigned to Blacks over the years contradict what one would normally expect among high-performance athletes. As the work of Hoberman (1997) shows, findings associating Blacks with inferior pulmonary capacity and weaker lungs persisted in the Western "scientific" literature well into the 1960s. Obviously Blacks must be "freaks of nature" to have weaker lungs and still be better endurance runners. If this does not surprise you, the nineteenth-century racist physician Samuel Cartwright's observation that a Black man's "blood is blacker than the White man's" would (quoted in Hoberman 1997: 127).

It is fair to acknowledge that not only Whites engage in this infatuation with Black physiology. Pre-eminent Black athletes, including the Olympic overachiever Carl Lewis, the notorious O.J. Simpson, and the Baseball Hall of Famer Joe Morgan, all have alluded to Blacks' superior physique. This is how O.J. formulates his position: "We are built a little differently, built for speed—skinny calves, long legs, high asses are all characteristics of Blacks.... I'll argue with any doctor that physically we're geared to speed, and most sports have something to do with speed" (*Time* 1977: 58). In a similar vein, Joe Morgan asserts that "Blacks, for physiological reasons, have better speed, quickness, and agility.... I don't know why, but we are clearly superior in that way" (quoted in Rhoden 1974: 137). At least, unlike O.J. Simpson, Joe Morgan admits his ignorance.

The question then is: Why has the *nature* argument—which indeed has made "nature" *the* N-word—become such a minefield for Whites, in particular? The answer lies in the law of compensation, which claims an inverse relationship between brain and brawn, between intelligence and physical ability. Many Blacks believe that behind the intricate maze of scientific technicalities about Black anatomy lies a hesitancy on the part of some Whites to credit Blacks with being smart. In fact, the belief that some Whites cannot bring themselves to appreciate any accomplishment made by Blacks is widespread. But, who can blame these Black cynics when we have people like Canadian Alliance MP Rob Anders branding a Black cultural and political icon like Nelson Mandela (a Nobel Peace Prize winner) as a "Communist and a terrorist"; and who can forget Toronto Mayor Mel Lastman's recent comments on Kenyans?[20] The perception in the nurture camp is that, by stressing Blacks' physicality, Whites are underhandedly underrating Blacks' intelligence. This is how Cashmore (1990: 88) captures this concern: "[I]f we accept as proof of the natural ability argument the outstanding results recorded by black sports performers then what are we to infer from the 'underachievement' of blacks in formal education? That they are naturally limited intellectually?"

The law of compensation was developed in the nineteenth century by Charles Darwin in his epochal *Descent of Man*. This anachronistic evolutionary folklore underlies much of what is being disseminated by some nature advocates; at least that is the belief among many sophisticated Blacks. Recent advocates of Darwin's law include Richard Herrnstein and Charles Murray in their notorious book, *The Bell Curve* (1994), which has been compared with Hitler's *Mein Kampf* and described as "Nazi propaganda wrapped in a cover of pseudo-scientific respectability."[21] *The Bell Curve* pontificates, quite laboriously, on racial disparities in both IQ scores and criminal behaviour. Typically, Blacks occupy the bottom rung in all indicators presented in the book.

Many other modern scientists have espoused the law of compensation, but none has been more outrageous than Philippe Rushton, a Canadian psychologist at the University of Western Ontario. In his *Race, Evolution, and Behaviour: A Life-History Perspective* (1995), Rushton argues that each race in the world evolved by relying on its own unique set of reproductive strategies to cope with its physical environment. Those who evolved in warm but unpredictable climates—notably Africans—adopted a strategy of high reproduction, whereas those who settled in the moderate cold of Europe and the more hostile environment of northern Asia took to reproducing fewer children but nurturing them more carefully. These strategies, according to Rushton, led to differences in brain size and intelligence, with Africans again occupying the lowest rung and having the lowest IQ, the highest sex drive, and the highest proclivity towards crime. Asians, in the Rushtonian voodoo theory of life-history, surpass Whites in brain size and intelligence and have the lowest sex drive.

One wonders why nearly 60 percent of the world's population is in Asia, while Africa has less than 15 percent. Also, any reading of the leading population theories, notably the Demographic Transition Model and the Malthusian Theory,[22] will quickly reveal the weaknesses of Rushton's life history. Both theories show that Europe was not immune to high birth rates or high population growth. Needless to say, the propensity to have more children has more to do with poverty, religion, and other cultural factors than Rushton's environmentalism. Rushton even contends that Hitler's army fought effectively because of its genetic purity (*Winnipeg Free Press* 1989: 11). Like many racist scientists, Rushton predicts that the ongoing Human Genome Project will tell us "more about ourselves than any of us are prepared to know" (*Calgary Herald* 1989: D7). If Rushton (or any of the extreme nature proponents) really thinks, for instance, that there is an "athletic gene" somewhere in the Black body to be discovered by the Genome project, then he is in for a long, tedious search.

Rushton has been bombarded by student demonstrations, investigated by provincial authorities, and severely chastised by Michael Ziegler, Frederic Weizmann, Neil Weiner and David Wiesenthal, who were among his academic colleagues at York University's psychology department. In fact, former Ontario Premier David Peterson even called for Rushton's dismissal. In a scathing joint article in *The Canadian Forum*, Ziegler et al. (1989) describe Rushton's work as shoddy and incompetent. In their view he either misunderstands the works he cites or he wilfully misinterprets them. They contend that Rushton often is selective in his use of evidence, largely ignoring counter-evidence. His work is essentially a voodoo science in which one takes "a tape measure, put[s] it around people's head" and tells us who is more intelligent (Ziegler et al. 1989: 20). In fact, Rushton admitted before a TV audience that his data leave a lot to be desired.[23]

The fact that Rushton received research funds from the eugenist Pioneer Fund[24] and published his tabloid-science papers in extreme right wing journals such as *Mankind Quarterly* is hardly surprising. What perplexes many observers, however, is how he was able to secure a tenured position at Western, win the prestigious Guggenheim Fellowship (1988–89), become a fellow of both the American and Canadian Psychological Associations, and pass all of his professional evaluations until 1990 when he became too scandalous to handle (Hoberman 1997; Entine, 2000; Ziegler et al. 1989).

Studies show that women have smaller brains than do men, even after controlling for body weight. Nevertheless, men and women score virtually the same on IQ tests (Jensen 1969). Until recently many were those who took as gospel truth the view that women were not as smart or as good in mathematics and science as men. Any objective contemporary teacher, or student, knows better now. Similarly, there are well-grounded scientific studies that indicate that Blacks and Whites exhibit some physiological differences. The fundamental question, though, is whether we now know enough about the physiological traits that produce good athletes to even start accounting for racial disparities in sport based on physiological difference. Also, are the observed physiological differences fundamental enough to justify our growing fixations with racial distinctions?

Interestingly, some of the most respected and often-cited scientific works on Black-White differences in muscles and metabolism are by Canadian scientist Pierre Ama and his colleagues Pierre Lagasse, Claude Bouchard, and Jena Aimé Simoneau at Laval University in Quebec City. In a 1986 study they compared the muscles of Black West African non-athletes with those of White French Canadian non-athletes and found that, on average, the Africans had 67.5 percent fast-twitch muscle fibre while the Whites had 59 percent, which led them to conclude that Blacks are "well endowed to perform in sports events of short duration" (Ama et al. 1986: 510).[25] Indeed, a study by Australian scientists North et al. (1999) lends some support to this conclusion. They found that more Asians and Whites than Black Africans tended to have what they dubbed "wimp genes."[26]

It is important to note that when the Laval University scientists replicated their study in 1990, they could not find any significant difference between the muscles of their West African and French Canadian subjects. Consequently, they readily admitted that this result contradicts earlier suppositions, including their own, that Blacks are naturally endowed with muscles that give them an advantage in sprints and jumps (Ama et al. 1990). They found, however, that their African subjects became tired quicker than their White Canadian counterparts.

Jon Entine summarizes the purported physiological difference between Black West Africans and "others" as follows:

Blacks with West African ancestry generally have relatively less
subcutaneous fat on arms and legs ... broader shoulders, larger
quadriceps, and bigger, more developed musculature in general.
[They also have] smaller chest cavities, a higher centre of gravity,
narrow hips and lighter calves ... greater body density ... modest,
but significantly higher, levels of plasma testosterone [and] ... a
higher percentage of fast-twitch muscles and more anaerobic
enzyme, which can translate into more explosive energy. (2000:
268–69)

Like many analysts, Entine presents these facts as though they are
gospel truths without cautioning readers about the availability of contradictory findings. His focus on West Africans is understandable as he traces
all of the outstanding sprinters and jumpers to that part of Africa, but he
refuses to say with which group he is comparing the West Africans. The
ambiguity in the statement "West Africans have smaller chest cavities"
cannot be ignored. Is he comparing West Africans with East or North
Africans, or Asians? Are we supposed to guess here? Most likely he has
Whites in mind, but the question remains, What makes Whites, or whatever
group he chooses, the standard human group against which he can
justifiably assert that the West African attributes are bigger, smaller, higher,
or longer? Why not consider the African features as the standard for once?
Also one is at a loss to discover what area Entine considers as West Africa;
he attempts no such geographic delimitation explicitly.

Do we really know which physiological attributes produce the
different proficiencies in sport? Do we have enough White athletes in elite-
level track and field, for instance, to make reasonably scientific comparisons? Do such dramatic physiological comparisons feed into the prejudice
that Blacks are inherently primitive, or not? Can we assume that all West
Africans—let alone all Blacks—are physiologically homogenous when we
consider the impact of environmental and cultural factors (diet, eating
habits, and child-rearing practices) on human biology? Put differently, is
there a single physical feature, including skin colour, that all Black have in
common? Do we even know how the relatively pampered life of
Westerners and the harsh rough-and-tumble life of Africans over the
centuries affect their respective athletic performances? Isn't the nature–
nurture schism a false dichotomy, after all?

In the final analysis, the nature–nurture debate amounts to nothing but
a futile effort to separate the inseparable. There is no real split between
biological and cultural factors, for all practical purposes; both are intrinsically implicated in the athleticism of both Blacks and Whites. The
feedback loops between the physiological and socio-cultural factors that

influence proficiency in sport are highly convoluted, and as the preceding discussion indicates the exact nature of the relevant variables from either camp, and their attendant forward and backward linkages, are not yet well understood. Indeed, as of now, we cannot even identify, let alone control for, all of the socio-cultural factors in our attempt to determine the exclusive role of human physiology in sport performance. In reality there is no separate nature or nurture camp. It so happens that some observers are seduced by the sheer simplicity and the intuitive, albeit problematic, appeal of the nature arguments. As Gunnar Myrdal points out in *An American Dilemma*, "To conceive that apparent difference in capacities and aptitudes could be cultural in origin ... requires difficult and complicated thinking about a multitude of mutually dependent variables, thinking which does not easily break into the lazy formalism of unintellectual people" (1944: 98–99).

Conclusion

The preceding analysis shows that not even in sport—the most level playing field—have Canadian Blacks escaped the shackles of racial discrimination and dehumanization. While systemic anti-Black exclusions, prohibitions, and stacking are virtually non-existent now in Canadian sport, there seems to be an increase in stereotypical and folkloric thinking concerning Black athleticism. We have noted that, although they are relatively few in number, Blacks have made an impressive contribution to elite sport in Canada, especially in disciplines such as track and field, football, and basketball, where the start-up resources for prospective athletes are not very costly.

The excellent achievements of Blacks in sport have spawned intense debate on Black athletic aptitude, a debate that so far has generated more heat than light. Worse still, there are indications that the competing camps of the dispute are being fortified, quite riskily, along racial lines. While a White person might consider it a compliment to say that a Black athlete has a "natural" ability in sport, the latter may, quite understandably, consider this as a denigration of his or her personal sacrifice and dedication; some may even consider it a racist comment, given the history of this "compliment" in the Western world. Many Black intellectuals accept Black "superiority" in sport, but they attribute this to socio-cultural variables rather than biological or genetic factors. It is reasoned that Blacks with the necessary physical attributes tend to work harder than their White counterparts in sport, as the latter usually have other things they would rather do.

The Black dominance in sport has created a discernible inferiority complex among many Whites, the corollary of which is the danger of a misguided sense of racial superiority or arrogance on the part of some Blacks. Especially vulnerable are gullible Black youths, many of whom are diverting all of their energies toward sport to the virtual neglect of intellectual endeavours. The unfortunate part of this sport obsession is that few Black intellectuals and parents are prepared to voice the pitfalls of this trend. British sport sociologist Ellis Cashmore writes in *Making Sense of Sport* (1990) that when he talked about the self-destructive nature of the Black obsession with sports in his earlier book *Black Sportsmen* (1982), he was summarily chastised by the British Black community. His critics contend that sport is one of the very few areas in which Blacks can feel superior and that Cashmore's book seems to have taken even that away from them.

At the risk of attracting such misguided, myopic criticism from the Canadian Black community, this author would like to add his voice to that of Cashmore and call for a calculated balance between Black athleticism and Black intellectualism. There is nothing intrinsically bad about sport; no one can deny that sport has been valuable to Blacks over the years. It has enhanced the sense of identity, community, and self-worth among many Blacks, not to mention the phenomenal economic and health benefits that sport has bestowed upon Blacks. After all, who can dispute the dictum *mens sana in corpore sano*.[27] The Black community here and elsewhere must learn to approach intellectual pursuit with the same vigour as it approaches sport, however. Otherwise, stereotypes of Black intellectual inability will persist, notwithstanding conclusive evidence of racial exclusions, which dissuade many Black youths from pursuing academically-oriented careers. Worse still, unless this infatuation with sport is squarely confronted and dealt with, the Black emancipatory project will remain a figment of our imagination. Harry Edwards' (1970: 70) scathing admonition is worth stressing here: "The only difference between the black man shining shoes in the ghetto and the champion black sprinter is that the shoe shine man is a nigger, while the sprinter is a fast nigger."

Notes

1. Entertainment may also be considered an area in which Blacks have outperformed their White counterparts.
2. Stacking refers to the disproportionate concentration of Blacks in non-central (as opposed to central) positions in team sports.
3. As preposterous as this condition may sound now, we must note that many Blacks had to agree to lose before they were allowed to fight Whites at the time (McPherson, et al. 1989).
4. African-American sprinters Tommie Smith and John Carlos, after winning gold and bronze medals, respectively, in the 200-metre went to the awards

podium and raised their fists (in the infamous Black power salute) in silent protest against racism, while the U.S. national anthem was being played. As Entine (2000: 229) points out, they offered themselves as public sacrifice for African-Americans frustrated by the racial injustice meted out to them in their own country.

5. Note that an NBA team was established in Toronto in 1949, but did not last long; the team was called the Toronto Huskies.

6. James (Jesse) Cleveland Owens (1913–1980), the African-American athlete single-handedly undermined Hitler's White supremacist ideology during the Berlin "Nazi Olympics" of 1936, by winning four gold medals—in the 100 m, 200 m, long jump, and 400 m relay. This recorded stood for 40 years.

7. The other person is obviously Donovan Bailey; both men have a personal best of 9.84 seconds.

8. At the 1988 Seoul Olympics, Jamaican-born Canadian Ben Johnson a won the 100-metre gold medal in the time of 9.79 seconds. Our collective and individual celebrations were short-lived, however, as Johnson tested positive for steroids and was stripped of his gold and suspended from competition for two years.

9. This is the logical fallacy of begging the question.

10. *Sport Canada Strategic Plan, 1998–2001*: 1–2, http://www.pch.gc.ca/sportcanada/SC_E/strate.htm [Accessed on June 26, 2001].

11. Sport Canada. 2001. *Athlete Assistance Program: Backgrounder.* http://www.pch.gc.ca/sportcanada/Sc_e/aapall.htm. [Accessed on June 26, 2001: 1.

12. Ibid, p. 1–2.

13. Earl Smith made this observation in his forward to Entine's *Taboo* (2000: ix)

14. "Muscular Christianity" refers to the use of the church to spread throughout the colonies the purported connection between healthy sport and the "civilizing" properties of Christianity. As part of this project, many Christian ministers became athletes or sport figures and vice versa. Examples include the Reverend A.V. Lyttleton, who became the president of the Wodehouse Cricket Club in the Kimberley region of South Africa in the 1890s. Also, C.T. Studd gave up a promising career in cricket to take up missionary work. See Stoddart 1988 for more examples of muscular Christians.

15. For a comprehensive coverage of these colonial conflicts, consult Robert Edgerton's *Like Lions They Fought* (1988). While the main focus of the book is on the Zulu War, there is extensive coverage of the Ashanti Wars and the Mau Mau uprising. In Chapter 1, writing under the dramatic title "Never Has Such a Disaster Happened to the English Army," Edgerton notes that more British officers died in a single battle during the Zulu War "than were killed in all the fighting at Waterloo" (4). Moreover, "no British battalion had ever before lost so many of its officers in a single battle. Six companies of a veteran British regiment had been killed to the last man. That too, was unheard of" (Edgerton 1988: 4).

16. See "Die Profis abkoppeln," *Der Speigel*, August 23, 1993: 144.

17. For a comprehensive listing consult the Canadian Outdoor All-time Rankings at http://home.eol.ca/~ontrack/all_time_men_2001.htm; accessed on June 15, 2001. For the women's record substitute "women" for "men" in the above web address.

18. The fact that White distance runners are being called "White-Kenyans" was noted by Hoberman (2000: 40).

19. Kenya has highlands, but obviously highlands are not unique to Kenya. In fact, the highest peak in Africa, Mount Kilimanjaro (5,895 metres) is in North Tanzania. This height is not even close to that of the highlands in the Himalayas, which peak at Everest in South Asia between Tibet and Nepal at the height of 8,848 metres. Even the Andes mountain system, which extends some 7,250 km along the entire west coast of South America with an average height of 3,900 metres, peaks at Aconcagua with the height of 6,960 m. Comparable heights can be found in the Cordillera of British Columbia.

20. Rob Anders' comment came during a parliamentary vote to grant Mandela an honorary citizenship of Canada. See the *Globe and Mail*, Thursday, June 7, 2001: A1 for the full story.

"What the hell would I want to go to a place like Mombasa.... I just see myself in a pot of boiling water with all these natives dancing around me" was Mayor Mel Lastman's words suggesting that he was afraid to go to Kenya as part of Toronto's 2008 Olympic bidding team. Believe it or not, Lastman was about to leave for Kenya to solicit support for Toronto's bid, and he just couldn't help himself. Situate this comment not only in the context of Kenya's accomplishments in the Olympics, but also in the fact that Lastman was going to plead for votes in Kenya, and you will realize the depth of the contempt he holds for Africans. Very likely Lastman's comment contributed, at least in part, to Toronto's defeat by Beijing for the 2008 Olympics. See the *Globe and Mail*, Friday June 22, 2001: A1, A14; *Ottawa Citizen* Online, Friday, June 22, 2001: 1–3) at http://www.ottawacitizen.com/sport/. Note that in the chapter, the word "some" is emphasized to stress that not all Whites hold such views; the biting criticisms levelled against Rob Anders and Mayor Lastman by most White Canadians attest to this.

21. Entine (200: 238) attributes this comparison and description to Steven J. Rosenthal of Hampton University, who reviewed *The Bell Curve*.

22. Consult any introduction to human geography text for more information on the Malthusian and Demographic Transition models. A good starting point is William Norton's *Human Geography* (Toronto: Oxford University Press, 1998).

23. He made this admission on the *Geraldo* show, hosted by Geraldo Rivera, in February 1989 (*Calgary Herald* 1989).

24. The secretive Pioneer Fund has provided research funding to many extreme right-wingers. Wickliffe Draper, a textile magnate who openly admired Hitler, established the fund in 1937.

25. Exercise physiologists usually divide muscles into two groups: Type I or fast-twitch and Type II or slow-twitch. It is generally believed that the former is good for explosive bursts of speed while the latter is good for endurance (Ama et al. 1986).

26. These are defective genes that limit the formation of a-acctinine-3, which is believed to be responsible for the explosive power of the human muscle.

27. This is the dictum that "a healthy mind can be found in a healthy body."

Chapter 8

Managing Race and Ethnic Relations in Canada

Official Multiculturalism and Blacks

The analyses pursued in nearly all of the preceding chapters suggest that a fundamental problem facing Blacks has to do with the entrapments of racial discrimination. Until the 1960s, racialized evaluations were used not only to restrict the flow of Blacks into Canada, but also to determine the types of jobs and incomes suitable for the few Blacks who lived in this country. The slow abandonment of racism in Canadian government policies started with the introduction of the *Canadian Bill of Rights* in 1960 and was followed by the removal of racial criteria from immigration policies in 1962 and the subsequent introduction of the point system in 1967. Other government initiatives in this area include the enunciation of official multiculturalism in 1971 and the enactment of the *Human Rights Act* in 1978, the *Charter of Rights and Freedoms* in 1982, the *Employment Equity Act* in 1986, and the *Multiculturalism Act* in 1988.

Notwithstanding these laudable endeavours, Blacks and other visible minorities are still victimized by racial discrimination in nearly all visages of Canadian society. Peter Li (1998) in his recent paper "The Market Value and Social Value of Race" demonstrates how Canadian society continues to attribute lower socio-economic worth to Blacks and other visible minorities despite its general acceptance of democratic principles such as equality and justice. As we noted in Chapter 2, Henry et al. (1995) have dubbed this apparent contradiction "democratic racism." Many expositors of race relations, including Li (1998), Allahar (1993), Nelson and Fleras (1995), and Satzewich (1993), are now convinced that racial problems are rooted not so much in personal attitudes as in societal structures and broader socio-economic and political pursuits. Indeed, the works of Li (1998) and Satzewich (1993) leave no escape from the conclusion that racial discrimination is used as a vehicle to procure cheap labour, to divide the working class, and, ultimately, to help consolidate the capitalist status quo. Heightened concern about the structural roots of racial problems has intensified the call for institutional reforms that reflect the differential access to social, economic, and political power at the societal level. Given the history of Canada, it is not irrational to assert that without government intervention racial discrimination could get worse, especially in times of economic downturn.

Of all the government initiatives for managing racial discrimination in Canada, few have received the same level of attention and notoriety as the policies of multiculturalism and employment equity (Fleras and Elliott 1992). This chapter examines the evolution, the pros, and the cons of official multiculturalism in Canada and concludes that, notwithstanding its problems, official multiculturalism is on the whole beneficial to Black Canadians.

Multiculturalism in Canada

The concept of multiculturalism continues to elude any straightforward definition, despite its popularity in Canadian social and political discourse. The difficulty here, as Fleras and Elliott (1992: 21; 1996: 324) rightly point out, is due partly to the definitional process itself: Should a definition focus on what a phenomenon or a thing looks like; how it is put together; how it is supposed to function; or how it really operates? Another part of the difficulty is due to the fact that discussions on multiculturalism are often loaded with myths and stereotypes (Musto 1997).

Liodakis and Satzewich (1998), Tepper (1997), and Fleras and Elliott (1996) suggest that "multiculturalism" has four main connotations in Canadian social discourse. First, multiculturalism can be conceptualized as a demographic reality: the Canadian population consists of people with multicultural backgrounds. Second, it can be viewed as an ideology: it involves some normative prescriptions about how Canadian society ought to be, especially regarding ethnic and racial relations. Third, it connotes a competitive process: groups of people struggle for access to scarce social, economic, and political resources. And, finally, multiculturalism can be seen as a government policy that seeks to manage race relations in Canada. Conceived in this way, multiculturalism becomes a multifaceted "ideology, based on Canadian social reality, that gives rise to sets of economic, political, and social practices" (Liodakis and Satzewich 1998: 96–97). It is pertinent to emphasize that multiculturalism is not only a government policy but also an empirically verifiable social reality in Canada that will arguably persist and even deepen with time (Tepper 1997).

The Evolution of Official Multiculturalism in Canada

Pierre Trudeau's Liberal government introduced official multiculturalism in 1971. Before the Second World War Canadian governments did not manage ethnic and racial diversity in any coherent and systematic fashion.

Cultural and religious differences were treated with an indifference couched in the belief that these were private matters and should not become policy. Canada was considered a bicultural nation in which British and to a lesser extent French cultures formed the basis of society. Any departure from these traditions was seen as a threat to national identity and national unity (Kallen 1987; Fleras and Elliott 1996).

By the late 1950s, however, the public consensus on the prevailing Anglo- and Franco-Canadian symbolic order had begun to crumble as more immigrants from a wide range of European and developing countries settled in Canada. Political agitation in the turbulent 1960s offered additional impetus to the demise of Canada's assimilationist stance and paved the way for official multiculturalism. The pressure for a change in the 1960s emanated from three main quarters: the forces of Quebec nationalism, following the Quiet Revolution,[1] intense lobbying by members of the "third force,"[2] notably Ukrainian- and German-Canadians, who resented the lack of recognition for their contribution to Canadian nation-building; and increased assertiveness by First Nations people over the government's inaction on Native issues (Liodakis and Satzewich 1998). To defuse the threat to national unity posed by these forces, Prime Minister Lester Pearson appointed the Royal Commission on Bilingualism and Biculturalism in 1963 to examine the state of Canada's bilingualism and biculturalism in relation to the contribution of other ethnic groups in Canada.

On October 8, 1971, Prime Minister Pierre Elliott Trudeau tabled the official response of his Liberal government to the recommendations of the Royal Commission and introduced Canada's policy of multiculturalism. Trudeau (Canada, House of Commons 1971: 8545–48) made several noteworthy points in this landmark speech, the most significant being that:

- Canada has two official languages—English and French—but has no official culture; and, therefore, all cultures are equal to each other in status.
- It is the responsibility of government to help everyone to enjoy full participation in Canadian life without discrimination.
- Cultural diversity, within the framework of two official languages and a set of Canadian values, constitutes the crux of Canadian identity.
- Confidence in one's own identity promotes respect for others, and, ultimately, national unity.

The underlying assumption of the entire speech is that multiculturalism and Canadianism interact, intersect and, most importantly, support each other. Unlike the critics who demonized multiculturalism as a vehicle for

Box 8.1
Excerpts from Prime Minister Trudeau's Speech on Multiculturalism to the House of Commons, October 8, 1971

I am happy this morning to be able to reveal to the House that the government has accepted all those recommendations of the Royal Commission on Bilingualism and Biculturalism as contained in Volume IV of its reports directed to federal departments and agencies. Honourable members will recall that the subject of this volume is "the contribution by other ethnic groups to the cultural enrichment of Canada and the measures that should be taken to safeguard that contribution...."

It was the view of the Royal Commission, shared by the government and, I am sure, by all Canadians, that there cannot be one cultural policy for Canadians of British and French origin, another for the original peoples and yet a third for all others. For although there are two official languages, there is not official culture, nor does any ethnic group take precedence over any other.

The Royal Commission was guided by the belief that adherence to one's ethnic group is influenced not so much by one's origin or mother tongue as by one's sense of belonging to the group, and by what the Commission calls the group's "collective will to exist." The government shares this belief.

The individual's freedom would be hampered if he were locked for life within a particular cultural compartment by the accident of birth or language. It is vital, therefore, that every Canadian, whatever his ethnic origin, be given a chance to learn at least one of the two languages in which his country conducts its official business and its politics.

A policy of multiculturalism within a bilingual framework commends itself to the government as the most suitable means of assuring the cultural freedom of Canadians. Such a policy should help to break down discriminatory attitudes and cultural jealousies; national unity if it is to mean anything in the deeply personal sense, must be founded on confidence in one's own individual identity; out of this can grow respect for that of others and a willingness to share ideas, attitudes and assumptions. In implementing a policy of multiculturalism within a bilingual framework, the government will provide support in four ways.

First, resources permitting, the government will seek to assist all Canadian cultural groups that have demonstrated a desire and effort to continue to develop, a capacity to grow and contribute to Canada, and a clear need for assistance....

Second, the government will assist members of all cultural groups to overcome cultural barriers to full participation in Canadian society.

Third, the government will promote creative encounters and interchange among all Canadian cultural groups in the interest of national unity.

Fourth, the government will continue to assist immigrants to acquire at least one of Canada's official languages in order to become full participants in Canadian society.

Mr. Speaker, I stated at the outset that the government has accepted in principle all recommendations addressed to federal departments and agencies. We are ready and willing to work cooperatively with provincial governments towards implementing those recommendations that concern matters under provincial or shared responsibility....

In conclusion, I wish to emphasize the view of the government that a policy of multiculturalism within a bilingual framework is basically the conscious support for individual freedom of choice. We are free to be ourselves. But this cannot be left to chance. It must be fostered and pursued actively. If freedom of choice is in danger for some ethnic groups, it is in danger for all. It is the policy of this government to eliminate any such danger and to "safeguard" this freedom.

Source: Canada, House of Commons 1971: 8545–48.

social division, Trudeau saw it as a realistic, inclusionary mechanism capable of mediating race and ethnic relations. Trudeau noted that federal government support for multiculturalism would include assistance for members of all cultural groups in Canada to overcome cultural barriers to their full participation in Canadian society; promotion of intercultural exchange; and aid to immigrants in learning at least one of Canada's official languages to facilitate their involvement in Canadian society. Excerpts of Trudeau's historic speech is provided in Box 8.1.

While the enunciation of official multiculturalism in October 1971 was certainly hastened by the recommendations of the Royal Commission on Bilingualism and Biculturalism, one cannot easily discount the allegation that political expediency was a significant impetus as well. Several observers, especially Francophones, believe that the policy undermines Quebec nationalism by reducing the Quebec factor to just another ethnic phenomenon in multicultural Canada (Labelle 1990; Harney 1985). A similar allegation has been made vis-à-vis the special claims of First Nations people in Canada (Abu-Laban and Stasiulis 1992). Other critics assert that the policy was used by the Liberal government not only to capture ethnic votes, but to boost Liberal political strength in Western Canada where official bilingualism was denounced (Fleras and Elliott 1992: 72). Whether or not Trudeau had a hidden political agenda in elevating multiculturalism to official government policy is hard to establish. However, few expositors will now deny that the policy has altered, perhaps forever, the symbolic order of Canada (Abu-Laban and Stasiulis 1992: 367).

The political implementation of official multiculturalism saw the creation of a Multicultural Directorate at the Department of the Secretary of State in 1972. Among other things, this directorate assisted ethnic and cultural groups in dealing with issues concerning human rights abuses, racial discrimination, citizenship involvement, and immigrant services (Fleras and Elliott 1996; Lupul 1982). Also, in May 1973, the Canadian Consultative Council on Multiculturalism was created to monitor the implementation of federal multicultural initiatives; this Council was revamped and renamed the Canadian Ethnocultural Council in 1983 (Lupul 1982; Fleras and Elliott 1996). As a policy, multiculturalism assumed an even higher official status in July 1998, following the enactment of the Canadian *Multiculturalism Act*. This Act reaffirmed multiculturalism as a fundamental characteristic of Canadian society, and it gave the policy a better sense of direction by outlining a specific framework and federal institutions for its implementation. The federal Department of Multiculturalism and Citizenship was created in 1991 but was disbanded two years later. Presently, multiculturalism is one of several portfolios within the federal Ministry of Canadian Heritage (Fleras and Elliott 1996: 332).

While the federal Liberals were the first to introduce official multiculturalism, both the New Democratic and Progressive Conservative parties—unlike the Parti Québécois and the Reform Party (now the Canadian Alliance Party)—generally have been supportive of the policy over the years. Furthermore, nearly all Canadian provinces have adopted some form of official multiculturalism since 1974 when Saskatchewan became the first to endorse the policy (Abu-Laban and Stasiulis 1992). Not surprisingly, Quebec has rejected official multiculturalism as presented by the federal government. Instead it has created its own version dubbed "interculturalism" with which it seeks to integrate allophones into French language and culture (Fleras and Elliott 1996: 332). More recently, several municipalities, businesses, and institutions have introduced multicultural packages of their own in response to the growing ethnoracial diversity in the country (Cardozo and Musto 1997).

Since the mid-1980s, public perception of and reaction to official multiculturalism have been ambivalent. While some have chastised the policy for reasons that we shall examine below, there are many who support, even apotheosize, the policy. A national attitudinal survey conducted by the Angus Reid Group in 1991 on behalf of Multiculturalism and Citizenship Canada found strong public support for the policy (Angus Reid Group 1991). Similarly, the *Canadian Ethnic Studies Bulletin* (1992: 3) reports that 77 percent of Canadians believe that official multiculturalism will enrich Canada's culture. According to the same bulletin, 73 percent of Canadians "agree that multiculturalism will ensure that people from various cultural backgrounds will have a sense of belonging [and will] provide greater equality of opportunity for all groups."

Conversely, a December 1993 poll released by the Decima Research Group found that three out of every four Canadians reject the notion of cultural diversity and think that racial and ethnic minorities should try harder to assimilate (*Ottawa Citizen* 1993: B1; Bergman 1993: 42). The same survey found that 54 percent of respondents believe that current immigration regulations allow too many people of different racial and cultural backgrounds into Canada. After reviewing opinion polls conducted by Ekos Research Associates and the Environics Research Group, Musto (1997) notes that "overall public support for the policy declined between 1989 and 1995." In his view, the decline is largely attributable to economic insecurity at the time.

As it now stands some Canadians see multiculturalism as a source of national disunity, while others view the policy as a realistic solution to the problems of racism and inequality in Canadian society. We will assess the value of official multiculturalism from the standpoint of Black Canadians, but first let us examine the main criticisms leveled against the policy and offer some arguments to counter these attacks.

Arguments for and Against Official Multiculturalism

As Abu-Laban and Stasiulis (1992: 337) remark, criticizing official multiculturalism has become a pastime for many Canadians. Some critics allege that multiculturalism depoliticizes social inequality; fosters cultural relativism and social division; creates ethnic ghettoes; commodifies ethnic culture; and reinforces cultural stereotypes. Others fault the policy for allegedly undermining the distinctiveness and special claims of Québécois and First Nations people in Canada. The most vocal and most caustic of the multiculturalism critics are novelist Neil Bissoondath in his *Selling Illusions: The Cult of Multiculturalism in Canada* (1994) and University of Lethbridge sociologist Reginald Bibby in his *Mosaic Madness* (1990). As we examine the attacks leveled against the policy and offer a comprehensive response to them, our counter-arguments will draw upon ideas that resonate in the works of such multiculturalism supporters as Nikolaos

Liodakis and Vic Satzewich (1998), Elliot Tepper (1997), Augie Fleras and
Jean Leonard Elliott (1996), Benet Davetian (1994), and Yasmeen Abu-
Laban and Daiva Stasiulis (1992). The various attacks are numbered for the
purposes of orderly presentation and reflect neither their relative magni-
tude nor their popularity. Furthermore, the coverage of criticism is by no
means exhaustive. The aim here is to present the prevalent attacks and to
respond to them as comprehensively as possible.

Attack #1: Multiculturalism abandons the pursuit of the best and promotes excessive relativism

The main thrust of this attack, popularized by Reginald W. Bibby in his
Mosaic Madness (1990), is that multiculturalism promotes excessive relativism and creates a situation in which we cheer "for all plays instead of the
best plays" (14).

> Since the 1960s, Canada has been encouraging the freedom of
> groups and individuals without simultaneously laying down
> cultural expectations. Canada has also been encouraging the
> expression of viewpoints without simultaneously insisting on the
> importance of evaluating the merits of those viewpoints. (Bibby
> 1990: 10)

In his view, while individual freedom is a good thing, too much of it has
led to excessive individualism and relativism, which has "slain moral
consensus [and] ... stripped us of our ethical and moral guidelines, leaving
us with no authoritative instruments with which to measure social life"
(Bibby 1990: 14). Bibby laments:

> Cultural relativism[3] is accepted as given; those who dare to assert
> that their culture [read as Anglo-Saxon culture] is the best is
> dubbed ethnocentric; those who dare to assert that they have the
> truth [read as those who share Bibby's view] are labeled bigots.
> Truth has been replaced by personal viewpoints. (1990: 2)

In illustrating the prevalence of "cultural relativism" in Canadian society,
Bibby cites as an example the lack of consensus on a wide range of issues
including abortion, homosexuality, and even the Ben Johnson doping
scandal at the 1988 Seoul Olympics. Not surprisingly, several antagonists
of multiculturalism—including Neil Bissoondath and the federal Reform
Party/Canadian Alliance—have echoed Bibby's views. Under the pithy
heading "Losing the Centre," Bissoondath (1994: 45) argues that

[Canada has gone] from a society of almost uniform colour to one that is multi-hued; from a society that was of almost uniform religion to one that is multi-faithed. The traditional notions of Canada, then, representing the centre of the nation's being, are being challenged, even effaced, by the need for transition—a need created to a large degree, *by multiculturalism.* (emphasis added)

While Bissoondath does not advocate a return to Anglo-conformity, he, like Bibby, believes that multiculturalism has caused excessive relativism and disunity among Canadians. Listen to how he concludes his treatise on "Losing the Centre":

A void remains, a lack of a new and definable centre. Multiculturalism, the agent of that change and the policy designed to be the face of the new Canada, has failed to acquire shape and shows no signs of doing so. Without a change in focus and practice, it is unlikely ever to coalesce into the centre—distinct and firm and *recognizably Canadian*—we so desperately need. (1994: 77; emphasis added)

In its 1989 and 1991 policy platforms the federal Reform Party launched a fairly similar attack, calling for an end to government funding for multicultural programs (Reform Party of Canada 1989; 1991).

Response
Many other criticisms of multiculturalism—it causes social division; it creates ethnic ghettoes; it undermines the special status of Québécois and First Nations—logically can be linked to one claim: multiculturalism promotes excessive relativism. Let us subject this criticism to an in-depth analytical scrutiny, asking: Can we blame multiculturalism for the rising incidence of relativism, assuming that the latter is necessarily a worrisome phenomenon? Does multiculturalism lead to an "everything goes" mentality, as these critics allege? What constitutes the "national culture," the "recognizably Canadian culture," or the "centre" that we are supposedly losing as a result of multiculturalism? Who decides the key components of this centre? And, lastly, who decides who decides?

Moral principles are best conceptualized as a continuum. On one extreme are the relativists who categorically deny the existence of a single moral standard that is equally applicable to all people, regardless of place and time. On the other are the moral absolutists who insist that there is but one eternally true and valid moral code applicable to all humans. While Bibby and many of his sympathizers strategically retreat from offering specific moral absolutes, one can clearly discern from their writings that they are generally situated closer to the absolutist end of the moral continuum than they are to the relativist end. The fact is, neither extreme absolutism nor extreme relativism is logically defensible. Interestingly, Bibby tactically admits this in his preface with this proviso: "Both approaches are equally closed-minded. More seriously, neither works" (1990: vii). Extreme moral relativism has serious problems, best encapsulated by Walter Stace (1967: 147):

> [T]aken seriously and pressed to its logical conclusion, extreme ethical relativism can only end in destroying the conception of morality altogether, in undermining its practical efficacy, in rendering meaningless many almost universally accepted truths about human affairs, in robbing human beings of any incentive to strive for a better world, in taking the life-blood out of every ideal and every aspiration which has ever ennobled man's [and woman's] moral feelings.

Likewise, the extreme absolutism towards which opponents like Bibby and Bissoondath are covertly, and sometimes overtly, tiptoeing is no better. With extreme absolutism, one is faced with the difficult task of discovering the foundation upon which to rest absolute moral principles, or the authority from which a universally binding moral code derives (Stace 1967: 145). Ultimately, the best way to proceed is to strike a compromise— something few antagonists of multiculturalism have attempted to date.

Some analysts may try to locate moral authority in religion. The issue then becomes which specific religion should be the authority in a demographically multicultural society like ours. Those who agitate over the growing lack of Anglo-conformity would implicitly call for the use of Christian principles in this context, with the usual assertion that God commanded us to live by some rules. But, as Harry Browne (1972: 177) pointedly queries in discussing what he calls the "Morality Trap":

> Who can be sure he knows exactly when and how and what God said and what he meant?... And if the code did come from God, it still had to be handled by human beings on its way to you. Whatever the absolute morality may be, you're relying upon someone else to vouch for its authority.... Suppose you use a holy book as your guide. I haven't yet seen one that doesn't have some apparent contradictions regarding conduct in it. Those contradictions may disappear with the proper interpretation; but who provides the interpretations?

Without turning the discussion into a philosophical treatise, suffice it to state that there are, indeed, many who doubt that we can reasonably situate universal moral laws in religion or in some form of a uniform command of God to all people, regardless of time and place. This philosophical issue goes back to Socrates' incisive question to Euthyphro[4] in Plato's *Last Days of Socrates*: "Is what is pious loved by the gods because it is pious, or it is pious because it is loved?" (plato 1954: 31). Put differently, is a pious deed pious and the gods simply acknowledge its inherent piety, or is a pious deed pious because the gods say so? After being entangled in a host of unimaginable contradictions while attempting to answer this question, the pompous Euthyphro, who is usually confident in his infallibility, admits: "But Socrates, I don't know how to convey to you what I have in mind. Whatever we put forward somehow keeps shifting its position and refuses to stay where we laid it down" (Plato 1954: 33). Euthyphro is not alone: this question of whether or not we can locate the foundation of morality in religion has exercised the minds of preeminent ethicists and theologians for centuries.

The absolutism/relativism dispute is a long-standing one, and it is certainly not peculiar to Canada. Consequently, attempts to draw a causal nexus between relativism, or even excessive relativism, and Canada's official multiculturalism are simplistic at best. Relativism is traceable to the works of the Greek Sophist Protagoras, who insisted that "Man is the measure of all things; of things that are that they are, and things that are not that they are not" (quoted in Pojman 1995: 690). Relativism has been gaining popularity around the world in recent years due to the ascendance of postmodernism in social discourse. Despite the diverse interpretations given to postmodernism in the available literature, nearly all the renowned postmodern theoreticians, including Michel Foucault, Fredric Jameson, Jacques Derrida, Charles Jencks, and Jean-François Lyotard,[5] stress the heterogeneous, fragmentary, subjective, and pluralistic character of reality.

Liodakis and Satzewich (1998: 103) write: "What is common [among these critics] is an appeal to the 'national' character of Canada, which is never defined … people expressing these critical views are always silent or purposefully vague in describing what constitutes Canadian culture…." Has it ever occurred to these critics that maybe, just maybe, Canada does not have or cherish any complicated set of central values except basic human decency; a respect for individual freedom and the rule of law; a commitment to equality of individuals; non-violence; and a collective urge to assist all Canadians, especially those who are most vulnerable, through social and welfare services (Sajoo 1994)?

Has multiculturalism led to an "everything goes" mentality? Has it really "made us fearful of defining acceptable boundaries," as Bissoondath

(1994: 143) asserts? Arguably, it has only made us thoughtful, and not fearful; it has certainly not led to a situation where everything goes. As Fleras and Elliott (1996: 354) point out:

> Multiculturalism does *not* endorse a mindless relativism in which anything goes in the name of tolerance. Multiculturalism is clear about what is permissible in Canada. It rejects any custom that violates Canadian laws, interferes with the rights of others, offends the moral sensibilities of most Canadians, or disturbs central institutions or core values. (original emphasis)

Interestingly, Bissoondath (1994: 143) admits that the acceptance of customs such as female circumcision and sex selection is a virtual impossibility in Canada. It is worth noting in this context that in May 1997 an amendment to Canada's Criminal Code categorically outlawed female circumcision on the grounds that it "violates the human rights of young women and offends notions of equality, human integrity, and other core values prevalent in Canada" (Liodakis and Satzewich 1998: 103). Undoubtedly, official multiculturalism seeks to balance the core principles of Canada with the rights of its immigrant groups.

The interpretable interplay between multiculturalism and the growing relativism in Canadian society is far more convoluted than what has been presented so far by the critics. For one thing, the link between these two phenomena can neither be viewed as unidirectional nor straightforward; rather it is "cumulative," "nested," and "reciprocal," to paraphrase Timothy Weiskel (1997: 220). It is cumulative in the sense that behavioural patterns of Canadians, like those of people elsewhere, change slowly and are greatly influenced by the past; therefore, it is hardly the case that relativism emerged only following the introduction of official multiculturalism in 1971. The relationship is nested in the sense that patterns of micro-behaviour in any particular place are conditioned by shifts in macro-behaviour and vice versa. Put differently, Canadian social dynamics are invariably shaped by global circumstances and vice versa, particularly in this era of globalization in which national and international factors shape one another in ways previously absent. The growing tendency towards relativism in Canada, therefore, has a lot to do with global paradigm shifts. Finally, the link is reciprocal in the sense that just as multiculturalism can promote excessive relativism (at least in the minds of critics), so can excessive relativism become the antecedent and foster the urge for multiculturalism in Canada. Thus, logically speaking, excessive relativism can be both the cause as well as the consequence of multiculturalism—there lies the intricate reciprocity. It is, therefore, a matter of great importance to avoid the kind of analysis that dwells on a simplistic, unidirectional causal link between official multiculturalism and relativism.

The works of Lionel Rubinoff (1982) and A.R.M. Lower (1946, 1953) suggest that the conditions that foster relativism and pluralism in Canada are reflected even in the physiography of the country. These authors strongly situate parts of Canada's diversity in its physical landscape. To them "the landscape itself is a model of diversity, defiant of any attempt to centralize power, and proud of the independent, pluralistic and unpredictable way of existence that it makes possible and indeed favours" (Rubinoff 1982: 125). Without question, for the sake of national unity, there is always the need to identify the distinctive values that bind the citizens of a country together. In the case of Canada, one can argue that our national glue is our unity in diversity; a unity couched in the belief that "the only freedom which deserves the name is that of pursuing our own good in our own ways, so long as we do not attempt to deprive others of theirs or impede their efforts to obtain it" (from the essay "On Liberty" by John Stuart Mill quoted in Rubinoff 1982: 130).

Attack #2: Multiculturalism fosters social division and ethnic ghettoization

This attack is closely related to the preceding one. It rebuffs multiculturalism on the grounds that it fosters social division and ethnic ghettoization. Like many other criticisms of multiculturalism, this one is in several parts, and it emanates from different directions with no discernible sign of abating in the near future. While the social division/ethnic ghettoization attack has been launched by several analysts and politicians (including Keith Spicer of the Spicer Commission;[6] Preston Manning and the erstwhile Reform Party; and John Nunziata, the former Liberal MP who was an independent MP until the year 2000), perhaps the most spirited among them has been Neil Bissoondath. In *Selling Illusions* [7] he argues that multiculturalism's "provisions *seem* aimed … at encouraging division, at ensuring that the various ethnic groups whose interests it espouses discover no compelling reason to blur the distinction among them" (43; emphasis added). If Bissoondath's use of "seem" suggests doubt about his views on the impact of multiculturalism on national unity, consider the following barb: "Multiculturalism has … heightened our differences rather than diminished them … and it is leading us into a divisiveness so entrenched that we face a future of multiple solitudes with no central notion to bind us" (Bissoondath 1994: 192). Indeed, he was equally acerbic in noting earlier in his book: "Differences between people are already obvious enough without their being emphasized through multiculturalism policy and its growing cult of racial and ethnic identity" (Bissoondath 1994: 122).

This attack also chides multiculturalism for crystallizing ethnic and racial groups into distinct enclaves or ethnoracial ghettoes by promoting an inward-looking mentality among immigrants. This attack, most commonly attributed to politicians such as John Nunziata, is discernible in the works of both Reginald Bibby and Neil Bissoondath also. Nunziata maintains that official multiculturalism has outlived its usefulness:

> I believe very strongly that the policy is no longer valid or appropriate today. In effect, the present policy of multiculturalism is divisive…. [It] is discriminatory because there is almost a suggestion that because one is part of the multicultural community, somehow one is inferior, is of a different class, is of inferior quality to Canadians who have origins that are French and English…. I think it is time we stopped segregating and ghettoizing Canadians of origins other than French and English. (House of Commons speech, quoted in Abu-Laban and Stasiulis 1992: 376)

Nunziata and other purveyors of this criticism, including some ethnic minority leaders, lament that multiculturalism is being used to marginalize ethnic minorities by isolating their concerns from those of the mainstream. What seems to bother many critics is the notion that government money allegedly is being used to foster diversity. The Spicer Commission, for example, noted that the use of tax dollars to enhance multicultural diversity is distasteful to many Canadians (Canada, Citizens' Forum on Canada's Future 1991). Accordingly the commission recommended that "federal government funding for multiculturalism activities other than those serving immigrant orientation, reduction of racial discrimination and promotion of equality should be eliminated…. The key goal of multiculturalism should be to welcome all Canadians to an evolving mainstream" (Canada, Citizens' Forum on Canada's Future 1991: 129). In an earlier article in the *Montreal Gazette*, Spicer (1989) called on the federal government to end its financial support for multicultural programs. In his view, state-funded multiculturalism is nothing more than a "multicultural zoo," which ends up creating "not Canadians but professional ethnics" (Spicer 1989: B3).

The Spicer Commission also notes another thing that rankles many Canadians: the growing trend towards hyphenated citizenship with divided loyalties among many newcomers. Bissoondath (1994) echoes this concern, characteristically lashing out at official multiculturalism as the main culprit, "Multiculturalism, with its emphasis on the importance of holding on to the former or ancestral homeland, with its insistence that

There is more important than *Here*, serves to encourage such attitudes" (133; original emphasis). Moreover, Bissoondath alleges that official multiculturalism is a political scheme designed not only to buy ethnic votes through a system of patronage and ethnic-based spending, but to "keep [ethnic groups] divided and therefore conquered" (1994: 43).

Response

Can we blame multiculturalism for national unity problems in Canada? Without question, there is some evidence of ethnic ghettoization, but is multiculturalism the culprit? Are the concerns about the use of tax dollars to "promote diversity," legitimate concerns? Finally, to what extent is the government using multiculturalism to buy "ethnic votes"?

Admittedly, Bissoondath's *Selling Illusions (1994)* makes some incisive points. However, like many uncompromising critics of multiculturalism, he sometimes goes too far or simply ignores any inclination towards a balanced assessment of issues and thereby ends up with some facile generalizations. Like many critics, Bissoondath sees multiculturalism as the main culprit for the country's unity problems. As Benet Davetian (1994) points out in his review of *Selling Illusions,* the fact that ethnoracial integration has not fully come about during the era of multiculturalism does not in any way mean that the latter is responsible for the former; to posit otherwise is to commit the fallacy of false cause[8] (i.e., *non causa pro causa*) or the "associative fallacy," to use Davetian's terminology (1994: 134). In the words of Davetian (1994: 134): "It is a little like walking into a forest where something is wrong, and, upon seeing a jagged rock, declaring that it is the rock's fault that the trees are ailing." Irving Copi (1978: 97) comments in his discussion of the fallacy of false cause that: "we should reject the ... claim that beating drums is the cause of the sun's reappearance after an eclipse, despite the evidence offered that every time drums have been beaten during an eclipse, the sun has reappeared!" No one would be misled by such argument, yet many are those who believe that official multiculturalism is the cause of Canada's unity problems just because the two seem to occur simultaneously. In examining the unity question can we reasonably overlook factors such as geographic segmentation; regionalism; uneven spatial development; socio-economic inequities; lack of strong leadership; the antiquated friction between English- and French-Canadians; racial discrimination; the hydra-headed problems of Aboriginal treaty negotiation; and the global paradigm shift towards postmodernism? One might even add to this list the argument that our high tax regime creates a climate of "every man and woman for him/herself" (Davetian 1994: 135).

The difficulty in identifying the leading cause of our national unity problems is obvious. University of Saskatchewan geographer Robert Bone believes that the "greatest challenge to Canadian unity comes from the cultural divide that separates French- and English-speaking Canadians and their respective visions of the country" (Bone 1999: 137). Political economists, in particular, contend that "a far bigger threat to Canadian unity and cohesion comes from the North American Free Trade Agreement and our associated political, economic, and cultural incorporation into the United States" (Liodakis and Satzewich 1998: 105). Fleras and Elliott (1996: 355) are convinced that "the real culprit is racism with its power to shunt minorities to the sidestream for reasons unrelated to merit." Unlike multiculturalism's opponents, Fleras and Elliott (1996: 355) opine that this policy offers avenues for patching over ethnic and racial divisions by removing exclusionary barriers.

Davetian (1994: 135) writes that Canada's official multiculturalism was adopted for two main purposes: "on one hand, it sought to assure prospective immigrants that Canada was committed to universal tolerance; on the other, it attempted to resocialize the indigenous population into accepting the presence of foreigners without falling into socially disruptive mind-sets." It is not quite clear what Davetian means by "the indigenous population." If the reference is to First Nations people and not to the charter groups, one wonders if there is a need for resocialization, as the former traditionally has been little disposed towards xenophobia. Furthermore, given the obvious lack of socio-economic and political power among Canada's Aboriginal people, it would be exceedingly hard for them to inflict any real harm or to translate "socially disruptive mind-sets" into practice, at least on any meaningful scale. Having said that, it is difficult to fault Davetian's first point, which sees official multiculturalism as Canada's commitment to "universal tolerance." Even a cursory reading of Trudeau's multicultural speech and the 1988 Multicultural Act will support this position. Official multiculturalism seeks to promote tolerance of, and to some extent respect for, foreigners and minorities within the framework of Canadian nationalism. Thus, it endorses diversity and tolerance only to the extent that they are couched in Canadian law and order.

As noted earlier, the proliferation of hyphenated citizenship (e.g., Jamaican-Canadian or Nigerian-Canadian) in Canada is another worrisome issue for critics who contend that it undermines our national identity, fosters divided loyalty, and promotes ethnic ghettoization. Read how Lee Morrison, a Reform Party official, chides Canada's multiculturalism on behalf of his party:

> It is the Reform Party's position that the federal Department of Multiculturalism is a divisive agency.... Thanks to the official

federal policy of multiculturalism, Canada is being divided as never before along racial, linguistic and cultural lines. We have Anglo-Canadians, French-Canadians, Native-Canadians, Chinese-Canadians and a host of other hyphenated nationalities, but apparently no plain, ordinary Canadians. (quoted in Kirkham 1998: 255).

These criticisms have some intuitive appeal, but we cannot blame the conferring (or even the proliferation) of hyphenated citizenship in Canada on official multiculturalism. For obvious reasons, critics such as Morrison would like to gloss over the fact that before official multiculturalism there still were French-Canadians, English-Canadians, German-Canadians, Ukrainian-Canadians, etc. Tracing the root cause of hyphenated citizenship in Canada to multiculturalism is an erroneous supposition by any stretch of the imagination. As a matter of fact, if hyphenation *per se* creates divided loyalty and disunity, then Canada was divided at birth, and one cannot therefore blame official multiculturalism for that. Perhaps the cogent questions here are: Why do more immigrants find it necessary to resort to hyphenated-citizenship, ethnic distinctions, and ethnic separations? Are ethnic distinctions and separations necessarily divisive? To what extent are these ethnic distinctions and separations self-imposed? Can we alleviate the problems of ethnic distinction and separation by abandoning official multiculturalism? And, more pointedly, does official multiculturalism cause ethnic ghettoization?

Some immigrants may find it irritating constantly to be seen as "some exoticism on two legs" (Bissoondath 1994: 113) or routinely to be drilled on what appears to be a standard conversational "Question and Answer":[9]

Q: "Where are you from?"
A: "Surrey, British Columbia, or anywhere in Canada, for that matter."
Q: "No, I mean where are you originally from?"

If you happen to be Black or a visible minority, then you better have your answers straight and ready. "Straight" in the sense that it is never enough to assert that you hail from anywhere in Canada; and "ready" in that such intrusions into your ancestry never end, as long as you choose to live in Canada. For Black Canadians, there is no way out: it matters not whether you or even your great-grandparents were born here, you will still be bombarded with such inquiries. Indeed, as part of a gradual discursive reinterpretation and re-articulation of ideological concepts in Canada, the term "immigrants" is increasingly becoming a code word for "Blacks" and "visible minorities" (Kirkham 1998; Agnew 1996).

Whether out of naiveté or plain misguided optimism, Bissoondath (1994: 111) predicts that "children [of immigrants], and their children after them, will in all likelihood shrug off the restraints of ethnicity.... They will, in a word, integrate." As Davetian (1994: 136) points out, not all immigrants share Bissoondath's desire to be completely integrated into the Canadian culture. In fact, for some, especially Blacks, total integration is next to impossible, due to their high visibility and the constant probe into their ancestry.

Arguably, no matter how troubling these intrusions may be to some immigrants, there is nothing necessarily wrong with people wanting to know about others' ancestry. Indeed, as many immigrants and ethnic minorities ask these questions as do "non-immigrant" Canadians. What is wrong, however, is that many of us Canadians want to play both sides. We want to remind ethnic minorities of their ancestry, their "otherness," but then we criticize their embracing of hyphenated citizenship as an indication that they are not making an effort to be part of the Canadian "mainstream."

While some Canadians may probe into immigrants' roots out of such innocent reasons as natural curiosity, solicitousness, fondness, or even as a means of initiating a conversation, others may use these intrusions as exclusionary tactics in the face of competition or adversity. Alan Simmons (1998: 87) calls this "othering." A classic example of "othering" is how, within a matter of twenty-four hours, media reports metamorphosed sprinter Ben Johnson from a Canadian into a Jamaican immigrant following his 1998 Seoul Olympic fiasco. Ironically, even Bissoondath was bemused by this: "The only thing swifter than Mr. Johnson's drug-enhanced achievement was his public demotion from 'one of us' to 'one of them'" (1994: 116).

Without question, some ethnic distinctions, ethnic separations, and hyphenated citizenship are voluntary. Others are impelled or involuntary; and still others lie somewhere in between. Many immigrants do not arrive here with a language, culture, and skin pigmentation that will permit them easily to "plunge into mainstream Canadian culture without a certain measure of self-protection" (Davetian 1994: 137). Some minority groups may find these exclusionary tactics useful in temporarily asserting control over their affairs or even in carving a niche for themselves in the social and economic spheres of multicultural Canada (Hiebert 1999b). The obvious risk here is marginalization and ghettoization, especially when the group involved already is beset with an acute lack of socio-economic and political resources, as in the case of Black Canadians.

The danger of multiculturalism degenerating into ethnic ghettoization is real and should not be taken lightly. Canada must guard against a situation in which minorities are compelled by the forces of oppression, repression, and alienation to resort to ethnic distinctions and separations, and the federal Liberal government has taken action to accomplish this. It has shifted its focus away from the celebration of our multicultural differences and centred it on society building through civic education and citizenship participation (Liodakis and Satzewich 1998; Cardozo and Musto 1997).

Without playing down the possibilities of ghettoization under official multiculturalism, one can still assert that multiculturalism *per se* is not the culprit. Rather, it is the manipulation of its principles by unscrupulous, opportunistic leaders that cause ethnic ghettoization. In fact, ethnic ghettoization conceivably can persist, and indeed intensify, in the absence of official multiculturalism. The situation in the United States corroborates this supposition. Regardless of what the apologists of the melting pot sophistry would have us believe, the level of ethnic ghettoization in Canada pales in comparison to the deep-seated racial hatred, ethnic ghettoization, and race-based segregation and socio-economic inequities in the United States. Considering this, it is amazing that critics such as the Reform Party of Canada[10] and Reginald Bibby can advocate the melting pot for Canada. Bibby (1990: 7) insists,

> In this country, there will be no pressure, as there is in some other countries—notably the United States—to discard one's cultural past, and conform to the dominant culture. The name of the Canadian cultural game is not *melting* but *mosaic*. (emphasis in original)

According to him, in the "zeal to promote coexistence, Canada may find itself a world leader in promoting the breakdown of group life and the abandonment of the pursuit of the best" (Bibby 1990: 15). What these critics don't understand is that the melting pot is an illusion. Nothing has really "melted" in the United States (Barbara Smith 1994), at least from the perspective of Blacks. Massey and Denton (1993: 2) write in their thought-provoking book *American Apartheid* that "not only is the depth of Black segregation unprecedented and utterly unique compared with that of other groups, but it shows little sign of change with the passage of time or improvements in socioeconomic status." Only by ignoring the massive, veritable evidence of ghettoization across America, and by overlooking the prevalence of "chocolate cities and vanilla suburbs" (West 1993: 5), can these critics argue in favour of the melting pot.

In addressing the concern that the federal government is using tax dollars to promote diversity and to drive wedges between ethnoracial groups, can we afford to accept the erstwhile Reform Party's (1991) nostrum to put an end to federal funding for multiculturalism?[11] Fleras and Elliott (1996: 330–35) have identified three major phases in the development of official multiculturalism in Canada: the folkloric, the institutional, and the civic. During the 1970s, the folkloric phase, multiculturalism focused on "celebrating our differences" based on the premise that cultural diversity is at the heart of the true Canadian identity. During the 1980s, the institutional phase, multiculturalism focused on managing diversity and race relations using institutional mechanisms such as the 1982 *Charter of Rights*, the 1986 *Employment Equity Act*, and the 1988 *Multiculturalism Act*. Then in the 1990s, Canada entered its "civic multiculturalism" phase with emphasis on society-building through citizenship and a sense of belonging Fleras and Elliott (1996: 334).

As emphasis shifts, so does government funding. Available data suggest that government funding for multiculturalism has shifted from programs relating to the so-called three D's (i.e., diet, dance, and dress) to those that foster race relations, national identity, citizenship, civic education, and ethnoracial harmony (Liodakis and Satzewich 1998; Cardozo and Musto 1997; Fleras and Elliott 1992).

The allegation that official multiculturalism is a political ploy to buy ethnic votes is difficult to tackle as no supporting evidence has ever been provided. Then, again, in fairness to the critics, it is always difficult to find such evidence, be it circumstantial or otherwise. Immigrant groups who are well organized and who can exert some political leverage through effective lobbying are most successful in securing multicultural funding. This has always been the case, whether one is dealing with immigrants or non-immigrants, and it does not by itself support the allegation that multicultural funds are being used to buy ethnic votes (Cardozo and Musto 1997). In a way this allegation does not insult the political intelligence and sophistication of immigrant groups, it simply assumes that they have none at all.

In the final analysis the issue boils down to whether official multiculturalism and Canadian national unity are mutually exclusive or not. Trudeau in his multiculturalism speech argued that "national unity ... must be founded on confidence in one's own individual identity; out of this can grow respect for that of others and a willingness to share ideas, attitudes and assumptions" (Canada, House of Commons 1971: 8545–48). Trudeau assumed that multiculturalism and Canadianism are mutually supportive. Others, including Keith Spicer (1989) and McGill University sociologist Morton Weinfeld (1988: 600) believe that this core assumption is invalid and that respect for diversity can lead only to disunity and antipathy between groups. To them, national unity cannot be attained without cultural homogeneity. This position is arguably erroneous, for "what unites a country is a common purpose [not a common culture] directed at some future goal" (Davetian 1994: 137). It probably is closer to the truth to assert that diversity is not the problem; people's reaction to diversity is. You decide!

Attack #3: Multiculturalism undermines the special claims of Quebec nationalists and Aboriginal people

Like the preceding attacks, this one is highly convoluted. Principally, it alleges that multiculturalism has an ulterior motive that seeks to undermine the special claims of Quebec nationalists and Aboriginal people by promoting the "notion of equivalence of cultures" (Fleras and Elliott 1992: 171).

From the standpoint of Quebec nationalists, multiculturalism threatens their special status both as a "distinct society" and as one of Canada's two charter groups. It is alleged that multiculturalism subverts the English-French biculturalism upon which the Canadian federation is founded by reducing the French culture to the level of other ethnic minority cultures under the domination of English Canada (Cummins and Danesi 1990). For the most part, Quebec nationalists see multiculturalism as a political ruse devised by glib federal politicians to undermine their right to self-determination. Many Quebec nationalists chide multiculturalism as nothing more than a federal intrusion into their internal politics (Labelle 1990). In the place of federal multiculturalism, Quebec endorses "interculturalism," a policy that affirms the preeminence of French language and culture while recognizing the cultural plurality of Quebec (Webber 1994; Hudson 1987).

Like Quebec nationalists, Aboriginal people see multiculturalism as an attempt to "minoritize" them, that is, to reduce them to "just another minority group" in the Canadian mosaic (Abu-Laban and Stasiulis 1992: 376). They contend, quite rightly, that as "natives," they have a distinct and unique set of rights that naturally derive from their aboriginality (Kallen 1987). Like Quebec nationalists, Aboriginal people prefer to negotiate with, or relate to, Canada in a framework that recognizes their special status and distinctiveness (Liodakis and Satzewich 1998).

Response

The attack that official multiculturalism undermines special claims is arguably the hardest to address. At the core of it lies several of the inconsistencies in Canada's attempt to marry its principles of bilingualism and biculturalism with those of multiculturalism. Several thorny questions spring up in conjunction with this attack: Is Trudeau's vision of "multiculturalism within a bilingual framework" logically sustainable? Given that language is a major, if not the leading, component of any culture, how can we logically assert the notion of cultural equivalence or parity within the confines of a French-English bilingualism? Can we candidly say that all cultures in the Canadian mosaic are of equal status? And, more importantly, can we uphold "the notion of cultural equivalence" without glossing over the distinctiveness of and special status for both Quebec and First Nations?

The concerns expressed by Quebec nationalists and Aboriginal people are not only closely related; they are competing and sometimes conflicting. The source of conflict and competition here is not hard to envisage: so long as both groups cast their attack in terms of power and resource distribution in Canada, the issue becomes a zero-sum game in which both groups cannot be winners: one can win only at the expense of the other. Indeed, one can postulate that the greater the number of groups seeking the "distinct society" status, the less powerful their respective positions become.

The criticism that official multiculturalism undermines, or, at the very least, complicates the special status of French Canadians and First Nations shores up the inconsistencies surrounding the Canadian federation more than anything else. At the crux of this attack are two diametrically opposed visions of the Canadian federation. On the one hand are those who see the Canadian federation as a "*contract* between federal and provincial authorities involving a specific division of responsibility and exclusive realms of jurisdiction" (Fleras and Elliott 1992: 170; emphasis added). The contract thesis is implicitly concordant with official multiculturalism, as it perceives Canada "as a multicultural quilt of diverse cultures," none of which is superior in status to anothers (Fleras and Elliott 1992: 167).

Opposed to adherents of the contract thesis are those who see the Canadian federation as a bicultural compact between the two charter groups: French- and English-speaking Canadians. In this vision, cherished by most Quebec nationalists, other cultures are important but subordinate to those of the two founding nations. Clearly, responses to the attack under consideration would vary depending on one's perspective of Canada. Indeed, whether or not the attack itself is logically sustainable depends on which of the two visions of Canada one holds. For those with the contract vision, the attack is somewhat inconsistent, if not self-contradictory, for one cannot plausibly posit that Canada is a (multicultural) nation in which all cultures are of equal status, and, at the same time, expect Quebec to be accorded a special or superior status.

For those favouring the compact or biculturalism thesis, however, the attack holds considerable logical legitimacy. There is no contradiction in the assertion that Canada is a bicultural society and that Quebec being one of the two founding nations deserves a special status. Perhaps it is in recognition of this legitimacy that Trudeau attempted, in his multiculturalism speech of 1971, to relax the notion of cultural parity by severing language from culture with the caveat that Canada's multiculturalism is couched in bilingualism. However, we do not need Quebec nationalists to inform us that their demands go beyond mere language rights or bilingualism into the realm of self-determination, sovereignty, and collective survival anymore than we need them to remind us that yesterday, today was tomorrow. Thus, the casting of official multiculturalism in a bilingual framework is at best superfluous from the standpoint of Quebec nationalists.

The ultimate question, though, is "Has Quebec's position in the federation been downgraded as a result of multiculturalism?" The straight answer here is both yes and no. We can answer yes, because the notion of cultural equivalence upon which multiculturalism is founded works in favour of English Canadians, as many of the contemporary immigrants have or choose English, as opposed to French, as their preferred official language. Given the intricate and mutually supportive interplay between language and culture, there is no denying that French Canadians stand to lose in this context. We can answer no in the sense that, unlike other ethnic groups and First Nations people, French Canadians enjoy preferential treatment with access to well-entrenched cultural, linguistic, religious, political, socio-economic and legal apparatuses in the Canadian mosaic. French Canadians have their own school systems, media support, and legislative instruments controlling their socio-economic and cultural environment. As Fleras and Elliott (1992: 173) aptly put it, for all practical purposes, "Quebec and Ottawa are first among equals in the corridors of power, with guaranteed rights to self-determination over specific areas of jurisdiction." In reality, official multiculturalism "has done little to camouflage the centrality of the French and English as the 'cement' that connects the tiles upon which our mosaic rests" (Fleras and Elliott 1992: 178).

Now let us turn our attention to the impact of multiculturalism on the special status of First Nations people. Aboriginal people, unlike Quebec nationalists, are particularly disadvantaged in Canadian society. They are marginalized not only in social and economic terms but also in spatial terms through the Indian reserve system. Their lives are characterized by extreme poverty, unemployment, substandard formal education, poor-quality housing, and limited access to medical services. The deplorable living circumstances of Aboriginal people should not be surprising in a society that traditionally has viewed First Nations people as second-class citizens and did not even allow them to vote until 1960 (Krahn and Lowe 1998: 130; Norton 1998: 7). In fact, Native issues have generally been peripheral to central Canadian issues. Events surrounding the Meech Lake[12] fiasco attest to the resentment harboured by Aboriginal leaders with respect to the perennial lack of commitment on the part of federal and provincial authorities in addressing native issues in Canada. One can argue that Native Canadians deserve special treatment to elevate their living conditions to the level of non-Native Canadians. Any special treatment accorded to Aboriginal people in this respect is not at odds with the notion of cultural equivalence upon which official multiculturalism is premised. "Cultural equivalence" implies that no cultural group is or should be treated as either superior or inferior to others.

But the question still remains as to whether or not multiculturalism is undermining the special claims of Natives Canadians. Given that, so far, the notion of cultural equivalence has been given a simplistic interpretation in which all cultural groups are supposedly equal, one can assert that the special claims of Aboriginal people are being undermined, if not neglected, by official multiculturalism. Unlike French Canadians, First Nations people lack the necessary institutional support to maintain their culture, and they continue to be bombarded with the school materials, the media, and the worldview of an anglophone culture. On the positive side, one can argue that official multiculturalism has provided Aboriginal people with steadfast ethnic-minority allies such as Blacks, who are more likely to understand and sympathize with the plight of First Nations people than are members of the dominant majority. Because First Nations people and ethnic minorities share class, social, and geographical spaces in many Canadian cities, they tend to have more opportunities to interact with each other. At times, this interaction generates friction and resentment, but often it fosters understanding of, and sympathy for, the other's struggle against the discrimination and oppression of the dominant majority. More importantly, the reciprocal sympathies among ethnic minorities and First Nations are usually stripped of condescension, as members of these groups are all at the bottom of the Canadian hierarchy of social standing and acceptance (Reitz and Breton 1998: 57).

Blacks and other minorities in Canada are more threatened by the Quebec nationalists' claim of "distinct society" than by the Aboriginal call for special status, given the occasional outburst of xenophobic frenzy in Quebec. Under Premier Robert Bourassa, Quebec declared itself a distinct society and restricted minority rights by invoking the Constitution's "notwithstanding clause" through the enactment of Quebec's infamous Bill 178. This bill, also called the French Sign Law of 1988, banned the use of any language other than French on outdoor commercial signs (Samuels and Craig 1998). Are Canadians prepared to sacrifice some minority and individual equality rights by submitting to Quebec's call for special status in the confederation? The Charlottetown and Meech Lake debacles as well as the events surrounding the recent sovereignty referendums in Quebec show how other Canadians feel about the distinct society claims of Quebec.

Attack #4: Multiculturalism promotes symbolic ethnicity, commodifies cultures, reinforces cultural stereotypes, and serves as an ideological ploy to depoliticize social inequality

The crux of this attack is that multiculturalism simplifies, commodifies, and devalues ethnic cultures and ultimately reinforces cultural stereotypes. Critics such as Bissoondath (1994), Burnet (1984), Peter (1981), and Hughes and Kallen (1974) argue that caravans and folk festivals, which are so commonly associated with Canada's multiculturalism, do not promote any serious cultural exchange. In their view, such celebrations only reinforce cultural stereotypes about ethnic minorities. Bissoondath (1994: 83) remarks that implicit in these festivities is "the peculiar notion of culture as commodity: a thing that can be displayed, performed, admired, bought, sold or forgotten." Similarly, Hughes and Kallen (1974: 190–91) write that ethnic folk dances and multicultural festivals give minorities only the illusion of preserving their cultural identity while at the same time ensuring Anglo-conformity.

Burnet (1984) and Peter (1981) denounce multiculturalism as a political hoax to ensure minority containment and co-option. It is used to steer ethnic minorities into specific occupational structures and residential arrangements and, thereby, to exclude them from full and equal participation in Canadian society. Other opponents discredit multiculturalism as a regressive ideology that endorses the symbolic, ornamental, and situational aspects of minority cultures and downplays the substantive and structural dimensions of minority demands (Kallen 1987). Kallen (1987), Ramcharan (1982), and Peter (1981) argue that official multiculturalism distracts ethnic minorities from challenging the social and economic inequalities, as well as the entrenched class system and its attendant imperialist privileges and, thereby, helps to perpetuate Canada's vertical mosaic.

In their thought-provoking paper "Exploring the Ideology of Canadian Multiculturalism," Roberts and Clifton (1982) question even the sociological credibility of official multiculturalism. According to these two authors, official multiculturalism "is not only muddled but misconceived" because it is based on the unrealistic assumption "that a variety of cultures can exist without separate institutions" (Roberts and Clifton 1982: 88–89). They forcefully argue that the conventional vision of a Canadian mosaic composed of viable ethnic groups is unattainable since very few ethnic groups have the necessary social structures to perpetuate cultural traditions. Therefore, only "symbolic ethnicity" is attainable under Canadian multiculturalism. The pursuit of symbolic ethnicity is not much different from the activities of voluntary organizations, they argue; and for this reason the government should not be involved in the promotion of multiculturalism.

Response

By chiding multiculturalism as an ideological ploy and a promoter of symbolic ethnicity, these opponents have gathered many powerful supporters even among minorities. Coupling this with the allegation that multiculturalism reinforces cultural stereotypes makes a potent force to counter. Indeed, key supporters of multiculturalism, including Elliot Tepper, Jean Leonard Elliott, Augie Fleras, E.D. Nelson and others, agree that multiculturalism is about symbolic ethnicity. Thus, in a way the critics are right; but, as Nelson and Fleras (1995: 263) point out, they are right "for the wrong reason." The government of Canada did not intend to use multiculturalism to enhance the collective rights of minorities nor to create autonomous minority groups with parallel institutions and power bases within Canada. Rather, the policy seeks to promote symbolic ethnicity.

In any case, it is instructive to note that "symbolic" is a relative concept imbued with a host of contextual interpretations. What may be symbolic to one group may very well be substantive to another. Consequently, any attempt to overstate this attack glosses over the substantive accomplishment of the policy (e.g., to establish an anti-racism campaign), at least from the standpoint of Blacks and other ethnic minorities. Moreover, assuming for the sake of argument that multiculturalism is only about symbolism, can we candidly assert that symbols are insignificant in a country where there is a considerable public uproar and emotional debate over the wearing of Sikh turbans in the RCMP and in the halls of the Royal Canadian Legion?

Has the policy really devalued ethnic culture and reinforced cultural stereotypes about minorities? Not to pose these questions is to evade the most crucial aspect of the entire discussion. Arguably, multiculturalism goes beyond pageantry and folk festivals. The policy now provides a legitimate platform and a coherent conceptual framework upon which ethnic minorities can articulate their points of view and their collective and individual concerns. Furthermore, there is a definite anti-racism component of contemporary multiculturalism, which seeks to break down institutional barriers that militate against the full and equal participation of ethnic minorities in Canadian society. Without question, the pattern of property ownership is ethnically lopsided; and without question, racial discrimination continues to be pervasive in Canadian society, as we saw in many of the previous chapters. While the anti-racism and the distributional accomplishments of official multiculturalism may not sound like much to these critics, others happen to be in favour of almost anything that mitigates the destructive, dehumanizing, debilitating, and downright degrading practices of racial discrimination.

As a result of the policy, several public and private institutions in Canada are now prepared to make the necessary adjustments to accommodate different cultures. Even long-standing traditions and symbols, such as the RCMP dress code, are being altered to accommodate different cultures and religions. Fleras and Elliott (1996) write that multiculturalism has not only made it possible for minorities to identify with their cultural backgrounds and at the same time participate in Canadian society, but it has also helped Canada manage its race relations in such a way as to avoid the violent ethnic clashes so prevalent in contemporary geopolitics. Supporters of multiculturalism will certainly say amen to that.

The Case for Multiculturalism from the Perspectives of Blacks

So far we have examined the main criticisms leveled against official multiculturalism, and we have offered some general responses to them. In this concluding segment we explore the relevance of multiculturalism from the perspective of Black Canadians. The term "perspective of Blacks" is used loosely to signify a narrative couched in, and informed by, the history and socio-economic circumstances of Black Canadians. The term does not assume a single Black position on official multiculturalism in Canada. In fact, there are as many Blacks in favour of the policy as there are against it. Moreover, while the specific case of Blacks remains the main focus here, several of the arguments are applicable to other visible minorities in Canada. Even though truth is sometimes a dichotomy of "either–or" or "black and white," much more often it stretches into a spectrum of colour (Fearnside and Holther 1959: 30). This is exactly what happens when exploring the usefulness of multiculturalism in the lives of Black Canadians. Logically speaking, the issue demands a relative judgment. It would, therefore, be fallacious to wrap an answer into one bundle that labels multiculturalism as good or bad, blameworthy or blameless, significant or insignificant. There is no simple affirmation nor rejection of this policy.

As a government policy, multiculturalism is beset by a host of troublesome ambiguities and contradictions for Canadians in general and for Blacks and other visible minorities in particular. Official multiculturalism has been limited in its capacity to respond to the problems of race- and ethnic-based inequalities and discrimination in Canada. Moreover, there is no denying that the policy has been abused and manipulated by opportunistic politicians and minorities for personal gains from time to time. Also, the potential for official multiculturalism to create ethnic ghettoes is real, and it should be acknowledged.

While some of the reservations about the policy are well founded, others emanate from what Michael Ignatieff (1996) has called the narcissism of minor difference—as cultures get closer through globalization, more people are becoming increasingly concerned about their group identities. What is worrisome is not that people are asserting their group identities, but that some are acting as though they can maintain their own identity only by undermining someone else's. Needless to say, this zero-sum approach is a recipe for prejudice. As Abu-Laban and Stasiulis (1992) point out, many of the criticisms of the policy are expressions of hostility—or xenophobic frenzy, to put it bluntly—over the growing number of Blacks and other visible minorities in Canada. Very often the criticisms are nothing more than "a thinly-veiled attack on the legitimacy of demands for full membership in the Canadian political community by groups which diverge from white British (or in Quebec, French) standards of physical or cultural acceptability" (Abu-Laban and Stasiulis 1992: 381).

Despite its pitfalls, however, official multiculturalism generally has been beneficial for Blacks, and vice versa, and it therefore should not be terminated, at least from the standpoint of Blacks. Contrary to common belief, Blacks and other minorities do not take their Canadian identity lightly; no wonder Jacques Parizeau blamed the "ethnic vote" for Quebec's sovereignty problems. As Calof (1997: 130) contends, while fear of their treatment in a separate Quebec contributed to their massive vote against separation, minorities' "pride in Canada itself seemed to be a major factor in the voting pattern of these groups." Under the banner and support of official multiculturalism, Blacks and other immigrants have made significant contributions to the Canadian economy, culture, social life, and sports (Calof 1997).

Similarly, Blacks and other minorities have used official multiculturalism to achieve tangible and practical goals in the Canadian mosaic. The work of Liodakis and Satzewich (1998) suggests that while cultural enhancement and cultural retention remain a significant component of contemporary multiculturalism, it has increased its emphasis on assisting Blacks and other minority groups to overcome racial barriers to full participation in Canadian society. This shift in emphasis can be traced to 1981 when the Multiculturalism Directorate (within the Department of the Secretary of State) commissioned reports on race relations in twelve major Canadian cities (Liodakis and Satzewich 1998: 105–106). Several of these reports noted that race relations were problematic or potentially problematic in many of those cities (Lowe 1982; Jobidon 1982; Malik 1982), which elevated issues of racial discrimination in the discourse of official multiculturalism. Contemporary multiculturalism is not only about "parades," "pizza," "polka," and "perogy," to use the playful words of Elliott and Fleras (1992: 287); it is concerned with the elimination of racism. In fact, the Multiculturalism and Citizenship Secretariat now has a Race Relations and Cross-Cultural Understanding Program to battle all forms of racial discrimination (Liodakis and Satzewich 1998: 106). As we shall see in the next chapter, the federal employment equity legislation introduced in 1986 reflects the growing awareness that racial discrimination and exploitation undermine the central tenets of multiculturalism. The basic point here is that multiculturalism is beneficial to the extent that it has been used as a tool to battle racism in employment, education, health care delivery, criminal justice, and the mass media, and it offers Blacks—most of whom are have-nots and have-too-littles—some ideological space to pursue their fair share of the expanding Canadian pie.

Official multiculturalism has established in Canada a new moral order in which the concerns of Blacks are no longer viewed with contempt and condescension, at least in official quarters. Black history and culture are now seen as a legitimate component of the Canadian mosaic and, therefore, worthy of institutional recognition and accommodation. Evidence of such institutional adjustments is now common in such areas as employment, law enforcement, formal education, and mass media. Indeed, the Canadian Radio-Television and Telecommunications Commission (CRTC), the Canadian Broadcasting Corporation (CBC), the National Film Board of Canada and other media-related federal bdoies now have programs that reflect and promote our multicultural mosaic (Cardozo and Musto 1997; Elliott and Fleras 1992).

Similarly, more Canadian schools are incorporating the perspectives of Blacks and other ethnic and racial minorities into their modes of operation, and several have broadened their curricula to reflect our growing cultural diversity. Now it is not uncommon to find Canadian schools and even municipal councils setting aside special days to celebrate and enhance multicultural awareness; the increasing popularity of Black History Month celebrations (usually in February) across the country is just one example. Also, police forces and fire departments in cities such as Toronto, Ottawa, Edmonton, and Vancouver now have recruitment programs that seek to reflect the cultural diversity of the communities they serve (Miner 1986; Scotti and Miller 1985). This is certainly commendable, especially in the case of Toronto where police shootings of Blacks have undermined Black confidence in the city's police force. Some of these institutional adjustments are mere window dressing, capable of appeasing only the most cursory glance. However, given the limited negotiating power of Blacks—as a result of their small numerical strength, immense cultural heterogeneity, spatial dispersion, and the racial oppression they face in Canada—we cannot realistically expect much at this early stage.

We have argued that multiculturalism has a significant role to play in the lives of Canadians, especially Blacks and other minorities, despite its pitfalls and ambiguities. While some of the criticism against multiculturalism is based on candid assessments of the workings of the policy over the years, some of it is rooted in a misguided fear that multiculturalism has given too much power to ethnic minorities. Indeed, it may well be that "multiculturalism is relatively easier to 'blame' for disunity, in part because there are fewer repercussions" (Abu-Laban and Stasiulis 1992: 378). The attacks on multiculturalism should not surprise any keen social observer, given the growing uneasiness over immigration, pluralism, and ethnoracial diversity in many Western developed countries. In fact, such attacks are equally prevalent in countries such as the United Kingdom and Australia where official multiculturalism initiatives have been implemented (Karim 1997).

In light of the emotional and sometimes vituperative repudiation of multiculturalism, it is quite astonishing that the avowed critics have not been able to articulate any workable alternative. This inability reinforces Lionel Rubinoff's contention that:

> the sustaining and characteristic feature of the Canadian experience has been more of a celebration than a homogenization of difference.... [Arguably, in Canada] unity is achieved not *in spite of* but *because of* the variety of irreconcilable differences which comprise the substance of this nation. (1982: 124; original emphasis)

And so Canada may be likened to an orchestra (Rubinoff 1982: 124–25) or, better still, to jazz music in which "individuality is promoted in order to sustain and increase the creative tension within the group—a tension that yields higher levels of performance to achieve the aim of the collective project" (West 1993: 105; original emphasis).

Notes

1. The Quiet Revolution was a period of rapid change experienced in Quebec from 1960 to 1966 under the Quebec Liberal government of Jean Lesage. During this period there were massive reforms to Quebec's electoral, educational, and health-care systems as well as to the province's labour code.
2. The "third force" refers to people who are neither aboriginal nor members of

the founding nations (Abu-Laban and Stasiulis 1992: 366; Fleras and Elliott 1992: 72).

3. "Cultural relativism" as used in this instance by Bibby is a bit ambiguous. Cultural relativism is an anthropological thesis that simply posits that moral rules differ from society to society. Obviously this is different from what Bibby implies here, for the objective fact of cultural relativism is accepted even by the non-relativist. Arguably, "ethical relativism"—the normative principle that "there are no universally valid moral principles," or that "morality lies in the eye of the beholder" (Pojman 1995: 690), or "that fundamental differences in ethical views and practices fall along cultural lines, to use Bibby's own definition (1990: 9)—would have been more appropriate in this context. And, of course, the distinction here can be deduced from Bibby's assertion: "We have decreed that what is descriptively obvious [i.e., cultural relativism] should be prescriptively valued [i.e., ethical relativism] (1990: 7).

4. Euthyphro was a seer and religious expert who sought to charge his own father with manslaughter after one of their family labourers, who had killed another labourer, died at the hands of Euthyphro's father. In this dialogue, Socrates inquires how Euthyphro can be so sure that his intended conduct is consistent with his religious duty. Much of the discussion centres on the true nature of *piety*. See Plato 1954.

5. None of these postmodern theoreticians is a Canadian. This suggests that the challenge to absolutism has long been going on in other places outside of Canada. It is, therefore, too simplistic to attribute the situation to multiculturalism. With or without multiculturalism, the anti-absolutist tendency will persist.

6. The Spicer Commission was appointed by the Mulroney Conservative government in 1990–91 to solicit Canadians' views on a wide range of issues relating to the country's future. Many believe that the commission—made up of Keith Spicer (chairman) and twelve appointed commissioners—was established primarily to answer criticism that the constitutional future of Canada was being negotiated by the Mulroney government in back rooms without public consultation. At the end of June 1991, the commission released its report, which according to the commission was based on the views of more than 400,000 Canadian groups and individuals. Among other things the Spicer Commission recommended that the government encourage a sense of country; that Quebec be recognized as unique; that there be a prompt settlement of Native land claims; and, most importantly, that the government cut down on multicultural spending relating to "the promotion of diversity." See Canada, Citizens' Forum on Canada's Future 1991.

7. Admittedly, this is a well-written book, albeit with some apparent and, indeed, real contradictions here and there.

8. The specific fallacy of false cause committed here is called *post hoc, ergo propter hoc,* translated as "after this, therefore because of this."

9. A version of this exchange was used by Bissoondath (1994: 111).

10. Tom Flanagan, a leading federal Reform policy analyst and former party director of policy, strategy, and communication, said in a 1993 interview with Della Kirkham that "there is fairly wide [party] support for a 'melting pot'

concept" (Kirkham 1998: 258).

11. In its Blue Book the Reform Party (1991: 35) emphatically asserts that the party "would end funding of the multiculturalism program and support the abolition of the Department of Multiculturalism. It is worth noting that, under intense pressure from the Reform Party, the short-lived Kim Campbell government dismantled the Department of Multiculturalism in 1993 and shifted some of department's programs over to other government ministries.

12. When Quebec refused to sign the 1982 Constitution because it did not allow the province to control its own future as a francophone society, Prime Minister Mulroney sought to bring Quebec into the "constitutional family" with an accord originally formulated at a meeting with the ten premiers at Meech Lake, Quebec, on April 30, 1987. Foremost among the provisions of the accord was the recognition that Quebec is a "distinct society" with powers beyond those of other provinces. To become law, the accord had to be ratified by the federal parliament and all provincial legislatures in accordance with the 1982 Constitution. Elijah Harper, the only Native member of the Manitoba legislature, would not support the accord, thus holding up its final ratification in that province; this eventually led to the demise of the accord. Harper withheld his consent on grounds that the constitutional process had ignored First Nations issues (Hiller 1991: 187; Denis 1991: 144–71).

Chapter 9

Employment Equity and Blacks in Canada

As with official multiculturalism, conversations and even academic discourse on Canada's employment equity policy often turn into heated debate imbued with value-laden assumptions and extreme opinions. This chapter examines the background, concepts, and rationale of Canada's Employment Equity program and offers a spirited response to the attacks leveled against it. The discussion does not belabour old-fashioned White supremacist doctrines and the exclusionary tactics they espouse with regard to Black employment. Rather it scrutinizes the subtle racism that underpins much of the prevailing criticism of employment equity in Canada, specifically the anti-employment equity arguments and ramblings emanating from the Canadian new right project spearheaded by Preston Manning and members of the erstwhile Reform Party. Like their counterparts in the United States and Britain, members of the Canadian new right are engaged in what Martin Barker (1983) calls the "new racism"—that is, racism that cunningly attempts to replace explicitly racist language with politically safe language, code words, and suppositions that appear race neutral when taken at face value. As Kirkham (1998: 248) points out, only a careful deconstruction of the underlying subtext of such arguments can unpack the racialized meanings they espouse.

Following Irving Thalberg (1976), a number of counter-polemics will be deployed not only to expose facts glossed over by opponents of Canada's employment equity policy, but also to reveal the implicit social alternatives and preferences one might have in opposing the policy.

Origins and Provisions

Canada's Employment Equity Act was passed in August 1986, largely in response to the recommendations of two landmark reports—*Equality Now!* (Canada, Special Committee on Visible Minorities in Canadian Society 1984) and *Equality in Employment* (Canada, Royal Commission on Equality in Employment 1984). The latter, chaired by Justice Rosalie

Silberman Abella, is known as the Abella Report. *Equality Now!* acknowledges the existence of a "vertical mosaic" in Canada, and offers eighty
recommendations to help contain and address the situation. Like *Equality
Now*, the Abella Report notes that race- and ethnic-based privileges are
entrenched in the Canadian workplace and, consequently, it calls for the
elimination of all systemic ethnoracial barriers in the job market. The term
"employment equity" was coined by the Abella Commission as a substitute
for the U.S. term "affirmative action," perhaps to reduce the negative
reactions and charges of reverse discrimination associated with the U.S.
project. But as we shall soon see, this change in nomenclature could not
shield Canada's employment equity from such attacks.

The Abella Report (Canada, Royal Commission on Equality in
Employment 1984: 254) views employment equity as a "strategy to
obliterate the present and the residual effects of discrimination and to open
equitably the competition for employment opportunities to *those arbitrarily
excluded"* (emphasis added). "Those arbitrarily excluded" in this context
include women, Aboriginal people, people with disabilities, and visible
minorities. Furthermore, in rejecting a program of voluntary compliance,
the Abella Report calls for the enactment of legislation requiring all
federally regulated employers and companies doing business with the
federal government to take proactive steps to eliminate discriminatory
barriers to employment, and to file an annual report outlining their
progress in this area. In addition, the Abella Report recommends that an
enforcement mechanism be established through the Canadian Human
Rights Commission. It was against the backdrop of these landmark reports
that the federal government enacted Canada's first Employment Equity
Act in August 1986; a new act came into effect in October of 1996.
The purpose of Canada's *Employment Equity Act* is:

> To achieve equality in the work place so that no person shall be
> denied employment opportunities or benefits for reasons unre-
> lated to ability and, in the fulfilment of that goal, to correct the
> conditions of disadvantage in employment experienced by women,
> aboriginal peoples, persons with disabilities and persons who are,
> because of their race or colour, in a visible minority in Canada by
> giving effect to the principle that employment equity means more
> than treating persons in the same way but also requires special
> measures and the accommodation of differences. (Canada, *Em-
> ployment Equity Act of 1986,* Section 2).

Clearly, Canada's employment equity is not a passive, nondiscrimina-
tory policy but a proactive one that seeks to assist women, persons with

disabilities, Aboriginal people, and visible minorities[1] to overcome current discrimination and to remedy the effects of past exclusionary measures on members of these groups. The provisions of the 1986 Act applied to all federally regulated employers with one hundred or more employees, public sector companies, Crown corporations, and federal contractors with at least a hundred employees that bid for government contracts worth $200,000 or more. The new *Employment Equity Act,* which came into effect in October 1996, brings almost all of the public service under its purview. Following the recommendations of the Abella Report, the *Employment Equity Act* requires all of these companies and employers to file an annual report on the composition of their work force, identifying the number and types of jobs performed by members of the designated groups. Any applicable employer who fails to produce this progress report is liable to a fine not exceeding $50,000. For the most part, the act is enforced based on complaints made to the Canadian Human Rights Commission.

Both the Canadian *Human Rights Act* of 1978 and the *Charter of Rights and Freedoms* of 1985 acknowledge the legitimacy, legality, and fairness of government measures to increase significantly the recruitment and up-grading of visible minorities, women, Aboriginal people, and persons with disabilities in the work force (Jain and Hackett 1989; Jain 1988). Section 41(2) of the *Human Rights Act,* for instance, specifically empowers human rights tribunals to impose remedial programs on employers in cases of systemic discrimination. Smilarly, the Canadian *Charter of Rights and Freedoms* exempts from its equality provisions all initiatives that seek to redress the disadvantages experienced by certain minorities (Elliott and Fleras 1992).

Underlying Assumptions and Concepts

Through employment equity, the government seeks to make the Canadian work force as diversified as the general population. The policy first and foremost is based on the assumption that without any government intervention, meritorious hiring and equality of opportunity will continue to elude minorities, women, disabled persons, and Aboriginal people in the Canadian labour market. Underneath this assumption is the realization that if discrimination did not exist, all sectors of the work force would exhibit the cultural diversity of the Canadian population. However, because of entrenched discrimination, members of the designated groups tend to be over-represented in less desirable jobs (Nelson and Fleras 1995). While ethnoracial traditions and preferences have channeled some groups into specific types of jobs (Hiebert 1999b), the fact remains that centuries of discrimination have forced members of the designated groups, especially Blacks, into the most miserable jobs in Canada. Employment equity is also based on the premise that institutional discrimination, which is far more damaging than individual discrimination, is prevalent in the workplace. As we learned in Chapter 6, institutional discrimination derives from employment practices that seem race neutral on the surface but nevertheless have a far-reaching, adverse impact on Blacks and other disadvantaged groups.

Canada's employment equity policy has been in place for more than a decade now. One would have expected—in debates and questions surrounding such a highly canvassed policy—that the meanings of all key terms, at least, should have been agreed upon among the opposing camps, and that our inquiries in the course of the last decade would have passed from semantics to the real subject of the controversy. Unfortunately, that is not the case. Ambiguity still surrounds the policy, as different disputants affix different connotations to some of the key terms used in the debate. Consequently, before we examine the arguments for and against the policy, let us establish some preliminary definitions of the main concepts: "equality," "equality of opportunities," and "equality of outcomes or results."

The Concept of Equality

The foundation of Canada's employment equity policy is equality. Many observers of Canada's socio-economic scene (e.g., Satzewich 1999; Krahn and Lowe 1998; Li 1998) agree that members of the designated groups generally have been denied equality in the labour market over the years. But what, in fact, is equality? What does it mean to demand to be treated as an equal? What kind of equality does Canada's employment equity seek? Finally, what are the best ways to achieve this equality? Equality in the workplace is interpreted differently, depending on one's political stance and philosophical convictions. Elliott and Fleras (1992: 254) have identified three main connotations of equality as used in the employment equity debate. First, there are those who see equality as sameness. According to this interpretation, the goal of equality is to treat everyone the same regardless of background. This implies giving individuals equal opportunities in the labour market by breaking down social, economic, and other barriers. Adherents of this view of equality usually advocate for equality of opportunity. Note that this interpretation does not call for any special steps to improve the lot of disadvantaged groups. Second, there are those who conceive of equality as numerical or proportional equivalence. In their estimation, members of disadvantaged groups should be given preferential treatment in hiring and promotion to reflect their relative share in the national population or in a particular work force. Third, some interpret equality as being different but equal. The proponents of this view contend that for the sake of genuine equality, backgrounds and circumstances of individuals and groups should be taken into consideration (Elliott and Fleras 1992: 254). As with the second connotation, this one permits the use of special measures to enhance the employment opportunities of members of the designated group.

That Canada's *Employment Equity Act* seeks to achieve equality is unequivocal. The burning issue, though, is "Which of the above three connotations of equality does the Act seek?" Indeed, all three versions can be deduced from the Act, albeit with varying degrees of accuracy, comprehensiveness, and logical consistency. The purpose of the Act (as stated in Section 2) is "to achieve equality in the work place so that no person shall be denied employment opportunities or benefits for reasons unrelated to ability...." Obviously, this statement chimes well with the first interpretation (i.e., equality as sameness), as the basic reference point is the individual and no preferential treatment is implied so far. But, then, Section 2 of the Act continues:

> and, in the fulfilment of that goal, to correct the conditions of disadvantage in employment experienced by women, aboriginal peoples, persons with disabilities and persons who are ... in a visible minority ... by giving effect to the principle that employment equity means more than treating persons in the same way but also requires special measures and the accommodation of differences.

Clearly, only the second and third connotations of equality can logically flow from the complete reading of the purpose of the Act, as we now have a categorical reference to groups and a tacit acknowledgment that employment inequality has a historical dimension that requires special remedial measures. Any forthright interpretation of the Act's stated and complete purpose suggests that the first interpretation (equality as sameness) alone does not withstand critical assessment.

Equality of opportunities versus equality of outcomes

Complicating the employment equity debate is the controversy of whether the Act should concentrate on individual rights, group rights, or both. This controversy underlies the now common distinction between equality of opportunities and equality of outcomes or results. Those who argue, as did members of the erstwhile Reform Party of Canada, that equality means sameness advocate for "equality of opportunities." Thus, they want employment equity programs to concentrate primarily on individuals (as opposed to groups), giving them equal opportunities and helping them to gain redress against discrimination. The underlying principle here is to treat everyone alike and let the market forces decide. Supporters of this view contend that employment inequalities are inevitable, if not necessary.

Equality of outcomes, on the other hand, places emphasis on the rights of groups rather than individuals. This perspective posits that for a genuine equality in employment to occur, disadvantaged groups ought to be treated differently, indeed, preferentially. Supporters of this position usually call for the setting up of specific timetables, targets, statistical outcomes or quotas for designated groups. In their view, equality of opportunity is inherently inadequate, as it leaves successive generations of disadvantaged groups to re-fight the same battles to win their place in society (Blakemore and Drake 1996). As it stands now, a compromise between these two opposing views is hard to come by, as neither side is willing to budge from what it sees as its well-grounded, morally defensible position. Not surprisingly, the controversy surrounding equality of outcomes and equality of opportunities underlies much of the employment equity debate in Canada, as we shall see in what follows.

Claims and Counter-claims from the Perspective of Blacks in Canada

Without question, employment equity remains the boldest policy pursued by the Canadian government to redress the long and woeful tradition of racism and discrimination in employment. However, like the policy of multiculturalism, employment equity has received an ambivalent reaction from the Canadian public, political parties, academia, and visible minority analysts. As in the United States, some visible minorities have repudiated the policy, and cries of reverse discrimination from White Canadians also abound. Drawing primarily from the affirmative action debate in the United States, some now argue that the policy has done more harm than good to Blacks and other minorities. Some critics allege that employment equity fosters inferiority and victim complexes among Blacks and reinforces White prejudice against Blacks. Others contend that the policy ultimately will lower standards of efficiency in Canadian institutions and workplaces. And still others, notably members of the erstwhile Reform Party of Canada, denounce the policy as a form of reverse discrimination that undermines the democratic principle of equality in Canada. In this section we examine these claims and offer responses from the standpoint of Black Canadians.

Attack #1: Employment equity is reverse discrimination
This is an old attack recycled from the U.S. affirmative action debate by Canadian critics such as Nathan Greenfield (1997) and members of the former Reform Party. The basic formulation of this criticism is that

employment equity operates as a zero-sum game in which Blacks and other designated groups win only at the expense of Whites (or more precisely White males). In the eyes of these opponents, the policy amounts to discrimination in reverse. As the avowed African-American critic Shelby Steele (1994: 225) puts it: "By making black the color of preference, these mandates have reburdened society with the very marriage of color and preference (in reverse) that we set out to eradicate. The old sin is reaffirmed in a new guise." It is argued that employment equity is unfair to Whites, as it somehow forces them to pay for the "sins" of their grandparents and great-grandparents. What is worse, some critics lament, is that the original victims of slavery and other such dehumanizing practices will not derive any direct benefit whatsoever from this "punishment" of Whites. Also, some contemporary Whites are quick to point out that they are not the direct descendants of the original perpetrators of these oppressive acts and, therefore, question why they have to pay for these perpetrators.

Some critics craftily cast this attack as a noble attempt to attain "equality" and "colour-blindness" in society—how ironic! They contend that employment equity undermines the democratic principle of "equality" by treating people differently based on race, gender, and other such variables. For instance, Carl Cohen, a leading U.S. critic, sums up his resentment over race-based hiring in these words: "Racial preference is good for nobody.... It will not integrate the races but will *disintegrate* them, forcing attention to race, creating anxiety and agitation about race,... exciting envy, ill-will, and widespread resentment of unfair penalties and undeserved rewards" (1980: 282; original emphasis). In launching their attacks on the preferential hiring of Blacks some critics go to the extent of quoting, or more precisely "twisting," the words used by civil rights leaders such as Martin Luther King Jr. The following quotation is from Frederick Lynch (1994: 233), a staunch opponent of preferential hiring in U.S. colleges and universities:

> My career has been badly damaged. Worse, I have watched a political steamroller flatten civil liberties and due process as it has moved through institutions designed to be bastions of traditionally liberal values and forums for the free discussion and rational analysis of ideas. The academic and intellectual communities which once embraced Martin Luther King's call to judge an individual by the content of his character, not the color of his skin, now do precisely the opposite.

Frankly, one wonders how Lynch can believe that U.S. academic institutions, including even the Black universities, really did judge individuals by the content of their character rather than the colour of their skin prior to the era of affirmative action. Then again, he did not see with the eyes of a "victim" then. There is also the possibility that Lynch was, and has been, so far removed from the circumstances of Blacks that the realities of their oppression escaped him. It is amazing how people suddenly can see the light as soon as the tables turn.

Similar cunning appeals to equality and colour-blindness have been trumpeted loudly by members of the former Reform Party and by other Canadian critics to chastise employment equity. Preston Manning, for instance, asserts that "Canada must be a country where race ... should not determine any individual's employment status" (quoted in Kirkham 1998: 260). And, Stephen Harper, a leading Reform/Canadian Alliance policy strategist, in an interview with Della Kirkham (1998: 259), encapsulated his party's position in the following bromide:

> The two views of equality that I think are most prevalent in our society are on the one hand, that government should pursue some kind of pattern of behaviour towards people that makes them more equal, or that government is prepared to provide different sets of rules and standards for people ... that would 'enhance their equality.' *There's another view that people should be treated identically or equally regardless of differences otherwise that they possess. More than any mainstream political party in Canada, the Reform Party subscribes to the second view.* (emphasis added)

The appeal to equality and race neutrality here is a classic example of what U.S. Senator Daniel Patrick Moynihan calls "semantic infiltration"— the appropriation of the language of one's political opponent "for the purpose of blurring distinctions and molding it to one's own political position" (quoted in Steinberg 1995: 23). Of course, even Manning and his "Reformers" should know that the argument that equality means treating people equally regardless of their differences is patently absurd. We thus find Aristotle, the master of those who know,[2] offering the following epigram in his famous *Nicomachean Ethics*: Injustices occurs when equals are treated unequally, or when unequals are treated equally. Needless to say, the "Reformers" are resorting to this erroneous connotation of equality only to camouflage their real racist intentions through semantic infiltration. As Della Kirkham (1998) points out, Reform's appeal to equality and colour-blindness in attacking Canada's policies on employment equity (and, indeed, those on immigration and multiculturalism as well) is a strategic re-articulation of the party's racist intentions in race neutral rhetoric. This is a common strategy deployed by perpetrators of the new racism (Martin Baker 1983). "Re-articulation," as used here, implies the "discursive reorganization and reinterpretation of ideological themes and interest" in such a way that they attain new meanings (Omi 1987: 16). Those who engage in this re-articulation usually abandon overtly or explicitly racist language in favour of covert, race-neutral language and politically safe semantics.[3] Again, only a resourceful deconstruction can reveal the full ramifications of the views espoused by such re-articulation.

One should never underestimate the ability of some Canadian politicians, especially the former "Reformers," to underrate the intelligence of the Canadian public when it comes to issues of race and ethnicity. Only by framing their attack in the simplistic connotation of equality as sameness can the party individualize employment equity, focusing on individual rights rather than group rights, and call for equality of opportunity as opposed to equality of outcomes. Desperate to avoid charges of racism and extremism, the Reform Party asserted in a 1992 document that "the Reform Party believes that women and men, disabled persons, and persons of all ethnic origins, contribute to the enhancement and productivity of Canadian society" (quoted in Kirkham 1998: 259). Then, quite predictably, the document goes on to launch an attack on employment equity: "Reformers also believe that government intrusions into a society of free individuals which attempt to impose a result rather than enhance equality of opportunity are undesirable" (quoted in Kirkham 1998: 259).

By adopting this simplistic interpretation of equality, these critics are pursuing equality as an end in itself. This approach is narrow-minded, for genuine democracies do not seek equality for its own sake. As the Alva Myrdal Report to the Swedish Social Democratic Party shrewdly points out, "Equality is not merely a goal in itself"; it is a means to an end—an end which ensures that all individuals in society *have the same rights to live a full and satisfying life*" (quoted in Struhl and Struhl 1980: 386; original emphasis). The Alva Myrdal Report further states that equality is a "means of changing human relations, of *creating a better social climate*" in society (quoted in Struhl and Struhl 1980: 387; emphasis added). Former U.S. President Lyndon Johnson expressed a similar view in a 1965 commencement speech at Howard University:

> You do not take a person who, for years, has been hobbled by chains and liberate him, bring him to the starting line of a race and then say, "you are free to compete with all the others," and still justly believe that you have been completely fair.... We seek not just freedom but opportunity ... *not just equality as a right and a theory but equality as a fact, as a result.* (quoted in Steinberg 1995: 165; emphasis added)

Reasoning such as that of the former Reform Party, which sees equality as sameness and calls for equality of opportunities rather than equality of outcomes is inherently biased against Blacks and other disadvantaged groups. As Elliott and Fleras (1992: 255) observe, this train of thought simply

> freezes the prevailing distribution of inequality without any appreciable change to the status quo.... After all, as ethnic groups move forward to improve their socio-economic status, their forward movement is matched by an equal move forward by those who already have benefited from the advantages of a head start. The numbers improve overall, the gap remains proportionately intact.

Due to their double sense—or, more accurately. their multifaceted connotations—words such as "equality" usually lead to disputable conclusions in reasoning. Yet, there can be no doubt that the conceptualization of equality as "sameness" in this context seeks to maintain the status quo in Canada. Such a position disregards a diachronic synthesis in favour of a synchronic one, which effectively ignores the historical and material sources of the inequalities faced by Blacks and other minorities in Canada. "Corrective justice," Charles Adams (1994: 230) writes:

> demands that ... institutions that have been "color struck" for generations must not all of a sudden pretend to be so "color blind" that they fail to make special provisions ... to help the historically racially excluded segment of the population catch up to an equal position at the starting line of competition.

It is amazing how the former "Reformers" and other critics can blame such flimsy and abstract notions as hyphenated citizenship and the wearing of turbans for Canada's unity problems and fail to see the interpretable interplay between entrenched socio-economic inequalities and national disunity.

Certainly, one cannot create a better social climate by maintaining a status quo of inequality. As Aristotle lucidly points out in *The Politics*,: inequality is generally at the bottom of national disunity, "for it is in their striving for what is fair and equal that men [and women] become divided" (1974: 191). That which causes conditions leading to revolution and social strife, according to Aristotle, "is chiefly and generally inequality. For those who are bent on equality start a revolution if they believe that they, having less, are yet the equals of those who have more" (1974: 192). It bears asking whether it is realistic, or fair, to expect Blacks and other minorities to remain loyal to a social, political, and economic system that neglects their demands for a socially dignified existence.

Many who see employment equity as reverse discrimination argue that it is intellectually inconsistent to fight for equality and colour-blindness when Blacks are the victims of discrimination and then to do nothing when Whites are the "victims." This is how Bissoondath (1994: 97) frames this attack: "That there are problems to be addressed there is no doubt. But simply changing the focus of discrimination, treating members of visible minorities as if their skin colour were a handicap, is no answer." One would simply have to agree to disagree with Bissoondath if he believes that, despite the voluminous empirical evidence for the enduring "liability" of non-White skin pigmentation in Canadian society, there are no serious disadvantages, if not strong penalties, for being Black or a visible minority in Canadian society (Li 1998; Henry 1989; Henry and Ginsberg 1985a, 1985b).

More substantially, the problem with this intellectual inconsistency attack is that it ignores a significant difference between the two situations. As Richard Wasserstrom (1980: 284) argues, the fundamental evil of the discriminatory practices perpetrated against Blacks is that these practices were part of a social universe that systematically concentrated socio-economic and political power in the hands of Whites (specifically, White males). Obviously this is not the case under employment equity. As Wasserstrom (1980: 284–85) points out: "There is simply no way in which all these programs taken together could plausibly be viewed as capable of relegating White males to the kind of genuinely oppressive status characteristically bestowed upon women and Blacks by the dominant social institutions and ideology."

Without question, the two situations are markedly different, and the supporters of employment equity are not guilty of any intellectual inconsistency. That aside, is it not hypocritical for White employers and White workers, many of whom have discriminated against Blacks over the years, to invoke the principle of equality now?

Let us now address the closely related criticism that employment equity is unfair because it seeks to "punish" contemporary Whites for the "sins" of their grandparents. This is how Neil Bissoondath (1994: 94) reasons this attack: "To force all white, English-speaking males to pay for the wrongs committed by others of their color, language and gender is like giving an entire class detention because one of its members scribbled a dirty word on the blackboard. It is juvenile and discriminatory."

Logically speaking, every analogy must break down at one point or another, since no two cases are perfectly identical. But in this instance, the properties of the two situations are so drastically different that Bissoondath is, indeed, committing a fallacy of faulty analogy. The only way out is for him to make the preposterous assumption that, first, all the members of this hypothetical class were physically present at the time; second, that the class acted responsibly and pinpointed the culprit involved; third, that no member of the class benefited or took advantage of the situation in any way; and finally, that no harm or potential harm was inflicted on any member of the class or the teacher by this dirty word and that, despite all this the teacher gave the entire class detention. In such a situation, the teacher involved must be power-drunk, if not insane! Needless to say, both White males and females have benefited and continue to enjoy race privileges engendered by the wrongs and "dirty words" scribbled on the blackboard of Canadian history and Canadian workplaces over the years.

Irving Thalberg (1976: 106) captures the flaws in this "unfairness argument," revealing how it starts from the true premise that contemporary Whites did not create the oppressive system under which Blacks are suffering and then ends up with the false conclusion that contemporary Whites therefore "are not responsible for the system, and have no obligation to alter it." The link that the unfairness argument draws between causation and accountability is based on the baneful assumption that only those who initiate harm are liable for the harm, regardless of who sustains and benefits from the inequities produced by this harm (Thalberg 1976: 106–07). Contemporary Whites should be partly liable not only because, by and large, they passively and sometimes actively benefit from past harms caused to Blacks, Aboriginal people, and other minorities, but also because some contemporary Whites have cherished and, indeed, reinforced the status quo. In any case, is the argument that contemporary Whites have nothing to do with the predicament of present-day Blacks and other ethnic minorities ethically or even empirically sustainable? The reader is urged to form his or her own opinion on this question. Furthermore, it is quite erroneous to conceptualize employment equity as a "punishment" for Whites. As Thalberg (1976: 106) queries, if there is marked inequality between Blacks and Whites due to a historical discrimination in favour of Whites, "how can it be a punishment when Whites are compelled to give up their privileged status" and play fair in their dealings with Blacks and other minorities?

Finally, let us grant for the sake of argument that employment equity is unfair to Whites. Still, are we ready to assert that this unfairness is anywhere near the unfairness engendered by the alternative, which amounts to a status quo of entrenched racial inequities? Of course not!

Attack #2: Employment equality will ultimately lead to institutionalized inefficiency

Another common criticism of employment equity in Canada is that it will eventually lower standards at our institutions and workplaces and that the level of competence that the Canadian public—implicitly, the White establishment—has come to expect from public institutions will decline. Thus, employment equity is objectionable because it allegedly bypasses people who are qualified and bestows a preference to others just because they are Black, from a visible minority group, disabled, female, or Aboriginal. Can this attack withstand intense analytical scrutiny?

More than anything else, this criticism is patently hypocritical. It is based on the false assumption that we live in a meritocracy that is being undermined by underhanded proponents of employment equity. But would anyone argue that we would have the best qualified person for each advertised job were it not for employment equity? Would anyone claim that every CEO, government minister, judge, and top-ranking official in Canada's private and public institutions is in such a prestigious position because he or she is the best qualified? Although each person's qualifications were not totally discounted in securing the appointment, who can deny that for the most part these qualifications were not the decisive factor. Indeed, Richard Wasserstrom was not far from the truth when he observed that generally

> the higher one goes up in terms of prestige, power and the like, the less qualifications seem ever to be decisive. It is only for certain jobs and certain places that qualifications are used to do more than establish the possession of certain minimum competencies. (1980: 285)

It is amazing how the opponents of employment equity can all of a sudden invoke this myth of meritocracy, knowing very well that many are hired into positions of power in Canada primarily on the basis of whom they know and not what they know, or will ever know. The enduring power of the patronage appointment, especially in the political arena, is now so prevalent in Canada that many hiring processes demonstrate no pretence of a qualification requirement.

Now, let us grant for the sake of argument that most Blacks and minorities are incompetent. Would it not still be a gross mismanagement of the nation's human resources to allow only the better-suited to develop their inherent talents and fully express themselves in society, while the talent, creativity, energy, and vitality of the rest, however small that may be, remain untapped just because we want to attain this utopian conception of institutional efficiency? Also, given the natural tendency for socio-economic inequality to limit, and sometimes poison, communication among different classes of society, can we expect any enduring economic or institutional efficiency under conditions of extreme ethnoracial inequality in employment?

As Elliott and Fleras (1992: 260) argue, employment equity does not dilute the competition for jobs; rather "it seeks to expand the number of applicants in the competition ... and to make the competition more equal by opening it up to those formerly excluded from fair and just application." One can argue that employment equity makes job competitions more intense, and, implicitly, leads to a more efficient and competent work force. And as Thalberg (1976: 110) suggests, anyone who is tempted to believe that Blacks and other ethnic minorities are inherently incompetent is simply urged, by way of counter-argument, to recall the many talentless, uninterested, and incompetent Whites he or she has encountered in many workplaces and academic environments, and realize that race or ethnicity has no causal link whatsoever with incompetence. The fact is, in Canada, as in several Western industrialized nations, many marginally competent or grossly ineffectual Whites, to put it bluntly, are hired over Blacks and other minorities simply because their skin colour suits the racial preferences of employers. Perhaps what is worse is that "White incompetence is always an individual matter, while for Blacks it is often confirmation of an ugly stereotype" (Steele 1994: 223).

Again, assuming that the hiring of Blacks and other minorities would dilute the level of efficiency in the workplace, are we prepared to accept the implicit and problematic premise that it is more important for us, as a demographically multicultural society, to maintain high standards of competence than to include ethnoracial minorities in our work force? Before offering any response here, ponder for a moment what the answer would be if Whites were the targets in this exclusionary scenario. It bears stressing that any efficiency enhancement that might emanate from the abolishment of employment equity will "weigh very little in the moral balance against the double accomplishment of preferential treatment: compensation to Blacks for past wrongs against them and achieving ... occupational integration [and] racial justice in the workplace" (Ezorsky 1991" 92). Finally, what are these opponents of employment equity doing about practices such as seniority ranking, hiring by personal contacts, and political patronage appointments, all of which obviously undermine the principle of meritocracy they seem to cherish so much?

Attack #3: Employment equity helps only advantaged Blacks

Some critics contend that employment equity benefits only the few well-educated, middle-class Blacks seeking academic and high-level professional employment and does little for the disadvantaged or poorly educated Blacks seeking low-end jobs. This criticism became popular following the 1987 publication of *The Truly Disadvantaged* by the eminent African-American sociologist William Julius Wilson. This book is a follow-up to *The Declining Significance of Race* (1978), in which Wilson argues that the problems of Blacks in America in the seventies and beyond can best be addressed not by tearing down racist barriers but by improving the skills and education of Blacks. According to Wilson, many Blacks are unemployed not because of racism, but because they lack the necessary skills and educational qualifications for the emerging knowledge-based economy. He contends that the civil rights movement resolved key racial issues in the U.S.; the hurdles facing Blacks now are issues of class.[4] In essence, race now has limited explanatory power or "significance" in our understanding of the employment situation of Blacks in America.

In *The Truly Disadvantaged*, Wilson examines the policy implication of "the declining significant of race" in America. His basic argument, as his title suggests, is that race-based employment programs mainly have benefited the well-educated, middle-class Blacks and not the truly disadvantaged Blacks. Most often Wilson uses the term "truly disadvantaged" to refer to the Black underclass—that is, Blacks outside the U.S. occupational mainstream, most of whom engage in street crime and other aberrant behaviour for their livelihood. Wilson argues in favour of "universal," class-based (rather than race-based) policies. In his view, the solution to Black unemployment lies in microeconomic policies that promote employment growth and job training for the underclass.

In opposition to Wilson, analysts such as Steinberg (1995), Hacker (1992), Ezorsky (1991), and Tollet (1990) have demonstrated through empirical and theoretical analyses that affirmative action has benefited not only advantaged Blacks, but also Blacks seeking blue-collar and low-end jobs. Tollet (1990) argues that Wilson's position that affirmative action programs are derisory because they neither promote employment growth nor address the job-training problems of the underclass is analogous to condemning penicillin for not anticipating and preventing AIDS and cancer. Similarly, Ezorsky (1991) uses the following analogy to show that it would be imprudent to adopt Wilson's policy of full employment as a substitute for preferential treatment:

> Before bus desegregation [in the U.S.], blacks could occupy only
> a relatively small number of seats in the back of a bus; hence they

often had to stand. If there were more buses, blacks would have gained more seats, but Wilson certainly would not have advocated building more buses as a substitute for desegregation, that is, as a substitute for racial justice, let us not conceive of expansion in the number of jobs as a substitute for racial justice in the workplace.

There is no denying that affirmative action programs have limited usefulness for the ghetto underclass, most of whom are too destroyed as persons to be reasonably employable or trainable. Unless one is willing and able to work, no amount of affirmative action enforcement can be of any use. Implicitly, therefore, increased employment opportunities through economic growth, as proposed by Wilson, can be of equally little help to the extreme ghetto underclass or the truly disadvantaged. Without doubt, as the number of job openings increases relative to the available labour forces, employers will be compelled to offer more positions to Blacks but, as Ezorsky demonstrates in the preceding analogy, it would be misguided to use the expansion in the number of jobs as a substitute for employment equity programs. Indeed, the issues cannot be framed in an either–or format, as Wilson seems to imply. There is nothing wrong with combining affirmative action programs with employment growth and job-training initiatives. Lessons from history suggest that affirmative action policies are no less significant in periods of economic boom than in times of depression.

When it comes to the underclass, one is tempted to side with Cornel West's (1993) call for a politics of conversion to combat the "nihilist threat" facing Blacks in the ghettoes. This conversion, according to West, involves "the turning of one's soul … through one's own affirmation of one's worth … fuelled by the concern for others" (1993: 18–20). While it is hard to fault West in his proposal for a "love ethic" and "a turning of the soul," there is no denying that his suggestion overlooks the political and economic undertones of the Black underclass. Quite uncharacteristically, West in this instance disregards the structural and material constraints that eat at the human soul in the confines of the Black American ghettoes.

To what extent are these arguments and counter-arguments germane to the Canadian context? Has employment equity benefited only advantaged Black Canadians? Should we, as a society, favour class-based employment equity programs over ethnic-, race-, and gender-based ones? Can we really solve the employment discrimination problems faced by Black Canadians through microeconomic and employment expansion policies alone?

While the limited scientific debate on employment equity in Canada has usually centred on jobs in academia and professional disciplines, the greatest employment equity-induced job opportunities for Blacks and other minorities in Canada seem to have occurred in blue-collar and low-end employment. Available research (e.g., Nelson and Fleras 1995) shows that several cities and municipalities across Canada, including Kitchener, Vancouver, and Ottawa, have used employment equity mechanisms in recruiting their police officers, firefighters, and paramedics, despite intense opposition from the usual beneficiaries of the status quo—White males. Notwithstanding the ongoing debate and attacks against these enforcement programs, one thing remains indubitable: these workplaces have become more diverse in recent years.

There are indications that low- and mid-level jobs in Canada have become far more diverse than their high-level counterparts, especially in federal government departments, academia, and the professions. While this supposition may surprise many Canadians, it is nothing new to ethnic and racial minorities, especially to members of the Black community. It is common knowledge among many Blacks that, all things being equal, it is far easier for them to get low- and mid-level jobs than it is to get high-level jobs. While empirical data on the subject are scarce, it is not hard to explain this state of affairs: high-end jobs invariably involve, and sometimes invoke, leadership, influence, sophistication, and power—attributes which many Canadians are not ready even to associate with Blacks, let alone to relinquish to them. More disturbingly, this condescending sentiment is far more prevalent in Canada's public service departments; how else can one explain the fact that they are among the worst violators of Canada's employment equity policy? In their report on employment equity in the public services of Canada, John Samuel and Associates found that "both visible minorities employees and public service managers, including EXs [i.e., assistant deputy ministers and directors general], expressed the view that racial discrimination against visible minorities is *prevalent* in the public service" (1997: 1; emphasis added). After thorough theoretical and empirical analyses, John Samuel and Associates (1997: 1) observed that "there are indications that the federally regulated private sector is doing much better [than the federal public sector] in hiring visible minorities."

Available evidence suggests that the employment equity situation in our institutions of higher learning is not any better (Shah and Svoboda 2000; Rossi-Wayne Report, quoted in *Canadian Association of University Teachers Bulletin* 2000: 3). With the aid of a simulation model based on a "minimum" hiring practice in which 15 percent of the new faculty are visible minorities, Shah and Svoboda (2000: 4) estimate that it would take between 25 and 119 years for the University of Toronto,[5] for instance, to reach its desired rate of 15 percent visible minority faculty. Empirical data in this area are lacking, for quite obvious reasons. Yet, anecdotal evidence suggests that Canadian universities and colleges do not have any problem hiring Blacks and other minorities for part-time, temporary, or sessional positions, but that these institutions are hesitant to hire Blacks and ethnic minorities for full-time, tenured positions. Often, as soon as positions become full-time, those in authority present convoluted, and sometimes concocted, academic explanations as to why they need to hire someone (usually a White male or female) from outside to teach the same course at the same level. These full-time positions are usually filled through a network of kinship, social ties, old boyism and, more recently, new-girlism, under the auspices of "objective" hiring committees.

The case of Dr. Kin-Yip Chun, a world-renowned[6] Chinese-Canadian geophysicist at the University of Toronto is a classic example of what visible minorities have to go through to scale the ivory towers of Canadian academia. Dr. Chung taught at the University of Toronto from 1985 until 1994, when he was denied tenure and terminated. The Ontario Human Rights Commission, the Canadian Association of University Teachers' (CAUT) Academic Freedom and Tenure (AF&T) Committee, and many other reports on the issue, including the University of Toronto's own internal report, found that Dr. Chun had been unfairly treated. Indeed the AF&T Committee observed some evidence of systemic discrimination at the university. Similarly, the Ontario Human Rights Commission noted that the "old boys network" and "cronyism," which work against minority applicants when it comes to faculty hiring, are prevalent at the university (*Canadian Association of University Teachers Bulletin* 2000: 14). Perhaps the most perturbing aspect of the Chun case was the fact that the University of Toronto authorities resorted to shredding records to thwart the investigatory process (*Canadian Association of University Teachers Bulletin* 2000: 1, 4). If this does not point to systemic discrimination, or at least to the spectre of it, then one is at a loss as to what does.

Clearly, the common belief that racism has an inverse relationship with one's level of education is problematic, to put it mildly. For one thing it overlooks the fact that while redneck, overt racism is uncommon among well-educated people, covert or hypocritical—and, ultimately, more damaging—racism is prevalent.[7]

For a variety of reasons, only a few people in the Canadian academic community are prepared to engage in any debate or informed dialogue on employment equity, especially on their own campus. Some are fearful of being branded "racist," "bigoted," "radical," or "ethnocentric" by opponents, many of whom harbour unflinching, dogmatic opinions. Others have sensed, rightly or wrongly, that whatever they say on the issue could amount to professional suicide and so refuse to take the chance. Notwithstanding this reluctance, Canadian academic institutions soon must face up to employment equity in all of its uncomfortable intricacies because of anticipated increases in faculty hiring in the next five to ten years, due to retirement (*Canadian Association of University Teachers Bulletin* 2000: 3; *Vancouver Sun* 2000).

Perhaps no where do Blacks and other visible minorities, especially those trained in Africa, Asia, and Latin America, face more blatant discrimination than in the Canadian medical profession. Regardless of the talk about employment equity and the shortage of medical practitioners within the past decade or so, the Canadian Medical Association has managed to restrict the entry into their profession for Blacks and other minorities trained elsewhere. These minority doctors face a revolving door or what Randall Collins (1990) calls "market closure": they are refused employment because they lack Canadian experience, and they cannot get this experience without proper Canadian internship and certification. Meanwhile, there is virtually no fair and open system through which these immigrant physicians can upgrade or requalify in Canada.

The argument that employment equity has been more beneficial to advantaged Blacks is especially weak in the Canadian context as compared to that of the United States, where Blacks and other minorities have gained access to a considerable amount of federal government employment over the years (Steinberg 1995; Ezorsky 1991). Indeed one can hypothesize, on the basis of the preceding analysis and available anecdotal evidence, that the much-touted brain drain from Canada to the U.S. has significant ethnoracial undertones. Without question, employment equity programs have steadily opened up the top-end of the Canadian employment hierarchy for some visible minorities, disabled persons, Aboriginals, and women. But the gains so far have been minuscule and uneven not only *within* but also *between* the designated groups; there are indications that since the mid-1980s White women, in particular, have been scaling the Canadian ivory towers and corporate ladders faster than and in greater numbers than other designated groups (Shah and Svoboda 2000; McQueen, 2000).

Attack #4: Employment equity reinforces stereotypes of Black inferiority

Some—notably, African-American critics such as Shelby Steele (1994), Thomas Sowell (1976; 1989), and Stephen Carter (1991)—contend that preferential treatment reinforces stereotypes of Black inferiority, perpetuates White prejudice, and invariably encourages a victim-complex among Blacks. Thomas Sowell (1976, 1989) agrees with William Wilson (1987) that affirmative action rarely benefits those in need, and Sowell further admonishes the policy on grounds that it undermines "the legitimacy of black achievements by making them look like gifts from the Government"

(1976: 15). Sowell is also convinced that affirmative action weakens Black activism through gestures of appeasement and that it fosters polarization and backlash from the White majority. Similarly, Shelby Steele (1994) argues that affirmative action creates self-doubt and fosters inferiority and victim complexes among Blacks.

Stephen Carter expresses the same sentiment in his hard-hitting *Reflections of an Affirmative Action Baby* (1991). He claims that affirmative action has a patronizing and demeaning effect not only on Black recipients but on all Blacks, who are invariably tainted with the suspicion that they cannot compete on a level playing field without government help. Neil Bissoondoth (1994: 95) echoes this assertion in the Canadian context:

> On a personal level, as a member of one of those targeted racial minorities, I can think of few things more demeaning to me than to be offered an advantage because of my skin colour. It is demeaning because, no matter what I have struggled to achieve, I am still being judged on the colour of my skin and not simply as a human being with strengths and weaknesses. I am still, even with the best of intentions, being viewed racially—and that is offensive to me.

One cannot chastise or show any harshness towards Neil Bissoondath for merely expressing his personal feelings. Indeed his self-doubt (to put it mildly), as exhibited in the above quotation, is totally disarming. As long as critics such as Bissoondath, Carter, Steele, and Sowell do not presume to be speaking for all minorities, we can leave them alone. But they certainly cross the line whenever they assert that just because preferential treatment is demeaning to *them* it should be abolished. Certainly those who choose to see affirmative action as demeaning are free to do so, but let us not permit these people to present themselves as restorers of Black dignity when they have simply woven a sophistry out of what is basically an idiosyncratic uneasiness with the policy. Perhaps what Blacks need is a far less complicated act of restoration: simply offering them job opportunities to situate them in a dignified position of being able to provide the basic needs of food, shelter, and clothing for their families.

While some minorities may be uncomfortable with the alleged demeaning implications of employment equity, others "may not give a damn what Whites think and find within themselves a sense of their personal worth and mission" (Steinberg 1995: 169). Many others may appreciate the fact that employment equity has opened up doors that would otherwise be slammed shut in their faces, because of their skin pigmentation. It is all too easy for people who are gainfully employed to be bothered by the "odious and demeaning qualities" of employment equity. Tell that to the Black man or woman who is informed that an advertised position is filled only to find out that a White colleague with a comparable, or even lower, qualification is hired minutes later. Tell it to the South Asian woman who is refused a job interview because her name and accent identify her as a visible minority (Henry and Ginzberg 1985b). What is demeaning is, arguably, in the eyes of the beholder. Nonetheless most Blacks and ethnic minorities would concur that any possible humiliation and dehumanization caused by employment equity pale in comparison with those wrought by both the subtle and not-so-subtle discriminatory practices that are so widespread in the Canadian labour market.

Employment equity was necessitated by the historical exclusion of Blacks and other minorities from the Canadian labour market, not by any perceived or real inability of minorities to compete on a level playing field. To the extent that these critics have chosen to ignore this fact by casting their attacks in an ahistorical fashion, their position is suspicious if not seriously flawed.

Other critics (e.g., Paul Starr 1992) chastise preferential treatment, not because it is unbeneficial to Blacks, but because they believe it can foster antagonism from Whites, reinforce White prejudice and stereotypes about Blacks and, eventually, poison race relations. The reverence that some Blacks, especially Black intellectuals, have for what Whites think about them is almost superstitious. To these Blacks, the counter-discourse offered so far may seem like a form of simony. But let us add one such simony to the list by querying how they can possibly conceive of asking Blacks to sacrifice their employment opportunities to appease Whites, most of whom are against the policy for their own self-interest. Instead of denouncing the racism inherent in some of the attacks against the policy, these critics find it more expedient to persuade the woefully powerless Blacks to relinquish their employment gains—a classic case of a "spineless capitulation to racial backlash" (Steinberg 1995: 174).

That a critic playing on the ideological team of White supremacy would use employment equity to buttress his or her allegations of Black inferiority should surprise no one. But any Black who falls for such twaddle, not only in spite of the dehumanizing history of the Black diaspora in Canada but, even more, in the face of the continuing racial discrimination against Blacks in the Canadian job market deserves some commiseration. With no theoretical status whatsoever, isn't the term "inferiority complex" even in its most effective deployment a polemical one? Assuming there is any objectivity in assessing who has or should have an "inferiority complex," can we still draw a causal link between employment equity and inferiority complex? Finally, given the long-standing preferential treatment accorded to Whites in the job market, wouldn't it be disingenuous, or a simple case of double standard, to allege that such a treatment breeds an inferiority complex in Blacks and never in Whites, thus assuming there is a sustainable causal connection between the two concepts? These questions, some of which are original and none of which is uncontentious, serve as powerful lens through which one can assess the veracity of the inferiority-complex gambit formulated by opponents of Canada's employment equity policy.

Conclusion

Indeed, any proposal that seeks to hire qualified Blacks or any other visible minority over qualified Whites is bound to be controversial, not only because it has to grapple with the thorny issues of fairness and equality, but also because it counteracts the Eurocentric ideology purveyed through the state, corporations, and other monoliths of institutionalized power in Canada. That employment equity exacerbates insecurity among those who have benefited or have vested interest in the status quo is hardly surprising. What is a bit surprising is the level of apprehension generated among Blacks and other visible minorities who are supposed to be the direct beneficiaries of the policy.[8]

There is no denying that employment equity involves a serious clash between individual and group rights. There are those who insist that the collective rights of Blacks and other designated groups must take precedence over the individual rights of White males if the historical injustice against the former is ever to be remedied. Others argue, or rather take for granted, that it is morally indefensible, if not reprehensible, to sacrifice the individual rights of any White person for the collective rights of Blacks or other designated groups. What, then, is the best way to proceed? How do we reconcile these competing rights? As a society, only a dialogue with our collective past can shed light on the best way to resolve this moral dilemma. Nelson and Fleras (1995: 373) write that "neither right is superior, and attempting to choose between either of them is a losing proposition." But wouldn't it be apt, at least from the standpoint of morality couched in a dialogue with our societal past, to favour collective rights over individual rights in this context, given the historical injustice perpetrated against visible minorities, Aboriginal people, disabled persons, and women in the Canadian labour market?

In the bid to achieve ethnoracial and gender equality in the workplace, some White males may be unfairly treated or adversely impacted. For these Whites, there is nothing wrong with instituting some government-funded compensatory mechanisms, as suggested by Ezorsky (1991), but we must not deceive ourselves. As a corrective project, employment equity is a form of creative destruction or destructive creation. It invariably involves the destruction of old structures, ideologies, and some individual rights, as well as the creation of new mentalities that embrace anti-authoritarian gestures, multicultural sensitivities, and even some iconoclastic social habits in the Canadian workplace. The fact is that, without creative destroyers like employment equity and multiculturalism, Canada's quest for ethnoracial diversity and equality would remain illusive. Although the notion of creative destruction is not intuitively self-evident—as we are used to conceptualizing destruction only in negative terms—we must not forget that one cannot make an omelette without breaking some eggs in a creatively destructive manner.

Despite the chorus of criticism against employment equity, some employers are realizing that the policy is good for business.[9] While those who are shielded by the prevailing exclusionary ideology may derive some benefits from the status quo, Canada as a whole stands to lose when talented and well-qualified visible minorities, women, Aboriginals, and disabled persons are excluded from the work force for reasons unrelated to work performance. Without employment equity, we deprive ourselves of multicultural viewpoints and dynamism and their related sensitivities. Obviously, these attributes cannot be ascertained in a dreary, monocultural work environment. Furthermore, members of under-represented groups tend to be more receptive of change and least threatened by new ideas and personalities in the workplace, as they have not been part of the entrenched status quo. Since it is impossible for Blacks and other minorities, and indeed any group, to create world-views that are wholly independent of their historical and cultural backgrounds, they usually have the tendency and the capacity to interrogate and challenge the discursive strategies of the White majority and to expose the Anglo-Saxon biases that are so prevalent in many Canadian workplaces and institutions. Given the right circumstance, such a counter-discourse can foster creativity in the workplace. At the same time the potential for explosive ethnoracial confrontations and upheavals cannot be overlooked.

Before drawing the discussion to a close, it is worth stressing that even though Blacks have been the main focus of the preceding discussion, it would be erroneous for any Black person to be like the cobbler who thinks leather is the only real thing and discount the fact that other members of the designated groups also face discrimination in the Canadian labour market. Having said that, one should still avoid the temptation of lumping Blacks and other visible minorities together in any discourse on racial oppression. Renowned U.S. sociologists Robert Blauner (1972) and

Stephen Steinberg (1995) have written extensively about the fundamental differences between the Black experience in the United States and that of other ethnic groups. Blacks are not just another minority. Unlike other immigrants, who came to the United States through voluntary migration, Blacks came by forced migration to serve as slaves and cheap labour for the budding industrial capitalism. And as Steinberg (1995: 87) puts it:

> From these different starting points, the histories of blacks and [other] immigrants proceeded along two different trajectories. [Other] immigrants *did* encounter prejudice and discrimination … but their troubles paled in comparison to the all-encompassing system of domination and exploitation that was the lot of the average Negro. (original emphasis)

This book suggests that the Black experience in Canada is not much different from the Black experience in the United States. Any interpretable difference may be a matter only of degree, certainly not in kind. While most of the original Black Canadians were not slaves, many came through impelled migration—as refugees and loyalists—and were invariably used as cheap or indentured labour in the worst, most hazardous, and lowest-paying jobs in Canada. Moreover, as in the United States, the racial division of labour has resulted in a system of prejudice, racial stereotyping, mythology, and insult for Blacks and other visible minorities. The term "visible minority" is best conceptualized as a continuum: different groups are located at different positions, and they face varying degrees of discrimination and social distance, not only from the White majority but also from the other minority groups that constitute the continuum. While the relative position of the various visible minority groups (e.g., Chinese, East Indians, Blacks, etc.) along this continuum changes from time to time, Blacks have generally occupied the lowliest position, due to their legacy of slavery and their physical visibility—this assertion is supported by the available empirical studies.[10] Consequently, the common tendency to lump Blacks and other visible minority groups together in pursuance of employment equity creates a crowding effect in which Blacks (and to a large extent Aboriginals) ultimately become the main losers.

Some analysts question why many in other visible minority communities, notably Chinese and East Indians, have succeeded without employment equity and Blacks have not. The simple answer is that the Black experience is fundamentally different from that of other visible minorities. One might add that some Blacks, albeit a relatively small number, also have made it without relying on employment equity. Still, we cannot take too lightly the depth and pervasiveness of racial oppression and dehumanization faced by both "successful" and "disadvantaged" Black Canadians. Writing in the context of the United States, Ezorsky (1991: 74) asserts that Blacks "still predominate in those occupations that in a slave society would be reserved for slaves." Is the situation in Canada any different, based on the theoretical arguments and empirical data provided in this book? You decide.

Employment equity is a worthwhile initiative because it has the potential to correct past injustices, diversify our work force, and help make our institutions and workplaces more efficient by increasing the pool of qualified job applicants. Despite these merits, and notwithstanding the spirited arguments made in favour of the policy, it is only fair to admit that Canada's employment equity policy is not a paragon of virtue or a template of excellence, at least not yet. This is why Fleras and Elliott (1996: 347) shrewdly caution that when it comes to a policy like employment equity "criticism and rebuttal are not mutually exclusive but complementary yet in opposition." Put differently, given the internal heterogeneity of the policy, one can simultaneously criticize some aspects of the policy and applaud other components without being inconsistent.

There are serious shortfalls in the way the policy is presently implemented. Of particular concern is the lack of specific targets, timetables, comprehensive monitoring mechanisms, and sanctions for non-compliance. In the absence of stringent enforcement procedures, Blacks and other designated groups are left with only the complaint approach to redress—a highly deficient approach in most racial discrimination cases. As it stands now, victims of discrimination are supposed to lodge formal complaints (with human rights commissions) against individuals and firms that violate their employment equity rights. In most cases, the plaintiffs have to prove—with hard facts and data—that the culprits involved acted from racial bias. This is certainly a daunting task under any circumstance, let alone in work environments where employers naturally have the power to conceal their racial prejudice. The current enforcement procedures are so weak that even federal government departments frequently violate the policy with impunity. Without pressure from, and accountability to, outside authorities, employers in both the private and public sectors would find it difficult to change their ingrained dirty tricks against ethnoracial minorities. Too much is at stake for anyone to attempt a premature, categorical judgment of Canada's employment equity policy. One can but assert, as vigorously as possible, that unless these problems are dealt with seriously, opponents can justifiably denounce the policy as a sham, a skimpy and threadbare veil used to disguise entrenched inequalities and to disarm the activism of Blacks and other ethnic and racial minorities.

Notes

1. Based on the specifications of the *Employment Equity Act*, the term "visible minority" includes Chinese, South Asians, Blacks, Arabs and West Asians, Filipinos, Southeast Asians, Latin Americans, Japanese, Koreans, and Pacific Islanders.

2. Dante, the famous Italian poet, was the first to describe Aristotle as such.

3. A fairly similar tactic was used by Gordon Campbell, the leader of British Columbia's Liberal Party to oppose the Nisga'a Treaty. Couching his opposition in the democratic principles of equality, Mr. Campbell called for a referendum on the treaty, asserting: "I want to be clear: we strongly support the goal of workable, affordable treaties that will provide certainty, finality and equality" (Gordon Campbell, Press Statement on Nisga'a Court Proceedings, October 19, 1998). One would like to know how he intends to get any treaty at all, let alone a workable one, by insisting on a referendum on what is obviously a minority right. Then, again, that is the principal tactic of the new racism.

4. But can we really draw any durable theoretical line between race and class, especially in the context of the United States?

5. The reader should note that the University of Toronto is among our leading universities. In fact, one can assert that U of T is the leading Canadian university, based on the diversity of undergraduate and graduate programs, student population, library resources, research grants and facilities, and many other relevant variables.

6. "World-renowned" was the adjective used to describe Dr. Chung in an article in the Canadian Association of University Teachers (CAUT) Bulletin. See *Canadian Association of University Teachers Bulletin* 2000: 3.

7. The volumes of sophisticated racism that, under the guise of science, have poured out of the pens of highly educated people is perhaps the best testimony one can offer for this supposition.

8. The available literature suggests that Aboriginals, persons with disabilities, and women do not seem to harbour such uneasiness with the policy. The reasons for this deserve further research.

9. John Samuel and Associates (1997) writes that Canadian banks, in particular, now believe that visible minority employees in their work force help to increase productivity and profitability. It is, therefore, not surprising that the main chartered banks had visible-minority employee representation levels that ranged from 10.7 percent to 18 percent in 1995, when there was only 4.1 percent visible minority representation in the Canadian public service (John Samuel and Associates 1997: 1).

10. See Pineo (1977) and Reitz and Breton (1998).

Bibliography

Abella, Rosalie Silberman. 1985. *Research Studies of the Commission on Equality in Employment*. Ottawa: Supply and Services Canada.

Abu-Laban, Yasmeen, and Daiva Stasiulis. 1992. "Ethnic Pluralism Under Siege: Popular and Partisan Opposition to Multiculturalism." *Canadian Public Policy* 27 (4): 363–86.

Adams, Charles G. 1994. "It's Past Time to Speak Out." In Gary Goshgarian and Kathleen Krueger (eds.), *Crossfire: An Argument, Rhetoric and Reader*. New York: Harper Collins.

Adilman, Tamara. 1984. "A Preliminary Sketch of Chinese Women and Work in British Columbia, 1858–1950." In B. Latham and R. Pazdro (eds.), *Not Just Pin Money: Selected Essays on the History of Women's Work in British Columbia*. Victoria: Camosun College.

Adjibolosoo, Senyo, and Joseph Mensah. 1998. "Demographic Profile and Settlement Problems of African Immigrants in the Vancouver Metropolitan Area of British Columbia: A Human Factor Assessment." *Review of Human Factor Studies* (4) 2: 32–63.

Agnew, Vijay. 1996. *Resisting Discrimination: Women from Asia, Africa, and the Caribbean and the Women's Movement in Canada*. Toronto: University of Toronto Press.

Agocs, Carol, and Monica Boyd. 1993. "The Canadian Ethnic Mosaic Recast: Theory, Research, and Policy Frameworks for the 1990s." In James Curtis et al. (eds.), *Social Inequality in Canada: Patterns, Problems, Policies*. Toronto: Prentice.

Alexander, Ken, and Avis Glaze. 1996. *Towards Freedom: The African-Canadian Experience*. Toronto: Umbrella.

Allahar, Anton L. 1993. "When Black First Became Worth Less." *International Journal of Comparative Sociology* 34 (1–2): 39–55.

Ama, Pierre F.M., Pierre Lagasse, Claude Bouchard, and Jean-Aimé Simoneau. 1990. "Anaerobic Performances in Black and White Subjects," *Medicine and Science in Sports and Exercise* 22: 508–11.

Ama, Pierre F.M., et al. 1986. "Skeletal Muscles Characteristics in Sedentary Black and Caucasian Males." *Journal of Applied Physiology* 61: 1758–61.

Amnesty International. 1984. *The Public Tribunals in Ghana*. June. New York: Amnesty International Publications.

Anderson, Wolseley W. 1993. *Caribbean Immigrants: A Socio-Demographic Profile*. Toronto: Canadian Scholars.

Andrew, Allan. 1993. "Auditing Race Relations Practices of Metro Police." *Currents* 8 (1): 14–16.

Angus Reid Group. 1991. *Multiculturalism and Canadians: Attitude Study, 1991 National Survey Report*. Ottawa: Multiculturalism and Citizenship.

Appiah, Kwame. 1990. "Racism." In David Theo Goldberg (ed.), *The Anatomy of*

Racism. Minneapolis: University of Minnesota Press.

Arat-Koc, Sedef. 1989. "In the Privacy of Our Own Home: Foreign Domestic Workers as a Solution to the Crisis in the Domestic Sphere in Canada." *Studies in Political Economy* 28 (Spring): 33–58.

Aristotle. 1974. *The Politics*. Trans. Desmond Lee. Harmondsworth: Penguin.

_____. 1976. "The Nichomachean Ethics." In Melvin Rader (ed.), *The Enduring Questions: Main Problems of Philosophy*. New York: Rinehart and Winston.

Armstrong, Pat, and Hugh Armstrong. 1998. "Health Care as Business." In Wayne Antony and Les Samuelson (eds.), *Power and Resistance: Critical Thinking about Canadian Social Issues*. Halifax: Fernwood.

Artibise, Alan F.J. 1988. "Canada as an Urban Nation." *Daedalus* 117 (Fall): 244–46.

Asante, Molefe Kete. 1987. *The Afrocentric Idea*. Philadelphia: Temple University Press.

Audi, Robert. 1995. "Postmodern." In Robert Audi (ed.), *The Cambridge Dictionary of Philosophy*. Cambridge: Cambridge University Press.

Bacchi, Carol. 1983. *Liberation Deferred? The Ideas of the English-Canadian Suffragists, 1877–1918*. Toronto: University of Toronto Press.

Bakan, Abigail B., and Daiva K. Stasiulis. 1995. "Making the Match: Domestic Placement Agencies and the Racialization of Women's Household Work." *Signs: Journal of Women in Culture and Society* 20 (21): 303–35.

Balakrishnan, T.R. 1982. "Changing Patterns of Ethnic Residential Segregation in the Metropolitan Areas of Canada." *Canadian Review of Sociology and Anthropology* 19: 92–110.

Balakrishnan, T.R., and F. Hou. 1995. *The Changing Patterns of Spatial Concentration of Residential Segregation of Ethnic Groups in Canada's Major Metropolitan Areas, 1981–1991*. Discussion Paper No. 95–2. London: Population Studies Centre, University of Western Ontario.

Balakrishnan, T.R., and J. Kralt. 1987. "Segregation of Visible Minorities in Montreal, Toronto, and Vancouver." In Leo Driedger (ed.), *Ethnic Canada: Identities and Inequalities*. Toronto: Copp Clark.

Bannerji, H. 1986. "Popular Images of South Asian Women." *Tiger Lily* November/December: 23–29.

Bannerji, H., D. Brand, P. Kholsla, and M. Silvera. 1983. "We Appear Silent to People Who Are Deaf to What We Say." *Fireweed: A Feminist Quarterly*. "Women of Colour" Special Issue. Spring: 8–12, 14–15.

Bantin, Michael. 1987. *Racial Theories*. London: Cambridge University Press.

Barber, Marilyn. 1991. *Immigrant Domestic Servants in Canada*. Ottawa: Canadian Historical Association.

Barker, Martin. 1983. *The New Racism: Conservatives and the Ideology of the Tribe*. London: Junction.

Barrett, Michele. 1980. *Women's Oppression Today: Problems in Marxist Feminist Analysis*. London: Verso.

Barris, Ted. 1998. "Jerome, Harry Winston." In *1999 Canadian Encyclopedia: World Edition*, produced on CD-Rom by McClelland and Stewart.

Barry, Vincent. 1978. *Personal and Social Ethics: Moral Problems with Integrated Theory.* Belmont, CA: Wadsworth.

Bastide, Roger. 1968. "Colour, Racism, and Christianity." In J.H. Franklin (ed.), *Color and Race.* Boston: Houghton.

Bawumia, Mahamadu. 1995. "Racism and Economic Development." *Review of Human Factor Studies* 1 (1): 91–98.

Beck, E.M., P. Horan, and C. Tolbert. 1978. "Stratification in a Dual Economy: A Sectoral Model of Earning Determination." *American Sociological Review* 43 (October): 704–20.

Berger, John. 1974. *The Look of Things.* New York: Viking.

Bergman, Brian. 1993. "Canada: A Nation of Polite Bigots?" *Maclean's Magazine* December 27: 42.

Berry, J.W., R. Kalin, and D.M. Taylor. 1977. *Multiculturalism and Ethnic Attitudes in Canada.* Ottawa: Supply and Services Canada.

Berry, J.W., and J.A. Laponce. 1994. "Evaluating Research on Canada's Multiethnic and Multicultural Society: An Introduction." In J.W. Berry and J.A. Laponce (eds.), *Ethnicity and Culture in Canada: The Research Landscape.* Toronto: University of Toronto Press.

Bibby, Reg. 1990. *Mosaic Madness.* Toronto: Stoddart.

Billson, Janet Mancini. 1991. "Interlocking Identities: Gender, Ethnicity and Power in the Canadian Context." *International Journal of Canadian Studies* 3 (Spring): 49–67.

Bissoondath, Neil. 1994. *Selling Illusions: The Cult of Multiculturalism in Canada.* Toronto: Penguin.

Black, Naomi. 1993. "The Canadian Women's Movement: The Second Wave." In Sandra Burt, Lorraine Code, and Lindsay Dorney (eds.), *Changing Patterns: Women in Canada.* Toronto: McClelland and Stewart.

Blakemore, Ken, and Robert F. Drake. 1996. *Understanding Equal Opportunity Policies.* London: Prentice.

Blauner, Robert. 1972. *Racial Oppression in America.* New York: Harper and Row.

Bloom, Marc. 1998. "Kenyan Runners in the US Face Bitter Taste of Success." *New York Times,* April 16: A1, C24.

Bolaria, B. Singh. 1991. *Social Issues and Contradictions in Canadian Society.* Toronto: Harcourt.

Bolaria, B. Singh, and Peter S. Li. 1988. *Racial Oppression in Canada.* Toronto: Garamond.

Bonacich, E. 1972. "A Theory of Ethnic Antagonism: The Split Labour Market." *American Sociological Review* 37: 547–59.

_____. 1975. "Abolition, the Extension of Slavery, and the Position of Free Blacks: A Study of Split Labour Markets in the United States, 1830–1836." *American Journal of Sociology* 81: 601–62.

_____. 1976. "Advanced Capitalism and Black/White Race Relations in the United States: A Split Labour Market Interpretation." *American Sociological Review* 41: 34–51.

_____. 1979. "The Past, Present, and Future of Split Labour Market Theory." In

C.B. Marrett and C. Leggon (eds.), *Race and Ethnic Relations*. Volume 1. Greenwich: JAI.

———. 1997. "Abolition, the Extension of Slavery, and the Position of Free Blacks: A Study of Split Labour Markets in the United States, 1830–1836." *American Journal of Sociology* 81: 601–28.

Bone, Robert M. 1999. *The Regional Geography of Canada*. Don Mills, ON: Oxford University Press.

Bordo, Susan. 1990. "Feminism, Postmodernism, and Gender-Skepticism." In L. Nicholson (ed.), *Feminism/Postmodernism*. New York: Routledge.

Boros, James M., and J.R. Parkinson. 1980. *How to Get a Fast Start in Today's Job Market*. Englewood Cliffs, NJ: Prentice.

Bourne, L.S., A.M. Baker, and W. Kalbach. 1985. *Ontario's Ethnocultural Population, 1981: Socio-Economic Characteristics and Geographic Distribution*. Ontario Ministry of Citizenship and Culture, Ethnocultural Data Base Series III, Special Report No. 3. Toronto: Ontario Ministry of Citizenship and Culture.

Boyd, Monica. 1992. "Gender, Visible Minority, and Immigrants Earning Inequality: Reassessing an Employment Equity Premise." In Vic Satzewich (ed.), *Deconstructing a Nation: Immigration, Multiculturalism, and Racism in '90s Canada*. Halifax: Fernwood.

Boyko, John. 1998. *Last Steps to Freedom: The Evolution of Canadian Racism*. Toronto: J. Gordon Shillingford.

Boyle, Paul, Keith Halfacree, and Vaughan Robinson. 1998. *Exploring Contemporary Migration*. New York: Longman.

Bristow, Peggy. 1993. "The Hour-a-day Study Club." In Linda Carty (ed.), *And Still We Rise: Feminist Political Mobilizing in Contemporary Canada*. Toronto: Women's.

Brookfield, H.C. 1969. "On the Environment as Perceived." *Progress in Geography* 1: 51–80.

Brouwer, Ruth. 1991. *New Women for God*. Toronto: University of Toronto Press.

Brown, Rosemary. 1989. *Being Brown: A Very Public Life*. Toronto: Random House.

Browne, Harry. 1972. "The Morality Trap." In John R. Burr and Milton Goldinger (eds.), *Philosophy and Contemporary Issues*. New York: Macmillan.

Burnet, Jean. 1984. "Myths and Multiculturalism." In Ronald J. Samuda, John W. Berry, and Michel Laferriere (eds.), *Multiculturalism in Canada*. Toronto: Allyn.

Cadwallader, M. 1985. *Analytical Urban Geography: Spatial Patterns and Theories*. Englewood Cliffs, NJ: Prentice.

Calgary Herald. 1989. "Controversial Prof Cool on Talk Show." February 17: D7.

Calliste, Agnes. 1993. "Women of 'Exceptional Merit': Immigration of Caribbean Nurses to Canada." *Canadian Journal of Women and the Law* 6 (1): 131–48.

———. 1993/94. "Race, Gender and Canadian Immigration Policy: Blacks from the Caribbean, 1900–1932." *Journal of Canadian Studies* 28 (Winter): 131–48.

———. 1996. "Canadian Immigration Policy and Domestics from the Caribbean: The Second Domestic Scheme." In Wendy Mitchinson et al. (eds.), *Canadian Women: A Reader*. Toronto: Harcourt.

Calof, Jonathan L. 1997. "The Role of Ethnic Minorities in Building a Stronger

Economy and a More United Country." Andrew Cardozo and Louis Musto (eds.), *The Battle Over Multiculturalism*. Ottawa: PSI.

Campbell, J.A., and D.N. Livingstone. 1983. "Neo-Lamarckism and the Development of Geography in the United States and Great Britain." *Transactions of the Institute of British Geographers* 8: 267–94.

Canada. 1906. *Revised Statutes of Canada*. Ottawa: King's Printer.

_____. 1986. *Employment Equity Act*. Chapter 31. Statutes of Canada. Assented to on June 27.

_____. 1988. *Multiculturalism Act*. Chapter 31. Statutes of Canada. Assented to on July 21.

Canada, Citizens' Forum on Canada's Future. 1991. *Report to the People and Government of Canada*. Ottawa: Supply and Services Canada.

Canada, Department of Citizenship and Immigration. [various years]. *Immigration Statistics*. Ottawa: Immigration and Demographic Policy Group, Employment and Immigration Canada.

Canada, Congress for Learning Opportunities for Women. 1986. *Decade of Promise: An Assessment of Canadian Women's Studies in Education Training and Employment, 1976–1985*. Toronto: Avebury Research and Consulting.

Canada, House of Commons. 1947. *Debates*. Speech by W.L.M. King. May 1. 2644–46. Ottawa: House of Commons.

_____. 1971. *Debates*. October 12. 8545–48. Ottawa: House of Commons.

Canada, Manpower and Immigration. 1974. *Immigration and Population Statistics*. Ottawa: Information Canada.

Canada, Royal Commission on Equality in Employment. 1984. *Report of the Royal Commission on Equality in Employment* [The Abella Report]. Ottawa: Supply and Services Canada.

Canada, Special Committee on Visible Minorities in Canadian Society. 1984. *Equality Now! Report of the Special Committee on Visible Minorities in Canadian Society*. Ottawa: Supply and Services Canada.

Canada, Statistics Canada. 1998. "1996 Census: Ethnic Origin, Visible Minorities." *The Daily*. February 17. Cat. no. CS11–001E.

_____. 1999a. *1996 Census Dictionary*. 1996 Census of Canada. Cat. no. 92–351–UPE. Ottawa: Industry Canada.

_____. 1999b. *Dimension Series. Canadian Demographic Characteristics (Including Language and Mobility). 1996 Census*. Cat. no. 94F0008XCB. Ottawa: Statistics Canada.

Canadian Association of University Teachers (CAUT) Bulletin. 2000. "Diversity Debate Finds New Ammo at U of T." 47 (2): 3.

Canadian Ethnic Studies Association. 1992. *Canadian Ethnic Studies Bulletin*. 19 (2): 3.

Cannon, L.W., E. Higginbotham, and M.L.A. Leung. 1988. "Race and Class Bias in Qualitative Research on Women." *Gender and Society* 2 (4): 449–62.

Carby, Hazel. 1986. "White Women Listen! Black Feminism and the Boundaries of Sisterhood." In Centre for Contemporary Culture Studies (ed.), *The Empire Strikes Back: Race and Racism in '70s Britain*. London: Hutchinson.

Cardozo, Andrew, and Louis Musto. 1997. "Introduction: Identifying the Issues." In Andrew Cardozo and Louis Musto (eds.), *The Battle Over Multiculturalism*. Ottawa: PSI.

Carmichael, Stokely, and Charles Hamilton. 1967. *Black Power: The Politics of Liberation in America*. New York: Vintage.

Carr, Edward. 1961. *What Is History?* New York: Vintage.

Carter, Stephen. 1991. *Reflections of an Affirmative Action Baby*. New York: Basic.

Carty, Linda. 1993. "Combining Our Efforts: Making Feminism Relevant to the Changing Sociality." In Linda Carty (ed.), *And Still We Rise: Feminist Political Mobilizing in Contemporary Canada*. Toronto: Women's.

Carty, Linda, and Dionne Brand. 1989. "'Visible Minority' Woman: A Creation of the Canadian State." *Resource for Feminist Research* 17 (3): 39–40.

Cashmore, Ellis. 1982. *Black Sportsmen*. London: Routledge.

_____. 1988. *Dictionary of Race and Ethnic Relations*. London: Routledge.

_____. 1990. *Making Sense of Sport*. London: Routledge.

Chazan, Naomi. 1983. *An Anatomy of Ghanaian Politics: Managing Political Recession, 1969–1982*. Boulder, CO: Westview.

Christensen, Carole P., and Morton Weinfeld. 1993. "The Black Family in Canada: A Preliminary Exploration of Family Patterns and Inequality." *Canadian Ethnic Studies* 25 (3): 26–44.

Christian, Barbara. 1987. "The Race for Theory." *Cultural Critique* 6: 51–63.

_____. 1989. "But What Do We Think We're Doing Anyway? The State of Black Feminist Criticism(s), or My Version of a Little Bit of History." In C. Wall (ed.), *Changing Our Own Words*. New Brunswick, NJ: Rutgers.

Clairmont, Donald H., and Dennis H. Magill. 1970. *Nova Scotian Blacks: An Historical and Structural Overview*. Halifax: Institute of Public Affairs, Dalhousie University.

Coakley, Jay J. 1978. *Sport in Society: Issues and Controversies*. St. Louis: C.V. Mosby.

Cobb, W.M. 1934. "The Physical Constitution of the American Negro." *The Journal of Negro Education* 3: 340–88.

_____. 1936. "Race Runners." *Journal of Health and Physical Education* 7: 3–7, 52–56.

Code, Lorraine. 1993. "Feminist Theory." In S. Burt, L. Code, and L. Dorney (eds.), *Changing Patterns: Women in Canada*. Toronto: McClelland and Stewart.

Cohen, Carl. 1980. "Equality and Preferential Treatment." In John R. Burr and Milton Goldinger (eds.), *Philosophy and Contemporary Issues*. New York: Macmillan.

Cohen, Marjorie Griffin. 1993. "The Canadian Women's Movement Document." In Ruth Roach Pierson et al. (eds.), *Canadian Women's Issues* 1: 1–31.

Collins, Patricia Hill. 1989. "The Social Construction of Black Feminist Thought." *Signs* 14 (4): 745–73.

_____. 1991. *Black Feminist Thought: Knowledge, Consciousness, and the Politics of Empowerment*. New York: Routledge.

_____. 1997. "Defining Black Feminist Thought." In Linda Nicholson (ed.), *The Second Wave: A Reader in Feminist Theory*. New York: Routledge.

Collins, Randall. 1971. "A Conflict Theory of Sexual Stratification." *Social Problems* 19: 3–21.

_____. 1990. "Market Closures and the Conflict Theory of Professions." In Michael Burrage and Rolf Torsten-dahl (eds.), *Professions in Theory and History: Rethinking the Study of the Professions*. London: Routledge.

Colombo, J.R. 1994. *The Canadian Global Almanac*. Toronto: Macmillan.

Combahee River Collective. 1997. "A Black Feminist Statement." In Linda Nicholson (ed.), *The Second Wave: A Reader in Feminist Theory*. New York: Routledge.

Copi, Irving. 1978. *Introduction to Logic*. New York: Macmillan.

Cornia, Giovanni Andrea, and Germano Mwabu. 2000. "Health Status and Policy in Sub-Saharan Africa: A Long-Term Perspective." In Dharam Ghai (ed.), *Renewing Social and Economic Progress in Africa*. New York: St. Martin's.

Cosentino, Frank. 1989. "Football." In Don Morrow et al. (eds.), *A Concise History of Sport in Canada*. Toronto: Oxford University Press.

_____. 1998. *Afros, Aboriginals and Amateur Sport in Pre World War One Canada*. Ottawa: Canadian Historical Society.

Cox, Oliver Cromwell. 1959. *Caste, Class, and Race: A Study in Social Dynamics*. New York: Monthly Review.

Creese, Gillian. 1992. "The Politics of Refugees in Canada." In Vic Satzewich (ed.), *Deconstructing a Nation: Immigration, Multiculturalism, and Racism in '90s Canada*. Halifax: Fernwood.

Cruz, Herman S. 1971. *Racial Discrimination*. New York: United Nations.

Crystal, David, ed. 1998. *The Cambridge Biographical Encyclopedia*. Second edition. Cambridge: Cambridge University Press.

Cumming, P.A., E.L.D Lee, and D.G. Orepoulos. 1989. *Access! Task Force on Access to Trades and Professions in Ontario*. Toronto: Ministry of Citizenship.

Cummins, Jim, and Marcel Danesi. 1990. *Heritage Languages: The Development and Denial of Canada's Linguistic Resources*. Toronto: Garamond.

Curtis, J., and J. Low. 1978. "Race/ethnicity and the Relative Centrality of Playing Positions in Team Sport." *Exercise and Sport Sciences Review* 6: 285–313.

Daenzer, Patricia. 1991. "Ideology and the Formation of Migration Policy: The Case of Immigrant Domestic Workers, 1940–90." Ph.D. Dissertation. Toronto: University of Toronto.

_____. 1997. "Challenging Diversity: Black Women and Social Welfare." In Patricia M. Evans and Gerda R. Wekerle (eds.), *Women and the Canadian Welfare State: Challenges and Change*. Toronto: University of Toronto Press.

Daly, Mary. 1978. *Gyn/Ecology: The Metaethics of Radical Feminism*. Boston: Beacon.

Darroch, Gordon A. 1979. "Another Look at Ethnicity, Stratification and Social Mobility in Canada." *Canadian Journal of Sociology* 4: 1–25.

Darwin, Charles. 1981. *The Descent of Man, and Selection in Relation to Sex*. Princeton, NJ: Princeton University Press.

Das Gupta, Tania. 1996. *Racism in Pain Work*. Toronto: Garamond.

Davetian, Benet. 1994. "Out of the Melting Pot and into the Fire." *Canadian Ethnic Studies* 26 (3): 135–40.

Davies, W.K.D., and R.A. Murdie. 1993. "Measuring the Social Ecology of Cities." In Larry S. Bourne and David F. Ley (eds.), *The Changing Social Geography of Canadian Cities*. Montreal and Kingston: McGill-Queen's University Press.

Davis, Angela. 1981. *Women, Race and Class*. London: Women's.

D'Costa, Ronald. 1989. "Canadian Immigration Policy: A Chronological Review with Particular Reference to Discrimination." In O.P. Dwivedi et al. (eds.), *Canada 2000: Race Relations and Public Policy*. Guelph: University of Guelph Press.

de Blij, Harm J. 1993. *Human Geography: Culture, Society and Space*. New York: John Wiley.

de Blij, Harm J., and Peter O. Muller. 1988. *Geography: Regions and Concepts*. New York: John Wiley.

de Gobineau, J. Arthur. 1853. *Inequality of the Human Races*. New York: Anchor.

Dei, George J. Sefa. 1996. *Anti-Racism Education: Theory and Practice*. Halifax: Fernwood.

Demont, John, Luke Fisher, and Anthony Wilson-Smith. 1997. "Somalia Inquiry's Damning Report." In *1999 Canadian Encyclopedia: World Edition*, produced on CD-Rom by McClelland and Stewart.

Denis, Wilfrid B. 1991. "The Meech Lake Shuffle: French and English Language Rights in Canada." In B. Singh Bolaria (ed.), *Social Issues and Contradictions in Canadian Society*. Toronto: Harcourt.

Depradine, L. 1995. "Nurse Wins $250,000." *Share* 17 (32): 2.

Doris Marshall Institute and Arnold Minors and Associates. 1994. *Ethno-racial Equality: A Distant Goal? An Interim Report to Northwestern General Hospital*. Toronto: Doris Marshall Institute and Arnold Minors and Associates.

Dowty, A. 1987. *Closed Borders: The Contemporary Assault on Freedom of Movement*. New York: Yale University Press.

Dwivedi, O.P., Ronald D'Costa, C.L. Stanford, and Elliot Tepper, eds. 1989. *Canada 2000: Race Relations and Public Policy*. Proceedings of the Canada 2000 Conference, Carleton University, October 30–November 1, 1987. Guelph: Department of Political Science, University of Guelph.

Edgerton, Robert B. 1988. *Like Lions They Fought: The Zulu War and the Last Black Empire in South Africa*. New York: Free.

Edwards, Harry. 1970. *The Revolt of the Black Athlete*. New York: Free.

_____. 1973. *Sociology of Sport*. Homewood, IL: Dorsey.

Edwards, Richard. 1979. *Contested Terrain*. New York: Basic.

Edwards, Susan. 1981. *Female Sexuality and the Law*. Oxford: Martin Robertson.

Eisenstein, Zillah. 1981. *The Radical Future of Liberal Feminism*. Boston: Northeastern University Press.

Elliott, Jean Leonard, and Augie Fleras. 1992. *Unequal Relations: Introduction to Race and Ethnic Dynamics in Canada*. Scarborough, ON: Prentice.

Engels, Friedrich. 1942. *The Origin of the Family, Private Property, and the State*. New York: Random.

_____. 1958. *The Condition of the Working Class in England*. Trans. W.O. Henderson and W. Chalenor. London: Blackwell.

English, Philip. 1984. *Canadian Development Assistance to Haiti*. Ottawa: North–South Institute.

Entine, Jon. 2000. *Taboo: Why Black Athletes Dominate Sports and Why We Are Afraid to Talk About It*. New York: Public Affairs.

Errington, Jane. 1993. "Pioneers and Suffragists." In Sandra Burt, Lorraine Code, and Lindsay Dorney (eds.), *Changing Patterns: Women in Canada*. Toronto: McClelland and Stewart.

Ezorsky, Gertrude. 1991. *Racism and Justice: The Case for Affirmative Action*. Ithaca: Cornell University Press.

Fainstein, Norman. 1986–87. "The Underclass/Mismatch Hypothesis as an Explanation for Black Economic Deprivation." *Politics and Society* 15 (4): 439–43.

Fanon, Frantz. 1963. *The Wretched of the Earth*. New York: Grove.

_____. 1967. *Black Skin, White Masks*. New York: Grove.

Fearnside, Ward, and William Holther. 1959. *Fallacy: The Counterfeit of Argument*. Englewood Cliffs, NJ: Prentice.

Febvre, L. 1925. A *Geographical Introduction to History*. New York: Knopf.

Fellmann, Jerome D., Arthur Getis, and Judith Getis. 1999. *Human Geography: Landscapes of Human Activities*. Boston: McGraw.

Fellows, D.K. 1967. *Geography*. New York: John Wiley.

Firestone, Shulamith. 1970. *The Dialectic of Sex: The Case for Feminist Revolution*. New York: Bantam.

Fisher, Luke. 1996. "Somalia Affair Cover-up Alleged." *Maclean's*, April 8.

_____. 1997. "Somalia Inquiry Heats Up." *Maclean's*, February 10.

Fitzgibbon, Louis. 1985. *The Evaded Duty*. London: Rex Collins.

Fleras, Augie, and Jean Leonard Elliott. 1992. *Multiculturalism in Canada: The Challenges of Diversity*. Scarborough, ON: Nelson.

_____. 1996. *Unequal Relations: An Introduction to Race, Ethnic and Aboriginal Dynamics in Canada*. Scarborough, ON: Prentice.

Forcese, Dennis. 1997. *The Canadian Class Structure*. Toronto: McGraw.

Fornos, Werner. 1992. "Population Politics." In John L. Allen (ed.), *Environment, 92/92 Annual Edition*. Guilford, CT: Dushkin.

Foucault, Michel. 1986. "Of Other Spaces." Trans. Jay Miskowiec. *Diacritics* 16: 22–27.

Francis, E.K. 1947. "The Nature of the Ethnic Group." *American Journal of Sociology* 52: 393–400.

Frankenberg, Ruth. 1993. *White Women, Race Matters: The Social Construction of Whiteness*. Minneapolis: University of Minnesota Press.

Freud, Sigmund. 1965. *New Introductory Lectures on Psychoanalysis*. Trans./Ed. James Strachy. New York: Norton.

_____. 1994. *Civilization and Its Discontents*. 1930. Trans. Joan Riviere. New York: Dover.

Frideres, James S. 1992. "Changing Dimensions of Ethnicity in Canada." In Vic Satzewich (ed.), *Deconstructing a Nation: Immigration, Multiculturalism and Racism in '90s Canada*. Halifax: Fernwood.

Friedman, John Block. 1984. *Staying Power: The History of Black People in Britain*. London: Pluto.

Gage, Frances D. 1978. "Reminiscences of Sojourner Truth." 1851. In Mari Jo Buhle and Paul Buhle (eds.), *The Concise History of Woman Suffrage: Selections from Classic Work of Stanton, Anthony, Gage, and Harper*. Urbana: University of Illinois Press.

Gannage, Charlene. 1986. *Double Day, Double Bind*. Toronto: Women's.

Geschwender, James A. 1994. "Married Women's Waged Labour and Racial/ethnic Stratification in Canada." *Canadian Ethnic Studies* 26 (3): 53–73.

Ghai, Dharam. 2000. "African Development in Retrospect and Prospect." In Dharam Ghai (ed.), *Renewing Social and Economic Progress in Africa*. New York: St. Martin's.

Ghalam, Nancy Zukewich. 1994. "Women in the Workplace." *Canadian Social Trends*. Volume 2. Toronto: Thompson Educational.

Gilroy, Paul. 1987. *There Ain't No Black in the Union Jack: The Cultural Politics of Race and Nation*. London: Hutchinson.

Giroux, Henry A. 1997. "White Squall: Resistance and the Pedagogy of Whiteness." *Cultural Studies* 11 (13): 376–89.

Glazer, Nona Y. 1991. "'Between a Rock and a Hard Place': Women's Professional Organizations in Nursing and Class, Racial, and Ethnic Inequalities." *Gender and Society* 5 (3): 351–72.

Globe and Mail. 1991. "Nova Scotia Blacks Demand Solutions to Discrimination." July 23: A1, A4.

Goldberg, Michael A., and John Mercer. 1986. *The Myth of the North American City*. Vancouver: University of British Columbia Press.

Goldberg, Steven. 1974. *The Inevitability of Patriarchy*. New York: William Morrow.

Gordon, David M., Richard Edwards, and Michael Reich. 1982. *Segmented Work, Divided Workers*. Cambridge: Cambridge University Press.

Gray, Stan. 1994. "Hospitals and Human Rights." *Our Times* December: 17–20.

Green, Joyce A. 1995. "Towards a Detente with History: Confronting Canada's Colonial Legacy." *International Journal of Canadian Studies* 12 (Fall): 85–105.

Greenfield, Nathan M. 1997. "Our Constitution Does Not Admit of Distinctions or Races." In Andre Cardozo and Louis Musto (eds.), *The Battle Over Multiculturalism*. Ottawa: PSI.

Greenglass, E. 1982. *A World of Difference*. Toronto: John Wiley.

Gregory, Derek. 1986. "Lamarck(ian)ism." In R.J. Johnston, D. Gregory, and D.M. Smith (eds.), *The Dictionary of Human Geography*. Oxford: Blackwell.

Grow, Stewart. 1974. "The Blacks of Amber Valley: Negro Pioneering in Northern Alberta." *Canadian Ethnic Studies* 6: 17–38.

Gruneau, R. 1976. "Class or Mass: Notes on the Democratization of Canadian Amateur Sport." In R. Gruneau and J. Albinson (eds.), *Canadian Sports: Sociological Perspectives*. Don Mills, ON: Addison-Wesley.

Gwaltney, John Langston. 1980. *Drylongso: A Self-portrait of Black America*. New York: Vintage.

Hacker, Andrew. 1992. *Two Nations*. New York: Macmillan.

Hale, S.M. 1995. *Controversies in Sociology: A Canadian Introduction*. Toronto: Copp Clark.

Hamilton, J. 1990/91. "Exiles in a Cold Land: Montreal's Haitian Community Faces a Double Barrier of Prejudice." *Canadian Geographic* December/January: 34–42.

Hamilton, Roberta. 1986. "The Collusion with Patriarchy: A Psychoanalytic Account." In Roberta Hamilton and Michele Barrett (eds.), *The Politics of Diversity*. London: Verso.

_____. 1996. *Gendering the Vertical Mosaic: Feminist Perspectives on Canadian Society*. Toronto: Copp Clark.

Hardin, Garrett. 1968. *Exploring New Ethics for Survival: The Voyage of the Spaceship Beagle*. Baltimore: Penguin.

_____. 1980. "Lifeboat Ethics: The Case Against Helping the Poor." In John R. Burr and Milton Goldinger (eds.), *Philosophy and Contemporary Issues*. New York: Macmillan.

Harding, Sandra. 1990. "Feminism, Science, and the Anti-enlightenment Critique." In L. Nicholson (ed.), *Feminism/Postmodernism*. New York: Routledge.

Harney, R.F. 1985. "Ethnicity and Neighbourhoods." In R.F. Harney (ed.), *Gathering Place: Peoples and Neighbourhoods of Toronto, 1834–1945*. Toronto: Multicultural History Society of Ontario.

Harvey, David. 1990. *The Condition of Postmodernity*. Oxford: Blackwell.

Hawkins, Freda. 1989. *Critical Years in Immigration: Canada and Australia Compared*. Montreal and Kingston: McGill-Queen's University Press.

Head, Wilson A. 1984. "Race Relations in Canada: A Re-appraisal." *Multiculturalism* 7 (2): 7–12.

_____. 1985a. "The Concept of Race and Racism in Society." In Rosalie Silberman Abella (ed.), *Research Studies of the Commission on Equality in Employment*. Ottawa: Supply and Services Canada.

_____. 1985b. *An Exploratory Study of Attitudes and Perceptions of Minority and Majority Group Healthcare Workers*. Toronto: Ontario Ministry of Labour.

Helmes-Hayes, R., and James Curtis, eds. 1998. *The Vertical Mosaic Revisited*. Toronto: University of Toronto Press.

Henry, Frances. 1989. *Housing and Racial Discrimination in Canada*. Ottawa: Multiculturalism and Citizenship.

_____. 1994. *The Caribbean Diaspora in Toronto: Learning to Live with Racism*. Toronto: University of Toronto Press.

Henry, Frances, and Effie Ginzberg. 1985a. *No Discrimination Here? Toronto Employers and the Multiracial Workforce*. Toronto: Social Planning Council of Metropolitan Toronto and Urban Alliance on Race Relations.

_____. 1985b. *Who Gets the Work? A Test of Racial Discrimination in Employment*. Toronto: Social Planning Council of Metropolitan Toronto and Urban Alliance on Race Relations.

_____. 1991. *Highlights of Attitudes about Multiculturalism and Citizenship*. Ottawa: Multiculturalism and Citizenship.

Henry, Frances, Carol Tator, Winston Mattis, and Tim Rees. 1995. *The Colour of*

Democracy: Racism in Canadian Society. Toronto: Harcourt.

Herberg, E.N. 1990. "The Ethno-Racial Socioeconomic Hierarchy in Canada: Theory and Analysis of the New Vertical Mosaic." *International Journal of Comparative Sociology* 31 (3–4): 206–21.

Herrnstein, Richard J., and Charles Murray. 1994. *The Bell Curve: Intelligence and Class Structure in American Life*. New York: Free.

Hiebert, Daniel. 1994. "Canadian Immigration: Policy, Politics, Geography." *The Canadian Geographer* 38 (3): 254–58.

_____. 1999a. "Immigration and the Changing Social Geography of Greater Vancouver." *BC Studies* 121 (Spring): 35–82.

_____. 1999b. "Local Geographies of Labour Market Segmentation: Montreal, Toronto, and Vancouver, 1991." *Economic Geography* 75 (3): 339–69.

Hill, Daniel. 1981. *The Freedom-Seekers: Blacks in Early Canada*. Agincourt, ON: Book Society of Canada.

Hiller, Harry H. 1991. *Canadian Society: A Micro Analysis*. Scarborough, ON: Prentice.

Hirsch, E.D. Jr. 1994. "Cultural Literacy." In Gary Goshgarian and Kathleen Krueger (eds.), *Crossfire: An Argument, Rhetoric and Reader*. New York: Harper Collins.

Hitch, P. 1983. "The Mental Health of Refugees: A Review of Research." In R. Baker (ed.), *The Psychosocial Problems of Refugees*. London: British Refugee Council.

Hoberman, John. 1997. *Darwin's Athletes: How Sport Has Damaged Black America and Preserved the Myth of Race*. Boston: Houghton.

hooks, bell. 1981. *Ain't I a Woman: Black Women and Feminism*. Boston: South End.

_____. 1984. *Feminist Theory from Margin to Center*. Boston: South End.

_____. 1988. *Talking Back: Thinking Feminist, Thinking Black*. Toronto: Between the Lines.

Hornby, Jim. 1991. *Black Islanders: Prince Edward Island's Historical Black Community*. Charlottetown: Institute of Island Studies.

Horowitz, Gad. 1977. *Basic and Surplus Repression in Psychoanalytic Theory*. Toronto: University of Toronto Press.

Hou, Feng, and T.R. Balakrishnan. 1996. "The Integration of Visible Minorities in Contemporary Canadian Society." *Canadian Journal of Sociology* 21 (3): 307–26.

Hudson, Michael R. 1987. "Multiculturalism, Government Policy and Constitutional Enshrinement: A Comparative Study." In Canadian Human Rights Foundation (ed.), *Multiculturalism and the Charter: A Legal Perspective*. Toronto: Carswell.

Hughes, David R., and Evelyn Kallen. 1974. *The Anatomy of Racism: Canadian Dimensions*. Montreal: Harvest House.

Hughes, Everett Cherrington, and Helen MacGill Hughes. 1952. *Where Peoples Meet: Racial and Ethnic Frontiers*. Glencoe, IL: Free.

Humphries, J.S., and J.S. Whitelaw. 1970. "Immigrants in an Unfair Environment: Locational Decision-Making Under Constrained Circumstances." *Geografiska Annaler* 61B.

Hurwitz, Samuel J., and E.F. Hurwitz. 1971. *Jamaica: A Historical Portrait*. New York: Praeger.

Ignatieff, Michael. 1996. *The Narcissism of Minor Differences: Clash of Identities*. Toronto: Prentice.

Immigration and Refugee Board Documentation Centre. 1990. *Ghana: Country Profile*. Ottawa: Immigration and Refugee Board Documentation Centre.

Isajiw, Wsevolod W., Aysan Sever, and Leo Driedger. 1993. "Ethnic Identity and Social Mobility: A Test of the 'Drawback Model.'" *Canadian Journal of Sociology* 18: 177–96.

Jackson, Richard A., and L.E. Hudman. 1990. *Cultural Geography: People, Places and Environment*. St. Paul: West.

Jain, Harish C. 1988. "Affirmative Action/Employment Equity Programs and Visible Minorities in Canada." *Current*: 3–7.

Jain, Harish C., and Rick D. Hackett. 1989. "Measuring Effectiveness of Employment Equity Programs in Canada: Public Policy and a Survey." *Canadian Public Policy* 15 (2): 189–204.

James, Allan. 1981. "'Black': An Inquiry into the Pejorative Associations of an English Word." *New Community* 9 (1): 19–30.

James, Carl E. 1998. "Up to No Good: Black on the Streets and Encountering Police." In Vic Satzewich (ed.), *Racism and Social Inequality in Canada: Concepts, Controversies and Strategies of Resistance*. Toronto: Thompson Educational.

Jean-Baptiste, Jacqueline. 1979. *Haitians in Canada*. Ottawa: Supply and Services Canada.

Jensen, Arthur R. 1969. "How Much Can We Boost I.Q. and Scholastic Achievement?" *Harvard Educational Review* 39 (Winter): 11–23.

Jiobu, R. 1988. "Racial Inequality in a Public Arena." *Social Forces* 67 (2): 524–34.

Jobidon, Odette. 1982. *Situation Report on the Current State of Race Relations in Vancouver, B.C.* Ottawa: Secretary of State.

John Samuel and Associates Inc. 1997. *Visible Minorities and the Public Services of Canada*. Ottawa: Canadian Human Rights Commission.

Jones, G. 1980. *Social Darwinism and English Thought: The Interaction Between Biological and Social Theory*. Brighton: Harvester.

Jones, J.M., and A.R. Hochner. 1973. "Racial Differences in Sport Activities: A Look at the Self-Paced Versus Reactive Hypothesis." *Journal of Personality and Social Psychology* 27 (1): 86–95.

Kain, J.F. 1968. "Housing Segregation, Negro Employment, and Metropolitan Decentralization." *The Quarterly Journal of Economics* 82 (2): 175–97.

Kallen, Evelyn. 1987. "Multiculturalism, Minorities, and Motherhood: A Social Scientific Critique of Section 27." In Canadian Human Rights Foundation (ed.), *Multiculturalism and the Charter: A Legal Perspective*. Toronto: Carswell.

Kane, Martin. 1971. "An Assessment of 'Black Is Best.'" *Sports Illustrated* January 18: 72–81.

Kant, Immanuel. 1983. "The Categorical Imperative." In Michael D. Bayles and Kenneth Henley (eds.), *Right Conduct: Theories and Applications*. New York: Random House.

Kaplan, Irving, Howard I. Blutstein, Kathryn T. Johnston, and David S. McMorris. 1976. *Area Handbook for Jamaica*. Washington, DC: U.S. Government Printing Office.

Karim, Karim H. 1997. "Multiculturalism in Australia, the United States and the United Kingdom: An Overview." In Andrew Cardozo and Louis Musto (eds.), *The Battle Over Multiculturalism*. Ottawa: PSI.

Kasarda, J.D. 1989. "Urban Industrial Transition and the Underclass." *Annals, American Association of Political and Social Science* 501 (January): 26–47.

Kazemipur, A., and S.S. Halli. 1997. "Plight of Immigrants: The Spatial Concentration of Poverty in Canada." *Canadian Journal of Regional Science* 20:1 (2): 11–28.

Kendall, P.R. 1992. *A Pilot Study of the Health and Social Needs of the Somali Community in Toronto*. Toronto: Department of Public Health.

Kenyon, G. 1977. "Factors Influencing the Attainment of Elite Status in Track and Field." *Proceedings of the 1976 Post Olympic Games Symposium*. Ottawa: Coaching Association of Canada.

Kew, Frank 1997. *Sport: Social Problems and Issues*. Oxford: Butterworth-Heinemann.

Keyes, Mary. 1989. "Sport and Technological Change." In Don Morrow et al. (eds.), *A Concise History of Sport in Canada*. Toronto: Oxford University Press.

King, Martin Luther, Jr. 1967. *Conscience for Change*. The Massey Lectures. Toronto: Canadian Broadcasting Corporation.

Kirkham, Della. 1998. "The Reform Party of Canada: A Discourse of Race, Ethnicity and Equality." In Vic Satzewich (ed.), *Racism and Social Inequality in Canada: Concept, Controversies and Strategies of Resistance*. Toronto: Thompson Educational.

Klineberg, Otto. 1971. *Race Differences*. New York and London: Harper.

Knowles, Valerie. 1992. *Strangers at our Gates: Canadian Immigration and Immigration Policy, 1540–1990*. Toronto and Oxford: Dundurn.

Kobayashi, A. 1988. "Asian Migration to Canada." *The Canadian Geographer* 32 (4): 351–62.

Konadu-Agyemang, Kwadwo. 1999. "Characteristics and Migration Excrescence of Africans in Canada with Specific Reference to Ghanaians in Greater Toronto." *The Canadian Geographer* 43 (4): 400–14.

Kopyto, H. 1966. "Victory Is for All." *Share* 18 (38): 7.

Krahn, Harvey J., and G.S. Lowe. 1998. *Work, Industry, and Canadian Society*. Scarborough, ON: ITP Nelson.

Krauter, Joseph F., and Morris Davis. 1978. *Minority Canadians: Ethnic Groups*. Toronto: Methuen.

Labelle, Micheline. 1990. "Immigration, culture et question nationale." *Cahiers de recherche sociologique* 14: 143–51.

Lam, L. 1983. "Vietnamese Chinese Refugees in Montreal." Unpublished Ph.D. Dissertation. Toronto: York University.

Lampkin, Lorna. 1985. "Visible Minorities in Canada." In Rosalie Silberman Abella (ed.), *Research Studies of the Commission on Equality in Employment*. Ottawa: Supply and Services Canada.

Lautard, Hugh E., and Donald J. Loree. 1984. "Ethnic Stratification in Canada, 1931–1971." *Canadian Journal of Sociology* 9: 334–43.

Lee, Roger. 1986a. "Colonialism." In R.J. Johnston, D. Gregory, and D.M. Smith (eds.), *The Dictionary of Human Geography*. Oxford: Blackwell.

_____. 1986b "Neo-Colonialism." In R.J. Johnston, D. Gregory, and D.M. Smith (eds.), *The Dictionary of Human Geography*. Oxford: Blackwell.

Lenin, V.I. 1921. *Women and Society*. New York: International.

Lewis, I.M. 1981. *Somalia Culture, History and Social Institutions: An Introductory Guide to the Somali Democratic Republic*. London: London School of Economics and Political Science.

Lewis, Oscar. 1966. *La Vida: A Puerto Rican Family in the Culture of Poverty*. New York: Random House.

Lewis, Stephen. 1992. *The Stephen Lewis Report on Race Relations in Ontario*. Toronto: Government of Ontario.

Ley, David, and Heather Smith. 1997. "Immigration and Poverty in Canadian Cities, 1971–1991." *Canadian Journal of Regional Science* 20 (1–2): 29–48.

Li, Peter S. 1988. *Ethnic Inequality in a Class Society*. Toronto: Thompson Educational.

_____. 1995. "Racial Supremacism Under Social Democracy." *Canadian Ethnic Studies* 27 (1): 1–18.

_____. 1998. "The Market Value and Social Value of Race." In Vic Satzewich (ed.), *Racism and Social Inequality in Canada: Concepts, Controversies and Strategies of Resistance*. Toronto: Thompson Educational.

_____. 1999. "Race and Ethnicity." In Peter Li (ed.), *Race and Ethnic Relations in Canada*. Toronto: Oxford University Press.

Liodakis, Nikolaos, and Vic Satzewich. 1998. "From Solution to Problem: Multiculturalism and 'Race Relations' as New Social Problems." In Les Samuelson and Wayne Antony (eds.), *Power and Resistance: Critical Thinking about Social Issues in Canada*. Halifax: Fernwood.

Lipset, Seymour Martin. 1989. *Continental Divide: The Values and Institutions of the United States and Canada*. New York: Routledge.

Lo, Lucia, and Shuguang Wang. 1997. "Settlement Patterns of Toronto's Chinese Immigrants: Convergence or Divergence?" *Canadian Journal of Regional Science* 20 (1–2): 49–72.

Lowe, Keith. 1982. *Race Relations in Metropolitan Toronto: A Situation Report*. Ottawa: Secretary of State.

Lower, A.R.M. 1946. *Colony to Nation: A History of Canada*. Toronto: Longmans.

_____. 1953. *Unconventional Voyages*. Toronto: Ryerson.

Lundahl, Mats. 1983. *The Haitian Economy: Man, Land and Markets*. New York: St. Martin's.

Lupul, Manoly. R. 1982. "The Political Implementation of Multiculturalism." *Journal of Canadian Studies* 17 (1): 93–102.

Lynch, Frederick. 1994. "Surviving Affirmative Action." In Gary Goshgarian and Kathleen Krueger (eds.), *Crossfire: An Argument, Rhetoric and Reader*. New York: Harper Collins.

Lyons, Terrence, and A.I. Samatar. 1995. *Somalia: State Collapse, Multilateral Intervention, and Strategies for Political Reconstruction*. Washington, DC: Brookings Institute.

Mabogunje, Akin L. 1970. "Systems Approach to a Theory of Rural-Urban Migration." *Geographical Analysis* 2 (1): 1–18.

Macintosh, Donald, and J. Albinson. 1985. "An Evaluation of the Athlete Assistance Program." In *Report to Sport Canada*. Kingston, ON: Social Program Evaluation Group, Queen's University.

Macintosh, Donald, and David Whitson. 1990. *The Game Planners: Transforming Canada's Sport System*. Montreal and Kingston: McGill-Queen's University Press.

Macionis, J.J., and L.M. Gerber. 1999. *Sociology*. Scarborough, ON: Prentice, Allyn.

Mackie, Marlene. 1974. "Ethnic Stereotype and Prejudice: Alberta Indians, Hutterites and Ukrainians." *Canadian Ethnic Studies* 10: 118–29.

MacRae, D.G. 1988. "Karl Marx, 1818–1883." In Antonio O. Donini and Joseph A. Novack (eds.), *Origins and Growth of Sociological Theory*. Chicago: Nelson-Hall.

Magnet, Myron. 1987. "America's Underclass: What to Do?" *Fortune Magazine* 115 (May 11): 130.

Makinda, S.M. 1993. *Seeking Peace from Chaos: Humanitarian Intervention in Somalia*. London: Lynne Rienner.

Malik, W. 1982. *A Study of Race Relations in Montreal*. Ottawa: Secretary of State.

Mannheim, Karl. 1936. *Ideology and Utopia*. Trans. Louis Wirth and Edward Shils. New York: Harcourt.

Manschreck, Clyde L. 1974. *A History of Christianity in the World: From Persecution to Uncertainty*. Englewood Cliffs, NJ: Prentice.

Marger, Martin. 1994. *Race and Ethnic Relations: American and Global Perspectives*. Belmont, CA: Wadsworth.

Marks, Jonathan. 1995. *Human Biodiversity: Genes, Race, and History*. New York: Aldine de Gruyter.

Marx, Karl. 1977a. *Capital*. Volume 1. Moscow: Progress.

_____. 1977b. *Capital*. Volume 3. Moscow: Progress.

_____. 1983. "Alienated Labor." In Michael D. Bayles and Kenneth Henley (eds.), *Right Conduct: Theories and Applications*. New York: Random House.

Marx, Karl, and Friedrich Engels. 1955. *The Communist Manifesto*. Chicago: Great Books Foundation.

_____. 1976. *The German Ideology*. In *Collected Works*. 50 volumes. New York: International.

Massey, Douglas S. 1981. "Social Class and Ethnic Segregation: A Reconsideration of Methods and Conclusions." *American Sociological Review* (46): 641–50.

_____. 1984. *Spatial Division of Labour: Social Structure and the Geography of Production*. London: Macmillan.

Massey, Douglas S., J. Arango, G. Hugo, A. Kouaouch, A. Pellegrino, and E. Taylor. 1997. "Migration Theory, Ethnic Mobilization and Globalization." In Montserrat Guibernau and John Rex (eds.), *The Ethnicity Reader: Nationalism,*

Multiculturalism, and Migration. Malden, MA: Blackwell.

Massey, Douglas S., and Nancy A. Denton. 1993. *American Apartheid: Segregation and the Making of the Underclass*. Cambridge: Harvard University Press.

McKenzie, Maxine. 1987. "You Mean, I Still Ain't?" *Breaking the Silence* 5 (3): 27–38.

McPherson, Barry D. 1975. "The Segregation of Playing Positions Hypothesis in Sport: An Alternative Explanation." *Social Science Quarterly* 55: 960–66.

McPherson, Barry D., James E. Curtis, and John W. Low. 1989. *The Social Significance of Sport: An Introduction to the Sociology of Sport*. Champaign, IL: Human Kinetics.

McQueen, Rod. 2000. "Cracking the Glass Ceiling: A New-Girls' Network of Top Women Takes Its Place in Canada's Business Firmament." *National Post,* March 4: E1–E9.

Medlin, Brian. 1967. "Egoism Claimed Inconsistent." In William P. Alston and Richard B. Brandt (eds.), *Problems of Philosophy: Introductory Readings*. Boston: Allyn and Bacon.

Meggs, Geogg. 1995. "Quality Caring." *Our Times* May/June: 43.

Memmi, Albert. 1993. *The Colonizer and the Colonized*. Trans. Howard Greenfeld. Boston: Beacon.

Mensah, Joseph. 1995. "Low Income Housing, Employment Opportunities, and the Perception of the Urban Poor." *Tijdschrift voor economische en sociale geografie* 86 (4): 368–81.

_____. 1997. "Colonialism and Human Factor Degradation in Africa." *Review of Human Factor Studies* 3 (1): 48–64.

Mensah, Joseph, and Senyo Adjibolosoo. 1998. *The Demographic Profile of African Immigrants in the Lower Mainland of British Columbia*. A Report to the Community Liaison Division of the Ministry Responsible for Multiculturalism and Immigration, British Columbia (Part I). Vancouver: Community Liaison Division, Ministry Responsible for Multiculturalism and Immigration.

Mensah, Joseph, and R.G. Ironside. 1994. "Employment Opportunities of the Urban Poor: An Assessment of Spatial Constraints and the Mismatch Hypothesis." In Jean Andrey and J. Gordon Nelson (eds.), *Public Issues: A Geographical Perspective*. Waterloo: University of Waterloo Press.

Miles, Robert. 1982. *Racism and Migrant Labour*. Boston: Routledge.

_____. 1989. *Racism*. London: Routledge.

Mill, J.S. 1970. "The Subjection of Women." 1869. In Alice Rossi (ed.), *John Stuart Mill and Harriet Taylor Mill: Essays on Sex Equality*. Chicago: University of Chicago Press.

Miner, Michael. 1986. *Police Intercultural Training Manual*. Ottawa: Canadian Association of Chiefs of Police with the support of the Multiculturalism Directorate of the Secretary of State.

Mitchinson, Wendy. 1977. "Social Reform in the Nineteenth Century: A Step Towards Independence." *Atlantis* 2 (2): 58–81.

Moghaddam, Fathali M., Donald M. Taylor, Peggy T. Pelletier, and Marc Shepanek. 1994. "The Warped Looking Glass: How Minorities Perceive Themselves,

Believe They Are Perceived, and Are Actually Perceived by Majority Group Members in Quebec, Canada." *Canadian Ethnic Studies* 26 (2): 112–23.

Monreau, Joanne. 1995. "Employment Equity." *Social Trends* 2: 147–49.

Montagu, Ashley. 1964. *Man's Most Dangerous Myth*. New York: Oxford University Press.

More, T.S., and A. Laramore. 1990. "Industrial Change and Urban Joblessness: An Assessment of the Mismatch Hypothesis." *Urban Affairs Quarterly* 25 (2): 640–58.

Morton, Suzanne. 1996. "Separate Spheres in a Separate World: African-Nova Scotian Women in Late-Nineteenth-Century Halifax County." In Wendy Mitchinson et al. (eds.), *Canadian Women: A Reader*. Toronto: Harcourt.

Murdie, Robert A. 1994. "'Blacks in Near-ghettos?' Black Visible Minority Population in Metropolitan Toronto Housing Authority Public Housing Units." *Housing Studies* 9 (4): 435–57.

_____. 1998. "The Welfare State, Economic Restructuring and Immigrant Flows." In Sako Musterd and Wim Ostendorf (eds.), *Urban Segregation and the Welfare State*. London: Routledge.

Murphy, Emily. 1973. *The Black Candle*. 1922. Toronto: Thomas Allen.

Musterd, Sako, and Wim Ostendorf. 1998. "Segregation, Polarisation and Social Exclusion in Metropolitan Areas." In Sako Musterd and Wim Ostendorf (eds.), *Urban Segregation and the Welfare State*. London: Routledge.

Musto, Louis. 1997. "Public Opinion on Multiculturalism and Canadian Identity." In Andrew Cardozo and Louis Musto (eds.), *The Battle Over Multiculturalism*. Ottawa: PSI.

Muszynski, Alicja. 1991. "Social Stratification: Class and Gender Inequality." In B. Singh Bolaria (ed.), *Social Issues and Contradictions in Canadian Society*. Toronto: Harcourt.

Myers, Linda James. 1988. *Understanding an Afrocentric World View: Introduction to an Optimal Psychology*. Dubuque, IA: Kendall/Hunt.

Myrdal, Gunnar. 1944. *An American Dilemma: The Negro Problem and the Modern Democracy*. New York: Harper.

_____. 1957. *Rich Lands and Poor*. New York: Harper and Row.

Nagel, Joane. 1984. "The Ethnic Revolution: The Emergence of Ethnic Nationalism in Modern States." *Sociology and Social Research* 68 (4): 417–34.

Nash, Alan. 1994. "Some Recent Developments in Canadian Immigration Policy." *The Canadian Geographer* 38 (3): 258–61.

Nelson, E.D., and Augie Fleras. 1995. *Social Problems in Canada: Issues and Challenges*. Scarborough, ON: Prentice.

Nkrumah, Kwame. 1962. *Towards Colonial Freedom: Africa in the Struggle Against World Imperialism*. London: Heinemann.

_____. 1963. *Africa Must Unite*. London: Heinemann.

_____. 1964. *Consciencism: Philosophy and Ideology for Decolonization and Development*. London: Heinemann.

_____. 1965. *Neo-Colonialism, the Last Stage of Imperialism*. London: Heinemann.

North, Kathryn N., et al. 1999. "A Common Nonsense Mutation Results in actinin-3 Deficiency in the General Population." *Nature Genetics* 21 (April): 353–54.

Norton, William. 1998. *Human Geography*. Toronto: Oxford University Press.

Nystrom Desk Atlas. 1994. Chicago: Nystrom.

O'Connor, James. 1973. *The Fiscal Crisis of the State*. New York: St. Martin's.

O'Donnell, Hugh. 1994. "Mapping the Mythical: A Geopolitics of National Sporting Stereotypes." *Discourse and Society* 5 (3): 345–80.

Ogden, Philip E. 1992. "Migration." In R.J. Johnston, Derek Gregory, and David M. Smith (eds.), *The Dictionary of Human Geography*. Oxford: Blackwell.

Ogmundson, Rick, and James McLaughlin. 1992. "Trends in the Ethnic Origins of Canadian Elites: The Decline of the Brits?" *Canadian Journal of Sociology and Anthropology* 29 (2): 227–42.

Olson, S.H., and A.L. Kobayashi. 1993. "The Emerging Ethnocultural Mosaic." In Larry S. Bourne and David F. Ley (eds.), *The Changing Social Geography of Canadian Cities*. Montreal and Kingston: McGill-Queen's University Press.

Omi, Michael. 1987. "We Shall Overturn: Race and the Contemporary American Right." Unpublished Ph.D. Dissertation. Santa Cruz, CA: University of California.

Omi, Michael, and Howard Winant. 1986. *Racial Formation in the United States from the 1960s to the 1980s*. New York: Routledge.

_____. 1998. "Racial Formation." In Paula S. Rothenberg (ed.), *Race, Class, and Gender in the United States: An Integrated Study*. New York: St. Martin's.

Ontario Human Rights Commission. 1983. *The Experience of Visible Minorities in the Work World: The Case of MBA Graduates*. Toronto: Ontario Human Rights Commission.

Opoku-Dapaah, Edward. 1995. *Somali Refugees in Toronto: A Profile*. Toronto: York Lanes.

Ottawa Citizen. 1993. December 31: B1.

Owusu, Thomas Y. 1998. "To Buy or Not to Buy: Determinants of Home Ownership among Ghanaian Immigrants in Toronto." *The Canadian Geographer* 42: 40–52.

_____. 1999. "Residential Patterns and Housing Choices of Ghanaian Immigrants in Toronto, Canada." *Housing Studies* 14 (1): 77–97.

Parai, L. 1965. *Immigration and Emigration of Professional and Skilled Manpower During the Post-war Period*. Ottawa: Economic Council of Canada.

Parin, Ingris, and Edgar Parin. 1962. *D'Aulaire's Book of Greek Myth*. New York: Dell.

Perera, Suveendrini, and Joseph Pugliese. 1997. "'Racial Suicide': The Relicensing of Racism in Australia." *Race and Class* 39 (2): 1–19.

Peter, K. 1981. "The Myth of Multiculturalism and Other Political Fables." In J. Dahlie and T. Fernando (eds.), *Ethnicity, Power and Politics in Canada*. Toronto: Methuen.

Petersen, Kirsten Holst. 1995. "First Things First: Problems of a Feminist Approach to African Literature." In Bill Ashcroft, Gareth Griffiths, and Helen Tiffin (eds.), *The Post-Colonial Studies Reader*. London: Routledge.

Phillips, Jock. 1987. *A Man's Country? The Image of the Pakeha Male: A History*. New York: Penguin.

Pineo, P. 1977. "The Social Standings of Ethnic and Racial Groupings." *Canadian Review of Sociology and Anthropology* 14: 147–57.

Pineo, Peter, and John Porter. 1985. "Ethnic Origin and Occupational Attainment." In Monica Boyd, John Goyder, Frank E. Jones, Hugh A. McRoberts, Peter C. Pineo, and John Porter (eds.), *Ascription and Achievement: Studies in Mobility and Status Achievement in Canada*. Ottawa: Carleton University Press.

Plato. 1954. *The Last Days of Socrates: Euthyphro, the Apology, Crito, Phaedo*. Trans. Hugh Tredennick. Harmondsworth: Penguin.

_____. 1974. *The Republic*. Trans. Desmond Lee. Harmondsworth: Penguin.

Pojman, Louis P. 1995. "Relativism." In Robert Audi (ed.), *The Cambridge Dictionary of Philosophy*. Cambridge: Cambridge University Press.

Polachek, S. 1979. "Occupational Segregation among Women: Theory, Evidence, and a Prognosis." In C. Lloyd, E.S. Andrews, and C.L. Gilroy (eds.), *Women in the Labour Market*. New York: Columbia University.

_____. 1985. "Occupational Segregation: A Defense of Human Capital Predictions and 'Reply to England.'" *Journal of Human Resources* 20: 437–40, 444.

Ponting, J.R., and R.A. Wanner. 1983. "Blacks in Calgary: A Social and Attitudinal Profile." *Canadian Ethnic Studies* 15 (2): 57–76.

Porter, John. 1965. *The Vertical Mosaic*. Toronto: University of Toronto Press.

_____. 1975. "Ethnic Pluralism in Canadian Perspective." In N. Glazer and D. Moynihan (eds.), *Ethnicity: Theory and Experience*. Cambridge: Harvard University Press.

Prentice, Alison, et al. 1988. *Canadian Women: A History*. Toronto: Harcourt.

Preston, Valerie, and Wenona Giles. 1997. "Ethnicity, Gender and Labour Markets in Canada: A Case Study of Immigrant Women in Toronto." *Canadian Journal of Urban Research* 6 (2): 135–59.

Rajagopal, Indhu. 1990. "The Glass Ceiling in the Vertical Mosaic: Indian Immigrants in Canada." *Canadian Ethnic Studies* 22 (1): 96–100.

Ralston, Helen. 1996. "Race, Class, Gender, and Work Experience of South Asian Immigrant Women in Atlantic Canada." In Wendy Mitchinson et al. (eds.), *Canadian Women: A Reader*. Toronto: Harcourt.

Ramcharan, Subhas. 1982. *Racism: Nonwhites in Canada*. Toronto: Butterworths.

Rand McNally. 1993. *World Facts and Maps*. Chicago: Rand McNally.

_____. 1998. *World Facts and Maps*. Chicago: Rand McNally.

Ravenstein, E.G. 1885. "The Laws of Migration." *Journal of the Royal Statistical Society* 48: 242–305.

Ray, Brian. 1992. *Immigrants in a "Multicultural" Toronto: Exploring the Contested Social and Housing Geographies of Post-War Italian and Caribbean Immigrants*. Unpublished Ph.D. Dissertation. Kingston, ON: Queen's University.

_____. 1994. "Immigrant Settlement and Housing in Metropolitan Toronto." *The Canadian Geographer* 38 (3): 262–65.

Ray, Brian, and E.G. Moore. 1991. "Access to Homeownership among Immigrant Groups in Canada." *Canadian Review of Sociology and Anthropology* 28: 1–29.

Reform Party of Canada. 1989. *Platform and Statement of Principles.*

_____. 1991. Principles and Policies: The Blue Book.

Regan, Tom. 1980. *Matters of Life and Death: New Introductory Essays in Moral Philosophy.* New York: Random House.

Reiman, Jeffrey. 1990. *The Rich Get Richer and the Poor Get Prison: Ideology, Class, and Criminal Justice.* New York: Macmillan.

Reitz, Jeffery G. 1980. *The Survival of Ethnic Groups.* Toronto: McGraw.

_____. 1990. "Ethnic Concentration in Labour Markets and Their Implications for Ethnic Inequality." In Raymond Breton et al. (eds.), *Ethnic Identity and Equality: Varieties in a Canadian City.* Toronto: University of Toronto Press.

Reitz, Jeffrey G., and Raymond Breton. 1998. "Prejudice and Discrimination in Canada and the United States: A Comparison." In Vic Satzewich (ed.), *Racism and Social Inequality in Canada.* Toronto: Thompson Educational.

Rex, John. 1983. *Race Relations in Sociological Theory.* London: Routledge.

Rex, John, and Sally Tomlinson. 1979. *Colonial Immigrants in a British City: A Class Analysis.* London: Routledge.

Rhoden, Bill. 1974. "Are Black Athletes Naturally Superior?" *Ebony* 30: 136–38.

Rich, Adrienne. 1980. "Compulsory Heterosexuality and Lesbian Existence." *Signs* 5 (Summer): 631–60.

Richmond, A.H. 1989. *Caribbean Immigrants: A Demographic Economic Analysis.* Ottawa: Statistics Canada.

_____. 1994. *Global Apartheid: Refugee, Racism, and the New World Order.* Toronto: Oxford University Press.

Ritchie, Andrew. 1988. *Marshall "Major" Taylor.* San Francisco: Bicycle.

Roberts, Lance, and Rodney Clifton. 1982. "Exploring the Ideology of Canadian Multiculturalism." *Canadian Public Policy* 8 (1): 88–94.

Rodney, Walter. 1974. *How Europe Underdeveloped Africa.* Washington: Howard University Press.

Rogge, J.R., ed. 1987. *Refugees: A Third World Dilemma.* Totowa, NJ: Rowman and Littlefield.

Rourke, John T. 1993. *International Politics on the World Stage.* Guilford, CT: Dushkin.

Rowbotham, Sheila. 1973. *Woman's Consciousness, Man's World.* Harmondsworth: Penguin.

Rubenstein, James M. 1996. *An Introduction to Human Geography: The Cultural Landscape.* Don Mills, ON: Macmillan.

Rubin, Gayle. 1975. "The Traffic in Women: Notes on the 'Political Economy' of Sex." In R. Reiter (ed.), *Towards an Anthropology of Women.* New York: Monthly Review.

Rubinoff, Lionel. 1982. "Multiculturalism and the Metaphysics of Pluralism." *Journal of Canadian Studies* 17 (1): 122–30.

Rushin, Donna Kate. 1983. "The Bridge Poem." In Laurel Richardson and Verta Taylor (eds.), *Feminist Frontier: Rethinking Sex, Gender, and Society.* Reading, MA: Addison-Wesley.

Rushton, J. Philippe. 1988. "Race Differences in Behaviour: A Review and

Evolutionary Analysis." *Personality and Individual Differences* 90: 1009–24.

_____. 1990. "Race and Crime: A Reply to Roberts and Gober." *Canadian Journal of Criminology* 32: 315–34.

_____. 1995. *Race, Evolution, and Behaviour: A Life-History Perspective*. New Brunswick, NJ: Transaction.

Ryan, William. 1980. "Blaming the Victim." In Paula Rothenberg Struhl and Karsten J. Struhl (eds.), *Philosophy Now: An Introductory Reader*. New York: Random House.

Sahnoun, Mohammed. 1994. *Somalia: The Missed Opportunities*. Washington, DC: United States Institute of Peace.

Sajoo, A.B. 1994. "New Dances with Diversity." *Policy Options* (December): 14–19.

Samuels, Barbara, and Cheryl Craig. 1998. *Multiculturalism in Canada: Images and Issues*. Calgary: Weigl Educational.

Sanders, Douglas. 1987. "Article 27 and the Aboriginal Peoples of Canada." In Canadian Human Rights Foundation (ed.), *Multiculturalism and the Charter: A Legal Perspective*. Toronto: Carswell.

Sandoval, Chela. 1984. "Comment on Krieger's 'Lesbian Identity and Community: Recent Social Science Literature.'" *Signs* 9: 725–29.

Sartre, Jean-Paul. 1963. Preface. *The Wretched of the Earth*. By Frantz Fanon. New York: Grove.

Satzewich, Vic. 1993. "Race and Ethnic Relations." In Peter Li and B. Singh Bolaris (eds.), *Contemporary Sociology: Critical Perspectives*. Mississauga, ON: Copp Clark.

_____. 1998. Introduction. *Racism and Social Inequality in Canada: Concepts, Controversies and Strategic Resistance*. Ed. Vic Satzewich. Toronto: Thompson Educational.

_____. 1999. "The Political Economy of Race and Ethnicity." In Peter Li (ed.), *Race and Ethnic Relations in Canada*. Toronto: Oxford University Press.

Satzewich, Vic, and Peter S. Li. 1987. "Immigrant Labour in Canada: The Cost and Benefit of Ethnic Origin in the Job Market." *Canadian Journal of Sociology* 12 (3): 229–41.

Scotti, Rosanna, and Earl Miller. 1985. "National Conference on Policing in Multicultural Urban Communities." *Currents* 3 (2): 44–45.

Sefa, George J. 1996. "Critical Perspectives in Antiracism: An Introduction." *The Canadian Review of Sociology and Anthropology* 33 (3): 247–67.

Semple, Ellen C. 1911. *Influences of Geographic Environment of the Basis of Ratzel's System of Anthropo-Geography*. New York: H. Holt.

Serge, Joe. 1993. *Canadian Citizenship Made Simple*. Toronto: Doubleday.

Seward, Shirley B., and Marc Tremblay. 1989. *Immigrants in the Canadian Labour Force: Their Role in Structural Change*. Montreal: Institute for Research on Public Policy.

Shah, Chandrankant, and Tomislav Svoboda. 2000. "A Question of Fairness: With the Increase in Faculty Hirings Now Is a Critical Time to Begin Correcting Inequalities in Faculty Composition." Toronto: University of Toronto. Available on-line (http://www.newsandevents.utoronto.ca/bin/thoughts/forum000110.asp); accessed March 2, 2000.

Shapiro, Leonard. 1994. "Nicklaus Clarifies Remarks on Blacks; Says He Was 'Misinterpreted.'" *Washington Post*, August 10: C6.

Shropshire, Kenneth L. 1996. *In Black and White: Race and Sports in America*. New York: New York University Press.

Shyllon, Folarin. 1993. "Blacks in Britain: A Historical and Analytical Overview." In Joseph E. Harris (ed.), *Global Dimensions of the African Diaspora*. Washington, DC: Howard University Press.

Simmons, Allan. 1998. "Racism and Immigration Policy." In Vic Satzewich (ed.), *Racism and Social Inequality in Canada: Concept, Controversies and Strategies of Resistance*. Toronto: Thompson Educational.

Sivanandan, A. 1981. "From Resistance to Rebellion: Asian and Afro-Caribbean Struggles in Britain." *Race and Class* 23 (2–3).

Skinner, Elliott P. 1993. "Dialectic Between Diasporas and Homelands." In Joseph E. Harris (ed.), *Global Dimensions of the African Diaspora*. Washington, DC: Howard University Press.

Smith, Barbara. 1983. "Notes for Yet Another Paper on Black Feminism, or Will the Real Enemy Please Stand Up?" In Laurel Richardson and Verta Taylor (eds.), *Feminist Frontier: Rethinking Sex, Gender, and Society*. Reading, MA: Addison-Wesley.

_____. 1994. "Cult-Lit." In Gary Goshgarian and Kathleen Krueger (eds.), *Crossfire: An Argument, Rhetoric and Reader*. New York: Harper Collins.

Smith, Samuel Stanhope. 1965. *Essay on the Causes of the Variety of Complexion and Figure in the Human Species*. 1787. Cambridge, MA: Belknap.

Smith, Valerie. 1989. "Black Feminist Theory and the Representation of the 'Other.'" In C. Wall (ed.), *Changing Our Own Words: Essays on Criticism, Theory, and Writing by Black Women*. New Brunswick, NJ: Rutgers University Press.

Sollors, Werner. 1999. "Who Is Ethnic?" In Bill Ashcroft, Gareth Griffiths, and Helen Tiffin (eds.), *The Post-Colonial Studies Reader*. London: Routledge.

Sowell, Thomas. 1976. "A Black 'Conservative' Dissents." *New York Times Magazine*, August 8: 15.

_____. 1989. *Preferential Policies: An International Perspective*. New York: Morrow.

Soja, Edward W. 1985. "The Spatiality of Social Life: Towards a Transformative Retheorisation." In D. Gregory and J. Urry (eds.), *Social Relations and Spatial Structures*. New York: St. Martin's.

_____. 1989. *Postmodern Geographies: The Reassertion of Space in Critical Social Theory*. New York: Verso.

Spicer, Keith 1989. "Ottawa Should Stop Money for Multiculturalism." *The Montreal Gazette*, March 9: B3.

Stace, Walter T. 1967. "Ethical Relativism: Pros and Cons." In William P. Alston and Richard B. Brandt (eds.), *The Problems of Philosophy: Introductory Readings*. Boston: Allyn and Bacon.

Stafford, James. 1992. "The Impact of New Immigration Policy on Racism in Canada." In Vic Satzewich (ed.), *Deconstructing a Nation: Immigration,*

Multiculturalism, and Racism in '90s Canada. Halifax: Fernwood.

Stampp, Kenneth. 1956. *The Peculiar Institution: Slavery in the Ante-Bellum South*. New York: Knopf.

Starr, Paul. 1992. "Civic Reconstruction: What to Do Without Affirmative Action." *The American Prospect* 8 (Winter): 7–14.

Stasiulis, Daiva. 1980. "The Political Structuring of Ethnic Community Action." *Canadian Ethnic Studies* 12 (3): 19–44.

_____. 1999. "Feminist Intersectional Theorizing." In Peter Li (ed.), *Race and Ethnic Relations in Canada*. Toronto: Oxford University Press.

Steele, Shelby. 1990. *The Content of Our Character*. New York: St. Martin's.

_____. 1994. "Affirmative Action: The Price of Preference." In Gary Goshgarian and Kathleen Krueger (eds.), *Crossfire: An Argument, Rhetoric and Reader*. New York: Harper Collins.

Stein, B. 1981. "The Refugee Experience: Defining the Parameters of a Field of Study." *International Migration Review* 15: 320–30.

Steinberg, Stephen. 1995. *Turning Back: The Retreat from Racial Justice in American Thought and Policy*. Boston: Beacon.

Stewart, Frances. 2000. "Civil Wars in Sub Saharan Africa: Counting the Economic and Social Cost." In Dharam Ghai (ed.), *Renewing Social and Economic Progress in Africa*. New York: St. Martin's.

Stimpson, Catherine R. 1993. "How Did Feminist Theory Get This Way?" In M. Poster (ed.), *Politics, Theory, and Contemporary Culture*. New York: Columbia University Press.

Stoddart, Brian. 1988. "Sport, Cultural Imperialism, and Colonial Response in the British Empire." *Comparative Studies in Society and History*. Part 30: 649–73. Ann Arbor: University of Michigan Press.

Stouffer, S.A. 1940. "Intervening Opportunities: A Theory Relating to Distance." *American Sociological Review* 5: 845–67.

Struhl, P.R., and K.J. Struhl. 1980. "Excerpt from the Alva Myrdal Report to the Swedish Social Democratic Party." In Paula Rothenberg Struhl and Karsten J. Struhl (eds.), *Philosophy Now: An Introductory Reader*. New York: Random House.

Taylor, John B., and David R. Johnson. 1997. *Principles of Macroeconomics*. Toronto: ITP Nelson.

Taylor, K.W. 1991. "Racism in Canadian Immigration Policy." *Canadian Ethnic Studies* 23 (1): 1–19.

Teixeira, Carlos, and Robert A. Murdie. 1997. "The Role of Ethnic Real Estate Agents in the Residential Relocation Process: A Case Study of Portuguese Homebuyers in Suburban Toronto." *Urban Geography* 18 (6): 497–520.

Tepper, Elliot L. 1989. "Demographic Change and Pluralism." In O.P. Dwivedi et al. (eds.), *Canada 2000: Race Relations and Public Policy*. Guelph: University of Guelph Press.

_____. 1997. "Multiculturalism as a Response to an Evolving Society." In Andrew Cardozo and Louis Musto (eds.), *The Battle Over Multiculturalism*. Ottawa: PSI.

Tepperman, Lorne. 1975. *Social Mobility in Canada*. Toronto: University of Toronto Press.

Thalberg, Irving. 1976. "Justifications of Institutional Racism." In Lawrence Habermehl (ed.), *Morality in the Modern World: Ethical Dimensions of Contemporary Human Problems*. Encino, CA: Dickenson.

Thomas, W.I. 1966. "The Relation of Research to the Social Process." 1931. In Morris Janowitz (ed.), *W.I. Thomas on Social Organization and Social Personality*. Chicago: University of Chicago Press.

Thornhill, Esmeralda. 1991. "Focus on Black Women." In Jesse Vorst et al. (eds.), *Race, Class, Gender: Bonds and Barriers*. Toronto: Garamond.

Time Magazine. 1977. "Black Dominance." May 9: 57–60.

Tollett, Kenneth. 1990. "Racism and Race-Conscious Remedies." *The American Prospect* 5: 92.

Tong, Rosemarie. 1989. *Feminist Theory: A Comprehensive Introduction*. Boulder, CO: Westview.

_____. 1995. "Feminist Philosophy." In Robert Audi (ed.), *The Cambridge Dictionary of Philosophy*. Cambridge: Cambridge University Press.

Toronto Star. 1991. "Nova Scotia Blacks Have 350 Years but Feel Like Strangers." July 23: A1, A14.

Troper, Harold Martin. 1972. *Only Farmers Need Apply*. Toronto: Griffin House.

Tulloch, Headley. 1975. *Black Canadians: A Long Line of Fighters*. Toronto: N.C.

Turner, Jonathan H. 1984. *Oppression*. Chicago: Nelson-Hall.

Tygiel, J. 1983. *Baseball's Great Experiment: Jackie Robinson and His Legacy*. New York: Oxford University Press.

Tyhurst, L. 1977. "Psychosocial First Aid for Refugees." *Mental Health and Society* 4: 319–43.

United Nations. 1986. *Report of the Group of Governmental Experts on International Cooperation to Avert New Flows of Refugees*. Document a/41/324. New York: United Nations.

United Nations Educational, Scientific and Cultural Organization (UNESCO). 1978. *Declarations on Race and Racial Prejudice*. Adopted by the General Conference, 20th Session, November. Paris: UNESCO.

United Nations High Commissioner for Refugees (UNHCR). 1987. "Geography of Exile." *Refugees* 48: 24–25.

_____. 1995. *The State of the World's Refugees: In Search of Solutions*. London: Oxford University Press.

University of Toronto. 1990. *Report of the Presidential Advisors on Ethno-cultural Groups and Visible Minorities at the University of Toronto* [The Rossi-Wayne Report]. Toronto: University of Toronto Press.

Valverde, Mariana. 1992. "When the Mother of the Race Is Free: Race, Reproduction, and Sexuality in First-Wave Feminism." In F. Iocovetta and M. Valverde (eds.), *Gender Conflicts: New Essays in Women's History*. Toronto: University of Toronto Press.

Vancouver Sun. 2000. "Universities Up Ante in Battle to Attract Top Academic Talent." Available on-line (www.vancouversun.com); accessed April 3, 2000.

van den Berghe, Pierre L. 1959. "The Dynamics of Racial Prejudice: An Ideal-Type Dichotomy." *Social Force* 37 (1–4): 138–41.

_____. 1966. "Paternalistic Versus Competitive Race Relations: An Ideal-Type Approach." In Bernard E. Segal (ed.), *Racial and Ethnic Relations: Selected Readings*. New York: Thomas Y. Crowell.

_____. 1967. *Race and Racism: A Comparative Perspective*. New York: John Wiley.

_____. 1981. *The Ethnic Phenomenon*. New York: Elsevier.

_____. 1984. "Race Perspective Two." In Ellis Cashmore (ed.), *Dictionary of Race and Ethnic Relations*. London: Routledge.

Vickers, Jill. 1992. "The Intellectual Origins of the Contemporary Women's Movement in Canada and the United States." In C. Backhouse and D. Flaherty (eds.), *Changing Times*. Montreal and Kingston: McGill-Queen's University Press.

Vogler, Conrad C., and Stephen E. Schwartz. 1993. *The Sociology of Sport: An Introduction*. Englewood Cliffs, NJ: Prentice.

Wakefield, Gibbon. 1849. *A View of the Art of Colonization*. London: John W. Parker.

Walker, James W. 1980. *A History of Blacks in Canada*. Ottawa: Minister of State and Multiculturalism.

_____. 1984. *The West Indians in Canada*. Ottawa: Canadian Historical Association.

_____. 1989. "Race Policy in Canada: A Retrospective." In O.P. Dwivedi et al. (eds.), *Canada 2000: Race Relations and Public Policy*. Guelph: University of Guelph Press.

Walsh, J.J., and H.L. Shapiro, eds. 1967. *Aristotle's Ethics*. Belmont, CA: Wadsworth.

Ward, D. 1989. *Poverty, Ethnicity, and the American City, 1840–1928*. Cambridge: Cambridge University Press.

Warner, Lloyd W. 1941. Introduction. *Deep South*. Ed. Gardner Davies and Lloyd Warner. Chicago: University of Chicago Press.

Wasserstrom, Richard A. 1980. "A Defense of Programs of Preferential Treatment." In John R. Burr and Milton Goldinger (eds.), *Philosophy and Contemporary Issues*. New York: Macmillan.

Webber, Jeremy. 1994. *Reimaging Canada: Language, Culture, Community, and the Canadian Constitution*. Montreal and Kingston: McGill-Queen's University Press.

Weber, Max. 1968. *Economy and Society*. Volume 1. New York: Bedminster.

Weil, Thomas E., et al. 1973. *Area Handbook for Haiti*. Washington, DC: U.S. Government Printing Office.

Weiner, Myron. 1999. "Migration and Refugee Policies: An Overview." In Ann Bernstein and Myron Weiner (eds.), *Migration and Refugee Policies*. London: Pinter.

Weinfeld, Morton. 1988. "Ethnic and Race Relations." In James Curtis and Lorne Tepperman (eds.), *Understanding Canadian Society*. Toronto: McGraw.

Weis, L., and M. Fine. 1996. "Notes on 'Whites' as 'Race.'" *Race, Gender and Class: An Interdisciplinary and Multicultural Journal* 3 (3): 5–9.

Weiskel, T.C. 1997. "Vicious Circles: African Demographic History as a Warning." In G. Pitzl (ed.), *Geography*. Guilford, CT: Dushkin.

West, Cornel. 1993. *Race Matters*. Boston: Beacon.

Wieler, Edith E. 1985. "The French in Western Canada." In John W. Friesen (ed.),

When Cultures Clash: Case Studies in Multiculturalism. Calgary: Detselig.

Wiggins, David K. 1997. *Glory Bound: Black Athletes in White America*. Syracuse, NY: Syracuse University Press.

Wilkins, Roger. 1994. "Harping on Racism." In Gary Goshgarian and Kathleen Krueger (eds.), *Crossfire: An Argument, Rhetoric and Reader*. New York: Harper Collins.

Williams, Chancellor. 1971. *The Destruction of Black Civilization: Great Issues of a Race from 4500 BC to 2000 AD*. Dubuque, IA: Kendall/Hunt.

Williams, Eric. 1966. *Capitalism and Slavery*. New York: Putnam's.

Williams, Gardner. 1967. "The Right Act Is to Promote One's Own Welfare: Egoism." In William P. Alston and Richard B. Brandt (eds.), *Problems of Philosophy: Introductory Readings*. Boston: Allyn and Bacon.

Wilson, William J. 1973. *Power, Racism, and Privilege*. London: Macmillan.

_____. 1978. *The Declining Significance of Race*. Chicago: University of Chicago Press.

_____. 1987. *The Truly Disadvantaged: The Inner City, the Underclass, and Public Policy*. Chicago: University of Chicago Press.

Winks, Robin W. 1971. *The Blacks in Canada: A History*. New Haven and London: Yale University Press.

Winnipeg Free Press. 1989. "Professor Credits Genetics for Might of German Military." February 14: 11.

Woddis, Jack. 1967. *An Introduction to Neo-Colonialism*. London: Lawrence and Wishart.

Wolpe, Harold. 1986. "Class Concept, Class Struggle and Racism." In John Rex and David Mason (eds.), *Theories of Race and Ethnic Relations*. Cambridge: Cambridge University Press.

Worthy, M., and A. Markle. 1970. "Racial Differences in Reactive versus Self-paced Sports Activities." *Journal of Personality and Social Psychology* 16: 439–43.

Wyse, Akintola J.G. 1993. "The Sierra Leone Krios: A Reappraisal from the Perspective of the African Diaspora." In Joseph E. Harris (ed.), *Global Dimensions of the African Diaspora*. Washington, DC: Howard University Press.

Yeates, M. 1990. *The North American City*. New York: Harper and Row.

Ziegler, Michael, Fredric Weizmann, Neil Wiener, and David Wiesenthal. 1989. "Philip Rushton and the Growing Acceptance of 'Race-Science.'" *Canadian Forum* September: 19–22.

Zipf, G.K. 1949. *Human Behaviour and the Principles of Least Effort*. Cambridge: Addison-Wesley.

Subject Index

Author Index